Lecture Notes in Computer Scie

Commenced Publication in 1973
Founding and Former Series Editors:
Gerhard Goos, Juris Hartmanis, and Jan van Leeuwen

Jesper Larsson Träff   Siegfried Benkner
Jack Dongarra (Eds.)

Recent Advances in the Message Passing Interface

19th European MPI Users' Group Meeting
EuroMPI 2012
Vienna, Austria, September 23-26, 2012
Proceedings

 Springer

Volume Editors

Jesper Larsson Träff
Vienna University of Technology
Faculty of Informatics
Institute of Information Systems
Research Group Parallel Computing
Favoritenstr. 16
1040 Vienna, Austria
E-mail: traff@par.tuwien.ac.at

Siegfried Benkner
University of Vienna
Faculty of Computer Science
Research Group Scientific Computing
Währinger Str. 29/6.21
1090 Vienna, Austria
E-mail: siegfried.benkner@univie.ac.at

Jack Dongarra
University of Tennessee
Department of Electrical Engineering
and Computer Science
Knoxville, TN 37996, USA
E-mail: dongarra@cs.utk.edu

ISSN 0302-9743   e-ISSN 1611-3349
ISBN 978-3-642-33517-4   e-ISBN 978-3-642-33518-1
DOI 10.1007/978-3-642-33518-1
Springer Heidelberg Dordrecht London New York

Library of Congress Control Number: Applied for

CR Subject Classification (1998): C.2.4, F.2, D.2, C.2, H.4, D.4

LNCS Sublibrary: SL 2 – Programming and Software Engineering

Typesetting: Camera-ready by author, data conversion by Scientific Publishing Services, Chennai, India

Printed on acid-free paper

Springer is part of Springer Science+Business Media (www.springer.com)

Preface

Extended message-passing style parallel programming with MPI remains the most important and successful paradigm for programming hybrid, distributed memory parallel systems and achieving high application efficiency. MPI, the Message-Passing Interface, introduced more than 20 years ago, has been an extremely efficient and productive interface (both in qualitative and quantitative terms), and proven surprisingly robust in the face of very radical changes in systems configurations, capabilities, and scale over the past decades. This has entailed an immense amount of work, both in improvement of the implementations of MPI, mostly done by research labs and in academic environments, but also in part by commercial vendors (that often base their developments on open implementations from labs and academe), and in exploration and extension of the standard itself often as driven by application needs. The EuroMPI conference series has provided and will continue to provide an important forum for MPI developers, researchers in message-passing parallel programming, application developers, users, and students to meet and discuss specific issues related to MPI; always with a look towards new trends and developments of related or alternative interfaces for high-performance parallel programming, and often in quite close interaction with important HPC vendors. In the past five years the MPI Forum has been active in revising and extending the MPI standard, addressing among others issues of scalability, and has brought out consolidated versions of MPI 2, as well as drafts for more significant extensions to go into an upcoming MPI 3.0 version of the standard. In this process EuroMPI has played a role in testing new proposals for MPI 3, for example on fault-tolerance, collective communication, interaction with threads, and other matters. EuroMPI is one of the few meetings where these kinds of specific explorations related to the concrete MPI standard can be discussed, and should be used also in the future for more such research. It is a community conviction that other paradigms and interfaces for highly parallel distributed memory programming must do as well as MPI in order to be successful, and that there is consequentially much to learn from MPI and ongoing research activities as presented at the EuroMPI conference.

EuroMPI 2012 featured 22 technical presentations on MPI implementation techniques and issues, benchmarking and performance analysis, programming models and new architectures, run-time support, fault-tolerance, message-passing algorithms, and applications. A special session on Improving MPI User and Developer Interaction (IMUDI), introduced with EuroMPI 2011, was dedicated to intensifying interaction between users and implementors of MPI, in particular to make user expectations and desiderata regarding the standard (and its implementations) explicit. The conference also featured four invited talks on MPI 3 and beyond (Gropp), the Fujitsu petaflop K computer and its MPI (Sumimoto), the impact of MPI on design of efficient interconnect hardware (Brüning), and the prospects of applying advanced compiler optimizations to MPI programs (Danalis), as well as two tutorials on advanced MPI and performance engineering. The conference was rounded off with a vendor session, a report from the MPI Forum, discussion slots, and a poster exhibition. Papers and abstracts can be found on the following pages. The meeting program and (most of) the talks can be found at www.eurompi2012.org.

EuroMPI is the successor to the EuroPVM/MPI user group meeting series (since 2010), making EuroMPI 2012 the 19th event of this kind. EuroMPI takes place each year at a different European location; the 2012 meeting was held in Vienna, Austria, organized jointly by Vienna University of Technology (TU Wien) and the University of Vienna. Previous meetings were held in Santorini (2011), Stuttgart (2010), Espoo (2009), Dublin (2008), Paris (2007), Bonn (2006), Sorrento (2005), Budapest (2004), Venice (2003), Linz (2002), Santorini (2001), Balatonfüred (2000), Barcelona (1999), Liverpool (1998), Cracow (1997), Munich (1996), Lyon (1995), and Rome (1994). The meeting took place at the Austrian Academy of Sciences, during September 23–26, 2012.

In reaction to the call for papers that was first published late 2011, we received a total of 47 submissions by the (extended) submission deadline on May 16th, clearly fewer than hoped for. The low number of submissions possibly reflects the universally more difficult funding situation for conference travel. EuroMPI has so far had a very good record with respect to attendance and presentation with as good as no no-shows; potential contributors who knew in advance that they might not be able to travel may have chosen to submit to geographically closer forums. It might also reflect the (positive) fact that good MPI work, whether in implementations or applications, can also be presented at broader parallel processing conferences. All 47 submissions were in scope, and were reviewed by program committee members (with only relatively few external referees) with each paper getting between 3 and 5 reviews. An effort was made to provide informative and helpful feedback to authors. Based on the reviews, the program chairs selected 22 submissions as regular papers, and 7 papers for presentation as posters. Regular papers were allotted 10 pages in the proceedings, and a 30 minute slot for presentation. Among the regular papers, a handful of the strongest and best presented are invited for a Special Issue of the Springer "Computing" journal. These extended papers will again be reviewed by members of the EuroMPI 2012 program committee as well as by new external reviewers.

The program chairs and general chair would like to thank all authors who submitted their contributions to EuroMPI 2012; the program committee members for their work in getting the submissions reviewed, mostly in time and with good-quality, informative reviews; our sponsors who contributed significantly toward making the conference feasible; and all who attended the meeting in Vienna. We hope that the EuroMPI 2012 conference had something to offer for all, and will remain a solid forum for high-quality MPI-related work as it goes into its third decade.

September 2012

Jesper Larsson Träff
Siegfried Benkner
Jack Dongarra

Organization

EuroMPI 2012 was organized jointly by Vienna University of Technology (TU Wien) and the University of Vienna, in association with the Innovative Computing Laboratory of the University of Tennessee.

General Chair

Jack Dongarra   University of Tennessee, USA

Program Chairs

Siegfried Benkner   University of Vienna, Austria
Jesper Larsson Träff   Vienna University of Technology, Austria

Program Committee

Pavan Balaji   Argonne National Laboratory, USA
Siegfried Benkner   University of Vienna, Austria
Gil Bloch   Mellanox Technologies, Israel
George Bosilca   University of Tennessee, Knoxville, USA
Ron Brightwell   Sandia National Laboratories, Albuquerque, USA
Darius Buntinas   Argonne National Laboratory, USA
Franck Cappello   INRIA, France and University of Illinois at
                                 Urbana-Champaign, USA
Gilles Civario   Irish Centre for High-End Computing, Ireland
Yiannis Cotronis   University of Athens, Greece
Jim Cownie   Intel, UK
Anthony Danalis   University of Tennessee, Knoxville, USA
Bronis R. de Supinski   Lawrence Livermore National Laboratory, USA
Luiz DeRose   Cray, USA
Edgar Gabriel   University of Houston, USA
Brice Goglin   INRIA, Bordeaux, France
David Goodell   Argonne National Laboratory, USA
Ganesh Gopalakrishnan   University of Utah, USA
Richard Graham   Oak Ridge National Laboratory, USA
William Gropp   University of Illinois at Urbana-Champaign, USA
Thomas Herault   University of Tennessee, Knoxville, USA
Torsten Hoefler   University of Illinois at Urbana-Champaign, USA
Yutaka Ishikawa   Universty of Tokyo, Japan

Michael Kagan   Mellanox Technologies, Israel
Rainer Keller   HFT Stuttgart, University of Applied Science,
                              Germany
Dries Kimpe   Argonne National Laboratory, USA
Jesus Labarta   Technical University of Catalonia, Barcelona
                              Supercomputing Center, Spain
Dong Li   Oak Ridge National Laboratory, USA
Ewing Rusty Lusk   Argonne National Laboratory, USA
Amith Rajith Mamidala   IBM, USA
Satoshi Matsuoka   Tokyo Institute of Technology, Japan
Guillaume Mercier   INRIA, France
Bernd Mohr   Jülich Supercomputing Centre, Germany
Matthias Mueller   TU Dresden, Germany
Rolf Rabenseifner   High Performance Computing Center Stuttgart
                              (HLRS), Germany
Thomas Rauber   University of Bayreuth, Germany
Rolf Riesen   IBM, Ireland
Robert Ross   Argonne National Laboratory, USA
Peter Sanders   Karlsruhe Institute of Technology, Germany
Mitsuhisa Sato   University of Tsukuba, Japan
Saba Sehrish   Northwestern University, USA
Christian Siebert   University of Aachen, Germany
Stephen Siegel   University of Delaware, USA
Anna Sikora   Autonomous University of Barcelona, Spain
Jeff Squyres   Cisco, USA
Shinji Sumimoto   Fujitsu Ltd., Japan
Rajeev Thakur   Argonne National Laboratory, USA
Vinod Tipparaju   AMD, USA
Carsten Trinitis   Technical University of Munich, Germany
Denis Trystram   Grenoble Institute of Technology, France
Jesper Larsson Träff   Vienna University of Technology, Austria
Keith Underwood   Intel, USA
Robert Van De Geijn   The University of Texas at Austin, USA
Alan Wagner   University of British Columbia, Canada
Roland Wismüller   University of Siegen, Germany
Xin Yuan   Florida State University, USA

External Referees

Sriram   Sascha Hunold   Hitoshi Sato
  Aananthakrishnan   Benny Koren   Subodh Sharma
Leonardo Bautista   Guodong Li   Keita Teranishi
Eduardo Cesar   Grant Mackey   Francois Trahay
Wei-Fan Chiang   Sabri Pllana
Aleksandr Drozd   Claudia Rosas

Local Organization

Jesper Larsson Träff, Vienna University of Technology
Siegfried Benkner, University of Vienna

Enes Bajrovic, University of Vienna
Christine Kamper, Vienna University of Technology
Margret Steinbuch, Vienna University of Technology
Angelika Wiesinger, University of Vienna

Sponsors

The conference would not have been possible without financial support from sponsors, and we therefore gratefully acknowledge the support and contribution of this years' sponsors to a successful meeting. Platinum and Gold sponsors also contributed with technically oriented talks in the vendor session, an important part of the conference for getting technically oriented information from relevant HPC and interconnect vendors and software developers.

Platinum level sponsor

Gold level sponsors

Silver level sponsors

MEGWARE

Table of Contents

Benchmarking and Performance Analysis

Programming Models and New Architectures

Run-Time Support

Posters

MPI 3 and Beyond: Why MPI Is Successful and What Challenges It Faces*

William Gropp

University of Illinois at Urbana-Champaign
wgropp@illinois.edu

Abstract. The Message Passing Interface (MPI) was developed over eighteen years ago and continues to be the preferred programming model for scientific computing. Contributing to that success was a combination of forward-looking features, precise definition, and judgment based on the experience of developers, vendors and users. Today, MPI continues to adapt to the changing needs of parallel programming, with MPI-3 introducing enhancements for collective and one-sided communication, multi-threaded programming, support of performance tools for MPI programming, etc. However, MPI faces many challenges as the nature of parallel computing changes more radically than at any time in the history of MPI. This talk will touch on some of the less obvious but important reasons for MPI success, discuss some of the challenges that MPI faces, and makes suggestions for future directions in MPI and parallel programming language research.

The Message Passing Interface (MPI) has been tremendously successful. First released over eighteen years ago, it continues to be the preferred programming model for parallel scientific computing. MPI is used in applications ranging from astronomy to zoology and on systems ranging from laptops to the world's fastest supercomputers. Yet MPI faces many challenges. Processor architectures are evolving dramatically as the end of Moore's Law approaches. The complexity of parallel programming, always considered a weak point of low-level programming models such as message passing, has become a major issue as all systems become parallel computers. And nearly two decades is a long time in computing — MPI represents the best ideas of an earlier era. This paper will discuss some of the reasons for the success of MPI and some of the challenges faced by MPI.

1   A Strong Base

One of the major reason for the success of MPI is that the original MPI standard (now called MPI-1) was built around a relatively small number of well defined and forward looking concepts. The core, two-sided message passing and collective communication and computation, had been well-established as an effective

---

* This work was supported in part by the Office of Advanced Scientific Computing Research, Office of Science, U.S. Department of Energy award DE-FG02-08ER25835 and award DE-SC0004131.

J.L. Träff, S. Benkner, and J. Dongarra (Eds.): EuroMPI 2012, LNCS 7490, pp. 1–9, 2012.

programming model. The MPI Forum built on this standard practice, but extended it in several ways. For example, MPI datatypes were introduced because it was recognized that data motion is expensive and there was an opportunity to eliminate some data motion by describing the data to be moved, even if non-contiguous, in the MPI communication routines. This can eliminate a extra copy performed by the user into a separate buffer (unfortunately, still commonly used, as in the NAS Parallel Benchmarks [1]), and permits the MPI implementation to pipeline data transfers. While MPI datatypes provided little performance benefit initially because few implementations optimized the use of MPI datatypes (and even those that did, such as MPICH, only did a small subset of possible types), it provided several important benefits. Perhaps most important, datatypes were critical to the description of parallel I/O in MPI-2, providing a way to concisely describe data motion from a file to a collection of processes in a way that enables high performance while preserving a canonical structure in a file. In addition, as the relative cost of memory motion has increased, the value of optimizations tied to MPI datatypes has increased, and this has been borne out in recent papers [2–5]. This is particularly important to note, because the value of MPI datatypes was based on a forward-looking view of where parallel computing was likely to go, not on measurements of the benefit of some implementation on the platforms of the day.

Similarly, the MPI communicator, and especially the communication context, provided a way to build modular software and encouraged an ecosystem of parallel software libraries by ensuring that software components could ensure that communication was not accidentally intercepted by the user's code or by another software component. Again, this was a forward-looking approach. There were few parallel libraries and the communication context added a small but real additional time cost to communication.

However, perhaps the most important feature of MPI has been the precise description of the behavior of each MPI routine. While there are some areas of ambiguity, particularly with respect to what is often called progress, what data gets moved and when that data can and cannot be referenced is precisely defined [6]. Not all parallel computing models have such precision. This has been critical for the long-term success of MPI because those precise semantics have ensured that, even with nearly two decades of change in computer hardware, programs continue to work and produce the same result.

Of course, other features of MPI were important in its success. Features such as portability, performance, support for modularity and composibility, and completeness of the interface were critical for the success of MPI [7], and it is the combination of all of these features into a single programming model that was important. MPI is by no means perfect; there are several key weaknesses of MPI. Perhaps the two most often mentioned are MPI's specification as a library, preventing close integration with the language, and MPI's lack of support for distributed (global) data structures.

1.1 Myths about MPI

Before discussing some of the challenges facing MPI, there are some persistent myths that should be dispelled.

MPI Requires p^2 Buffering for p Processes. This is a typical claim that confuses decisions taken by a particular implementation with requirements of the MPI standard. There is no such requirement in MPI. However, there are some performance tradeoffs for the implementation; the use of an internal buffer for each process simplifies the code and can reduce the complexity of the critical path. Providing a fast yet scalable approach is a challenge [8].

MPI Is Not Fault-Tolerant. What is meant by this is that the standard does not describe what happens when certain kinds of faults or errors occur [9]. Few standards do. The efforts of the MPI Forum at providing fault tolerance strive to specify the behavior of MPI after certain types of faults (primarily so that the failure of an MPI process does not force the other processes to fail).

MPI Does Not Have Scalable Startup. Like statements about buffering, this myth comes from examining how one or even several MPI implementations currently manage process startup and then making a blanket claim based on that examination. MPI in fact does not say anything about how processes are started, and different implementations have selected different tradeoffs between scalability and simplicity. A scalable startup mechanism, particularly one that is robust in the face of errors, is more complex to design, build, and maintain.

MPI RMA Has Complex Rules. This statement is correct, but the inference that this makes MPI RMA (Remote Memory Access) more complex to use than some other one-sided programming mode is highly misleading. The MPI RMA model strives for precision about when data can be referenced with used with one-sided operations, and in the standard, provides detailed information that an implementor of MPI needs when considering possible optimizations. Like many other one-sided programming models, there are simple subsets that are often all that a programmer needs (it is in that sense that the statement that "MPI RMA has complex rules" is incorrect).

MPI Requires Ordering of Messages in the Network. This statement is incorrect. MPI requires that some operations be ordered with respect to others, but says nothing about the order in which data is moved on the network. It is true that an easy way to ensure the ordering that MPI requires is to use a transport layer that provides ordering, but this is not necessary. This permits an MPI implementation to make efficient use of fast networks for data transfers.

What most of these myths have in common is that an examination of the current behavior of some version of MPI is used to draw conclusions about the MPI programming model. This kind of faulty reasoning is still seen in papers published today that compare different approaches (not just those about MPI), and can lead to decisions based on short term features of current hardware and software.

In contrast, the evaluation of current implementations can provide valuable insight into implementation issues and can be critical in identifying directions for implementation research. Perhaps the major challenge facing any designer is to balance quantitative thinking about the future with experiments that can be run today.

2   Challenges for MPI 3 and Beyond

As MPI approaches its third decade, it faces greater challenges than ever before. The end of Dennard (frequency) scaling and the growing challenges of power consumption and heat dissipation in processors are forcing radical changes in processor architecture. In turn, programming models and algorithms are changing rapidly, perhaps more radically than anytime since vectorization over thirty years ago.

2.1   Changes in Processor Architecture

MPI was defined in an era when a single processor often required multiple chips and there was at most one program counter per chip. Many systems ran exactly one user process on each processor, leading to the confusion in many early works on MPI between process and processor (MPI describes communication between processes, not processors). Today, there are no single "core" chips. There are many different ways to organize processing elements, including multicore, "manycore", GPU, FPGA, and embedded memory processing (also called processor in memory). The MPI programming model remains a single process programming model (with one exception in MPI-3, discussed below), and leaves the details of programming the processor to the programming language used for that process; this is only C, Fortran, and in MPI-2, C++. All of these languages are quite old and have few if any features to support parallel programming within a process. This approach of relying on a *composition of programming models* has been both a strength and a weakness of MPI. The strength is that MPI and the languages can evolve independently. The weakness is that MPI depends on the language and cannot take full advantage of it. One example that illustrates this is the decisions made in MPI-2 about non-blocking operations and threading. Nonblocking routines are provided in MPI for two reasons: they significantly simplify correctness with respect to point-to-point communication and internal buffering and they provide for performance for critical routines, by permitting communication/computation overlap and eliminating extra memory copies to internal buffers. However, they introduce complexity into the programming model, in part because the programming languages do not have corresponding language features (such as futures). For nonblocking operations that the MPI Forum felt were less performance sensitive, and for which correctness in the blocking case was easier to ensure, the MPI-2 Forum expected programmers to use threads and that this would spur MPI implementations to offer full thread safety (MPI_THREAD_MULTIPLE). Unfortunately, this was not the case.

The thread model introduces significant overheads as well as programmer complexity, and several major HPC systems choose to limit processes to one thread per core. This makes threads useless as a portable method to implement non-blocking communication and collective I/O, and has led to a substantial increase in the number of MPI routines in MPI-3. In addition, users that have tried using threads for computation, for example, by mixing MPI with OpenMP, have found that the composition of programming models introduces a new challenge, that of coordinating the use of resources. In this case, the MPI and OpenMP runtimes may assume that their runtime is the only performance critical runtime, and optimized the use of cores under that assumption. This can lead to competition between programming models for resources and remains a challenge for programming models.

2.2   Remote Direct Memory Access

Remote Direct Memory Access (RDMA) challenges MPI in two ways: making efficient use of RDMA hardware and providing an effective (for the user) RDMA programming model. In hardware, the development of RDMA (also called one-sided) hardware has a long history, including distributed shared memory and explicit remote put/get support. Infiniband provides a commodity network that supports RDMA, making hardware for this model widely available and not just limited to the very high end of computing systems. The challenge here is in the details. While the basic operations for moving data are similar in different hardware, the handling of control and synchronization information is different, and performance is extremely sensitive to subtle details of these choices. This of course impacts the programming model, which can specify a one-sided model that is difficult to implement efficiently.

The one-sided programming model can be a better match to distributed data structures where it is easy for each process or thread to determine where a data item resides on another process. Two-sided works well when that is not the case, as is true in more dynamic data structures. The challenge is to develop a programming model that can make efficient use of RDMA hardware, not just now but five to ten years in the future, provides a clean way to reason about one-sided operations (which means providing a precise definition of the behavior, or at least a precise specification of the ambiguities), and interfaces cleanly with the two-sided and collective communication in MPI (see [10] for an evaluation of the MPI-2 RMA interface from the point of view of a parallel language implementor). Programming *correctly* with one sided operations is difficult; see [11] for an introduction to some of the issues in the context of shared memory. Any RDMA programming model must address correctness as well. MPI-3 introduces a few features to enable MPI processes to share memory; to address some of the issues of shared memory programming, the MPI RMA model is used to enforce completion of shared memory operations.

2.3 Issues at Scale

MPI was originally designed when a massively parallel system had 128 nodes (with one core per node). While MPI was designed to be scalable, some collective operations have arguments whose size is proportional to the number of processes (e.g., MPI_Alltoallv). Such interfaces are not viable as system exceed a million processes [12]. Of course, in many ways, these very operations are not scalable. The challenge here is to determine how best to replace or supplement these collectives; the topological or sparse collectives in MPI-3 are one possibility. The implementation of collective operations in a way that is scalable, works efficiently with complex processor architectures (and composed programming models) and provides effective communication/computation overlap for scalable algorithms remains a challenge.

A more difficult issue is that of matching the algorithm and program to the interconnect topology. MPI provides some support for virtual process topologies (and extended it in MPI-2.2 [13]), but it tries to both provide performance and a specific abstract model, and cannot excel at either. Complicating this is that mapping a process (or thread) to compute resource (core) depends on many features of the code and algorithm, and may be affected by dynamic events outside of the programmers control. A challenge is to develop an effective approach for this problem and provide the support for it from the programming models (MPI and anything with which it is composed).

Systems at extreme scale are likely to experience failures. The best way to handle this is not clear. Many current systems cause a process to exit when there is a failure; many MPI implementations then abort the parallel program. But in the future, failures might be finer grained — processes may recover from some faults without failing; other failures may be more widespread. A challenge here is to define the fault model and the programming model features that address the likely faults.

2.4 Library and Language

Because MPI is a library, it appears easy to add routines. However, each routine needs to be written, tested, tuned, and documented, and users must be supported. In addition, there is the potential of interference with other routines or unanticipated performance impacts. A challenge is to strike a balance between "My user needs X, and I want MPI to provide it" and the potential impacts. Also, as noted above, one of the strengths of MPI is completeness: there are a limited number of basic concepts; MPI (in most cases) specifies *all* of the routines that apply those concepts. Adding individual routines breaks this model and introduces additional complexity for the programmer.

The interaction between MPI and the programming language used for the MPI process has become more complex. Most obvious from the changes to the MPI standard in MPI 2.2 is the proliferation of language datatypes. When MPI-1 was created, both C and Fortran had a small number of basic datatypes.

Now there are many types, some with specific sizes (representing a convergence in computing to 8-bit bytes) and some whose size is specified only in relation to others. MPI 2.0 attempted to handle this for Fortran by specifying routines to create a datatype matching parameters, such as precision and range, given by the user and matching those in Fortran. This approach is more easily extensible but more complex for both implementors and users. MPI 2.2 added a large set of specific MPI datatypes to match new types in C.

Many difficulties remain. For example, there was until very recently no way to support nonblocking operations within the Fortran standard (even for nonblocking I/O; this was not only a limitation for MPI). The travails of the MPI binding for C++ illustrate another problem. MPI provides a very low-level model; this has been one reason for its success. But more modern programming models provide a rich set of operations. A challenge is how to match MPI to a modern programming language. The MPI-2 binding for C++ took a low-level approach; however, many people felt that this did not offer enough benefit over the C binding. In addition, some C++ features, such as throwing exceptions instead of returning an error code, can cause problems when MPI code using C++ is mixed with code in C or Fortran. Higher level bindings are possible, but often are specialized to particular domains. How should such a language binding be defined?

2.5   Productivity

Despite the success of MPI, many complain about the low-productivity of MPI. Some have argued that this is really due to the complexity of parallel programming. Others, including this author, have noted that, since programs are expressions of data structures and algorithms, and parallel programs require parallel (thus distributed) data structures, providing support for distributed data structures is important for a productive programming environment. MPI (with the partial exception of the darray and subarray MPI datatypes) provides no support for distributed data structures. It was the expectation of the MPI Forum that libraries would be written to provide such support, and in some cases, that has happened (e.g., PETSc and Trilinos). However, where no library exists, the developer using MPI must start from scratch.

Parallel programming languages such as HPF, CoArray Fortran (now part of Fortran), and UPC all provide some set of distributed data structures and convenient operations on them. The advantage is that if those are the data structures you want, then the language is likely to be more productive for you. The disadvantage is that if those are not what you need, then productivity is lost. The challenge for any parallel programming approach is to provide aids to productivity without limiting the applicability of the language, or alternately, providing some subset and the ability to work with programming models providing other distributed data structures.

3   Conclusions

This paper has touched on some of the challenges facing MPI as a programming model. Many of these apply to any parallel programming model; the successes and failures of MPI provide valuable guidance for the future. Some of the key items include:

- Better support for composition of programming models, including resource sharing, precise memory model,
- Language support for nonblocking operations (e.g., futures),
- Support for both static and dyanamic analysis of correctness,
- Performance as a first class object (recognizing that parallelism is used to achieve performance), permitting formal analysis of performance correctness.

While there are many challenges, MPI's focus on programming in the large, with support for software libraries, programming with multiple programming languages, and support for threads, positions MPI well for the future.

References

1. Kjolstad, F., Hoefler, T., Snir, M.: Automatic datatype generation and optimization. In: Ramanujam, J., Sadayappan, P. (eds.) PPOPP, pp. 327–328. ACM (2012)
2. Träff, J.L., Hempel, R., Ritzdorf, H., Zimmermann, F.: Flattening on the Fly: Efficient Handling of MPI Derived Datatypes. In: Dongarra, J., Luque, E., Margalef, T. (eds.) PVM/MPI 1999. LNCS, vol. 1697, pp. 109–116. Springer, Heidelberg (1999)
3. Byna, S., Sun, X.-H., Thakur, R., Gropp, W.D.: Automatic Memory Optimizations for Improving MPI Derived Datatype Performance. In: Mohr, B., Träff, J.L., Worringen, J., Dongarra, J. (eds.) PVM/MPI 2006. LNCS, vol. 4192, pp. 238–246. Springer, Heidelberg (2006)
4. Ross, R., Miller, N., Gropp, W.D.: Implementing Fast and Reusable Datatype Processing. In: Dongarra, J., Laforenza, D., Orlando, S. (eds.) EuroPVM/MPI 2003. LNCS, vol. 2840, pp. 404–413. Springer, Heidelberg (2003)
5. Hoefler, T., Gottlieb, S.: Parallel Zero-Copy Algorithms for Fast Fourier Transform and Conjugate Gradient Using MPI Datatypes. In: Keller, R., Gabriel, E., Resch, M., Dongarra, J. (eds.) EuroMPI 2010. LNCS, vol. 6305, pp. 132–141. Springer, Heidelberg (2010)
6. Li, G., Palmer, R., Delisi, M., Gopalakrishnan, G., Kirby, R.M.: Formal specification of MPI 2.0: Case study in specifying a practical concurrent programming API. Sci. Comput. Program. 76(2), 65–81 (2011)
7. Gropp, W.D.: Learning from the Success of MPI. In: Monien, B., Prasanna, V.K., Vajapeyam, S. (eds.) HiPC 2001. LNCS, vol. 2228, pp. 81–92. Springer, Heidelberg (2001)
8. Goodell, D., Gropp, W., Zhao, X., Thakur, R.: Scalable Memory Use in MPI: A Case Study with MPICH2. In: Cotronis, Y., Danalis, A., Nikolopoulos, D.S., Dongarra, J. (eds.) EuroMPI 2011. LNCS, vol. 6960, pp. 140–149. Springer, Heidelberg (2011)
9. Gropp, W.D., Lusk, E.: Fault tolerance in MPI programs. International Journal of High Performance Computer Applications 18(3), 363–372 (2004)

10. Bonachea, D., Duell, J.: Problems with using MPI 1.1 and 2.0 as compilation targets for parallel language implementations. IJHPCN 1(1/2/3), 91–99 (2004)
11. Boehm, H.J., Adve, S.V.: You don't know jack about shared variables or memory models. Commun. ACM 55(2), 48–54 (2012)
12. Balaji, P., Buntinas, D., Goodell, D., Gropp, W., Hoefler, T., Kumar, S., Lusk, E., Thakur, R., Träff, J.L.: MPI on millions of cores. Parallel Processing Letters 21(1), 45–60 (2011)
13. Hoefler, T., Rabenseifner, R., Ritzdorf, H., de Supinski, B.R., Thakur, R., Träff, J.L.: The scalable process topology interface of MPI 2.2. Concurrency and Computation: Practice and Experience 23, 293–310 (2011)

MPI Functions
and Their Impact on Interconnect Hardware

Ulrich Brüning

University of Heidelberg
ZITI Department of Computer Engineering
Computer Architecture Group
B6, 26, Building B
68159 Mannheim, Germany
ulrich.bruening@ziti.uni-heidelberg.de

Abstract. High performance computing requires optimized interconnects in order to serve the increasing computing power from multi and many core CPUs. MPI is one of the most prominent programming models used for HPC systems. In order to achieve very low latency and high message rates, the functions of MPI must be implemented in a very efficient way. The specification of various MPI functions is analyzed and the impact to interconnect hardware is presented. A careful analysis of latency components and pipeline structure must be done in order to map the MPI functions to hardware in an efficient way.

J.L. Träff, S. Benkner, and J. Dongarra (Eds.): EuroMPI 2012, LNCS 7490, p. 10, 2012.
© Springer-Verlag Berlin Heidelberg 2012

The MPI Communication Library
for the K Computer:
Its Design and Implementation

Shinji Sumimoto

Fujitsu Ltd.
1-1, Kamikodanaka 4-chome, Nakahara-ku, Kawasaki
211-8588, Japan
s-sumi@labs.fujitsu.com

Abstract. This talk presents the overall design and implementation of the MPI communication library for the K computer. The K computer introduces the Tofu interconnect, 6D torus/mesh topology, for higher performance and availability for peta-scale systems, however, present several issues to increase performance, availability and usability. In this talk, these issues, approaches, designs and implementations are discussed. Performance evaluation results are also presented.

J.L. Träff, S. Benkner, and J. Dongarra (Eds.): EuroMPI 2012, LNCS 7490, p. 11, 2012.

MPI and Compiler Technology: A Love-Hate Relationship

Anthony Danalis

Inovative Computing Laboratory
University of Tennessee
Knoxville, TN, 37996
adanalis@eecs.utk.edu

MPI has been the de facto standard for parallel computing for over a decade now, and remains mostly unchallenged as the only viable options for harnessing the processing power of massively parallel supercomputers. Alternative parallel programming paradigms have existed for quite some time, mainly in the form of PGAS languages [4,7], but have yet to deliver the necessary performance, robustness and portability needed to drive developers away from MPI.

However, despite its success, MPI has several shortcomings, some in its very design, that could be addressed if we learn from the experiences gained by the PGAS languages. Specifically, MPI is focused strictly on the library, run-time and operating system layers and makes no effort to utilize advanced compiler technologies. Research has shown that the data-flow of MPI programs can be analyzed [1,2,6,5], albeit with limitations, and compiler technology can modify MPI programs to reduce the communication delays through techniques such as communication-computation overlapping [10,3] and communication restructuring [8,9].

As we move to increasingly complicated hardware systems, developers will need all the help they can get in order to achieve high efficiency at scale. One way to achieve this is to rely on more sophisticated run-time systems, such as task scheduling engines, that run on top of MPI and try to dynamically adapt the execution and communication to the hardware resources. However, pure MPI applications can remain competitive, if we utilize the whole development stack, from kernel modules to compilers and auto-tuning benchmarks. This integration can be achieved by exposing to the compiler and auto-tuning layers more information about the internals of MPI libraries and the way MPI functions interact with, and modify, the application that calls them.

References

1. Bronevetsky, G.: Communication-sensitive static dataflow for parallel message passing applications. In: Proceedings of the 7th annual IEEE/ACM International Symposium on Code Generation and Optimization, CGO 2009, pp. 1–12. IEEE Computer Society (2009)
2. Shires, D., Pollock, L., Sprenkle, S.: Program Flow Graph Construction for Static Analysis of MPI Programs. In: Parallel and Distributed Processing Techniques and Applications (PDPTA 1999), pp. 1847–1853 (June 1999)

J.L. Träff, S. Benkner, and J. Dongarra (Eds.): EuroMPI 2012, LNCS 7490, pp. 12–13, 2012.
© Springer-Verlag Berlin Heidelberg 2012

3. Danalis, A., Pollock, L., Swany, M., Cavazos, J.: Mpi-aware compiler optimizations for improving communication-computation overlap. In: Proceedings of the 23rd International Conference on Supercomputing, ICS 2009, pp. 316–325. ACM, New York (2009)
4. El-Ghazawi, T.A., Carlson, W.W., Draper, J.M.: UPC Specification v. 1.1 (2003), http://upc.gwu.edu/documentation
5. Kreaseck, B., Strout, M.M., Hovland, P.: Depth Analysis of MPI Programs. In: Proceedings of the First Workshop on Advances in Message Passing (AMP 2010 co-located with PLDI) (June 2010)
6. Strout, M.M., Kreaseck, B., Hovland, P.D.: Data-Flow Analysis for MPI Programs. In: International Conference on Parallel Processing (ICPP 2006), pp. 175–184 (August 2006)
7. Numrich, R.W., Reid, J.K.: Co-Array Fortran for parallel programming. ACM Fortran Forum 17(2), 1–31 (1998)
8. Preissl, R., Schulz, M., Kranzlmüller, D., de Supinski, B.R., Quinlan, D.J.: Transforming mpi source code based on communication patterns. Future Gener. Comput. Syst. 26, 147–154 (2010)
9. Preissl, R., de Supinski, B.R., Schulz, M., Quinlan, D.J., Kranzlmuller, D., Panas, T.: Exploitation of dynamic communication patterns through static analysis. In: Proceedings of the 2010 39th International Conference on Parallel Processing, ICPP 2010, pp. 51–60. IEEE Computer Society (2010)
10. Sancho, J.C., Barker, K.J., Kerbyson, D.J., Davis, K.: Quantifying the potential benefit of overlapping communication and computation in large-scale scientific applications. In: SC 2006: Proceedings of the 2006 ACM/IEEE Conference on Supercomputing, p. 125. ACM Press, New York (2006)

Advanced MPI Including New MPI-3 Features

William Gropp[1], Ewing Lusk[2], and Rajeev Thakur[2]

[1] University of Illinois at Urbana-Champaign
`wgropp@illinois.edu`
[2] Argonne National Laboratory
`{lusk,thakur}@mcs.anl.gov`

Abstract. This tutorial will cover several advanced topics in MPI. We will cover one-sided communication, dynamic processes, multithreaded communication and hybrid programming, and parallel I/O. We will also discuss new features in the newest version of MPI, MPI-3, which is expected to be officially released a few days before this tutorial. The tutorial will be heavily example driven; we will introduce concepts by using code examples based on scenarios found in real applications. The example codes will be available for attendees to run on their laptops.

J.L. Träff, S. Benkner, and J. Dongarra (Eds.): EuroMPI 2012, LNCS 7490, p. 14, 2012.
© Springer-Verlag Berlin Heidelberg 2012

Hands-on Practical Hybrid Parallel Application Performance Engineering

Markus Geimer[1], Michael Gerndt[2], Sameer Shende[3],
Bert Wesarg[4], and Brian Wylie[1]

[1] Jülich Supercomputing Centre
{m.geimer,b.wylie}@fz-juelich.de
[2] Technical University of Munich
gerndt@in.tum.de
[3] University of Oregon
sameer@cs.uoregon.edu
[4] Technical University of Dresden
bert.wesarg@tu-dresden.de

This tutorial presents state-of-the-art performance tools for leading-edge HPC systems founded on the Score-P community instrumentation and measurement infrastructure, demonstrating how they can be used for performance engineering of effective scientific applications based on standard MPI or OpenMP and now common mixed-mode hybrid parallelizations. Parallel performance evaluation tools from the Virtual Institute – High Productivity Supercomputing (VI-HPS) are introduced and featured in hands-on exercises with Periscope, Scalasca, Vampir and TAU. We cover all aspects of performance engineering practice, including instrumentation, measurement (profiling and tracing, timing and hardware counters), data storage, analysis and visualization. Emphasis is placed on how tools are used in combination for identifying performance problems and investigating optimization alternatives, illustrated with a case study using a major application code.

To prepare participants to locate and diagnose performance bottlenecks in their own parallel programs, the tutorial prominently features hands-on exercises with the tools. Participants will use their own notebook computers with a provided Linux Live-ISO image booted natively from DVD/USB or running within a virtual machine (e.g., VirtualBox). Due to limited time and network bandwidth available during tutorials, those who intend to install a virtual machine and download the 4GB ISO disk image to their notebook computers should do so in advance.

For further information visit http://www.vi-hps.org/training/material.

J.L. Träff, S. Benkner, and J. Dongarra (Eds.): EuroMPI 2012, LNCS 7490, p. 15, 2012.
© Springer-Verlag Berlin Heidelberg 2012

Adaptive Strategy
for One-Sided Communication in MPICH2

Xin Zhao, Gopalakrishnan Santhanaraman, and William Gropp

University of Illinois at Urbana-Champaign, Urbana IL 61801, USA
{xinzhao3,gopalsan,wgropp}@illinois.edu

Abstract. The one-sided communication model supported by MPI-2 can be more convenient to use than the regular two-sided communication model and has potential to provide better performance. The MPI-2 standard gives flexibility about when RMA operations can be issued and completed. The current MPICH2 implementation employs a lazy approach, in which operations are queued up and issued in the later synchronization phase. This has certain benefits for small data transfers because of reduced network operations, but for large data transfers, issuing operations in an eager fashion could achieve better performance. In this paper we describe our design and implementation of an adaptive strategy for one-sided operations and synchronization mechanisms (fence, post-start-complete-wait, lock-unlock) supported by MPI-2, which combines benefits from both lazy and eager approaches. Our performance results demonstrate that our approach performs as well as the lazy approach for small data transfers and achieves similar performance as the eager approach for large data transfers. In addition, it achieves good overlap of communication with computation.

Keywords: One-sided communication, MPI implementation, adaptive strategy, MPI-2.

1 Introduction

The original MPI standard provided only two-sided and collective communication. The MPI-2 standard, released in 1997, added functionality for one-sided communication (also called remote memory access (RMA)). One-sided communication allows one process to specify all communication parameters, both for the source and destination processes (called origin and target in the MPI-2 standard). One-sided communication also has the potential to deliver higher performance than regular two-sided communication, particularly on networks that natively support one-sided communication.

MPI-2 provides three operations (put, get, accumulate) and three synchronization mechanisms (fence, post-start-complete-wait, lock-unlock) for one-sided communication. These synchronization mechanisms ensure the correct semantics of one-sided operations. The MPI-2 standard gives much flexibility on when a one-sided operation completes, which permits an MPI implementation to be optimized internally, particularly in terms of when data transfers are initiated

J.L. Träff, S. Benkner, and J. Dongarra (Eds.): EuroMPI 2012, LNCS 7490, pp. 16–26, 2012.

within one communication epoch (an epoch is the period between synchronization calls; MPI further distinguishes between access and exposure epochs but in the interests of space, we will use the term epoch). A detailed description of one-sided communication in MPI-2 can be found in [1].

For small number of operations with short data, issuing them at the end of the epoch (the closing synchronization call) permits aggregation of the RMA operations into fewer communication steps, significantly improving performance. For either large number of operations or significant amounts of data, however, issuing them as early as possible may be beneficial, since their transmission latency is expensive, and issuing them early provides opportunities to overlap communication with computation within the epoch.

In many situations, it is not obvious beforehand whether issuing operations early or late is better, due to the nature of communication pattern. Therefore, it is desirable to design an adaptive strategy that can automatically select the most suitable one. In this paper, we address this issue by designing and implementing an adaptive approach for one-sided communication in MPI.

2   Related Work

There are several studies regarding the implementation of one-sided communication in MPI-2. Some MPI-2 implementations which support one-sided communication are MPICH2 [2], OpenMPI [3] and NEC [4]. In [11,12], the design choices and issues in implementing one-sided communication in MPI are described. The authors in [13] have studied optimizations for reducing the synchronization overhead involved in implementing one-sided communication. Designs for MPI RMA in InfiniBand clusters is described in [14,15]. In [16,17], the authors describe a design for efficient passive synchronization using hardware support from InfiniBand atomic operations. In [18], some performance guidelines for one-sided communication in MPI are discussed. Besides MPI, other programming models that also provide one-sided communication include CRAY SHMEM [5], ARMCI [6], GASNET [7] and BSP [8]. Some BSP papers, particularly [9,10], discuss the benefits of aggregating and scheduling communication operations for better performance as well as contention avoidance.

3   Adaptive Strategy Design

3.1   Lock-Unlock

The existing implementation of lock-unlock in MPICH2 uses a *lazy* strategy. In MPI_Win_lock, the origin process does nothing but enqueues the lock request. During the following epoch, the origin process also enqueues puts, gets and accumulates. In MPI_Win_unlock, the origin process issues the lock request and waits for the lock granted message from the target. After that, it issues all queued operations to the target and sets a field in the packet header of the last operation to notify the target that all operations have already been issued out. In this way, the *lazy* approach combines the last synchronization message with the last operation. The *lazy* approach also includes an optimization for single short operation: if there is only one operation between lock and unlock, the data size is small and the MPI data type is predefined, the origin process sends that operation together with the lock request in `MPI_Win_unlock`. In this case, both synchronizations at the beginning and at the end are eliminated.

Another choice for lock-unlock is an *eager* approach. In `MPI_Win_lock`, the origin process issues the lock request immediately and waits for lock to be granted. For the following puts, gets and accumulates, it issues them as soon as they occur. In `MPI_Win_unlock`, the origin process sends an additional 0-byte message to release the lock. The *eager* approach needs two synchronizations (and three messages): one for the lock request and the lock grant, and one for the unlock at the end. Besides, since it issues the lock request and operation separately, optimization for single operation is impossible.

Our design for lock-unlock eliminates the synchronization message at the end and preserves the optimization for single short operation. In `MPI_Win_lock`, the origin process enqueues the lock request, just like *lazy*. Subsequent RMA operations are also enqueued (*lazy* mode). If the number of queued operations reaches the threshold, which is a certain value of operation number or message size, the origin first issues the lock request, but does not wait for the lock-granted response. Instead, it continues to enqueue RMA operations until the lock is granted. Once the lock is granted, it issues all queued operations, switches from *lazy* to *eager* mode, and issues the following operations immediately. Even though the rest of operations are issued in an *eager* fashion, we still avoid the last synchronization message by introducing a `last_rma_op` pointer, which keeps one operation not being issued until `MPI_Win_unlock`. We also preserve the optimization of single short operation, because the lock request is not issued in `MPI_Win_lock`, if only one short operation exists, it will be issued together with the lock request in `MPI_Win_unlock`.

The semantic of `MPI_Win_unlock` requires that when the function returns, one-sided operations are completed at both origin and target. We use an optimization strategy in the original implementation to guarantee this. For shared lock, when it encounters a get operation, the origin keeps it in a buffer and issues it at last, otherwise the target needs to send an acknowledgement message to the origin after receiving the last operation. This strategy assumes that the network is ordered. If the network is unordered, the acknowledgement message is always needed. For exclusive lock, no acknowledgement is needed.

3.2   Post-Start-Complete-Wait (PSCW)

The current implementation of PSCW in MPICH2 also uses a *lazy* strategy. In `MPI_Win_post`, processes in the target group sends a synchronization message to each process in the origin group, and sets the counter of the window to the size of the origin group. In `MPI_Win_start`, processes in the origin group do nothing. The subsequent puts, gets and accumulates are enqueued. In `MPI_Win_complete`, every process in the origin group is blocked until it receives the synchronization message from all processes in the target group, and then it issues all queued operations. For target process of each operation, the origin process sets a field in the packet header of the last operation to decrement the counter of the window. In MPI_Win_wait, every process in the target group is blocked until the counter reaches zero. For each pair of processes, only one synchronization message is needed. If the origin process has no operation destined to a target process, it needs to send an additional 0-byte message to that target, which means they need two synchronization messages in total.

Another choice for the implementation of PSCW is an *eager* approach. In MPI_Win_start (or the first one-sided operation function, if exists), the origin process is blocked until it receives the post message from all processes in the target group. After that, puts, gets and accumulates are issued immediately without queuing. Because of this, in MPI_Win_complete, the origin process needs to send an additional 0-byte message to all processes in the target group to decrement the counter. The *eager* approach always needs two synchronization messages.

Like the *lazy* approach, our design for PSCW needs one synchronization if the origin process has operations to a target process, and needs two synchronizations when the origin has no operation destined to a target. In MPI_Win_start, processes in the origin group do nothing. During the following epoch, each origin process begins with the *lazy* mode: queuing up operations. When number of queued operations reaches the threshold, the origin process is blocked to wait for the synchronization message from all target processes of those queued operations, and then issues all queued operations and switches from *lazy* to *eager* mode. For the following puts, gets and accumulates, the origin process issues them as they occur. Like lock-unlock, we avoid sending another synchronization message by introducing a last_rma_op pointer for each target.

3.3   Fence

As for the lock-unlock and PSCW cases, the current implementation of fence in MPICH2 also uses a *lazy* approach. In the MPI_Win_fence that begins an RMA epoch, the processes perform no communication. The following puts, gets and accumulates are enqueued. In the next MPI_Win_fence, each process first goes through all queued operations to determine, for each other process i, how many operations have i as the target, and it stores this information in an array. Then all processes perform a reduce-scatter communication (with sum operation on this array) over the communicator of the window. After that, each process knows how many processes have operations targeting this process, and stores this information in the counter of the window. Then each process issues all queued operations, and the counter is decremented when all operations from the same process have been arrived (indicated by the packet header of the last operation from that process). Thus, in the *lazy* approach, only one synchronization (reduce-scatter) is needed.

Another choice for implementing fence is an *eager* approach, in which all one-sided operations are issued as early as possible. In the MPI_Win_fence that begins an epoch, all processes perform a barrier synchronization over the communicator of the window. After that, every process issues operations as they occur.

At the next `MPI_Win_fence`, all processes perform another barrier synchronization to guarantee that no process leaves this fence before all other processes have finished accessing the window. Therefore, in the *eager* approach, two synchronizations (barriers) are needed. Our design for fence needs one synchronization

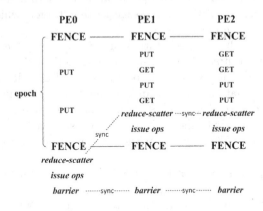

Fig. 1. Adaptive fence

(reduce-scatter) when number of operations is small, and two synchronizations (one barrier and one reduce-scatter) when number of operations reaches the threshold. As is shown in Fig. 1, in the beginning `MPI_Win_fence`, every process does no communication. For the following puts, gets and accumulates, the process initially enqueues them. If number of queued operations does not reach the threshold (the case for PE0), the process just goes into the next `MPI_Win_fence` and is blocked at the reduce-scatter in it. If the number reaches the threshold during the epoch (the case for PE1 and PE2), the process is blocked at the reduce-scatter in the operation function. Therefore, PE1 and PE2 are synchronized by reduce-scatter with PE0. After the reduce-scatter completes, PE0 issues all queued operations, whereas PE1 and PE2 also immediately issue queued operations as well as the operations after the reduce-scatter. When PE1 and PE2 enter the next fence, they do not need to perform the reduce-scatter in it. At the end of fence, all processes need to be synchronized again by calling a barrier. This strategy applies to ordered networks, or networks with remote completion mechanisms, in which processes can wait for all remote completion events and then call barrier. On an unordered network without such mechanisms, however, barrier cannot guarantee the correct completion and all processes need to perform an all-to-all communication acknowledgement after completing all operations instead. It is notable that full ordering for all data is not required to be imposed on the communication, just ordering of particular transfers with respect to others should be respected.

If every process has small number of operations (fence is always in *lazy* mode), they only need one synchronization, which is the reduce-scatter in the second fence. An additional value in the reduce-scatter is used to indicate whether some process called reduce-scatter before the closing MPI_Win_fence; this is how the processes know whether a barrier synchronization is also required.

3.4 Comparison

For all three synchronization mechanisms discussed above, the general approach for *lazy* is to do nothing in the first synchronization, enqueue the following operations, and do everything in the second synchronization. The general approach for *eager* is to perform synchronization in the first call, issue the following operations as they occur, and do another synchronization at end. Compared with *lazy*, *eager* has more synchronization steps and there is no opportunity to aggregate or schedule operations. However, *eager* eliminates the cost of enqueuing operations and has the advantage of issuing operations immediately, which means they can arrive the target and be completed as early as possible. This is desirable when there are large number of operations and/or the amount of data to transfer is large. *Eager* also enables the overlap of communication and computation which is not possible in *lazy*. Our *adaptive* design combines features of *lazy* and *eager*, while introducing a modest overhead.

4   Performance Results

We implemented our *adaptive* approach based on the MPICH2-1.4.1p1 release and added a new configure option: --enable-hybridrma. For each synchronization mechanism, we also implemented the *eager* version(with--enable-eagerrma option) to compare with *lazy* and *adaptive*. Our implementation uses the CH3 device in MPICH2.

We run benchmarks on two different architectures: (i) an SMP machine with 4 Intel Core i5 CPU (2.67 GHz) and 8GB memory, we use it to simulate a architecture with a very fast interconnect network; (ii) the "breadboard" cluster at Argonne National Laboratory on which each node has two Intel Xeon quad-core processors (2.66 GHz) and 16GB memory, and nodes are connected with Ethernet, we use it to examine the performance on a slow interconnect network.

While all experiments make use of a simple communication layer, the idea applies even to one-sided transports, particularly those that can implement the one-sided semantics by directly exploiting the hardware features. Note that the *lazy* mode allows the use of a single remote direct memory access operation (as long as the MPI semantics are observed) while the *eager* mode permits the use of asynchronous communication for one-sided communication.

4.1   Latency Impact

Single-op Results. We first measured the latency between two processes when only one operation issued between synchronization calls. Fig. 2 (log-log plot) shows the put latency for lock-unlock, with message size varying from 1 byte to 2^{18} bytes. On SMP and breadboard, *adaptive* and *lazy* perform better than

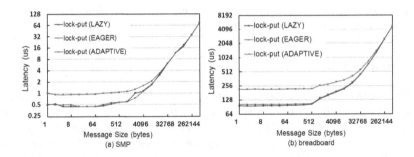

Fig. 2. Single-op results on SMP and breadboard

eager when message size is small, because of the optimization for single short operation. Similar results are observed for get and accumulate operation, in the interests of space we do not show them here.

Many-ops Results. We also measured the latency with increased number of short operations between synchronization calls. Fig. 3 and Fig. 4 show the put latency for lock-unlock and PSCW on SMP and breadboard. Since fence is commonly used for communication with many neighbors, we did not tested it here.

On SMP, when number of operations is small, data transmission speed is very fast and there is no distinct difference between *lazy* and *eager*. When number of operations is large, *eager* and *adaptive* are better than *lazy*. This is due to the extra queuing overhead in *lazy*. On breadboard, Fig. 4 shows that *lazy* and

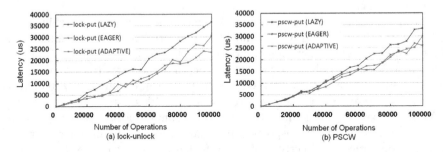

Fig. 3. Many-ops results on SMP

adaptive are better than *eager* when number of operations is small, because of the extra synchronization cost in *eager*; when number of operations is large, *eager* and *adaptive* are better than *lazy*, because the extra synchronization cost can be ignored due to the large number of operations. Here we used number of operations as the threshold for *adaptive*. Similar results are observed for get and accumulate operations, in the interests of space we do not show them here.

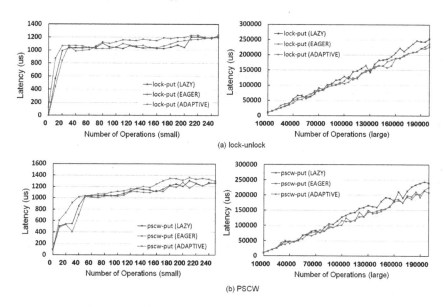

Fig. 4. Many-ops results on breadboard

4.2   Overlapping Impact

We validated overlapping performance by modifying the previous many-ops benchmark. We first measured the latency (t_1) for fixed number of operations plus synchronization calls between two processes, with no computation inserted. After that, we inserted after one-sided operations certain amount of computation corresponding to t_1. If the total latency does not change, it means all computation is absorbed and the overlapping percentage is 100%. If not, we decreased the amount of computation until it is completely absorbed by communication. Suppose now time corresponding to the inserted computation is t_2, then the overlapping percentage equals to $\frac{t_2}{t_1}$. Table. 1 shows the overlapping results of the *adaptive* approach for put operation on breadboard (number of operations is 4096). Percentage for accumulate operation is similar with put

Table 1. Overlapping results on breadboard

Message Size(bytes)	Put(lock)	Put(fence)	Put(pscw)
2^{10}	30%	30%	15%
2^{11}	25%	25%	20%
2^{12}	60%	50%	50%
2^{13}	70%	60%	60%
2^{14}	70%	70%	65%
2^{15}	70%	75%	80%
2^{16}	70%	85%	80%
2^{17}	70%	70%	75%

operation, whereas percentage for get operation is half that of put operation. This is because for get operation, the second synchronization needs to spend certain amount of time waiting for returning data, which cannot be overlapped with the computation in between. For *lazy*, there is nearly no overlapping observed and for *eager*, the overlapping percentage is similar to *adaptive*.

4.3   Performance Impact

We measured the performance impact of *adaptive* strategy on Graph 500 benchmark [19] and MPPTEST benchmark [20]. Graph 500 benchmark is designed to demonstrate the suitability of systems for data-intensive applications (by running BFS on a randomly generated graph). The one-sided version of BFS in Graph 500 is implemented by fence and accumulate operations. Between each pair of fence calls, every process issues multiple short operations to many other neighbors. MPPTEST benchmark includes an implementation of halo exchange, which can reflect common communication pattern in many simulation applications. In halo exchange, one process exchanges data with several neighbors with multiple short data transfers in between. We use halo exchange to measure the impact of *adaptive* PSCW. All benchmarks are run on breadboard machine.

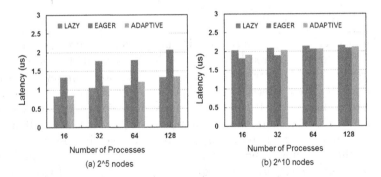

Fig. 5. Graph 500 results on breadboard

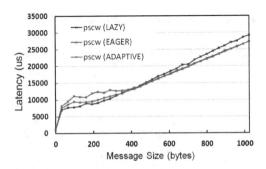

Fig. 6. Halo exchange results on breadboard

Fig. 5 shows the results of Graph 500 and Fig. 6 shows the results of halo exchange with 128 processes and 8 neighbors. For halo exchange, we use message size instead of number of operations as the threshold in *adaptive* approach.

5 Conclusion and Future Work

In this paper, we describe the design and implementation of an *adaptive* strategy for one-sided communication in MPI, which combines features of *lazy* and *eager* approach while introducing a modest overhead. The queuing threshold must be chosen appropriately for a given system and runtime condition. Currently we use a fixed value for it. We are considering to build a reasonable model for choosing threshold and to dynamically adjust it during runtime. We will explore these possibilities in future.

References

1. Message Passing Interface Forum, MPI-2: A Message Passing Interface Standard. High Performance Computing Applications 12, 1–299 (1988)
2. Argonne National Laboratory, MPICH2,
   http://www-unix.mcs.anl.gov/mpi/mpich2/
3. Barrett, B.W., Shipman, G.M., Lumsdaine, A.: Analysis of Implementation Options for MPI-2 One-Sided. In: Cappello, F., Herault, T., Dongarra, J. (eds.) PVM/MPI 2007. LNCS, vol. 4757, pp. 242–250. Springer, Heidelberg (2007)
4. Traff, J., Ritzdorf, H., Hempel, R.: The Implementation of MPI-2 One-Sided Communication for the NEC SX. In: Proceedings of Supercomputing 2000 (2000)
5. Cray Research Inc., Cray T3E C and C++ optimization guide (1994)
6. Nieplocha, J., Carpenter, B.: ARMCI: A Portable Remote Memory Copy Library for Distributed Array Libraries and Compiler Run-Time Systems. In: Rolim, J.D.P. (ed.) IPPS-WS 1999 and SPDP-WS 1999. LNCS, vol. 1586, pp. 533–546. Springer, Heidelberg (1999)
7. Bonachea, D.: GASNet Specification, v1.1. Technical Report UCB/CSD-02-1207, Computer Science Division, University of California at Berkeley (October 2002)
8. Goudreau, M., Lang, K., Rao, S.B., Suel, T., Tsantilas, T.: Portable and Efficient Parallel Computing Using the BSP Model. IEEE Transactions on Computers, 670–689 (1999)
9. Hill, J.M.D.: Lessons learned from Implementing BSP. Oxford University Technical Laboratory, Technical report 21-96
10. Hill, J.M.D., McColl, B., Stefanescu, D.C., Goudreau, M.W., Lang, K., Rao, S.B., Suel, T., Tsantilas, T., Bisseling, R.H.: BSPlib: The BSP programming library. Parallel Computing 24(14), 1947–1980 (1998)
11. Gropp, W.D., Thakur, R.: Revealing the Performance of MPI RMA Implementations. In: Cappello, F., Herault, T., Dongarra, J. (eds.) PVM/MPI 2007. LNCS, vol. 4757, pp. 272–280. Springer, Heidelberg (2007)
12. Gropp, W.D., Thakur, R.: An Evaluation of Implementation Options for MPI One-Sided Communication. In: Di Martino, B., Kranzlmüller, D., Dongarra, J. (eds.) EuroPVM/MPI 2005. LNCS, vol. 3666, pp. 415–424. Springer, Heidelberg (2005)
13. Thakur, R., Gropp, W.D., Toonen, B.: Minimizing Synchronization Overhead in the Implementation of MPI One-Sided Communication. In: Kranzlmüller, D., Kacsuk, P., Dongarra, J. (eds.) EuroPVM/MPI 2004. LNCS, vol. 3241, pp. 57–67. Springer, Heidelberg (2004)

14. Liu, J., Jiang, W., Jin, H.-W., Panda, D.K., Gropp, W., Thakur, R.: High Performance MPI-2 One-Sided Communication over InfiniBand. In: International Symposium on Cluster Computing and the Grid (CCGrid 2004) (April 2004)
15. Jiang, W., Liu, J., Jin, H.-W., Panda, D.K., Buntinas, D., Thakur, R., Gropp, W.D.: Efficient Implementation of MPI-2 Passive One-Sided Communication on InfiniBand Clusters. In: Kranzlmüller, D., Kacsuk, P., Dongarra, J. (eds.) EuroPVM/MPI 2004. LNCS, vol. 3241, pp. 68–76. Springer, Heidelberg (2004)
16. Santhanaraman, G., Narravula, S., Panda, D.K.: Designing passive synchronization for MPI-2 one-sided communication to maximize overlap. In: IPDPS 2008 (April 2008)
17. Santhanaraman, G., Balaji, P., Gopalakrishnan, K., Thakur, R., Gropp, W., Panda, D.K.: Natively Supporting True One-sided Communication in MPI on Multi-core Systems with InfiniBand. In: CCGRID 2009 (May 2009)
18. Traff, J.L., Gropp, W.D., Thakur, R.: Self-Consistent MPI Performance Guidelines. IEEE Trans. Parallel Distrib. Syst., 698–709 (2010)
19. The Graph 500 List, http://www.graph500.org/index.html/
20. Argonne National Laboratory, MPPTEST - Measuring MPI Performance, http://www.mcs.anl.gov/research/projects/mpi/mpptest/

A Low Impact Flow Control Implementation for Offload Communication Interfaces

Brian W. Barrett[1], Ron Brightwell[1], and Keith D. Underwood[2]

[1] Sandia National Laboratories*
P.O. Box 5800, MS-1319
Albuquerque, NM, 87185-1319
{bwbarre,rbbrigh}@sandia.gov
[2] Intel Corporation
Hillsboro, OR, USA
keith.d.underwood@intel.com

Abstract. Message passing paradigms provide for many to one messaging patterns that result in receive side resource exhaustion. Traditionally, MPI implementations layered over the Portals network programming interface provided a large default unexpected receive buffer space, the user was expected to configure the buffer size to the application demand, and the application was aborted when the buffer space was overrun. The Portals 4 design provides a set of primitives for implementing scalable resource exhaustion recovery without negatively impacting normal operation. A resource exhaustion recovery protocol for MPI implementations is presented, as well as performance results for an Open MPI implementation of the protocol.

1 Introduction

The usage model for message passing paradigms inherently makes it possible for a large number of tasks in a system to overwhelm a single node with traffic and cause resource exhaustion at the receiver. In the two-sided MPI semantics, resource exhaustion is most likely to occur due to a large number of "unexpected messages". For network APIs that directly implement two-sided matching semantics, there is often a fixed pool of resources to deal with unexpected messages. Historically, the Portals network API [2,4] handled resource exhaustion by dropping the offending message and notifying the receiver that the message had been dropped. At that point, MPI had little choice but to abort the application, since the ordering semantics could no longer be guaranteed. The philosophy was that applications could code to a finite buffering requirement and could allocate a sufficient receive buffer to meet that requirement. In practice, most applications had no problem with this; however, some applications have infrequent,

---

* Sandia National Laboratories is a multi-program laboratory managed and operated by Sandia Corporation, a wholly owned subsidiary of Lockheed Martin Corporation, for the U.S. Department of Energy's National Nuclear Security Administration under contract DE-AC04-94AL85000.

J.L. Träff, S. Benkner, and J. Dongarra (Eds.): EuroMPI 2012, LNCS 7490, pp. 27–36, 2012.
© Springer-Verlag Berlin Heidelberg 2012

transient demands on network resources that require more resources than can (or should) be dedicated in steady state. In these cases, the alternative to aborting the application is invoking some form of flow-control.

In a connectionless model like Portals 4, it is challenging to create a mechanism to properly implement flow-control. For example, the receiver-not-ready (RNR) approach used in InfiniBand depends on a connection context, since a single process running out of resources cannot be allowed to impact the entire node. Building a flow-control mechanism that can easily be used in a design exploiting extensive parallelism can also pose challenges. As with other types of processing, processing network packets is increasingly dependent on parallelism. As hardware architecture evolves, both pipelined parallelism and task parallelism become critical. Pipelined datapaths will be needed for functionality that is shared across a "node", such as end-to-end reliability, and then multiple processing elements will be needed to handle per process functionality like matching logic.

In the Portals 4 design, two principles were treated as sacrosanct. First, the solution must be scalable. Flow-control issues are most prominent at scale, and traditional approaches work worst at scale. Second, the solution must not penalize the performance of applications that worked well with a limited, fixed buffer, but it may have a high cost for recovery. The solution we chose has two key components: new message reception is disabled in a compartmentalized way when flow-control is invoked, and the sender is informed of all messages that are dropped due to flow-control. Together, these capabilities enable MPI to recover from flow-control events without incurring any overhead during normal operation.

2   Related Work

Flow control for user-level networks has been an active area of research for nearly two decades. Flow control strategies for Fast Messages (FM) were studied in [5]. A single pool of packet buffers was managed between all communicating peers, and a dynamic flow control protocol was employed to ensure that these buffers were not exhausted. Originally, FM used a static credit-based scheme where peers were given a fixed allocation of packet buffers. This scheme limited the achievable link bandwidth and caused bandwidth to degrade as the system size increased. The dynamic credit-based approach would allocate credits to senders based on the size of and number of incoming messages. The dynamic scheme improved the achievable bandwidth as the number of network endpoints increased.

The popularity of user-level networking hardware and the emergence of MPI as the *de facto* standard for message passing created a new flow control challenge. Because MPI is a fully-connected model that supports the concept of unexpected messages, flow control was needed to manage the amount of space needed for unexpected message buffers.

The Quadrics [8] network mapped a segment of the host's address space into the network interface controller (NIC) to use for unexpected messages. If this buffer space was about to be exhausted, the driver would simply allocate more memory for the NIC to use. Eventually, the driver would move the physical memory pages to disk and map them into the host process' address space when the unexpected messages needed to be received. This approach allowed for a nearly unlimited amount of memory to be used for unexpected messages, albeit at a large performance cost if message buffers were paged out to disk.

Liu [7] explored different software-based flow control strategies for MPI over InfiniBand, examining the trade-offs between static and dynamic credit-based approaches. For the static approach, the number of buffers per connection is established during MPI initialization and does not change. Control messages, which can either be sent explicitly or piggy-backed on other messages, are used to communicate the number of free credits back to the sender. The dynamic credit-based strategy they employed in this work increased the number of credits, and hence message buffers, when a low-water mark was reached. The dynamic scheme was shown to outperform a static credit-based scheme in terms of latency and bandwidth performance. Unlike the previous work mentioned above, this work focused on point-to-point flow control within a single connection. The problem of managing a set of buffers used for all potential senders in a connectionless environment is more complex.

Farreras [6] explored an acknowledgment-based protocol that considers the amount of memory available for unexpected messages and employs different protocols when memory is abundant versus when it is scarce. The key insight in this work is that the receiver can update the MPI matching structures independent of message delivery. In this strategy, a sender will send a control message containing the MPI envelope information. The receiver will process this message, updating the MPI matching structures. If there is room to buffer an unexpected message, the receiver will send a control message back to the sender indicating that the message can be sent. If there is no room, the control message will instead tell the sender to buffer the message locally and try to send it again at a later time.

The fundamental assumption in these user-level credit- and acknowledgment-based approaches is that senders need to be constrained so that they do not overwhelm receivers with too many unexpected messages. In our experience, a large number of unexpected messages is a characteristic of a poorly designed application whose performance and scalability will be inherently limited. Rather than constrain well-behaved applications with protocols designed for misbehaving applications, our strategy of recovering when the space for unexpected messages has been exhausted preserves correctness for the applications that need it without impacting the applications that do not.

3   MPI Flow Control with Portals 4.0

The implementation of MPI over Portals 4.0 is similar to the implementation over Portals 3.3 [3]; however, unlike Portals 3.3, Portals 4.0 provides support for managing unexpected message queues as part of its interface. Figure 1 shows the Portals constructs used to build MPI matching. An incoming message first traverses the match list entries in the priority list, which provide matching information and pointers to user buffers to enable direct data delivery for expected messages. Each match list entry in the priority list corresponds to a single posted MPI receive. If a match is not found, the overflow list is then traversed. Short messages match overflow list entries that are configured to deliver the message data for a number of incoming messages in a temporary buffer provided by MPI, while long messages match an entry that causes the data to be discarded. In either case, the match information for the incoming message is placed in the unexpected headers list.

When the user posts a new MPI receive, the unexpected headers list is first searched for a matching header. If a match is found, an event notifying the MPI is generated and the MPI moves the data into the user buffer, either copying it from the short message buffer or issuing an RDMA get from the sender for a long message. If no match in the unexpected headers list is found, a new match list entry is posted in the priority list. The search and post behavior is handled atomically by the Portals implementation. Portals will generate an event when a match in the unexpected headers list is found, when no match in the unexpected headers list is found and the match list entry is appended to the priority list, and when an incoming message matches the priority list. Events are delivered into a fixed-sized event queue (not shown in Figure 1).

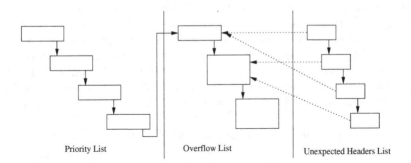

Priority List   Overflow List   Unexpected Headers List

Fig. 1. Portals structures used in implementing receive side message handling

The buffers in the overflow list for temporarily storing short unexpected messages, the unexpected headers list, and the event queue are all of finite size. In large systems, any one of the resources may be exhausted, either by many-to-one communication patterns or by communication during periods of application non-responsiveness to the network. Traditionally, such resource exhaustion in Portals 3.3 has resulted in an application abort, which lead to very high static resource allocation to prevent what are often transient spikes in resource usage.

In addition to the handling of unexpected messages, Portals 4.0 added a mechanism for handling this resource exhaustion. A portal table index (similar to a TCP port, used for selecting the proper match list) may optionally enable flow control.

If an incoming message was not matched in the priority or overflow list, exhausts the unexpected headers list, or exhausts space in the event queue, the portal table entry is disabled. The offending message and all future messages are dropped with an error delivered to the sender (similar to InfiniBand's RNR ACK mechanism, but without automatic recovery). A new operation, `PtlPTEnable()`, allows the receiver to re-enable the portal table entry for handling incoming messages after the exhaustion situation is solved. If it is necessary to prevent the reordering of messages that are in flight, the receiver should wait for all pending messages to complete before re-enabling the portal table entry. This typically requires coordination with the senders.

Two options were examined for handling flow control in a pipelined, parallel network architecture: a credit based transfer protocol and a receiver managed protocol.

3.1   Credit-Based Flow Control

A credit based flow control protocol avoids resource exhaustion by limiting the number of messages in transit at any time. The receiver must allocate sufficient unexpected buffer space, event queue space, and unexpected header space for each available send credit. A straight-forward static allocation of credits results in memory usage scaling according to the following equation:

$$memory = credits \times eager\ threshold \times number\ of\ peers \qquad (1)$$

The number of peers is growing rapidly with increasing processor counts and cores per processor. At the same time, the increasing bandwidth delay product of networks is increasing the eager threshold. Therefore, maintaining a reasonable memory footprint yields a very small number of credits available to each peer. Multiple strategies are available for controlling the number of outstanding credits, including lazy connection establishment and dynamic sharing of credit pools across multiple nodes. However, these strategies all suffer from scalability losses during the all-to-all or all-to-one patterns most likely to result in resource exhaustion.

3.2   Receiver-Managed Flow Control

The ability of a portal table entry to disable matching based on resource exhaustion provides the possibility of a more scalable flow control protocol. Unlike credit based flow control, in which resources are constrained to prevent resource exhaustion from occurring, receiver managed flow control allows resource exhaustion and provides the capability to gracefully recover.

As described in Section 3, communication operations notify the upper layer protocol of completion by generating events in an event queue. An application may utilize a number of event queues and the communication API allows the upper layer protocol to determine where an operation's completion notification will be delivered. In the case of MPI over Portals 4, three event queues are utilized: a receive queue for all receive queue related events, a send queue for all send events and for retrieving data for long unexpected messages, and a small event queue for handling flow control recovery.

Flow control is enabled for the portal table entry used for incoming MPI messages and the Portals implementation therefore ensures that the receive event queue will not overflow.[1] A credit protocol is utilized to ensure that the send event queue does not overflow. The event queue can be sized to cover the worst case in outstanding credits, since the resource utilized (event queue entry space) is small, all credits will be returned without requiring remote processes to enter the MPI library (that is, they are returned in bounded time), and the sizing of the event queue is based on message rate of the network interface and not the number of nodes in the system. All communication in the flow control recovery protocol is $log(N)$, so the flow control event queue may be sized extremely small without worry of overflow.

If a receiver side generated acknowledgement indicates that the remote process has entered flow control, the message is queued for later delivery and the process enters flow control recovery. As part of the message generate process, each outgoing message is assigned a 64 bit sequence number, which can be used by the sender to retransmit messages in order after a flow control event.

When a process receives an event indicating that its receive portal table entry has been disabled due to resource exhaustion, it notifies all connected processes through an asynchronous broadcast based on triggered operations [9] to enter flow control recovery. The steps in flow control recovery are outlined below:

1. All new MPI send operations are queued locally.
2. The triggered operations necessary for the notification broadcast are reset for the next occurrence of resource exhaustion.
3. MPI waits for acknowledgments from all in-flight send operations and sends which were not successfully delivered are queued for retransmission.
4. The receive event queue is drained to recover receive resources.
5. If required, more buffer space for short unexpected messages is posted.
6. All processes enter a barrier to signal the end of flow control recovery.
7. The list of messages queued for retransmission is sorted based on sequence number, ensuring message ordering on the receiver and are retransmitted.

The receiver maintains MPI message ordering semantics by disabling all incoming messages on the receiver experiencing resource exhaustion until the network is completely quiesced. The sender only needs to track the number of currently in-flight messages and a rolling 64-bit message counter in steady state. When the sender enters flow control recovery, it can determine no in-flight messages remain through the counter of in-flight messages, and can later determine the original transmission order based on the 64 bit counter.

The flow control recovery protocol may be executed in either a dedicated exception handling thread or as part of the normal message event handling path.

---

[1] Event queues are fixed size and an overflow results in lost events, which likely results in lost messages. Portals reports such a loss to the MPI implementation, which is likely to abort, as recovery is extremely difficult without flow control.

Portals 4 provides a blocking mechanism for waiting on new events `PtlEQWait()`, allowing the exception handling thread to sleep until recovery is necessary, resulting in low steady-state overhead. Although point-to-point message transmission is disabled during recovery, other communication mechanisms which are not layered on point-to-point messaging may progress during recovery.

4 Results

This section measures the impact of flow control on steady-state performance. Recovery from resource exhaustion is expected to be a rare event and, while the protocol has been thoroughly tested for correctness, performance results during recovery are not presented. All experiments were run on a cluster of dual socket Intel Xeon X5570 processors with InfiniBand ConnectX adapters. The Intel X5570 is a 2.93 GHz, quad-core part and the nodes have 24 GB of memory. Development versions of both Portals 4 over InfiniBand and Open MPI were used, with subversion revision numbers r1844 and r26439, respectively.

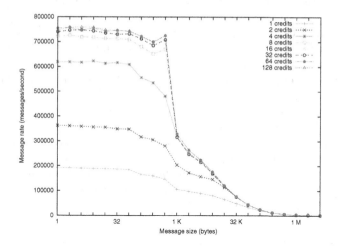

Fig. 2. Effect of available credits on message rate for a credit based flow control protocol

Figure 4 demonstrates the effect of limited credit availability on message rate. The peak message rate of approximately 750,000 messages per second is achievable with as few as 16 send credits. At 8 send credits, there is a drop in message rate, and at 2 credits, only half of the peak message rate is achieved. The results suggest that while 16 credits per connected peer is the minimum necessary to avoid impacting message rate performance, satisfactory results may be found with 8 credits if necessary.

The Portals 4 over InfiniBand implementation is still in development and currently provides a message rate well under that of MPI over raw InfiniBand.

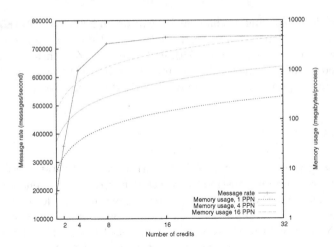

Fig. 3. Effect of credit management on receive-side buffer memory usage. We assume a 9,216 node machine with a 1 KB eager threshold.

As the message rates of Portals 4 implementations improve, greater numbers of send credits will be required to maintain peak message rates.

Figure 4 highlights the dangers of increasing credit counts on large scale machines. Assuming a 1 KB eager message threshold and a 9,216 node machine,[2] the effect of varying available send credits on message rate is compared to the computed effect of send credit count on receive buffer memory usage. Three use cases are demonstrated: one process per node (1 PPN), one process for every four cores (4 PPN), and one process per core (16 PPN). While 16 PPN may seem extreme if multi-threaded programming models are employed on modern systems, future many core systems are likely to leverage more than one process per node. The graph shows how much memory *each process* will need for the unexpected message state at each credit level, and indicates an unsustainable trend as core counts and socket counts grow — even if a small number of credits are used. Even dynamic credit schemes typically allocate at least a few credits to every peer.

The ping-pong bandwidth of a Open MPI with no flow control, credit-based flow control, and receiver managed flow control are presented in Figure 4. The 8 byte half round trip latency for the three protocols is consistent at 3.92 μs. Not surprisingly, there is little difference in performance between the three protocols, as none have more than one message in flight at a given time.

Unlike ping-pong bandwidth, streaming bandwidth is affected by the limited resources available in the credit based flow control protocol, as seen in Figure 4. Having only 8 available credits provides nearly the performance of the no flow control or receiver managed flow control cases. However, the 2 credit case sees a decrease in bandwidth due to the gap necessitated by waiting for credits.

---

[2] The ASC Cielo machine, Sandia's current generation supercomputer, is 9,216 nodes. All road maps point to larger node counts in the next 5 years.

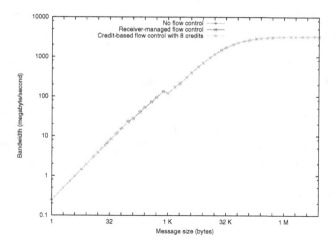

Fig. 4. Bandwidth comparison between flow control protocols for ping-pong bandwidth

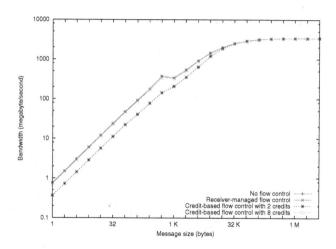

Fig. 5. Bandwidth comparison between flow control protocols for streaming bandwidth

5   Conclusions

The Portals 4 specification adds a mechanism for handling resource exhaustion suitable for use by a number of different upper layer protocols. By disabling the portal table entry to all new incoming operations automatically until the upper layer protocol explicitly re-enables message handling, Portals allows the upper layer protocol to determine how to handle message retransmission. MPI's strict message ordering requirements requires an ordered retransmission after quiescing the traffic to the affected node. In contrast, the active message protocol in GASNet[1] can create similar infrequent, transient resource exhaustion scenarios; however, GASNet active messages do not require ordering and the receiver can re-enable the portal table entry as soon as resources have been replenished.

This paper presents a receiver managed protocol for handling resource exhaustion in Open MPI running over Portals 4. The protocol requires a minimal amount of additional sends-side state that is independent of the system size and no additional receive-side state. Performance impacts are negligible, particularly when compared to a credit based flow control protocol. Unlike credit based flow control protocols, the protocol does not require unexpected receive buffer space that expands in a non-scalable fashion. Further, because resource exhaustion is no longer a fatal event for MPI implementations over Portals, the buffer space allocated for unexpected receive messages can actually be reduced compared to previous implementations.

References

1. Bonachea, D.: Gasnet specification, v1.1. Tech. Rep. UCB/CSD-02-1207 (October 2002)
2. Brightwell, R., Lawry, W., Maccabe, A.B., Riesen, R.: Portals 3.0: Protocol building blocks for low overhead communication. In: Proceedings of the 2002 Workshop on Communication Architecture for Clusters (April 2002)
3. Brightwell, R., Hudson, T., Pedretti, K., Riesen, R., Underwood, K.: Implementation and performance of Portals 3.3 on the Cray XT3. In: Proceedings of the 2005 IEEE International Conference on Cluster Computing (September 2005)
4. Brightwell, R., Maccabe, A.B., Riesen, R.: Design, implementation, and performance of MPI on Portals 3.0. International Journal of High Performance Computing Applications 17(1), 7–20 (2003)
5. Canonico, R., Cristaldi, R., Iannello, G.: A scalable flow control algorithm for the Fast Messages communication library. In: Proceedings of the Workshop on Communication, Architecture and Applications for Network-based Parallel Computing (CANPC 1999), pp. 77–90 (1999)
6. Farreras, M., Cortes, T., Labarta, J., Almasi, G.: Scaling MPI to short-memory MPPs such as BG/L. In: Proceeding of the International Conference on Supercomputing, pp. 209–218 (June 2006)
7. Liu, J., Panda, D.K.: Implementing efficient and scalable flow control schemes in MPI over InfiniBand. In: Proceedings of the 2004 Workshop on Communication Architecture for Clusters (April 2004)
8. Petrini, F., Chun Feng, W., Hoisie, A., Coll, S., Frachtenberg, E.: The Quadrics network: High-performance clustering technology. IEEE Micro 22(1), 46–57 (2002)
9. Underwood, K.D., Coffman, J., Larsen, R., Hemmert, K.S., Barrett, B.W., Brightwell, R., Levenhagen, M.: Enabling flexible collective communication offload with triggered operations. In: IEEE Symposium on High-Performance Interconnects (HotI 2011) (August 2011)

Improving MPI Communication Overlap
with Collaborative Polling

Sylvain Didelot[1,3], Patrick Carribault[2,1],
Marc Pérache[2,1], and William Jalby[1,3]

[1] Exascale Computing Research Center, Versailles, France
{`sylvain.didelot,william.jalby`}`@exascale-computing.eu`
[2] CEA, DAM, DIF F-91297, Arpajon, France
{`patrick.carribault,marc.perache`}`@cea.fr`
[3] Université de Versailles Saint-Quentin-en-Yvelines (UVSQ), Versailles, France

Abstract. With the rise of parallel applications complexity, the needs in term of computational power are continually growing. Recent trends in High-Performance Computing (HPC) have shown that improvements in single-core performance will not be sufficient to face the challenges of an Exascale machine: we expect an enormous growth of the number of cores as well as a multiplication of the data volume exchanged across compute nodes. To scale applications up to Exascale, the communication layer has to minimize the time while waiting for network messages. This paper presents a message progression based on Collaborative Polling which allows an efficient auto-adaptive overlapping of communication phases by performing computing. This approach is new as it increases the application overlap potential without introducing overheads of a threaded message progression.

Keywords: HPC, Overlap, MPI, High-Speed Network, Polling.

1 Introduction

The scalability of a parallel application is mainly driven by the amount of time wasted in the communication library. One solution to decrease the communication cost is to hide communication latencies by performing computation during communications. From the application developer's point of view, parallel programming models offer the ability to express this mechanism through non-blocking communication primitives. One of the most popular communication libraries, Message Passing Interface (MPI), allows the programmer to use non-blocking send and receive primitives (i.e., `MPI_Isend` and `MPI_Irecv`) to enable overlapping of communication with computation. For example, Figure 1-a exposes one MPI task performing a non-blocking communication without overlapping capabilities. In such a situation, the message is actually received from the network during the `MPI_Wait` call. On the other hand, the same example with overlapping shows a significant improvement reducing the overall time consumed (see Fig. 1-b).

Achieving overlap usually requires a lot of code restructuring and transformations. Users are often disappointed after spending a lot of time to enforce overlap because the runtime does not provide an efficient support for asynchronous

J.L. Träff, S. Benkner, and J. Dongarra (Eds.): EuroMPI 2012, LNCS 7490, pp. 37–46, 2012.

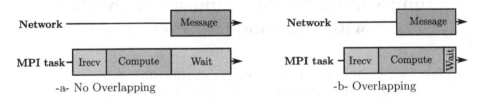

Fig. 1. Influence of Communication/Computation Overlapping in MPI

progress [1,2]. The MPI standard does not define a clear implementation rule for asynchronous communications but only gives recommendations. Most of the current MPI libraries does not support true asynchronous progression and performs message progression within MPI calls (i.e., inside `MPI_Wait` or `MPI_Test` functions). The main difficulty with these implementations occurs when an MPI task performs a time consuming function with no call to MPI routines for progressing messages (i.e., calls to BLAS).

In this paper, we propose a collaborative polling approach for improving the communication overlap without disturbing compute phases. This runtime optimization has been implemented inside a thread-based MPI runtime called MPC (Multi-Processor Computing [3]). Collaborative polling allows message progression when a task is blocked waiting for a message, enabling overlapping with any other task within the same compute node. This method expresses a significant message-waiting reduction on scientific codes. In this paper, we focus on the MPI standard and Infiniband network but the collaborative polling could be adapted to any network interconnect and could be extended to other distributed-memory programming models.

2 Related Work

2.1 Message Progression Strategies

Researches provide significant speedups using overlap of communication on large scale scientific applications [4,5]. For common MPI runtimes, message progression is accomplished when the main thread calls a function from the MPI library. To achieve overlap at user level, MPI applications may be instrumented with repeated calls to the `MPI_Test` function to test all outstanding requests for completion. This solution is not convenient for the developer and irrelevant for not MPI-aware functions. For implementations supporting the `MPI_THREAD_MULTIPLE` level of thread safety, Thakur et al. [6] present an alternative overlapping technique. Hager et al. [7] investigate a Hybrid MPI/OpenMP implementation with explicit overlap optimizations. However, both techniques rely on source-code modifications and involve multiple programming models.

Recent Host Channel Adapters (HCAs) provide hardware support for total or partial independent progress but rely on specific network hardware capabilities [8]. To enable software overlapping without user source code modifications, MPI libraries investigate a threaded messages progression. Additional threads (also known as progression threads) are created to retrieve and complete outstanding messages even if large computation loops prevent the main thread to call the runtime library. For accessing the network hardware, progression threads may be set to use the polling or the interrupted-driven methods.

The polling access approach increases performance on a spare-core thread subscription where the progression thread is bound on a dedicated core. It was for example adopted by IBM in the Bluegene systems [9]. Because only a part of the cores participates to computation, the spare-core mode is barely used on regular HPC clusters. MPI is often used in a fully subscribed mode sharing the progression thread and the user thread on the same core. However the decision when and how often the polling function should be called is non-trivial. Too many calls may cause overhead and not enough calls may waste the overlap potential.

The interrupted-driven message detection is different from the polling approach since it allows the sender or the receiver to have an immediate notification of completed messages [10]. If no work has to be done, the progression thread enters into the wait queue and goes to sleep. When a specific event is generated from the network card (i.e., an incoming message), an interruption is emitted and the progression thread goes back to the run queue. Because generating an interruption for each message may be costly, MPI runtimes often implement a selective interrupt-based solution [11, 12]. Only messages which are critical for overlapping performance may generate an interruption.

For the fairness of the CPU resource sharing, each process has a maximum time to run on a CPU: the time-slice. For example on a Linux kernel, it varies from 1 to 10 milliseconds. Once the time-slice is elapsed, the scheduler interrupts the current running thread, places it at the end of the run queue for its static priority and schedules a new runnable thread. When an interruption occurs, the progression thread has to be immediately scheduled, raising two main concerns. First, it is unclear how much time is required to switch from the active thread to the progression thread: the scheduler may wait for the running thread to finish its time-slice and it is uncertain that the progression thread is the next to be scheduled. Second, one time-slice may be insufficient to receive the entire message. One solution to increase the reactivity would be to use real-time threads. However, this might increase the context switching overheads since the progression thread is scheduled every time an interrupt occurs [13].

The approach most closely related to ours is described in the I/O Manager PIOMan [14] where the preemptive scheduler is able to run tasks in order to make the communication library progress. This previous work is able to efficiently overlap messages in a multi-threaded context but does not allow a MPI rank to steal tasks from another MPI rank.

2.2   Thread-Based MPI

In a thread-based MPI library, each MPI rank is a thread. All threads (MPI ranks) share the same memory address space within a unique UNIX process on a compute node. AMPI [15], AzequiaMPI [16], MPC [3], TOMPI [17], TMPI [18], USFMPI are some thread-based MPI implementations.

Because of the implicit shared-memory context among tasks, thread-based runtimes are well suited for implementing global policies, such as message progression, within a compute node. We implemented our contribution in the MPC framework, an hybrid parallelism framework exposing a thread-based MPI 1.3 runtime. According to our needs, MPC brings two main features:

- Customizable two-level thread scheduler (help for tuning the message progression strategies).
- Support for a high-speed and scalable network (access to the Infiniband network using the OFA IBverbs library with an OS-bypass technology).

3   Our Contribution: Collaborative Polling

During the execution of a parallel MPI application, the time spent while waiting for messages or collective communications is wasted. This idle time is often responsible for the poor scalability of the application on a large number of cores. Even on a well balanced application at user level, some imbalance between tasks may appear from several factors such as:

- The distance between communicating MPI peers.
- The number of neighbors.
- Micro-imbalance of communication (network links contentions, topology).
- Micro-imbalance of computation (non-deterministic events such as preemption) [5].

The main idea of the collaborative polling is to take advantage of idle cycles due to imbalance for progressing messages at the compute node level. During its unused waiting cycles, an MPI task is able to collaborate on the message progression of any other MPI task located on the same compute node. Fig. 2 compares the processing of messages arriving from a Network Interface Controller (NIC) with a regular message progression and with the collaborative polling method.

The algorithm depicted in Fig. 2 at application level is the following: each MPI task executes a non MPI-aware function (Compute) with an unbalanced workload between tasks before waiting for a message and calling a synchronization barrier. On the left part, a regular message progression is presented. On the right part, the collaborative polling method is used. Collaborative polling allows task 1 to benefit from the unused cycles while waiting its message: it can poll, receive and match messages for task 0 which is blocked into a non-interruptible computation loop. Once the computation loop is done on task 0, the expected message has already been retrieved by task 1 and the MPI_Wait primitive immediately returns.

As described in section 2.1 most message progression methods require to suspend the computing phase (with an interruption, an explicit call to MPI or a context switch to the progression thread) to perform progression. Collaborative polling does not require these interruptions as it only uses idle time to perform progression. Thus, the impact of collaborative polling on compute time

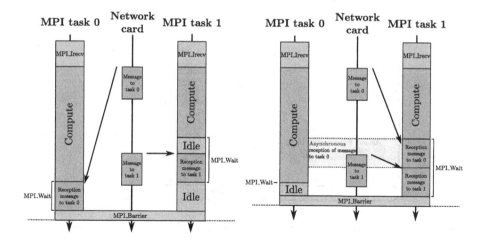

Fig. 2. MPI runtime without collaborative polling (left) and MPI with collaborative polling (right)

is reduced compared to other methods. Collaborative polling also provides an auto-adaptive polling frequency. Indeed, the frequency of calls to polling method is directly linked to the amount of tasks waiting for a communication. For example, when the number of tasks waiting on a barrier increases, the frequency of calls to the message progression method increases as well.

4   Implementation

We designed and implemented our collaborative polling approach into MPC. Since the Infiniband implementation of MPC uses the Reliable Connection (RC) service, the message order is guaranteed and messages are reliably delivered to the receiver. Three message transfer protocols are available: eager, buffered eager (split a message into several eager messages) and Rendezvous based on RDMA write. To guarantee the order across these three protocols, the high level reordering interface of MPC is in charge of sorting incoming messages.

Modern interconnects such as Infiniband usually exploit Event Queues. When a message is completed by the NIC, a new completion descriptor is posted to the corresponding completion queue (CQ). Then, the CQ is polled to read incoming descriptors and process messages. MPC implements two CQ: one for send, another for receive. Both of them are shared among tasks meaning that all notifications are received and multiplexed into the same CQ.

As depicted on Fig. 3, each MPI task implements two pending lists: one private for point-to-point messages and one global for collective operations. To ensure the message progression, the MPC scheduler calls the polling function every time a context switch occurs. The polling function is divided into three successive operations. *First* the task tries to access the CQ and returns if another task is already polling the same CQ. We limit to one the number of tasks authorized

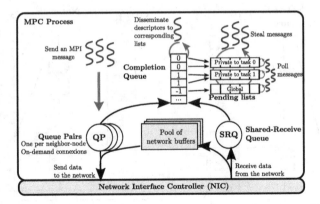

Fig. 3. Collaborative-Polling Implementation inside MPC Infiniband Module

to simultaneously poll the NIC because we observed a performance-loss with a concurrent access to the same CQ. Then, each completed Work Request (WR) found from the CQ is disseminated and enqueued to the corresponding pending list. At this time, the message is not processed. *Secondly*, the global and the private pending lists are both polled. *Thirdly*, with collaborative polling, if a task does not find any message to process, it tries to steal a WR for a task located on the same NUMA node before lastly trying another NUMA node.

4.1   Extension to Process-Based MPI

Collaborative polling requires the underlying MPI runtime to share some internal structures among tasks located on the same node. Within a regular process-based MPI runtime, collaborative polling could be implemented by mapping the same shared-memory segment in each process. The cumbersome job here is to extract the polling-related structures from the existing runtime and place them into the shared memory. Another approach would to use the Linux XPMEM Linux kernel that enables a process to expose its virutal address space to other MPI processes [19].

5   Experiments

This section presents the impact of collaborative polling on three MPI applications: EulerMHD [20], BT from the NAS Parallel Benchmark suite [21], and Gadget-2 [22] from the PRACE benchmarks. These codes run on the Curie supercomputer owned by GENCI and operated into the TGCC by CEA. This is a QDR Infiniband cluster with up to 360 nodes equipped with 4 Intel Nehalem EX processors for a total of 32 cores per node. We compare our approach (MPC w/ CP) against the regular version of MPC (MPC w/o CP), MVAPICH 1.7, Open MPI 1.5.4 and Intel MPI 4.0.3.088.

5.1   Block Tridiagonal Solver (NAS-BT)

The Block Tridiagonal Solver solves three sets of uncoupled systems of equations. It uses a balanced three-dimension domain partition in MPI and performs coarse-grained communications.

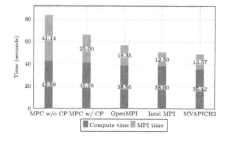

Function	w/o CP	w/ CP	Speedup
Execution time	83.73	66.19	1.26
Compute time	42.59	41.19	1.03
MPI time	41.14	25	1.65
MPI_Waitall	8.06	6.6	1.22
MPI_Reduce	$1.29 \cdot 10^{-3}$	$1.28 \cdot 10^{-2}$	0.1
MPI_Allreduce	$2.39 \cdot 10^{-2}$	$6.59 \cdot 10^{-2}$	0.36
MPI_Wait	30.11	15.97	1.89
MPI_Isend	2.65	2.01	1.32
MPI_Irecv	0.29	0.33	0.88
MPI_Barrier	$4.37 \cdot 10^{-3}$	$1.53 \cdot 10^{-2}$	0.29
MPI_Bcast	$1.12 \cdot 10^{-2}$	$3.5 \cdot 10^{-3}$	3.2

Fig. 4. BT Evaluation (class D)   **Fig. 5.** BT MPI Time Showdown (class D)

Figure 4 illustrates the results obtained running the BT benchmark with class D on 1024 cores on several MPI implementations. It decomposes the time spent inside the MPI runtime from the computational time. Collaborative polling allows a significant speed-up compared to regular MPC implementation. In comparison to other MPI implementations, we can however notice an overhead in MPC with collaborative polling. This is because the Message Passing layer of MPC is not well-optimized for the message sizes used by the NAS-BT benchmark in this configuration. We are currently investigating this issue.

Figure 5 exposes the details of the time spent in the MPI runtime. The gain comes from the time spent inside the *wait* functions (`MPI_Wait` and `MPI_Waitall`) because the messages have already been processed by another task when reaching such function. Indeed, Fig. 6 shows the amount of messages stolen per task (locally on the same NUMA node or remotely on another NUMA node located on the same computational node). It clearly states that the number of stolen messages is high, leading to the acceleration of the wait functions.

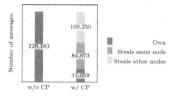

Fig. 6. Steal statistics (BT)

5.2   EulerMHD

EulerMHD is an MPI application solving both the Euler and the ideal magneto-hydrodynamics (MHD) equations at high order on a two dimensional Cartesian mesh. At each iteration, the ghost cells are packed into contiguous buffers and sent to neighbors through non-blocking calls with no-overlap capabilities. Furthermore, each timestep, a set of global reductions on one float number each is performed.

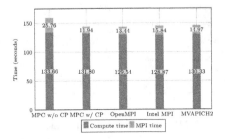

Function	w/o CP	w/ CP	Speedup
Execution time	159.41	143.74	1.11
Compute time	133.66	131.8	1.01
MPI time	25.76	11.94	2.16
MPI_Allreduce	3.12	2.75	1.13
MPI_Wait	21.86	8.45	2.59
MPI_Isend	0.57	0.49	1.16
MPI_Irecv	0.21	0.24	0.87

Fig. 7. EulerMHD Evaluation   **Fig. 8.** EulerMHD MPI Time Showdown

In these experiments, we use a mesh of size 4096 × 4096 for a total of 1024 MPI tasks and 193 timesteps. As depicted in Fig. 7, the collaborative polling decreases the time spent in MPI functions by a factor of 2. Details of time decomposition is illustrated in Table 8. The first time-consuming MPI call, the MPI_Wait function, shows a significant speedup by more than 2.5. The computation loop is also impacted and exhibits a minor improvement. This may be due to the polling function which is less aggressive while waiting messages with collaborative polling enabled, diminishing the memory traffic.

5.3   Gadget-2

Gadget-2 is an MPI application for cosmological N-body smoothed particle hydrodynamic simulations. At each timestep, the domain is decomposed and the work-load is balanced across MPI tasks using a combination of Allgather, Allgatherv and Ssend/Recv functions. During the force computation, each task exchanges the number of outgoing particles with a call to MPI_Allgather before sending a point-to-point message to each neighbor containing the new positions of the moving particles. From a task to another, the construction of the local tree differs causing an imbalanced work-load and a variation in the number of neighors. The configuration simulates $1e^7$ particles for 16 timesteps on 256 cores.

Collaborative polling exhibits an improvement in message-waiting time (see Fig. 9). Table 10 details the time acceleration of MPI functions: collaborative polling allows speed-up on MPI_Recv and MPI_Sendrecv functions leading to a 7% improvement for the MPI time compared to regular MPC run.

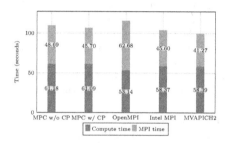

Function	w/o CP	w/ CP	Speedup
Execution time	109.87	106.8	1.03
Compute time	61.18	61.09	1
MPI time	48.69	45.7	1.07
MPI_Reduce	1.03	0.83	1.25
MPI_Allreduce	3.81	4.24	0.9
MPI_Recv	2.62	1.31	2
MPI_Barrier	6.55	6.56	1
MPI_Bcast	0.32	0.25	1.26
MPI_Allgather	9.07	9.22	0.98
MPI_Sendrecv	6.25	5.06	1.24
MPI_Gather	$4.62 \cdot 10^{-3}$	$3.8 \cdot 10^{-3}$	1.21
MPI_Ssend	0.18	0.18	0.99
MPI_Allgatherv	18.85	18.05	1.04

Fig. 9. Gadget Evaluation   **Fig. 10.** Gadget MPI Time Showdown

6   Conclusion and Future Work

In this paper, we proposed a transparent runtime optimization called Collaborative Polling. This solution does not require to modify the source code of the application nor the programming model. The experiments on scientific codes show a significant improvement of the MPI time with collaborative polling. Many kinds of MPI calls can benefit from this optimization: blocking/non-blocking point-to-point as well as global collectives such as barrier and allreduce. Additionally to this paper, collaborative polling was designed for MPI and Infiniband but may be extended to any programming model and any interconnect which does not implement a full independent message progression.

In the worst case of a perfectly well-balanced application, collaborative polling fails to progress message asynchronously. We plan to investigate a mixed-solution with an interrupt-based polling in a future work. We also plan to focus on hydrid MPI/OpenMP code where idle OpenMP would participate to collaborative polling and progress messages of any MPI task located on the same compute node.

Acknowledgements. This paper is a result of work performed in Exascale Computing Research Lab with support provided by CEA, GENCI, INTEL, and UVSQ. Any opinions, findings, and conclusions or recommendations expressed in this material are those of the author(s) and do not necessarily reflect the views of the CEA, GENCI, INTEL or UVSQ. We acknowledge that the results in this paper have been achieved using the PRACE Research Infrastructure resource Curie based in France at Bruyres-le-Châtel.

References

1. Iii, J.B.W., Bova, S.W.: Where's the overlap? - an analysis of popular MPI implementations. Technical report (August 12, 1999)
2. Brightwell, R., Riesen, R., Underwood, K.D.: Analyzing the impact of overlap, offload, and independent progress for message passing interface applications. IJHPCA (2005)
3. Pérache, M., Carribault, P., Jourdren, H.: MPC-MPI: An MPI Implementation Reducing the Overall Memory Consumption. In: Ropo, M., Westerholm, J., Dongarra, J. (eds.) PVM/MPI. LNCS, vol. 5759, pp. 94–103. Springer, Heidelberg (2009)

4. Bell, C., Bonachea, D., Nishtala, R., Yelick, K.A.: Optimizing bandwidth limited problems using one-sided communication and overlap. In: IPDPS (2006)
5. Subotic, V., Sancho, J.C., Labarta, J., Valero, M.: The impact of application's micro-imbalance on the communication-computation overlap. In: Parallel, Distributed and Network-based Processing (PDP) (2011)
6. Thakur, R., Gropp, W.: Open Issues in MPI Implementation. In: Choi, L., Paek, Y., Cho, S. (eds.) ACSAC 2007. LNCS, vol. 4697, pp. 327–338. Springer, Heidelberg (2007)
7. Hager, G., Jost, G., Rabenseifner, R.: Communication characteristics and hybrid MPI/OpenMP parallel programming on clusters of multi-core SMP nodes. In: Proceedings of Cray User Group (2009)
8. Graham, R., Poole, S., Shamis, P., Bloch, G., Bloch, N., Chapman, H., Kagan, M., Shahar, A., Rabinovitz, I., Shainer, G.: Connectx-2 infiniband management queues: First investigation of the new support for network offloaded collective operations. In: International Conference on Cluster, Cloud and Grid Computing, CCGRID (2010)
9. Almási, G., Bellofatto, R., Brunheroto, J., Caşcaval, C., Castaños, J.G., Crumley, P., Erway, C.C., Lieber, D., Martorell, X., Moreira, J.E., Sahoo, R., Sanomiya, A., Ceze, L., Strauss, K.: An overview of the bluegene/L system software organization. In: Parallel Processing Letters (2003)
10. Amerson, G., Apon, A.: Implementation and design analysis of a network messaging module using virtual interface architecture. In: International Conference on Cluster Computing (2004)
11. Sur, S., Jin, H.W., Chai, L., Panda, D.K.: RDMA Read Based Rendezvous Protocol for MPI over InfiniBand: Design Alternatives and Benefits. Alternatives (2006)
12. Kumar, R., Mamidala, A.R., Koop, M.J., Santhanaraman, G., Panda, D.K.: Lock-Free Asynchronous Rendezvous Design for MPI Point-to-Point Communication. In: Lastovetsky, A., Kechadi, T., Dongarra, J. (eds.) EuroPVM/MPI 2008. LNCS, vol. 5205, pp. 185–193. Springer, Heidelberg (2008)
13. Hoefler, T., Lumsdaine, A.: Message progression in parallel computing – to thread or not to thread? In: International Conference on Cluster Computing (2008)
14. Trahay, F., Denis, A.: A scalable and generic task scheduling system for communication libraries. In: International Conference on Cluster Computing (2009)
15. Huang, C., Lawlor, O., Kalé, L.V.: Adaptive MPI. In: LCPC (2004)
16. Rico-Gallego, J.-A., Díaz-Martín, J.-C.: Performance Evaluation of Thread-Based MPI in Shared Memory. In: Cotronis, Y., Danalis, A., Nikolopoulos, D.S., Dongarra, J. (eds.) EuroMPI 2011. LNCS, vol. 6960, pp. 337–338. Springer, Heidelberg (2011)
17. Demaine, E.: A threads-only MPI implementation for the development of parallel programming. In: Proceedings of the 11th International Symposium on High Performance Computing Systems (1997)
18. Tang, H., Yang, T.: Optimizing threaded MPI execution on SMP clusters. In: International Conference on Supercomputing, ICS (2001)
19. Brightwell, R., Pedretti, K.: An intra-node implementation of openshmem using virtual address space mapping. In: Fifth Partitioned Global Address Space Conference (2011)
20. Wolff, M., Jaouen, S., Jourdren, H., Sonnendrcker, E.: High-order dimensionally split lagrange-remap schemes for ideal magnetohydrodynamics. Discrete and Continuous Dynamical Systems - Series S (2012)
21. Bailey, D., Harris, T., Saphir, W., van der Wijngaart, R., Woo, A., Yarrow, M.: The NAS Parallel Benchmarks 2.0 (1995)
22. Springel, V.: The cosmological simulation code gadget-2. Monthly Notices of the Royal Astronomical Society 364 (2005)

Delegation-Based MPI Communications for a Hybrid Parallel Computer with Many-Core Architecture

Kazumi Yoshinaga[1,5], Yuichi Tsujita[1,5], Atsushi Hori[2,5],
Mikiko Sato[3,5], Mitaro Namiki[3,5], and Yutaka Ishikawa[4]

[1] Kinki University
[2] Advanced Institute for Computational Science, RIKEN
[3] Tokyo University of Agriculture and Technology
[4] The University of Tokyo
[5] JST CREST

Abstract. Many-core architecture draws much attention in HPC community towards the Exascale era. Many ongoing research activities using GPU or the Many Integrated Core (MIC) architecture from Intel exist worldwide. Many-core CPUs have a great deal of impact to improve computing performance, however, they are not favorable for heavy communications and I/Os which are essential for MPI operations in general.

We have been focusing on the MIC architecture as many-core CPUs to realize a hybrid parallel computer in conjunction with multi-core CPUs. We propose a delegation mechanism for scalable MPI communications issued on many-core CPUs so as to play delegated operations on multi-core ones. This architecture also minimizes memory utilization of not only many-core CPUs but also multi-core ones by deploying multi-layered MPI communicator information. Here we evaluated the delegation mechanism on an emulated hybrid computing environment. We show our innovative design and its performance evaluation on the emulated environment in this paper.

Keywords: many-core architecture, MPI, inter-core communication, delegation, multi-layered MPI communicator information.

1 Introduction

MPI [8] is the de-facto standard communication interface in parallel computing nowadays. Especially collective communications are widely used in large scale parallel computations.

Towards the exascale era, we should tackle serious problems in poor scalability and large inter-process communication overhead. For example, collective MPI communication functions include optimized communication algorithms. Even in the optimized method, we may have large overhead due to hardware heterogeneity in parallel computers consisting of large number of computing nodes. As a result, increasing the number of computing nodes or multi-core CPUs does not scale effectively.

J.L. Träff, S. Benkner, and J. Dongarra (Eds.): EuroMPI 2012, LNCS 7490, pp. 47–56, 2012.

Recently many-core CPUs has been focused for its highly optimized architecture. For example, the MIC architecture from Intel will play a big role as a computing accelerator in 10 PFlops class parallel computer named Stampede [11].

When we have more than millions of CPU cores, we may have difficulty in managing an MPI communicator information because its size per MPI process is proportional to the number of MPI processes in the current MPI implementations [1]. The authors pointed out some possibilities or technical challenges to have scalability.

We believe that a hybrid parallel computer with many-core and multi-core architectures will reach to the Exaflops era. We consider to utilize the MIC architecture [5] as computing accelerators for the hybrid computer. Our motivation for this research activity is having an MPI library which harnesses existing MPI applications from current homogeneous supercomputers to the state-of-art hybrid parallel computer with many-core CPUs based on the MIC architecture. In the hybrid architecture, MPI processes will be initiated on every core of many-core CPUs. We do not handle any threads in our framework.

For this purpose, we have been implementing a delegation mechanism which transfers an MPI function request from MPI processes on many-core CPUs to multi-core ones seamlessly. The delegation mechanism will also minimize communication cost by merging MPI requests from many-core CPUs on every delegatee process running on a multi-core CPU. We have started this research in parallel with R & D of our OS kernel to organize the whole system software with forthcoming MIC architecture as soon as possible. Therefore, we have evaluated performance of the delegation-based MPI infrastructure on a PC cluster which imitated our target hybrid architecture. Here we observed not only its performance advantages but also effective memory utilization relative to the original MPI implementation.

In this paper, we describe our motivation for this research and development, and explain software design of the delegation one in Sec. 2. Later we discuss performance evaluation results in Sec. 3. Related work is mentioned in Sec. 4, and finally we summarize our paper in Sec. 5.

2   Delegation-Based MPI Communication Infrastructure: Motivation and Design

It is expected to achieve Exaflops performance around 2018, and one of the key devices is a many-core CPU which is so-called a computation accelerator. In general, multi-core CPUs as host managers control the many-core CPUs in the form of a PCIe card. GPGPU is one of the advanced techniques for this purpose, and it is widely used in high performance computing community. Meanwhile Intel has announced the MIC in 2010, where the first substantiation named Knights Ferry was announced [5]. It is a development platform to evaluate scientific applications and system software to prepare for the forthcoming products. Intel will soon release a product based on the MIC architecture named Knights Corner later, and a parallel computer named Stampede [11] in TACC will utilize it as a computing accelerator.

When we use many-core CPUs based on the MIC architecture, we may deploy computation threads by using Pthreads, OpenMP, or Cilk plus in general. However we address to deploy an MPI process on every computing core, thus eliminating to have computation threads at least in the MPI program layer for sustainable use of existing MPI programs. In order to exploit high performance computing power of many-core CPUs, we propose a delegation-based MPI middleware for our target hybrid supercomputer. We are expecting that most of user's MPI applications can run faster with the help of the middleware.

A system architecture of our target parallel computer is shown in Figure 1. We have been designing a hybrid operating system for this architecture [10]. Every node has multi-core CPUs as host CPUs and many-core ones on PCIe cards for high performance computations. We will have a newly designed light-weight OS and a customized common Linux kernel for many-core and multi-core ones, respectively. R & D of them is in progress at this moment [10]. Communications in a user space between multi-core and many-core CPUs via a PCIe bus are realized by the inter-kernel communication support. We call this "inter-core communication" in a user level. Every process on many-core CPUs (hereafter many-core process) can access a sort of virtual memory address space of processes on multi-core CPUs (hereafter multi-core processes) and vice versa. Furthermore every many-core process has a shared memory address space on the same many-core CPU. Thus, such address space can be used for MPI communications inside the same many-core CPU in order to minimize latency of MPI communications.

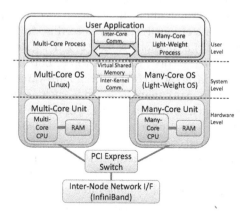

Fig. 1. Architecture of a target hybrid parallel computer system

We propose to deploy delegation processes (hereafter delegatees) to realize flexible and scalable MPI communications among computation nodes instead of direct communications among many-core processes as shown in Figure 2. Once an MPI start-up program is initiated (1), every delegatee is invoked by the MPI start-up program (2), followed by invocation of many-core processes by each delegatee (3).

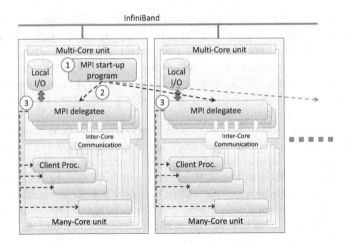

Fig. 2. Delegation mechanism in MPI communications

Another technical challenge is effective management of MPI communicator information. We can not keep existing MPI communicator management scheme in the Exascale era due to the limited memory resources of many-core CPUs. Therefore, we need to minimize communicator information on many-core CPUs by delegating most of the information to multi-core CPUs. In this strategy, we have been designing a multi-layered MPI communicator.

Figure 3 depicts a rough sketch of our multi-layered communicator table. The communicator table consists of four hierarchy according to node grouping manner in the current design; (1) a top-node table, (2) a delegatee-group table, (3) a delegatee table, and (4) a many-core table from top to bottom layers. The reason why we separate into four layers was coming from hardware hierarchy in the hybrid system. Information in every many-core table such as the number of cores, an assigned unique-ID of each core, MPI rank-ID, or an MPI attribute are stored in it. This table is managed by "super-process" on a dedicated core on a many-core CPU for delegation-based communications. Every delegatee shares a delegatee table which stores a pointer to an assigned many-core table. Besides, every slot has the number of processes which the assigned delegatee has in order to figure out the number of processes. Inside a delegatee group, one of the delegatees is assigned for "super-delegatee" which manages every delegatee table information and data communications among delegatee groups. Data communication from/to other group are carried out by the super-delegatee. The top-node table has information about every delegatee-group and we can easily access every group.

For preliminary performance evaluation in this paper, we have just implemented a pseudo communicator information table which consisted of node and many-core tables. The full-scale MPI communicator information mechanism was not implemented yet because we did not have enough number of processes to use the four-layered MPI communicator information. When we have more than 1 million processes for example, we may need such multi-layered table.

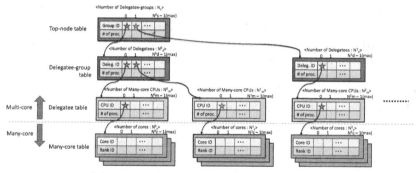

(a) Proposed multi-layered communicator table

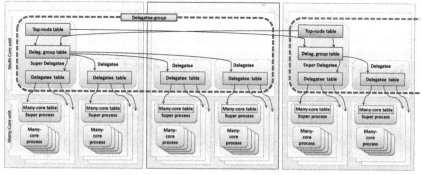

(b) Multi-layered communicator table and processes placement pattern

Fig. 3. Design of our multi-layered communicator table

3   Performance Evaluation on an Emulated Environment

We deployed an emulated environment which imitated the proposed hybrid architecture on a PC cluster system at Information Technology Center, the University of Tokyo. Every node had two Intel 6-core Xeon X5680 CPUs with 96 GB memory. PC nodes were connected via 4×QDR InfiniBand. MVAPICH2 ver. 1.6rc1 [12] was used on 24 nodes for this evaluation. MPI start-up program initiated one pseudo delegatee process on each node, thus one delegatee per node. Later every delegatee invoked pseudo many-core processes on vacant CPU cores with the help of CPU affinity control API. Polling scheme by using a user-level shared memory emulated inter-core communications.

We have evaluated our preliminary implementation in several collective MPI communications with and without delegatees, hereafter we describe delegation mode and normal mode, respectively. We deployed pseudo many-core processes in (a) round-robin and (b) block manner to evaluate impact of process locality. Every node had one delegatee process each, which managed multiple pseudo many-core processes.

Figure 4 shows communication times obtained by MPI_Bcast. Here **deleg** and **normal** denote the delegation mode and normal mode, respectively. Operation sequence of MPI_Bcast in the delegation mode is as follows: (1) Once many-core processes issue the MPI function, delegatees catch this function call and issue MPI_Bcast. The delegatee which manages the root many-core process works as a root process. (2) After the data communication, non-root many-core processes copy the received data from the delegatee to a local receive-buffer.

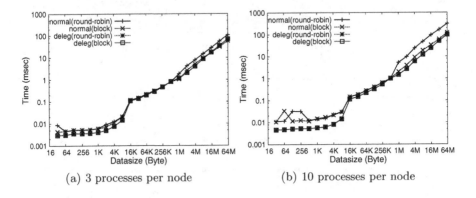

(a) 3 processes per node   (b) 10 processes per node

Fig. 4. Communication time of MPI_Bcast with and without delegatees, where (a) 3 and (b) 10 many-core processes per node

Vertical and horizontal axes denote communication time and message size specified in the MPI function, respectively. With more than 16 MB message size, Fig. 4(a) shows performance degradation in the delegation mode relative to the normal mode in a block manner. However the delegation mode outperformed the normal mode in round-robin manner. This performance gap was coming from process placement mismatch regarding communication scheme used in the function. The delegation mode in Fig. 4(b) outperformed the normal one in both placement manners.

Here, we note that the delegation mode could minimize communication time independent of process placement patterns because the delegatee eliminated unnecessary communications by many-core processes inside the same node.

We also evaluated MPI_Allgather as shown in Figure 5. Operation sequence of MPI_Allgather in delegation mode is as follows: (1) Once many-core processes issue the MPI function, every delegatee gathers data to be sent from many-core processes and stores them together to delegatee's send-buffer. (2) Delegatees issue MPI_Allgather. (3) If the many-core processes are allocated in round-robin manner, delegatees rearrange the received data in order of rank-ID. (4) Many-core processes copy the received data from the delegatee to a local receive-buffer specified in the MPI function.

With the help of collecting small data in the delegation mode, the delegation mode outperformed the normal mode with smaller message size less than 2 KB.

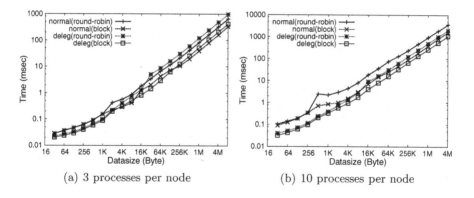

(a) 3 processes per node   (b) 10 processes per node

Fig. 5. Communication time of MPI_Allgather with and without delegatees, where (a) 3 and (b) 10 many-core processes per node

On the other hand, for larger message size more than 256 KB, delegation mode in each allocation manner were inefficient compared to the normal mode in Fig. 5(a) because the impact of additional processing such as memory copy is large. Whereas, Fig. 5(b) shows that the delegation mode outperformed the normal mode in each allocation manner.

The evaluation results show that the delegation mechanism could provide effective communication with the larger number of many-core processes. Since our target hybrid computer will have around 50 many-core processes per many-core CPU, the delegation mechanism is expected to provide efficient data communication for the target computer.

At this moment, we have just two-layers separated into many-core and node tables as we mentioned in Sec. 2. However we believed that it was worth to know how much MPI processes consumed memory resources. We have evaluated utilized memory resources of our implementation and the normal MVAPICH2 library by extracting /proc interface information. Since utilized physical memory size was observed only as a total value, we could not distinguish used memory size for a delegatee process and many-core processes in our implementation. Therefore we discuss size of mapped virtual memory space of each process through /proc interface.

Figure 6 shows measured values. Here the original MPI increased resource utilization with an increase in the number of MPI processes. While our delegation scheme did not increase as the original one did. It is noted that the delegation mode could minimize size of used memory on many-core processes, while the delegatees exhausted a sort of memory because every delegatee should have almost of all the communicator information.

Once we suppose to have 1 EFlops with 1 TFlops many-core CPUs, we may need 1 M CPUs. In this case, there will be 50 M processes in total if one many-core CPU has 50 cores. In case of 4 CPUs per computation node, we need 250,000 nodes. When we have one delegatee process per one many-core CPU, we need 1,000,000 delegatees. Since every delegatee process is an MPI process, it is very

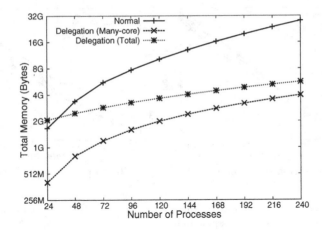

Fig. 6. Utilized memory size in collective MPI communications

hard to organize a flat MPI due to limited memory resources because we may need about 200 GB per process according to our estimation based on the evaluation in Fig. 6. Therefore we propose to divide a delegatee table into "delegatee groups" along with hardware affinity such as computation nodes under the same interconnection switch, for example, in order to minimize memory utilization. We also expect that this approach will minimize information retrieval time according to the nature of data-locality. Every delegatee group has a "super delegatee" to manage every delegatee information in the same group. In this scheme, we may have about 200 MB per group if each delegatee group has 1,000 delegatees. Towards the Exascale era, we are considering to have more layers by grouping in the node table layer.

4   Related Work

Kamal et al. have realized a scalable MPI implementation in communicator and group management [6]. They have focused on reducing memory utilization for communicator and groups towards effective and scalable management of a large number of MPI processes. Their principal idea is based on multi-layered communicator management, and it is similar with ours, however our target computer is different from their target. Since we have heterogeneity not only in hardware architecture but also among OSs, we should pay much attention to seamless operations among a light-weight OS on many-core architecture and a normal Linux kernel OS on multi-core one.

Locality-aware deployment is a very important aspect in such hybrid architecture. Authors in [4] proposed Locality-Aware Mapping Algorithm named LAMA to deploy MPI processes with locality-awareness across processing elements spreading among compute nodes. Their basic idea to utilize hwloc [2] is coming from a NUMA architecture of recent multi-core CPUs. It has incorporated in OpenMPI [9]. KNEM [7] is also focusing on locality-awareness, however its interest is within intra-node MPI communications.

On the other hand, our proposed communication infrastructure has addressed to have scalable MPI communications on a hybrid architecture with many-core and multi-core CPUs. We should pay attention to heterogeneity not only among the same kind of CPUs but also between many-core and multi-core CPUs. Primal goal of this infrastructure is work-sharing by delegating MPI communications from many-core to multi-core units.

Reducing memory utilization for MPI communicator information is a critical issue in scalability aspects. Goodell et al. proposed a virtual connection in the MPICH2 implementation [3]. Our multi-layered communicator management is similar with their scheme. However our proposal is based on delegation mechanism for MPI communications from many-core CPUs to multi-core ones.

5   Concluding Remarks

In this paper, we describe design of our delegation-based MPI communication middleware suitable for a hybrid parallel computer consisting of many-core and multi-core CPUs. We have addressed to utilize the MIC architecture from Intel as accelerators in our target parallel computers. Due to concurrent R&D with a light-weight OS for the MIC architecture, we evaluated our implementation on an emulated hybrid parallel computing system. Through the evaluation, we observed that our delegation mechanism was better than the communications without delegatees in mismatch process placement. Furthermore performance of our mechanism was not degraded by process placement patterns because delegatees minimized communication cost by merging MPI function calls and data movement by many-core processes.

We also proposed multi-layered MPI communicator management for the hybrid parallel computer. Since we did not have enough computing nodes on the emulated computing environment, we had only two layers in the communicator. However minimization of memory utilization was observed in our multi-layered MPI communicator management. Because many-core CPUs will have very limited memory resources in general, it is effective to deploy most of the communicator information on multi-core CPUs by using the communicator management scheme.

We also argued technical challenges to be done in our design through the evaluation and we will evaluate the full-scale MPI communicator information mechanism on a big parallel computer as a future work. Implementation of other MPI functions is also our future work.

Acknowledgment. This research work is partially supported by the support program for young and women researchers of the University of Tokyo and JST CREST.

References

1. Balaji, P., Buntinas, D., Goodell, D., Gropp, W., Hoefler, T., Kumar, S., Lusk, E.L., Thakur, R., Träff, J.L.: MPI on millions of cores. Parallel Processing Letters 21(1), 45–60 (2011)
2. Broquedis, F., Clet-Ortega, J., Moreaud, S., Furmento, N., Goglin, B., Mercier, G., Thibault, S., Namyst, R.: hwloc: A generic framework for managing hardware affinities in hpc applications. In: Proceedings of the 18th Euromicro Conference on Parallel, Distributed and Network-based Processing, PDP 2010, Pisa, Italy, February 17-19, pp. 180–186. IEEE Computer Society (2010)
3. Goodell, D., Gropp, W., Zhao, X., Thakur, R.: Scalable Memory Use in MPI: A Case Study with MPICH2. In: Cotronis, Y., Danalis, A., Nikolopoulos, D.S., Dongarra, J. (eds.) EuroMPI 2011. LNCS, vol. 6960, pp. 140–149. Springer, Heidelberg (2011)
4. Hursey, J., Squyres, J.M., Dontje, T.: Locality-aware parallel process mapping for multi-core hpc systems. In: Proceedings of 2011 IEEE International Conference on Cluster Computing (CLUSTER), Austin, TX, USA, September 26-30, pp. 527–531. IEEE (2011)
5. Intel: Intel unveils new product plans for high-performance computing (2010), http://www.intel.com/pressroom/archive/releases/2010/20100531comp.htm
6. Kamal, H., Mirtaheri, S., Wagner, A.: Scalability of communicators and groups in MPI. In: Proceedings of the 19th ACM International Symposium on High Performance Distributed Computing, pp. 264–275. ACM, New York (2010)
7. KNEM: High-performance intra-node MPI communication, http://runtime.bordeaux.inria.fr/knem/
8. MPI Forum, http://www.mpi-forum.org/
9. Open MPI: Open Source High Performance Computing, http://www.open-mpi.org/
10. Sato, M., Fukazawa, G., Nagamine, K., Sakamoto, R., Namiki, M., Yoshinaga, K., Tsujita, Y., Hori, A., Ishikawa, Y.: A design of hybrid operating system for a parallel computer with multi-core and many-core processors. Accepted to ROSS 2012 (2012)
11. Texas Advanced Computing Center: Stampede, http://www.tacc.utexas.edu/stampede
12. The Ohio State University: MVAPICH: MPI over InfiniBand, 10GigE/iWARP and RoCE, http://mvapich.cse.ohio-state.edu/index.shtml

Efficient Multithreaded Context ID Allocation in MPI*

James Dinan[1], David Goodell[1], William Gropp[2],
Rajeev Thakur[1], and Pavan Balaji[1]

[1] Argonne National Laboratory
{dinan,goodell,thakur,balaji}@mcs.anl.gov
[2] University of Illinois at Urbana-Champaign
wgropp@illinois.edu

Abstract. An important aspect of support for multithreaded MPI executions is the management of communication context identifiers (IDs), which are used to associate MPI communication operations with a communicator. New communicator creation functionality in MPI 3.0 adds complexity to this core resource management problem. We present an efficient algorithm for multithreaded context ID allocation that builds on an existing production algorithm developed to support MPI 2.2. Through this work, we have discovered a subtle concurrency bug in the existing algorithm that can result in deadlock. We correct this bug and develop methods to overcome the performance impact of deadlock prevention. We evaluate the performance of the new algorithm and prove that it is free from deadlock.

1 Introduction

Hybrid parallel programming that combines MPI with a shared-memory programming model, such as threads or OpenMP, has become a popular paradigm for constructing scalable and efficient high-performance applications. In this model, MPI is used for internode coordination and data movement, while hardware-supported shared memory is leveraged to achieve efficient intranode execution. The adoption of such hybrid programming techniques has been driven by sustained increases in the number of cores and hardware threads provided per processor. This trend indicates not only that MPI must interoperate well with a variety of shared-memory programming models but also that MPI must efficiently manage increasing levels of concurrency within the MPI library [6].

The MPI 2.2 standard [7] defined the interaction of MPI with threads, and significant effort was invested to extend MPI implementations to support this new hybrid execution model [5,8,9]. An important component of this effort was the development of multithreaded context identity (ID) allocation algorithms [5].

---

* This work was supported in part by the U.S. Department of Energy under contract DE-AC02-06CH11357 and the Advanced Scientific Computing Research program, Office of Science, U.S. Department of Energy award DE-FG02-08ER25835.

J.L. Träff, S. Benkner, and J. Dongarra (Eds.): EuroMPI 2012, LNCS 7490, pp. 57–66, 2012.

MPI uses context IDs internally to match communication operations with communicators; a new context ID must be generated each time MPI constructs a new communicator.

The MPI 3.0 specification that is nearing completion contains new functionality that will require modification to how an MPI implementation allocates context IDs. Among these changes is a new, noncollective communicator creation routine that supports multiple concurrent invocations that are differentiated by using a tag argument [3]. Traditional communicator creation routines are collective over all processes in a parent communicator; in contrast, this new routine is collective over only the group of processes that will be members of the new communicator. The functionality of this routine is expected to address several key application needs, as explained in detail in [3]. For example, when a node failure occurs, processes must create a new communicator to re-establish collective communication; however, traditional communicator creation would require participation from failed processes. This routine also enables the use of load balancing techniques that asynchronously reassign idle processes to heavily loaded execution teams [2]. Moreover, this routine can significantly reduce the cost of communicator creation by including only processes that will be members of the new communicator.

We have extended the MPICH2 [1] multithreaded context ID allocation routine to support this new functionality. Through this work, we discovered a bug in the production algorithm that can result in deadlock. We correct this bug and discuss techniques to eliminate the performance impact of deadlock prevention. We prove that the new algorithm meets all constraints and is free from deadlock. We compare the performance of native noncollective communicator creation with the user-level algorithm [3] and demonstrate that the native implementation provides a significant speedup by eliminating $O(\log n)$ communicator creation operations. Furthermore, we show that noncollective communicator creation can provide a several-fold speedup over collective communicator creation when the output group is smaller than the parent communicator.

This paper is organized as follows. In Section 2 we discuss the interaction of MPI with threads and the new, noncollective communicator creation routine that will be added in MPI-3. Section 3 presents the enhanced multithreaded context ID allocation algorithm, which prevents the deadlock condition that was possible in the existing algorithm. In Section 4 we prove correctness and deadlock freedom for this new routine. An optimization to eliminate deadlock prevention overheads is presented in Section 5. We evaluate the performance of our implementation in Section 6 and summarize our conclusions in Section 8.

2   Multithreading and MPI

The MPI 2.0 standard defined MPI's interaction with threads; several levels of multithreading are supported depending on the needs of the application. In this work, we consider the case where MPI is initialized to support MPI_THREAD_MULTIPLE because other, more restrictive threading levels don't subject the MPI implementation to a level of concurrency that necessitates these techniques.

Of particular importance to this work is the interaction of MPI collectives with threads. The MPI standard states that a program may perform only one collective operation per communicator at a time. If the application uses threads, the programmer must ensure that threads do not perform multiple collectives concurrently on the same communicator. However, multiple collectives can be issued concurrently on different communicators. In the MPI-2 standard, communicator construction is a collective operation that is performed on a parent communicator. Thus, when threads are in use, multiple communicator construction operations can be issued concurrently if the parent communicators are different.

A new routine, MPI_Comm_create_group, which was proposed by the authors, is anticipated in MPI 3.0. The input to this routine is a parent communicator, a group of processes (represented by an MPI_Group object) that will be members of the new communicator, and a tag argument. All processes in the input group must call this routine with the same arguments. A new communicator containing the processes in this group is returned as output; if a process is not a member of the group, MPI_COMM_NULL is returned. In contrast with other collective operations, this routine can be invoked concurrently by multiple threads on the same parent communicator. In such a case, each call must use a distinct tag argument, which is used to distinguish operations. Communication generated by this routine is defined not to interfere with other point-to-point communication on the parent communicator, even if the same tag (or MPI_ANY_TAG) is already in use.

3   Multithreaded Context ID Allocation Algorithm

Communicators are internally identified by an integer context ID in most MPI runtime systems. The context ID value uniquely identifies a given communicator on all processes that are members of the communicator's group. This value is included as a part of the message envelope and is used to ensure that communication operations match only within the same communicator. Allocation of the context ID is at the core of all communicator creation operations. To ensure efficient message matching, all known MPI implementations use context ids that are unique and uniform across all involved processes.

In MPI-2, a parent communicator that contains all processes in the output communicator's group is used to perform any communication needed to select the context ID—typically a collective allreduce operation. Multiple communicator creation operations can be issued concurrently by different threads on different parent communicators; however, the user must ensure that operations are ordered such that only one collective operation is performed on a given parent communicator at any time. In contrast with these semantics, the new MPI_Comm_create_group routine permits threads to issue multiple such operations concurrently on the same parent communicator, and individual operations are distinguished through an additional tag argument.

```
1   /* Input: my_comm, my_group, my_tag.  Output: integer context ID      */
    /* Shared variables ( shared by threads at a each process )           */
3   mask                       /* Bit array, indicates if each context ID is free  */
    mask_in_use   = 0          /* Flag, indicates if mask is in use       */
5   lowest_ctx_id = MAXINT     /* Indicates which thread has the highest priority  */
    lowest_tag                 /* Breaks lowest_ctx_id priority ties      */
7
    /* Private variables ( not shared across threads )                    */
9   local_mask                 /* Thread private copy of the mask         */
    i_own_the_mask = 0         /* Flag indicating if this thread holds the mask   */
11  context_id     = 0         /* Output context ID                       */

13  MPIR_Barrier_group(my_comm, my_group, my_tag) /* new barrier, prevents deadlock */
    while ( context_id == 0 ) {
15    Mutex_lock ()
      if ( my_comm->context_id < lowest_ctx_id
17         || ( my_comm->context_id == lowest_ctx_id && my_tag < lowest_tag ) ) {
        lowest_ctx_id = my_comm -> context_id
19        lowest_tag    = my_tag
      }
21    if ( !mask_in_use
           && my_comm->context_id == lowest_ctx_id && my_tag == lowest_tag ) {
23      local_mask    = mask
        mask_in_use = 1, i_own_the_mask = 1
25    }
      else {
27      local_mask  = 0, i_own_the_mask = 0
      }
29    Mutex_unlock ()
      MPIR_Allreduce_group ( local_mask, MPI_BAND, my_comm, my_group, my_tag )
31    if ( i_own_the_mask ) {
        Mutex_lock ()
33      if ( local_mask != 0 ) {
          context_id      = location of first set bit in local_mask
35        mask[context_id] = 0
          if ( lowest_ctx_id == my_comm->context_id && lowest_tag == my_tag ) {
37          lowest_ctx_id = MAXINT
          }
39      }
        mask_in_use = 0
41      Mutex_unlock ()
      }
43  }
```

Listing 1.1. Multithreaded context ID allocation algorithm

We have extended the existing multithreaded MPICH2 context ID allocation algorithm [5] to include support for MPI_Comm_create_group; we present the modified algorithm in Listing 1.1. In this algorithm, the state of all context IDs is tracked through a vector of Boolean entries, called mask. The context ID mask vector is an array of bits, where the nth bit identifies whether the context ID value n is unused. To allocate a context ID, processes perform a bitwise AND allreduce on the full vector and select the first context ID corresponding to the first nonzero bit.

Group-collective allreduce and barrier routines were created that include only the processes specified by a group argument. Multiple group-collective operations can occur concurrently in different threads, and operations are distinguished by using the tag argument provided by the user. One bit in the tag space was reserved to indicate messages using the given tag correspond to group-collective operation traffic. Thus, we ensure that messages generated during context ID allocation do not conflict with application-generated point-to-point operations.

Concurrent attempts to allocate context IDs by multiple threads in the same process are managed by allowing only one thread to access the context ID mask at any given time. If a thread is not able to gain access to the mask, it must still participate in the allreduce to prevent another thread in its communicator creation operation from blocking indefinitely while holding the mask. Threads that are unable to access the context ID mask pass a vector of zeroes to the allreduce, indicating that no context IDs are currently available and effectively aborting the attempt to allocate the context ID. Thus, multiple attempts may be needed for a successful allreduce to occur; threads continue to retry until a context ID is successfully allocated. In order to prevent livelock where threads cause each other to mutually abort indefinitely, a simple prioritization scheme is used where the threads whose parent communicator has the lowest context ID are given priority for access to the context ID mask.

Two components of the existing algorithm were modified to support the new MPI_Comm_create_group routine. A group-collective version of allreduce was substituted for the communicator-collective implementation. In addition, the prioritization scheme was modified to prioritize threads based on the ⟨$context id, tag$⟩ pair.

Freeing a given context ID, n, requires simply acquiring the mutex and marking $mask[n] = 1$ without waiting for the mask to be available. Threads update only one bit in the mask at a time while holding the mutex. If a context ID, n, is freed during a concurrent allocation attempt, the ongoing allocation attempt will continue to use the initial value $n = 0$ of the given context ID. Context ID n will be observed as available during the next allocation attempt.

3.1   Deadlock Issue and Prevention Mechanism

The existing version of this multithreaded context ID algorithm has been deployed in production for several years in MPICH2, and it was verified by a student collaborator using model checking [5]. However, while extending the algorithm to support noncollective communicator creation, we discovered a subtle bug that can lead to deadlock in the multithreaded case The existence of this bug for several years indicates that the algorithm may not have been used extensively in the field in multithreaded situations, and that the model used for verification did not capture the case that leads to the deadlock.

The existing algorithm did not contain the beginning in Listing 1.1, line 13. In the absence of the barrier, a thread is permitted to reserve the context ID mask and perform the collective allreduce even though the other threads may not have made matching calls to the communicator creation routine, introducing the possibility of a hold-and-wait scenario. If another thread in the same process attempts to perform a second communicator creation operation, a circular wait can occur, resulting in deadlock. One such scenario is illustrated in Figure 1, where there are two processes and two threads per process; each thread executes the following code.

```
if (thread_id == mpi_rank) { MPI_Comm_dup(MPI_COMM_SELF, &self_dup); }
MPI_Comm_dup(thread_comm, &thread_comm_dup);
```

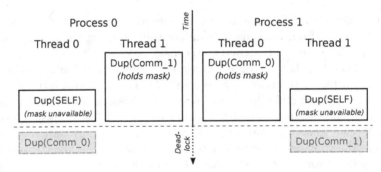

Fig. 1. Deadlock scenario with two processes and two threads per process. Blocked threads hold the mask, preventing other threads from making matching collective calls.

Here, thread_comm is a communicator of the threads at all processes with the same thread ID. In this scenario, calls to duplicate thread_comm block in the allreduce while holding the mask, preventing the calls to duplicate MPI_COMM_SELF from successfully allocating a context ID.

To avoid this deadlock scenario, we break the hold-and-wait condition by ensuring that all threads have arrived before allowing them to reserve the mask. This is accomplished by performing a barrier before entering the allocation loop. Once threads have completed the barrier, they can perform the allreduce and reserve the mask without risk of deadlock. The addition of the barrier, can have a negative impact on performance; in Section 5 we present an optimization that avoids this barrier in many cases while still avoiding the deadlock.

4   Proof of Correctness

We demonstrate that the multithreaded context ID allocation algorithm guarantees progress and ensures that allocation invariants are not violated under a failure-free assumption. MPICH2 requires that the following conditions are satisfied for a context ID allocation to be correct.

Property 1. For a given operation, all processes select the same context ID and this ID is allocated at most once at every process.

Uniform context IDs are guaranteed through the allreduce, which ensures that the output mask is the same at all processes. In addition, the locking discipline and bitwise AND reduction operation ensure that if the given context ID is unavailable (the corresponding bit is zero) at any process, it will be observed as unavailable in the output mask at all processes.

4.1   Proof of Progress

To prove global progress, we must first prove the following liveness property, which did not hold in the original version of the algorithm:

Property 2. No thread can block indefinitely.

The initial barrier added to the algorithm ensures that all processes with the same parent communicator, group, and tag arguments are present before they can reserve the mask or be prioritized for access to the mask. If the mask has been reserved by another thread, threads supply a zero mask to indicate that the mask is locally unavailable. These mechanisms ensure that all necessary threads participate in the ensuing allreduce operation.

Property 3. Threads with the globally highest priority will eventually succeed.

Access to the mask is prioritized according to the ⟨*context id, tag*⟩ pair. This prioritization is critical to ensure that threads do not enter a livelock situation where allocation attempts repeatedly fail because all threads in a given group are unable to obtain the mask at the same time. As threads iterate in the allocation loop, they update the ⟨*context id, tag*⟩ pair when their value is less than the current minimum. Threads are permitted to reserve the mask only when they have the highest priority, and they must release the mask after an allocation attempt if they no longer have the highest priority. A total ⟨*context id, tag*⟩ ordering can be imposed across all threads. The prioritization scheme ensures that threads with the globally highest priority will eventually be able to acquire the mask at all processes involved in the given operation. Assuming that a common, free context ID exists, the globally highest priority operation will eventually succeed.

Property 4. The highest priority thread at a process will eventually succeed.

Once the globally highest priority operation succeeds, the priority variables are reset, and the next ⟨*context id, tag*⟩ pair in the total ordering has the highest priority. A consequence of a prioritization scheme based on such a total ordering of operations is that a low-priority operation can be starved by repeated arrivals of higher-priority operations. Since realistic MPI programs perform a finite number of communicator creation operations, this starvation is bounded in practice. If we assume such finite MPI programs, we observe that as the globally highest-priority operations complete, a locally highest-priority operation will eventually become the globally highest priority and also complete.

Property 5. Every allocation attempt will eventually succeed.

When a locally highest-priority operation completes, the next highest-priority operation becomes the locally highest priority. Thus, assuming finite MPI programs, every operation eventually gains the locally highest priority and completes.

5   Eliminating the Overhead of Deadlock Avoidance

As discussed in Section 3, a synchronization step before entry to the context ID allocation loop is necessary to avoid deadlock. In Listing 1.1 a barrier is used as a

```
     /* Shared variables ( shared by threads at a each process )           */
2    eager_split              /* Reserves mask[0..eager_split-1] for eager alloc.*/
     eager_mask_in_use = 0    /* Flag, indicates if eager mask is already in use */
4
     /* Private variables ( not shared across threads )                     */
6    i_own_eager_mask  = 0    /* Flag, indicates if this thread has eager mask   */

8    Mutex_lock ( eager_lock )
     if ( ! eager_mask_in_use ) {
10      eager_mask_in_use = 1, i_own_eager_mask  = 1
        local_mask            = mask[0..eager_split-1]
12   } else {
        local_mask            = 0
14   }
     Mutex_unlock ( eager_lock )
16   MPIR_Allreduce_group ( local_mask , MPI_BAND , my_comm, my_group, my_tag )
     if ( i_own_eager_mask ) {
18      Mutex_lock ( eager_lock )
        eager_mask_in_use = 0, i_own_eager_mask  = 0
20      context_id        = location of first set bit in local_mask
        mask[context_id]  = 0
22      Mutex_unlock ( eager_lock )
     }
```

Listing 1.2. Multithreaded context ID allocation algorithm

simple solution; however, any operation that synchronizes all threads is sufficient to prevent them from entering the context ID allocation loop until all threads have made matching calls. We use this observation to attempt allocation of a context ID during the synchronization step itself. In most MPI programs, this method results in successful context ID allocation in a single step and eliminates the additional overhead incurred by the new synchronization step.

This *eager* mode of context ID allocation is achieved by splitting the context ID mask into *eager* and *base* segments. During the synchronization step, an allreduce on the eager context ID space is performed. If eager allocation fails, the allreduce effectively acts as a barrier and threads proceed to the base allocation algorithm, which utilizes the base segment of the mask. Many variations of this optimization are possible, and an important property is the method used to divide the context ID space between eager and base protocols. Dynamic approaches where each process selects the first n available context IDs are possible. However, fragmentation in the context ID mask due to repeated communicator creation and destruction can cause individual masks to diverge and render this approach ineffective. Static allocation approaches are not as susceptible to this issue, but they limit the number of context IDs available to each protocol.

We define a static allocation strategy that reserves the first n context IDs for eager allocation and utilizes the remaining $max\_id - n$ IDs for the base protocol, where n is a configurable parameter. This strategy maximizes the likelihood of successful eager allocation and, as a tradeoff, in the worst case reduces the size of the context ID space to $max\_id - n$. The algorithm is shown in Listing 1.2, and this code is substituted in place of the barrier in Listing 1.1, line 13. In addition, line 23 in Listing 1.1 must be modified as follows.

```
local_mask[ 0..eager_split-1 ] = 0
local_mask[eager_split..MAXID] = mask
```

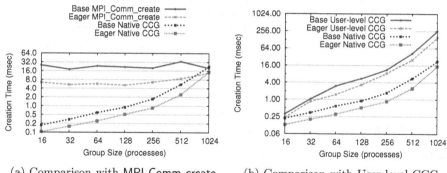

(a) Comparison with MPI_Comm_create   (b) Comparison with User-level CCG

Fig. 2. Comparison of native MPI_Comm_create_group (CCG) performance with two other communication creation routines. The impact of eager versus baseline context ID allocation is shown for each algorithm.

6 Experimental Evaluation

We compare the cost of several communicator-creation operations on a QDR InfiniBand cluster. Each node is configured with two 2.6 GHz, quad-core Intel Nehalem processors, and 36 GB memory. In Figure 2, we use MPI_COMM_WORLD as the parent communicator and vary the size of the output communicator. We compare the execution time of MPI_Comm_create with MPI_Comm_create_group (CCG) in Figure 2a. Two implementations of MPI_Comm_create_group are evaluated in Figure 2b, a user-level implementation that performs recursive intercommunicator merging presented in [3] and a direct implementation that uses the new context ID allocation algorithm. For each comparison, we show the impact of the eager allocation optimization.

From these results, we see that MPI_Comm_create_group provides a significant performance advantage over MPI_Comm_create, whose cost is always proportional to the size of the parent communicator. In addition, we see that there is a $O(\log p)$ performance advantage of the direct $O(\log p)$ MPI_Comm_create_group algorithm over the $O(\log^2 p)$ user-level algorithm. Moreover, the eager-allocation protocol accomplishes allocation in one, rather than two, allreduce operations, yielding a factor of two or more improvement in communicator-creation cost.

7 Related Work

Open MPI [4] utilizes a similar approach to context ID allocation, however rather than considering the full context ID mask when performing allocation, one context ID is evaluated at a time. In this algorithm, each thread starts with its lowest available context ID and a MAX allreduce is performed. A second AND allreduce is performed to determine if the operation succeeded at all threads and, if not, the process is repeated with the next highest context ID. Assuming a fixed-size context ID space, this algorithm is also susceptible to the deadlock scenario presented in Section 3.1 when the number of threads attempting allocation approaches the number of available context IDs at any process. In comparison with the algorithm presented in this work, the algorithm currently used by Open MPI always performs two allreduce operations (on a single integer, rather than the full mask) and can require multiple iterations if the context ID space becomes fragmented. This algorithm can also be extended to support MPI_Comm_create_group through the same the priority and tag space approaches presented in Section 3.

8   Conclusions

We have presented an efficient, multithreaded context ID allocation routine that includes support for new functionality in MPI 3.0. This work builds on the existing MPICH2 algorithm that was found to contain a subtle deadlock bug. We corrected this bug and proposed an eager allocation protocol that eliminates the performance impact of deadlock avoidance. We prove correctness of the new algorithm and evaluate its performance relative to existing approaches. Results indicate that the MPI_Comm_create_group routine built on top of the multithreaded context ID allocation algorithm significantly reduces the cost of communicator creation when the output group is smaller than the parent communicator's group.

References

1. MPICH2 Project Website,
   http://www.mcs.anl.gov/research/projects/mpich2/
2. Arafat, M.H., Dinan, J., Krishnamoorthy, S., Windus, T., Sadayappan, P.: Load balancing of dynamical nucleation theory Monte Carlo simulations through resource sharing barriers. In: Proc. 26th Intl. Par. and Distrib. Processing Symp. (May 2012)
3. Dinan, J., Krishnamoorthy, S., Balaji, P., Hammond, J.R., Krishnan, M., Tipparaju, V., Vishnu, A.: Noncollective communicator creation in MPI. In: Recent Adv. in the Message Passing Interface - 18th European MPI Users' Group Mtg. (2011)
4. Gabriel, E., Fagg, G.E., Bosilca, G., Angskun, T., Dongarra, J., Squyres, J.M., Sahay, V., Kambadur, P., Barrett, B., Lumsdaine, A., Castain, R.H., Daniel, D.J., Graham, R.L., Woodall, T.S.: Open MPI: Goals, Concept, and Design of a Next Generation MPI Implementation. In: Kranzlmüller, D., Kacsuk, P., Dongarra, J. (eds.) EuroPVM/MPI 2004. LNCS, vol. 3241, pp. 97–104. Springer, Heidelberg (2004)
5. Gropp, W., Thakur, R.: Thread-safety in an MPI implementation: Requirements and analysis. Parallel Computing 33(9), 595–604 (2007)
6. Kamal, H., Mirtaheri, S.M., Wagner, A.: Scalability of communicators and groups in MPI. In: Proceedings of the 19th ACM International Symposium on High Performance Distributed Computing, pp. 264–275. ACM, New York (2010)
7. MPI Forum: MPI: A Message-Passing Interface Standard. Version 2.2 (September 4, 2009)
8. Protopopov, B.V., Skjellum, A.: A multithreaded message passing interface (MPI) architecture: Performance and program issues. Journal of Parallel and Distributed Computing 61(4), 449–466 (2001)
9. Tang, H., Yang, T.: Optimizing threaded MPI execution on SMP clusters. In: Proc. 15th ACM International Conference on Supercomputing, pp. 381–392 (June 2001)

Collectives on Two-Tier Direct Networks

Nikhil Jain, JohnMark Lau, and Laxmikant Kale

Department of Computer Science
University of Illinois at Urbana-Champaign, Urbana, IL 61801, USA
{nikhil,johnlau,kale}@illinois.edu

Abstract. Collectives are an important component of parallel programs, and have a significant impact on performance and scalability of an application. To obtain best performance, platform specific implementations of various parallel programming frameworks, such as MPI and Charm++, are done. As a result, when systems with new network topologies are built, new topology aware algorithms for collectives are added to these frameworks that also contain the topology oblivious algorithms. In this paper, we propose topology aware algorithms for collectives performed on two-tier direct networks such as IBM PERCS and Dragonfly. We observe that, for large message operations, significant performance gains can be made by taking advantage of large number of links in a two-tier direct network. We evaluate proposed algorithms using an analytical model based on link utilization.

Keywords: Collectives, Topology, Two-tier networks, PERCS, Dragonfly.

1 Introduction

On the road to Exascale, there is a strong possibility that parallel machines of the future will have a large number of fast cores on each node and a low network bytes-to-flop ratio. Communication is becoming expensive whereas computation continues to become cheaper. Hence, scalable, low-diameter and fast networks will be desirable for building multi-Petaflop/s and Exaflop/s capability machines. New designs have been proposed recently by IBM (the PERCS topology [2]), and by the DARPA sponsored *Exascale Computing Study* on technical challenges in hardware (the dragonfly topology [6]). Both these topologies are two-tier direct networks with all-to-all connections at each level.

Many scientific applications use data movement collectives such as *Broadcast, Scatter, Gather, Allgather, All-to-all,* and computation collectives such as *Reduce, Reduce-scatter, and Allreduce* [1]. The performance of these MPI collectives is critical for improved scalability and efficiency of parallel scientific applications. In recent years, there have been an increasing number of applications such as web analytics, micro-scale weather simulation and computational nanotechnology, that involve processing extremely large scale data requiring collective operations with large messages. Performance of such large message collectives is significantly affected by network bandwidth constraints.

J.L. Träff, S. Benkner, and J. Dongarra (Eds.): EuroMPI 2012, LNCS 7490, pp. 67–77, 2012.

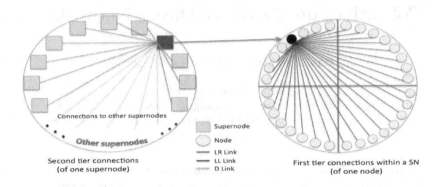

Connections to other supernodes

Other supernodes

Supernode

Node

LR Link

LL Link

D Link

Second tier connections
(of one supernode)

First tier connections within a SN
(of one node)

Fig. 1. The PERCS network – the right side shows first-level connections within a supernode; the left side shows second-level connections across supernodes (we show connections of only one node and one supernode respectively for clarity)

Most of the existing networks such as torus and fat-trees are low radix, and have constant number of links attached to a node. As such, transmitting packets from a source to destination involve traversal through a large number of nodes/switches. The multiplicity of hops makes these networks congestion prone, especially when performing collectives on large data/messages. To counter the effects of congestion, carefully designed topology aware algorithms have been used for collectives on such networks [4,5]. In addition, there is a set of topology oblivious algorithms which perform reasonably well on most systems [7,8,3]. However, most of these algorithms do not seem to be a good fit for two-tier direct networks as they may not be able to make full use of the all-to-all connectivity in two-tier direct networks. In this paper, we propose a new set of topology aware algorithms, which we refer to as *two-tier algorithms*, for collectives on two-tier direct networks for large messages. These algorithms exploit the high radix nodes and the multi-level structure of a two-tier direct network. Hence, they are better suited for two-tier direct networks, and as we demonstrate later should perform significantly better than other algorithms. A cost model based on the link utilization is used to evaluate the effectiveness of proposed algorithms in comparison to general topology oblivious algorithms. To best of our knowledge, this is the first paper which deals with collectives on two-tier direct networks.

2   Two-Tier Direct Networks

In this section, we provide an introduction to two-tier networks using IBM's PERCS network as an example. The elementary unit is called a node: a multi-core chip with connection to and from the system network. Any communication initiated by the cores is sent to the network manager of the node. In a two-tier direct network, nodes at the first level are grouped logically to form cliques. These cliques are further grouped to form larger clusters. In the PERCS topology, these logical groups are called drawers and supernodes whereas in the dragonfly topology they are called groups and racks (or cabinets). The supernodes are connected at the second level to form a larger clique.

As a concrete example, in the right side of Figure 1, we show one supernode of the PERCS topology. Within the supernode, a circle represents a node. Eight nodes in each quadrant constitute a drawer. Every node has a hub/switch that has three types of links originating from it - LL, LR and D links. LL and LR links constitute the first tier connections that enable communication between any two nodes in one hop. On the left side of Figure 1, the second tier connections between supernodes are shown. Every supernode is connected to every other supernode by a D or L2 link. These inter-supernode connections originate and terminate at hub/switches connected to a node; a given hub/switch is directly connected to only a fraction of the other supernodes. Any packet which is to be sent from a node (N1) in a supernode(S1) to a node (N2) in another supernode (S2) first need to be sent to that node in S1 which is connected to S2. Thereafter, the packet is sent to S2 and forwarded to N2 if required using the first level links.

In this paper, we do not differentiate among first level links (LL and LR) and denote them by L1 links. The links at second level are denoted as L2 links. We also stick to core, node and supernode terminology of PERCS, but the same principles apply to Dragonfly or any other two-tier direct network. We also assume that a node is capable of sending data simultaneously on all links originating from it.

3   Cost Model and Assumptions

We assume an inorder mapping of MPI ranks or cores onto the system. Consider a system with sn supernodes, each consisting of nps (nodes per supernode) nodes with cpn (cores per node) cores each. Hence, we have $p = sn * nps * cps$ cores whose inorder mapping is performed as following. Consider a global numbering of supernodes from 0 to $sn - 1$. Within a supernode and a node, nodes and cores are locally numbered from 0 to $(nps - 1)$ and from 0 to $(cpn - 1)$ respectively. In the global space, cores are numbered (by MPI) from 0 to $(p - 1)$ using the core's supernode, node and position within the node as the key. For example, cores in supernode 0 get ranks from 0 to $(nps * cpn - 1)$. Following which, cores in supernode 1 get ranks from $nps * cpn$ to $(2 * nps * cpn - 1)$ and so on.

Further, we assume a two-tier network with round robin connection for L2 links at node level. A connection from supernode $S1$ to supernode $S2$ originates at node ($S2$ modulo nps) in supernode $S1$. This link connects to node ($S1$ modulo nps) in supernode $S2$. Therefore, each node is connected to $spn = \frac{sn}{nps}$ supernodes. We consider the case in which job allocation onto nodes and supernodes happen in a uniform manner. To keep things simple, we assume the cases where the entire machine is being used by an application. Algorithms and results for the other case, where allocation is not uniform, can be derived with minor variations and will be discussed in a future work.

As we focus on large message collectives, we use a bandwidth based model to estimate the cost of a collective algorithm. The start up cost and latency effects are ignored as the bandwidth term dominates for large messages. We assume that the time taken to send a message between any two nodes is $n\beta$, where β is the transfer time per byte, if only 1 link is being used to send n bytes of data. In case of a computation operation, we add a γ computation cost component per byte. We also use a two step approach to find link utilization which provides a more accurate estimate of performance of an algorithm. In the first step, given a collective operation, the algorithm to use, number of MPI ranks or cores and the data length information (required by the operation), *pattern-generator* generates a list of communication exchange between every pair of MPI ranks. The data generated by *pattern-generator* is fed to *linkUsage*. Given a list of communication exchange, *linkUsage* generates the amount of traffic that will flow on each link in the given two-tier network.

4   Topology Oblivious Algorithms

This section lists the algorithms which are generally used to perform various collective operations in a topology oblivious manner for large message sizes. Many of these algorithms, which are listed in Table 1, are used in MPICH as the default option [8].

Table 1. Commonly used Algorithms

Operation	Algorithm	Cost (n bytes)
Scatter	Binomial Tree	$\frac{p-1}{p}n\beta$
Gather	Binomial Tree	$\frac{p-1}{p}n\beta$
Allgather	Ring, Recursive Doubling	$\frac{p-1}{p}n\beta$
Broadcast	DeGeijn's Scatter with Allgather [3]	$2\frac{p-1}{p}n\beta$
Reduce-Scatter	PairWise Exchange	$\frac{p-1}{p}(n\beta + n\gamma)$
Reduce	Rabenseifner's Reduce-Scatter with Gather [7]	$\frac{p-1}{p}(2n\beta + n\gamma)$

5   Two-Tier Algorithms

Given the clique property and the multiple levels of connections, the two-tier networks naturally leads to a new set of algorithm which we refer to as *two-tier algorithms*. The common idea in any two-tier algorithm is stepwise dissemination, transfer or aggregation (SDTA) of data. SDTA refers to simultaneous exchange of data within a level in order to optimize the over all data exchange. Performing SDTA ensures that the algorithms use maximum possible links for best bandwidth, and collate information to minimize the amount of data exchanged at higher levels. Without loss of generality let us assume that the root of any operation is core 0 of node 0 of supernode 0. In our discussion, we use core to refer to any entity which takes part in the collective operation. An MPI Rank and Charm++ Chare are examples of such entities.

5.1   Scatter and Gather

Scatter is a collective operation used to disseminate core specific data from a source core to every other core. The two-tier algorithm for Scatter using SDTA is as follows:

1. Core 0 of node 0 of supernode 0 sends data to core 0 of every other node in supernode 0. The data sent to a core is the data required by the cores residing in the supernodes connected to the node of that core.
2. Core 0 of every node within supernode 0 sends data to core 0 of every node outside supernode 0 that the node is connected to. The data sent to a node is the data required by the cores in the supernode to which this destination node belongs.
3. Core 0 of every node that has data (including node 0 of supernode 0) sends data to core 0 of every other node within its supernode. This data is required by the cores within the node that the data is being sent to.
4. Core 0 of every node shares data, required by the other cores, with all other cores in their node.

The four step process described above implies that the source core first spreads the data within its supernode. The data is then sent to exactly one node of every other supernode by the nodes which received the data. Thereafter, nodes which have data to be distributed within their supernode spreads the data within their supernodes. Gather can be performed using this algorithm in the reverse order.

For collectives with personalized data for each core such as Scatter, the dissemination of data can also be done using direct message send. The data will take exactly the same path as described in the above scheme. We have described our approach using Scatter because of its simplicity, and ease of understanding.

5.2   Broadcast

Broadcast can be performed using the approach used for Scatter if the entire data, without personalization, is sent in the four steps. We refer to this type of Broadcast as *base broadcast*. However, using the following scheme better performance can be obtained.

1. Core 0 of node 0 of supernode 0 divides the data to be broadcasted into nps chunks and sends chunk i to core 0 of node i of supernode 0.
2. Core 0 of every node within supernode 0 sends data to core 0 of exactly one node outside supernode 0 that the node is connected to. Exactly one node is chosen to avoid duplication of data delivery in following steps.
3. Core 0 of every node that received data in the previous step sends data to core 0 of every other node within their supernode.
4. Core 0 of all the nodes that received data in Step 2 and Step 3 send data to core 0 of all other nodes outside their supernode that they are connected to.
5. Now, these cores share data with core 0 of all other nodes in their supernode.
6. Core 0 of every node shares data with all other cores in their node.

This algorithm begins with the source core dividing the data into chunks, and distributing it within its supernode (as if performing Scatter over a limited set of cores). In the second step, every node in supernode 0 share the chunk with exactly 1 node outside their supernode. Thereafter, the nodes which received the chunk in the previous step share the data with other nodes in their supernode. As a result, all nodes in some of the supernodes have a chunk of initially divided data which needs to be sent to other supernodes. This is done in the next step, following which all nodes, which have received a chunk so far, share these chunks with other nodes in their supernode.

5.3 Allgather

An Allgather operation is equivalent to Broadcast being performed by all cores simultaneously. The SDTA based algorithm begins with all cores within every node exchanging data and collecting it at core 0 of the node. In the second step, all nodes within a supernode exchange data in an all-to-all manner using L1 links, and thus every node in every supernode contains the data which a supernode wants to broadcast to other supernodes. In the following step, supernodes exchange data in an all-to-all manner in parallel. Finally the nodes which receive data in the previous step disseminate this data to other nodes within its supernode. In addition, core 0 of every node has to share this data with all other cores in its node. This algorithm can be seen as a base broadcast being done by all nodes simultaneously (refer to §5.2).

Please note that many a times, multiple steps of SDTA can be performed by a send from the source of one step to eventual destination of the following step. An example case will be when core 0 of node 0 of supernode 0 has to send data to core 0 of nodes that are connected to other nodes of supernode 0. We have presented them as separate steps in which initially core 0 of node 0 sends the data to core 0 of other nodes of supernode 0. These nodes then forward the data to core 0 of nodes of other supernodes. This has been done only for ease of understanding, and comparison results will not reflect them.

5.4 Computation Collectives

Although the same two-tier approach presented in the previous section can be used to perform computation collectives such as Reduce, it may not result in the best performance. The inefficiency in the previous approach derives from the fact that computation collectives require some computation on the incoming data, and therefore if some node receives a lot of data from multiple sources, the computation it has to perform on the incoming data will become a bottleneck. We assume that the multiple cores do not share memory, and hence will not be able to assist in the computation to be performed on the incoming data. Also, the presented algorithms assume commutative and associative reduction operation.

Let us define an owner core as the core that has been assigned a part of the data that needs to be reduced. This core receives the corresponding part of the data from all other cores and performs the reduction operation on them.

Consider a clique of k cores on which a data of size m needs to be reduced, and be collected at core 0. The algorithm we propose for such a case is the following:

1. Each core is made owner of $\frac{m}{k}$ data - assume a simple rank based ownership.
2. Every core sends the data corresponding to the owner cores (in their data) to the owner cores.
3. The owner cores reduce the data they own using the corresponding part in their data, and the data they receive.
4. Every owner core sends the reduced data to core 0.

Essentially, what we are doing is a divide and conquer strategy. The data is divided among cores, and they are made responsible for reduction on that data. Every core divides their data, and sends the corresponding portion to the owner cores. The owner cores reduce the data, and eventually send it to core 0.

Reduce - The above strategy can be used in multiple stages to perform the overall reduction in a two-tier network:

1. Perform reduction among cores of every node; collect the data at core 0.
2. Perform reduction among nodes of every supernode - owners among nodes are decided such that instead of collecting data at node 0, the data can be left with the owner nodes and directly exchanged in the next step. This may require a node to be owner of scattered chunks in the data depending on the supernode connections.
3. Perform reduction among supernodes and collect the data at supernode 0.

Reduce-Scatter - We can use the same algorithm as above to perform Reduce-scatter with a minor modification. Since the Reduce-scatter requires the reduced data to be scattered over all cores, in the last phase of reduction (i.e. reduction among supernodes), we decide owners of data such that a supernode becomes owner of the data which its cores are required to receive in a reduce-scatter. Thereafter, instead of collecting all data at supernode 0 in the final step, the algorithm scatters the data within every supernode as required by Reduce-scatter.

6   Experiments

This section presents the details and results of the experiments we have conducted. The two-tier network that has been simulated for these experiments consists of 64 supernodes. Each supernode consists of 16 nodes each of which has 16 cores. The given configuration implies that there are 4032 L2 links and 15360 L1 links in the system. Note that we ignore the time spent in sharing data within a node by the cores.

6.1   Cost Comparison

In Table 2, we present comparison of the two-tier algorithms with other algorithms using the cost model mentioned in §3. Among the data collectives, for

Scatter and Gather, we observe that the two-tier algorithms which distributes data using all L1 links simultaneously within a source supernode provides theoretical speedup of factor nps i.e. nodes per supernode. This speedup may be affected by sn, i.e., the number of supernodes. If there are too few L2 links, they may become the bottleneck, and the speedup hence is bounded by $min\{nps, sn\}$. For Allgather, we find that the speedup provided by two-tier algorithms depends on both sn and nps. For Broadcast, which happens in three phases, the theoretical speedup is $\frac{nps}{3}$. Finally, for computation collectives, we observe that our approach leads to more computation being performed. This is because the reduction happens in two phases and some computation, which could have been avoided, is performed. However, as with data collectives, the speedup for data transfer is substantial and should mask the effect of increase in computation.

Table 2. Cost Model based Comparison

Operation	Base Cost	Two Tier Cost
Scatter	$\frac{p-1}{p}n\beta$	$n\beta * max\{\frac{1}{nps}, \frac{1}{sn}\}$
Gather	$\frac{p-1}{p}n\beta$	$n\beta * max\{\frac{1}{nps}, \frac{1}{sn}\}$
Allgather	$\frac{p-1}{p}n\beta$	$n\beta(\frac{1}{nps} + \frac{1}{sn} + \frac{1}{sn*nps})$
Broadcast	$2\frac{p-1}{p}n\beta$	$n\beta(\frac{3}{nps})$
Reduce-Scatter	$\frac{p-1}{p}(n\beta + n\gamma)$	$n\beta(\frac{1}{nps} + \frac{1}{sn} + \frac{1}{sn*nps}) + 2n\gamma$
Reduce	$\frac{p-1}{p}(2n\beta + n\gamma)$	$n\beta(\frac{1}{nps} + \frac{2}{sn}) + 2n\gamma$

6.2 Scatter, Gather and Broadcast

We consider a Scatter operation in which the root sends 64 KB data to each of the remaining cores. In Table 3, we present a comparison of binomial algorithm link utilization with the two-tier algorithm. The important thing to note in the comparison is the maximum load binomial algorithm puts on a link in comparison to what two-tier algorithm puts. For L1 links, we find that two-tier algorithm puts a maximum load of 64 MB whereas binomial algorithm performs much worse, and puts a load of 141 MB. The difference is much more significant when it comes to L2 links where binomial algorithm puts a factor 32 times more load. Exactly same results are found for Gather operation due to its inverse nature to Scatter.

We also present the link utilization statistics for a 1 GB Broadcast in Table 3. Link utilization improves substantially both in terms of number of links used and the load which is put on links when two-tier algorithm is used. We expect an order of magnitude improvement in the execution time as the worst case link load goes down from 1.1 GB to 128 MB.

6.3 Allgather

As mentioned earlier, we study the performance of Allgather using two algorithms - recursive doubling and ring. The amount of data that each MPI

Table 3. Link Usage Comparison for Scatter and Broadcast

	Scatter		Broadcast	
	Binomial	Two-tier	DeGeijn	Two-tier
L1 Links Used	1036	960	1588	15360
L1 Links Min Traffic	1 MB	1 MB	2 MB	64 MB
L1 Links Max Traffic	141 MB	64 MB	1.1 GB	128 MB
L2 Links Used	56	63	95	3937
L2 Links Min Traffic	16.7 MB	1 MB	32 MB	64 MB
L2 Links Max Traffic	520 MB	16 MB	1.09 GB	64 MB

rank/core wants to send is 64 KB. In Table 4, we present comparison of two-tier algorithm with the recursive doubling and ring algorithm. It can be seen that while two-tier algorithms uses all the available L1 and L2 links in the system, the other two algorithms use a very small fraction of available links. Moreover, the load which two-tier algorithm puts on the links is orders of magnitude smaller in comparison to the other algorithms. It strongly suggests that the two-tier algorithm will outperform the other two algorithms. These results also conforms with the fact that for large messages, ring algorithm is better than recursive-doubling [8].

Table 4. Link Usage Comparison for Allgather

	Recursive Doubling	Ring	Two-tier Algorithm
L1 Links Used	10496	1080	15360
L1 Links Min Traffic	16 MB	1 GB	65 MB
L1 Links Max Traffic	15.1 GB	1 GB	65 MB
L2 Links Used	384	634	4032
L2 Links Min Traffic	4.2 GB	1 GB	16 MB
L2 Links Max Traffic	4.3 GB	1 GB	16 MB

6.4   Computation Collectives

In the Table 5, we present a comparison of link utilization for Reduce-scatter and Reduce. For this experiment, the overall reduction size is 1 GB, and hence each core receives 64 KB reduced data when Reduce-Scatter is performed. We observe an order of magnitude difference in the load put on the links by two-tier algorithms in comparison to other algorithms. This can be attributed to the step wise manner in which two-tier algorithms perform reduction. Only the necessary data go out of a node or a supernode, and hence two-tier algorithm reduces the load put on the links significantly. Given this large difference in communication load, two-tier algorithms should outperform most other algorithms despite the additional computational load they put on the cores.

Table 5. Link Usage Comparison for Reduce-scatter and Reduce

	Reduce-Scatter		Reduce	
	Pairwise Exchange	Two-tier	Rabenseifner	Two-tier
L1 Links Used	15360	15360	15360	15360
L1 Links Min Traffic	2 GB	65 MB	2 GB	66 MB
L1 Links Max Traffic	2 GB	65 MB	3 GB	130 MB
L2 Links Used	4032	4032	4032	4032
L2 Links Min Traffic	4 GB	16 MB	4 GB	16 MB
L2 Links Max Traffic	4 GB	16 MB	5 GB	32 MB

7   Conclusion and Future Work

In this paper, we presented a new set of algorithms for two-tier networks, which takes advantage of the topology. A comparison, based on a cost model and network utilization, has been done to assess the performance of these new algorithms in comparison to well know algorithms. We focused on collectives for large data sizes, and showed that the two-tier algorithms significantly outperform most other algorithms for a two-tier direct network. In future, we plan to focus on collectives for small data sizes, and potentially improve the performance for large data size. We also plan to look at cases in which only a (non uniform) part of system is allocated to an application.

Acknowledgement. This project was initiated as part of a course taught by Professor Josep Torrellas, whom the authors gratefully thank. This research was supported in part by the Blue Waters: Leadership Petascale System project (which is supported by the NSF grant OCI 07-25070).

References

1. MPI: A Message Passing Interface Standard. MPI Forum
2. Arimilli, B., Arimilli, R., Chung, V., Clark, S., Denzel, W., Drerup, B., Hoefler, T., Joyner, J., Lewis, J., Li, J., Ni, N., Rajamony, R.: The PERCS High-Performance Interconnect. In: 2010 IEEE 18th Annual Symposium on High Performance Interconnects (HOTI), pp. 75–82 (August 2010)
3. Barnett, M., Gupta, S., Payne, D.G., Shuler, L., Geijn, R., Watts, J.: Interprocessor Collective Communication Library (InterCom). In: Proceedings of the Scalable High Performance Computing Conference, pp. 357–364 (1994)
4. Faraj, A., Kumar, S., Smith, B., Mamidala, A., Gunnels, J., Heidelberger, P.: Mpi collective communications on the blue gene/p supercomputer: algorithms and optimizations. In: Proceedings of the 23rd International Conference on Supercomputing, ICS 2009, pp. 489–490 (2009)
5. Jain, N., Sabharwal, Y.: Optimal bucket algorithms for large mpi collectives on torus interconnects. In: Proceedings of the 24th ACM International Conference on Supercomputing, ICS 2010, pp. 27–36 (2010)

6. Kim, J., Dally, W.J., Scott, S., Abts, D.: Technology-driven, highly-scalable drag-onfly topology. SIGARCH Comput. Archit. News 36, 77–88 (2008)
7. Rabenseifner, R.: A new optimized MPI reduce algorithm (1997)
8. Thakur, R., Gropp, W.D.: Improving the Performance of Collective Operations in MPICH. In: Dongarra, J., Laforenza, D., Orlando, S. (eds.) EuroPVM/MPI 2003. LNCS, vol. 2840, pp. 257–267. Springer, Heidelberg (2003)

Exploiting Atomic Operations for Barrier on Cray XE/XK Systems

Manjunath Gorentla Venkata[1], Richard L. Graham[1], Joshua S. Ladd[1], Pavel Shamis[1], Nathan T. Hjelm[2], and Samuel K. Gutierrez[2]

[1] Oak Ridge National Laboratory*, Oak Ridge TN 37830, USA
{manjugv,rlgraham,laddjs,shamisp}@ornl.gov
[2] Los Alamos National Laboratory**, Los Alamos NM 87545, USA
{hjelmn,samuel}@lanl.gov

Abstract. *Barrier* is a collective operation used by many scientific applications and parallel libraries for synchronization. Typically, a *Barrier* operation is implemented by exchanging a short data message that requires demultiplexing, thereby adding undesired latency to the operation. In this work, we reduce the latency of *Barrier* operations for *Cray XE/XK* systems by leveraging the atomic operations provided by the *Gemini* interconnect, tailoring algorithms to utilize these capabilities, and utilizing a hierarchical design to arrive at an efficient implementation. Our micro-benchmark evaluation shows that for a 4,096 process *Barrier* operation, the atomic-operations-based *Barrier* outperforms the data exchange *Barrier* by 52% and the native *Barrier* by 111%.

Keywords: Collectives, Barrier, Cray, Gemini, Atomic Operations, MPI.

1 Introduction

The *Barrier* collective is used by many scientific applications and parallel system software stacks for synchronization purposes. Typically, a *Barrier* collective is implemented by exchanging a short data message amongst all participating processes. The data sent typically includes a small amount of header information used for message demultiplexing and dispatch. For example, Open MPI adds 20 bytes of header information when exchanging a message over the *Gemini* network interface [1].

Many modern network interfaces provide atomic network operations that can be used to implement collective operations. For example, in addition to the *Gemini* network, InifiniBand networks also provide atomic network operations enabling processes to perform many simple arithmetic and boolean operations remotely and atomically. Using atomic operations for non-data collectives, such

* This research used resources of the Center for Computational Sciences at Oak Ridge National Laboratory, which is supported by the Office of Science of the U.S. Department of Energy under Contract No. DE-AC05-00OR22725.
** Work supported by the Advanced Simulation and Computing program of the U.S. Department of Energy's NNSA. Los Alamos National Laboratory is operated by Los Alamos National Security, LLC for the NNSA. LA-UR-12-21410.

J.L. Träff, S. Benkner, and J. Dongarra (Eds.): EuroMPI 2012, LNCS 7490, pp. 78–88, 2012.
© Springer-Verlag Berlin Heidelberg 2012

as *Barrier*, can potentially reduce collective latency, as there is no need for network message demultiplexing by the communication library to determine message completion. Instead, message completion is determined by simply polling on atomic counters.

Implementing a *Barrier* with atomic operations, however, presents two challenges. The first being the management of intra-node *Barrier* latency. Network atomic operations involve traversing the network interface for communication and may not be faster than a conventional shared-memory-aware *Barrier*. The second challenge is in managing the overhead associated with atomic counter initialization. For example, an atomic *Barrier* requires a memory buffer that acts as a counter whose initial value must be agreed upon by all participating processes.

In this paper, we optimize the *Barrier* operation for *Cray XE/XK* systems by 1) leveraging atomic operations on *Gemini* 2) using a hierarchical design to provide an efficient implementation for multi-core systems and 3) tailoring algorithms to take advantage of parallelism in the network interface card (NIC). We generalize the commonly used recursive doubling algorithm to a *Recursive K'ing* algorithm, which reduces to the common case when $k = 2$. Further, we compare the *Recursive K'ing* algorithm with the *n-ary* algorithm, which like the *Recursive K'ing*, provides flexibility by allowing the radix to be varied, but requires $2log_k(n)$ steps. We implement both blocking and non-blocking versions of the *Barrier* operation. All implementations of the *Barrier* operation in this paper refer to MPI_Barrier() and MPI_Ibarrier(), as defined in the message passing interface (MPI) specification[1].

The rest of the paper is organized as follows. Section 2 provides the relevant background and related works information. Section 3 describes the collectives framework, various *Barrier* algorithms and their implementations. Section 4 describes the experimental test bed and provides an evaluation of various *Barrier* implementations. Section 5 analyzes the results. Section 6 concludes and discusses future work.

2   Background and Related Work

Gemini Network Interface and Atomic Operations: The *Cray XE/XK* network infrastructure is arranged as a 3D torus built from *Gemini* application-specific integrated circuits (ASICs) that provide two network interface controllers (NICs) and a 48-port router [2]. Each *Gemini* provides ten torus connections and connects two Opteron nodes [2].

Cray exposes two application programming interfaces (APIs) for *Gemini*: the Generic Network Interface (GNI) and DMAPP. The GNI is designed for message passing communication models, and DMAPP for PGAS communication models. GNI exposes low-level interfaces that provide two mechanisms for remote direct memory access (RDMA): *Fast Memory Access* (FMA) and *Block Transfer Engine* (BTE). In addition to the RDMA interfaces, GNI exposes an interface

---

[1] The non-blocking version of *Barrier* is slated for inclusion into the MPI 3.0 specification.

for two-sided communication called Short message (SMSG) and an interface for atomic operations. GNI supports atomic operations such as ADD, AND, Compare and Swap (CSWAP), XOR, OR, and atomic AND and XOR (AX). Details regarding the use of this API can be found in [3].

Open MPI: A popular open source implementation of the MPI specification, Open MPI's design and implementation revolves around the concept of a modular component architecture (MCA). Functionality is provided by self-contained software modules with well-defined interfaces. Within Open MPI exists the following three important communication abstractions: the point-to-point management layer (PML), byte transfer layer (BTL), and the BTL management layer (BML). The PML layer provides MPI like semantics, the BML layer is responsible for multiplexing MPI messages, and the BTL layer is responsible for transferring data between communication endpoints. More details regarding Open MPI's architecture and implementation can be found in [1].

Related Work: There is a large body of research on *Barrier* algorithms [4] [5] and some research on *Barrier* implementations based on hardware primitives. Multiple network interfaces, including InfiniBand, Quadrics/Elan3, and BlueGene/L's network, provide hardware support or atomic operations [6] [7]. Hoefler [4] studied a broad range of synchronization algorithms, including the MPI barrier implementation based on the InfiniBand atomic operations. Yu et al. [8] compared network offloaded *Barrier* on Myrinet LANai-XP and Qlogic Elan3, which were based on a set of atomic operations implemented on the NIC. Almasi [6] et al. showed the advantage of using BlueGene/L's hardware support for implementing MPI_Barrier().

Our research here explores leveraging the *Gemini* interconnect's atomic operations to implement a logarithmic tree-based MPI_Barrier() algorithm. In addition, we study the advantages of using a *Hierarchical* design, where we combine an atomic-operations-based *Barrier* for inter-node synchronization with a shared-memory-aware *Barrier* for intra-node synchronization. As far as we are aware, this is the first such study to explore the use of *Gemini* atomic operations to implement a *Barrier* primitive on *Cray XE/XK* system.

3   Design

Barrier algorithms are implemented in *Cheetah*, a framework for implementing scalable hierarchical collectives. Cheetah provides infrastructure for implementing both blocking and non-blocking versions of collectives. This section first provides a brief overview of the Cheetah framework, and extensions to the framework to implement *Barrier* operations based on *Gemini*'s atomic operations.

3.1   Cheetah: A Framework for Collective Operations

Cheetah is implemented as an extension to Open MPI. In Cheetah, a hierarchical collective is expressed as a group of independently progressed collective

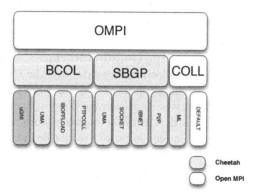

Fig. 1. The figure shows various components in the Cheetah framework and how components fit with other Open MPI components. The blue component, *uGNI BCOL*, was added for implementing atomic-operations-based *Barrier* operations.

primitives over different communication substrates, which include caches, inter central processing unit (CPU) socket communication interfaces, and network topologies. Figure 1 shows the various frameworks and components that make up the Cheetah framework. The Cheetah framework consists of two frameworks, BCOL and SBGP, and a component, ML.

The BCOL framework provides a collection of components, where each component represents a particular communication substrate and contains implementations of the collective primitives optimized for that particular level. In the current implementation, the Cheetah framework supports the BASESMUMA, IBOFFLOAD, and PTPCOLL components. The collective primitives in the BASESMUMA component are tailored for shared-memory communication, the primitives in IBOFFLOAD take advantage of Mellanox CORE-*Direct*'s [9] collective offload capabilities, and PTPCOLL is a generic point-to-point component. PTPCOLL uses Open MPI's PML component for communication, and, as a result, supports all the network interfaces supported by Open MPI.

SBGP provides the functionality responsible for grouping processes into subgroups based on the communication substrate shared by them. The Cheetah framework currently supports UMA, SOCKET, IBNET, and P2P subgroups. The UMA subgroup is defined over processes sharing the same memory, the SOCKET subgroup is defined over processes sharing the same CPU socket, the IBNET subgroup is defined over processes that can communicate over Mellanox CORE-*Direct*, and the P2P subgroup is defined over processes sharing network interfaces that are supported by Open MPI.

The ML component combines the collective primitives provided by BCOL and the subgrouping functionality provided by SBGP, and implements collective operations over these subgroups. This design decouples the collective operation implementation from the topological organization of the processes. For example, an MPI_Barrier() operation over a multi-core cluster can be defined by combining a shared-memory barrier primitive (BASESMUMA BCOL and UMA subgroup) and a network barrier primitive (PTPCOLL BCOL and P2P subgroup). More details about Cheetah's design and implementation are provided in one of our previous papers [9].

uGNI BCOL and Subgroup for the Gemini Interface: To take advantage of *Gemini*'s atomic operations for collectives, we extended the Cheetah framework with *uGNI BCOL* and subgrouping support over the *Gemini* interconnect. *uGNI BCOL* provides collective primitives that leverage *Gemini* atomic operations. In the next subsections, we provide details of the memory store required for atomic operations and various *Barrier* implementations available in the *uGNI BCOL*.

3.2   Memory Store for Atomic Operations

The *uGNI BCOL* provides a memory store, which implements the counters required for *Barrier* implementations based on atomic operations. Each process in the P2P subgroup, during job initialization, registers a block of memory with its *Gemini*, and shares this registration information with all other processes in the job. This memory block is divided into banks, which are further divided into buffers that act as counters. Each invocation of *Barrier* consumes only one memory buffer. When a *Barrier* consumes the last buffer in the bank, the buffers are recycled and reinitialized. Buffer recycling and reinitialization is a local operation, but does, however, require global synchronization to ensure that all processes have recycled their buffers. During recycling and reinitialization, the buffers from a different bank can be used without the need to block the *Barrier* operation. The size of the memory store, buffers, number of buffers in the bank, and the number of banks are all configurable during runtime.

The per-process memory footprint of the memory store is insignificant, as each atomic counter only requires eight bytes of memory. The number of counters required by a *Barrier* operation is dependent on the algorithm. For example, the *n-ary Barrier* and *Recursive K'ing Barrier* described below require two and $\lceil \log_k(n) \rceil$ counters per process, respectively. For a 300,000-process *Barrier*, the memory required for the *n-ary* algorithm is 16 bytes, and 152 bytes for the *Recursive K'ing* algorithm with radix 2.

3.3   Barrier Algorithms and Implementations

The atomic-based MPI_Barrier is implemented within the *uGNI BCOL*. Members participating in this operation are contained in the P2P subgroup. We explored four implementations of the *Barrier* in Cheetah, namely *Recursive K'ing Atomic Barrier*, *n-ary Atomic Barrier*, *Recursive K'ing p2p Barrier*, and *Hierarchical Barrier*.

Recursive K'ing Atomic Barrier (Recursive K'ing Barrier): Figure 2 shows the communication pattern of a nine-process *Barrier* with radix 3 where at each step all processes must synchronize with $k - 1$ processes. In total, the algorithm requires $\lceil \log_k(n) \rceil$ such steps. When n is not a power of k, the algorithm requires two extra steps.

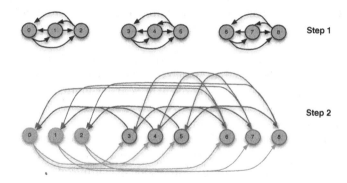

Fig. 2. The communication pattern of the *Recursive K'ing Barrier* with nine processes and radix 3

The *Recursive K'ing Barrier* implementation uses atomic operations provided by GNI. For $n = k^m$ processes and radix k, the *Recursive K'ing Barrier* implementation requires $\lceil \log_k(n) \rceil$ counters, when n is a power of k. When n is not a power of k, the implementation requires $\lceil \log_k(n) \rceil + 1$ counters. In step s, a process participating in the *Barrier* operation synchronizes with $k - 1$ processes by updating the counter, s, on the remote processes, and waiting until its counter reaches $k - 1$. The processes update the counter by posting *Gemini* atomic ADD operation using the $GNI\_PostFMA()$ primitive.

***n*-ary Atomic *Barrier* (*n*-ary *Barrier*):** The processes participating in an *n-ary Barrier* are organized into an *n-ary* tree for communication. Each process is designated as either a leaf, root, or interior process. The *Barrier* operation here is a two-phase process: fan-in and fan-out. The *n-ary Barrier* requires only two counters irrespective of the radix – one for the fan-in phase and one for the fan-out phase.

During the fan-in phase, the leaf processes update a fan-in counter on their interior, or parent process, using an atomic ADD operation. The interior processes, after receiving updates from their k children (where k is the radix of the tree), update their respective parents. The root process, after receiving updates from its k children, switches to the fan-out phase. During the fan-out phase of the algorithm, the root process updates its children's fan-out counters and exits, thus completing the *Barrier* operation. The interior processes, after receiving the update from their respective parents, update their children's fan-out counters and exit the *Barrier*. The leaf processes, after receiving the update from their respective parents, exit the *Barrier*, thus completing the *Barrier* operation.

***Recursive K'ing* p2p *Barrier* (*p2p Barrier*):** The communication pattern of this algorithm is similar to *Recursive K'ing Barrier*'s, however the implementation varies. Instead of using *Gemini*'s atomic operations for synchronization, it uses *Gemini* RDMA or SMSG for synchronization. For two processes to synchronize using SMSG, the sender sends a message using $GNI\_SmsgSendWTag()$ and the receiver polls the local completion queue for message arrival.

Hierarchical Barrier: This *Barrier* is implemented by combining one of the above *Barrier* primitives with a shared-memory *Barrier* primitive. On a system with multiple cores on single node, the intra-node *Barrier* will use a shared-memory-aware *Barrier* and the inter-node *Barrier* will use one of the above *Barrier* primitives. The shared-memory *Barrier* uses *mmap*ed memory for shared-memory communication. We implement and evaluate three hierarchical *Barrier*s, namely *Two-level Recursive K'ing Barrier* (*Recursive K'ing Barrier* for inter-node synchronization and shared-memory *Barrier* for intra-node synchronization), *Two-level n-ary Barrier* (*n-ary Barrier* for inter-node synchronization and shared-memory *Barrier* for intra-node synchronization), and *Two-level p2p Barrier* (*p2p Barrier* for inter-node synchronization and shared-memory *Barrier* for intra-node synchronization).

4   Evaluation

This section presents results evaluating the performance of various *Barrier* implementations after describing the experimental test bed. First, the overhead of native atomic operations is compared with the overhead of native data exchanging operations on *Gemini*. Next, the latency of the shared-memory *Barrier* is compared with the latency of the atomic-operations-based *Barrier*. Finally, the performance characteristics of various *Barrier* implementations are evaluated.

4.1   Test Bed

System Description: To evaluate the performance of the various *Barrier* implementations we used Jaguar, a Cray XK6 system located at the National Center for Computational Sciences (NCCS) at ORNL. It has 18,688 compute nodes, each containing one 2.2 GHz AMD Opteron Interlagos processor along with 32 GB of memory. Each AMD Opteron processor has 16 compute cores and 3 levels of cache memory. Out of the 18,688 compute nodes, 960 nodes also have a single NVIDIA graphical processing unit (GPU). Jaguar uses the *Gemini* interconnect for network communication.

Micro-benchmarks: To establish the performance of the native operations on *Gemini*, we implemented a simple benchmark, `Native_perf`, where one process is designated as the leader and all other processes as non-leaders. A non-leader communicates with the leader by either atomically updating a counter or sending a message (we implemented both versions for our experiments). The leader blocks until it gets an update from all other processes in the job, and reports its wait time.

To evaluate the latency of the *Barrier* operations, we ran MPI_Barrier() in a tight loop and measured its execution time. The performance reported is an average latency over many thousands of iterations. We further averaged these average latencies over three runs to in an attempt to account for variable network loads.

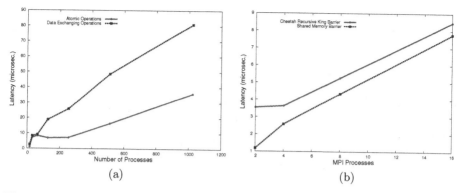

Fig. 3. Graph 3(a) shows the latency of native atomic and data operations as the number of processes are increased. Graph 3(b) shows the latency of the shared-memory *Barrier* alongside the atomic-based *Barrier*.

4.2   Performance Characteristics

Performance of Native Atomic and Data Exchange Operations: Figure 3(a) shows the overhead of native atomic and native data exchanging operations. The experiment is aimed at measuring the overhead for a process to receive synchronization information from other processes. The overhead is measured using `Native_perf`, as the number of synchronizing processes are increased. In the case of atomic operations, the leader waits for its counter to reach the target value, which indicates that all other processes have updated the counter. In the case of data exchanging operations, the leader counts message completions from all other processes. For the 16-process configuration, the latency of atomic operations is 1.2 μs and data exchanging operations is 2.69 μs. For the 1024-process configuration, the latency of atomic operations is 35.93 μs and data operations is 81.05 μs.

Performance of Shared-Memory *Barrier*: Figure 3(b) shows the latency of the shared-memory *Barrier* compared with the *Recursive K'ing Barrier*. As expected, the shared-memory *Barrier* performed better than the atomic *Barrier*. For a 16-process *Barrier* operation, the shared-memory *Barrier*'s latency is 7.77 μs and the *Recursive K'ing Barrier*'s latency is 8.47 μs.

Performance of *Barrier* Implementations: Figure 4(a) shows the latency of various *Barrier* implementations. The *Recursive K'ing Barrier* and *Two-level Recursive K'ing Barrier* perform the best. For the 4096-process *Barrier* operation, the latency of *Recursive K'ing Barrier*, *Two-level Recursive K'ing Barrier*, *n-ary Barrier*, *Two-level n-ary Barrier*, *Two-level p2p Barrier*, and Cray MPI's *Barrier* are 52.27 μs, 52.74 μs, 73.25 μs, 75.40 μs, 79.49 μs, and 110.48 μs, respectively. The performance of the *Recursive K'ing Barrier* is 52% and 111% better than the data-passing *Two-level p2p Barrier* and Cray MPI's *Barrier*, respectively. For this experiment, all our *Barrier* implementations used a radix of 2 for the tree. The non-blocking and blocking versions of the *Barrier*

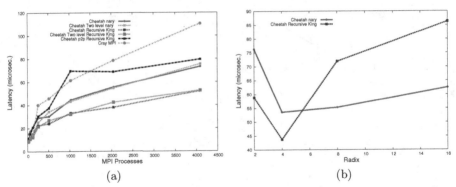

(a)   (b)

Fig. 4. Graph 4(a) shows the performance of the Cheetah uGNI *Barrier* compared to the Cheetah p2p *Barrier* as a function of problem size. Graph 4(b) shows the latency of the 4,096 process *Barrier* as the radix of the tree is varied.

implementations exhibit similar performance characteristics and, as a result, have not been included.

Latency of *Barrier* with Varying Radix: In this experiment, we varied the radix of *n-ary Barrier* and *Recursive K'ing Barrier* to understand how the tree's topology affects performance. Figure 4(b) shows the performance of a 4,096 process *Barrier* operation as we vary the radix of the tree. *n-ary Barrier* has the best performance when the radix of the tree is 4 and 8. Similarly, *Recursive K'ing Barrier* performs best when the radix of the tree is 4.

5   Analysis

Results in Figure 3(a) and 4(a) demonstrate the advantage of using atomic operations for *Barrier* operations. The *Recursive K'ing* atomic *Barrier* outperforms the data exchanging *Barrier* and Cray MPI's *Barrier* by 52% and 111%, respectively. The *n-ary* atomic *Barrier* outperforms the data exchanging *Barrier* by 8%, even though the runtime of the *n-ary* algorithm is $2log\ n$ and data exchanging *Barrier* is $log\ n$. Providing further basis for this performance advantage are the results shown in 3(a). We can observe that as we increase number of synchronizing processes, the atomic operations provide lower latency when compared to the data exchanging operations. From the results, we see that having 1023 processes sending updates to a single process required 35.93 μs when using atomic operations and 81.05 μs when using data exchanging operations.

Results in Figure 3(a) and 3(b) indicate that it would be advantageous to use a hierarchical design. That is, a shared-memory *Barrier* for intra-node synchronization and an atomic-operations-based *Barrier* for inter-node synchronization (*Two-level Recursive K'ing Barrier*). Figure 3(b) shows that for intra-node *Barrier* implementations, the shared-memory-based *Barrier* outperforms the atomic-operations-based *Barrier*. The *Two-level Recursive K'ing Barrier* performs better than the one-level atomic *Barriers* up to 512 processes. At 1024 processes and above, however, the performance of the one-level atomic *Barrier* and *Two-level Recursive K'ing Barrier* is very similar.

Hierarchical Barrier performing on-par with the one-level atomic *Barrier* at scale is surprising. It could very well be that for non-data type collectives the better scaling and cache characteristics of the atomic operations coupled with the relatively small performance difference between shared-memory *Barrier* and atomic *Barrier* may negate the performance advantages of the shared-memory *Barrier* at higher scale.

Results in 4(b) show the advantage of the flexibility provided by the *Recursive K'ing* and *n-ary Barrier*. As the degree of algorithms' graphs are increased, the *Barrier* implementation takes advantage of the network hardware's parallelism up to certain limit, which translates into decreased latency. The performance of *n-ary Barrier* is best at radix 4 and 8, and is diminished at other radices. The performance of *Recursive K'ing Barrier* is best at radix 4.

6 Conclusion and Future Work

The experimental results demonstrate that using atomic operations to implement a *Barrier* collective on *Cray XE/XK* systems provides better scalability and performance. The atomic-operations-based *Barrier* performed 52% better than the data-passing-based *Barrier*, and 111% better than the native implementation's *Barrier*. Furthermore, the advantages of leveraging atomic operations combined with a hierarchical design was explored. The two-level *Recursive K'ing Barrier* performed better than the one-level *Recursive K'ing Barrier* at smaller scales and on-par at higher scales. In the future, we plan to evaluate this implementation within scientific applications, and extend this work to explore the advantages of using the *Gemini* interconnect's atomic operations for other collective operations (e.g., short-data MPI_Allreduce and MPI_Reduce).

References

1. Gabriel, E., Fagg, G.E., Bosilca, G., Angskun, T., Dongarra, J., Squyres, J.M., Sahay, V., Kambadur, P., Barrett, B.W., Lumsdaine, A., Castain, R.H., Daniel, D.J., Graham, R.L., Woodall, T.S.: Open MPI: Goals, Concept, and Design of a Next Generation MPI Implementation. In: Kranzlmüller, D., Kacsuk, P., Dongarra, J. (eds.) EuroPVM/MPI 2004. LNCS, vol. 3241, pp. 97–104. Springer, Heidelberg (2004)
2. Alverson, R., Roweth, D., Kaplan, L.: The Gemini System Interconnect. In: 2010 IEEE 18th Annual Symposium on High Performance Interconnects (HOTI), pp. 83–87 (August 2010)
3. Cray Inc.: Using the GNI and DMAPP APIs. In: Cray Software Document, vol. S-2446-4002 (December 2011)
4. Hoefler, T.: Evaluation of publicly available Barrier-Algorithms and Improvement of the Barrier-Operation for large-scale Cluster-Systems with special Attention on InfiniBand Networks, Chemnitz, Germany (2005)
5. Hensgen, D., Finkel, R., Manber, U.: Two algorithms for barrier synchronization. International Journal of Parallel Programming, 1–17 (February 01, 1988)

6. Almási, G., Heidelberger, P., Archer, C.J., Martorell, X., Erway, C.C., Moreira, J.E., Steinmacher-Burow, B., Zheng, Y.: Optimization of MPI collective communication on BlueGene/L systems. In: Proceedings of the 19th Annual International Conference on Supercomputing, ICS 2005. ACM, New York (2005)
7. Petrini, F., Coll, S., Frachtenberg, E., Hoisie, A.: Hardware- and Software-Based Collective Communication on the Quadrics Network. In: Proceedings of the IEEE International Symposium on Network Computing and Applications (NCA 2001), Washington, DC, USA (2001)
8. Yu, W., Buntinas, D., Graham, R.L., Panda, D.K.: Efficient and Scalable Barrier over Quadrics and Myrinet with a New NIC-Based Collective Message Passing Protocol. CoRR (2004)
9. Graham, R., Venkata, M.G., Ladd, J., Shamis, P., Rabinovitz, I., Filipov, V., Shainer, G.: Cheetah: A Framework for Scalable Hierarchical Collective Operations. In: CCGRID 2011 (2011)

Exact Dependence Analysis
for Increased Communication Overlap*

Simone Pellegrini[1], Torsten Hoefler[2,3], and Thomas Fahringer[1]

[1] Institute of Informatics, University of Innsbruck, Austria
{spellegrini,tf}@dps.uibk.ac.at
[2] University of Illinois at Urbana-Champaign, IL, USA
htor@illinois.edu
[3] Department of Computer Science, ETH Zurich, Switzerland
htor@inf.ethz.ch

Abstract. MPI programs are often challenged to scale up to several million cores. In doing so, the programmer tunes every aspect of the application code. However, for large applications, this is often not practical and expensive tracing tools and post-mortem analysis are employed to guide the tuning efforts finding hot-spots and performance bottlenecks. In this paper we revive the use of compiler analysis techniques to automatically unveil opportunities for communication/computation overlap using the result of exact data dependence analysis provided by the polyhedral model. We apply our technique to a 5-point stencil code showing performance improvements up to 28% using 512 cores.

Keywords: Message passing, Compiler Analysis, Data Dependence Analysis, Polyhedral Model.

1   Introduction

The Message Passing Interface (MPI [12]) Standard defines a distributed memory library interface for use in performance-critical environments such as High Performance Computing (HPC). One of its main strengths is that the interface spans several abstraction layers, from very low level constructs (e.g., point-to-point messaging or simple one sided accesses) to high level performance-portable functionality (e.g., collective operations or derived datatypes). Highly optimized implementations exist for several supercomputer architectures and interconnects (e.g., Myrinet, InfiniBand). Performance and scalability are becoming critical aspects for tackling the challenges of exascale computing [14]. Thus, most of the latest research efforts have been spent in the runtime system.

However, the runtime system cannot overcome performance bugs in the application code. Performance analysis and profiling tools have been proposed over the years with the goal of helping developers to improve scalability of their

---

* This research has been partially funded by the Austrian Research Promotion Agency under contract nr. 824925 (OpenCore) and under contract 834307 (AutoCore).

J.L. Träff, S. Benkner, and J. Dongarra (Eds.): EuroMPI 2012, LNCS 7490, pp. 89–99, 2012.
© Springer-Verlag Berlin Heidelberg 2012

```
1  for(unsigned iter=0; iter<NUM_ITERS; iter++) { S0
2  MPI_Sendrecv(&A[ROWS-2][0], COLS, MPI_DOUBLE, top, 0,
3                  &A[0][0], COLS, MPI_DOUBLE, bottom, 0, MPI_COMM_WORLD,
                   &s);
4  S1   MPI_Sendrecv(&A[1][0], COLS, MPI_DOUBLE, bottom, 1,
5                  &A[ROWS-1][0], COLS, MPI_DOUBLE, top, 1, MPI_COMM_WORLD
                   , &s);
6       for(unsigned i = 1; i<ROWS-1; ++i)
7           for(unsigned j = 1; j<COLS-1; ++j)
8  S2          tmp[i][j] = A[i][j] + 1/4*(A[i+1][j]+A[i-1][j]+A[i][j-1]+A[i
           ][j+1]);
9       double** ttemp=A; A=tmp; tmp=ttemp; // swap arrays
10 }
```

Listing 1.1. 5-points stencil code

codes [13,15,7]. Such tools are often very helpful to determine performance bottlenecks or root causes for performance issues, however, the programmer has to adapt the code eventually. In addition, tracing and post mortem analysis, may be extremely time- and resource-consuming. Tuning the code for a particular architecture (e.g., determine software pipeline depths and optimal loop arrangement) is thus a very labor-intensive process and is often simply not applied in production environments.

Compiler technology has been used in the past to optimize MPI programs [6,4,2,3,11]. The main idea is to extend the compiler analysis module to understand the semantics of MPI routines and treat them not just like a library call but as a language construct. In doing so, existing compiler analysis can be utilized to uncover optimization potentials hidden within the input code.

In this work we show an approach based on compiler analysis, and specifically *exact* data dependency analysis to maximize the computation/communication overlap for a given input code. Indeed, increasing the time window on which computation and communication can be performed in parallel (or overlapped) is one of the well known rules of thumb used to optimize MPI codes. As opposed to the previous compiler-based approaches, we utilize finer-grain *exact* analyses using the polyhedral model [1]. Unlike the traditional dependence graph, which contains data dependency information between the program statements, the *dependence polyhedron* lists dependencies on the basis of *statement instances* [16]. An instance of a statement is a particular dynamic execution of that statement. For example, the body of a loop has as many instances as there are iterations. By using this more detailed analysis our approach increases the overlap window between generating the data or buffer availability and the final consumption of the data.

2   Motivation and State of the Art

MPI programs often exhibit recurring code patterns which are direct consequences of the programming paradigm. For example, many programs read the data right after receiving it from a peer process by iterating over the received array elements. Similarly, data is usually sent right after the sender process finishes the computation that writes to array elements being transmitted. A concrete and relevant example is represented by a standard parallelization of a 5-point stencil code depicted in Listing 1.1. Stencil codes are very important in computational sciences and we show a common way to parallelize such a code [9]. We have communication statements at the beginning of the loop, statements S0 and S1, which exchange data being computed in the previous iteration. Right after the communication is performed, data is updated by a computational loop, statement S2. In both case the compiler sees a *true*, or *Read-After-Write* (RAW), data dependence on the elements of array A from statement S0 to S2 and between S1 and S2.

Traditional compiler analyses usually derive dependence information on a per-statement basis. For the 5-point stencil code in Listing 1.1 the data dependence graph (DDG) built by classical data dependence analysis [10] is represented in Figure 1(a). We neglect, in this analysis, the swap statements in line 10 since it introduces data dependencies between successive iterations of the iter loop which are irrelevant since our focus is in maximizing the overlap within the loop body. The DDG shows three types of dependencies present in the code:

RAW : Read-After-Write dependencies (a.k.a. true-dependencies);
WAR : Write-After-Read dependencies (a.k.a. anti-dependencies);
WAW : Write-After-Write dependencies (a.k.a. output-dependencies);

Each dependence type is associated with a *distance vector* represented in brackets which, in the case of non loop-carried dependencies, is zero. We see that there are two, non loop-carried, RAW dependencies from statement S0 to S2 and between S1 and S2, respectively. This is caused by the receive operation (implicit in the MPI_Sendrecv routine) writing elements of the array A. More precisely, the receive operation in S0 writes A's array elements in the range $A[0][0 : COLS]$. Same elements which are going to be read later in the first iteration of the stencil loop – and thus Read-After-Write – by statement S2. Although correct,these results are too conservative and coarse grained *inhibiting any kind of automatic optimization*. As a matter of fact, every dependence in the DDG exists for all the dynamic executions, or instances, of interested statements, however this is not the case. For example the dependence between S0 and S2 only applies to the first iteration of the stencil loop, all the remaining dynamic executions of statement S2 are not dependent on S0. Similar considerations can be done for statement S1, for which the data dependence applies solely to the last iteration of the stencil loop.

The polyhedral model enables novel data analysis and transformation techniques by representing dependencies at the finest detail in an instance-based fashion. This technique is also referred to as *exact* data dependence analysis [16]. This allow a compiler to relax some of the constraints and apply more aggressive transformations at the array element level which would not be supported by a more coarse level of analysis at the object level. An example of the dependence polyhedron for the stencil code is shown in Figure 1(b). The graph contains the exact same key dependencies but it carries more information for each of them. An *expression predicate* states which subset of the statement instances are affected by the dependence. When the predicate is missing, then the dependence

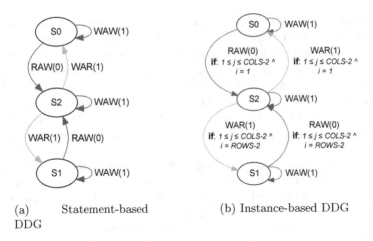

(a)   Statement-based
DDG

(b) Instance-based DDG

Fig. 1. Data Dependency Graph (DDG) for 5-points stencil code in Listing 1.1

applies to every instance of that couple of statements. For example, the non loop-carried RAW dependence between statements S0 and S2 exists for all the instances of S2 where iterator i is 1 and j is between 1 and COLS-2 inclusive. This means that the remaining instance of the stencil loop are not dependent on the communication statements and therefore can be used to hide communication costs.

3   The Polyhedral Model and Integration of MPI Semantics

The polyhedral model represents, in an algebraic way, the execution of a program composed of arbitrary nested loops with affine loop indexes. It captures both the control-flow and data-flow of a program using three compact linear algebraic structures, i.e. the *iteration domain*, the *scheduling* (or *scattering*) *function* and the *access function*. The main idea is to define, for a statement S, a *space* in Z^N where each point correspond to an execution, or *instance*, of S. The value of the coordinates of a point within this space represents the value of the N loop iterators spawning statement S. In order to keep the representation compact, the space, called *polyhedron*, is defined by a set of bounding *affine inequalities*.

Iteration Domain. The space on which a statement is defined is also referred to as its *Iteration Domain*, $\mathcal{D}_S$. For example consider the stencil code in Listing 1.1. Each statement is defined within an iteration domain which is bound by the surrounding control flow statements. For example the iteration domains for S0, S1 and S2 are defined as follows:

$$\mathcal{D}_{S_0} = \{ iter \mid 0 \le iter < NUM\_ITERS\}$$
$$\mathcal{D}_{S_1} = \{ iter \mid 0 \le iter < NUM\_ITERS\}$$
$$\mathcal{D}_{S_2} = \{ iter, i, j \mid 0 \le iter < NUM\_ITERS \wedge 1 \le i < ROWS - 1 \wedge 1 \le j < COLS - 1\}$$

Iteration domains are represented by an integer matrix A, multiplied by a so called *iteration vector* x. The iteration vector determine the dimensionality of the space on which a statement is defined (composed by the loop iterators enclosing that statement). For example the iteration domain for statement S2 in Listing 1.1 is defined by the vector $x_{S_2} = \begin{pmatrix} iter \\ i \\ j \end{pmatrix}$.

Scheduling Function. The second piece of information which is required to describe the semantics of a program are the so-called *scheduling* (or *scattering*) *functions*. Intuitively, statements belonging to a loop body, and subject to the same control flow, will share identical iteration domains. The information of the order on which statement instances are executed is not represented. A *schedule*, $\theta(x)$, is a function which associates a logical *execution date*, or *time-stamp*, to each instance of a statement. This allows the ordering of the instances defined by the iteration domain and furthermore it defines an execution order for instances of different statements.

Access Function. One last function is also required to capture the data locations on which a statement operates. The *access* (or *subscript*) *function* describes the index expression utilized to access an array, and therefore memory locations, within a statement. For compactness reasons, it is represented as a matrix. Access functions also store the information whether a particular memory location is being read (i.e., USE) or written (i.e., DEF). This kind of information is utilized by the polyhedral model to compute exact data dependency analysis for a given input code.

3.1   Instance-Based Data Dependence Analysis

A statement R *depends* on a statement S if there exists an operation $S(x_1)$, an operation $R(x_2)$, and a memory location m such that:

- $S(x_1)$ and $R(x_2)$ refer to the same memory location m, and at least one of them writes to that location;
- x_1 and x_2 respectively belong to the iteration domain of S and R;
- $S(x_1)$ precedes $R(x_2)$.

Dependence information is computed on the basis of the three data structures presented earlier in this section. Intuitively, every point of the iteration domain is projected into a different space using the affine linear transformation represented by the access functions. The domain of this transformation is defined by the statement instances and the co-domain is the memory elements being accessed by that particular statement. Intersecting the co-domains obtained for every statement yields the set of memory elements for which a data dependence may occur. Finally combining this information with the statement execution dates, given by the scheduling matrix, makes it possible to determine the *source* and the *sink* for every dependence.

This complex capability to perform data dependence analysis is implemented in the majority of the libraries supporting the polyhedral model. In our work we utilized the Integer Set Library (ISL) [17] currently employed in several mainstream compilers like GCC and LLVM.

3.2 Limitations of the Polyhedral Model

As mentioned above, the polyhedral model requires affine constraints to describe control- and data-flow. Thus, not every program can be completely represented in the polyhedral model. To maximize the applicability to arbitrary programs, the program is typically split into *Static Control Parts* (SCoPs) that are defined to be the maximal set of consecutive instructions such that: loop bounds, conditionals, and subscript expression are all affine functions of the surrounding loop iterators and global variables; loop iterators and global variables cannot be modified [1]. Girbal et al. demonstrated that SCoPs capture a large portion of the computation time in scientific applications [8].

3.3 Integration of MPI Semantics

Another limitation of a SCoP is the absence of any function or library call. However, if the body of the invoked function is available at compile time, *inlining* can be used to increase the size of the SCoP. This technique is applicable only if the function is not recursive and it has a single-entry and single-exit point. In order to overcome the problem with library routines, for which the source code is not available at compile time, our compiler pre-processes the input program and replaces MPI communication routines with semantically equivalent loop statements. Indeed our prototype deals with MPI_Send and MPI_Recv statements using plain datatypes for now. Under these circumstances, a send(&buff[offset], size) operation is semantically equivalent to a for loop *reading*, i.e., USE, elements buff[i] $\forall\ i \in [offset, offset + size)$. Similarly, a receive(&buff[offset], size) operation will be replaced by a loop *writing*, i.e., DEF, the same range of array elements. In this form, programs containing MPI routines can be handled by the polyhedral model and existing analysis and transformation tools can be utilized. While this transformation is sound for most MPI codes, it neglects the message tag and the communicator. To maintain the original relative ordering, additional data dependencies must be introduced between the generated loops for communication routines to enforce MPI's matching rules. Determining the value of the message tag at a specific program point requires, in the general case, dataflow analysis reaching beyond the SCoP boundaries (e.g. *aliasing* detection).

4 Implementation and Evaluation

In this section we propose a compiler transformation which based on the result of the instance based data dependence analysis obtained by the polyhedral model, maximize the communication/computation overlap by accordingly transforming the input program.

Algorithm 1. Transformation flow for maximizing communication/computation overlap

```
 1: Input: P = Syntax Tree of the input program; MOD = modified AST
 2: Output: T = Syntax Tree of the transformed program
 3: T = P
 4: repeat
 5:    MOD = false; G = extractDDG(T)
 6:    for all dep ∈ G do
 7:       if dist(dep) is 0 && src(dep) is MPI routine && sink(dep) is loop body && dep applies
          to a subset of the instances then
 8:          T = applyLoopFission(T, sink(dep), findCut(dep)); MOD = true
 9:       end if
10:    end for
11: until MOD is false
12: for all dep ∈ G do
13:    if dist(dep) is 0 && src(dep) is MPI routine && sink(dep) is loop body then
14:       {COMM_STMT, WAIT_STMT} = toAsynchronous(src(dep))
15:       T = removeStmt(T, src(dep))
16:       T = moveToEarliestSchedule(T, COMM_STMT)
17:       T = moveToLatestSchedule(T, {WAIT_STMT, sink(dep)})
18:    end if
19: end for
```

4.1   Implementation

The entire approach is implemented in the *Insieme Compiler and Runtime* infrastructure [5]. The *Insieme* project aims to provide an easy to use, powerful framework for source-to-source transformations and program analysis for heterogeneous multi-core parallel computers. It consists primarily of two components: the *Insieme Compiler* and the *Insieme Runtime System*. The *Insieme Compiler*, on which our work relies, fully integrates the polyhedral model analysis and transformations and provides a foundation for source-to-source program optimization. Its architecture is designed to support the processing of hybrid input codes that can include MPI, OpenMP and OpenCL written in C/C++.

Normal Form. Before applying any transformation, the input code is preprocessed into a normal form. In this, an MPI program only contains MPI_Send and MPI_Recv statements so that successive steps of the analysis process are simplified. It is worth noting that the normalized program could have different buffering requirements and therefore may lead to deadlocks if executed. However, the program is kept in this normalized form only for the sake of performing static analysis. The shape of an MPI program in normal form is described by the following rules:

- Non-blocking point-to-point operations are rewritten to use the corresponding blocking version. This is obtained by replacing every asynchronous routine with the synchronous counterpart and by removing every MPI_Wait statement in the input code.
- MPI_Sendrecv operations are split into the corresponding MPI_Send and MPI_Recv operations.
- MPI_Ssend, MPI_Rsend or MPI_Bsend are rewritten to plain MPI_Send.

```
1   for(unsigned iter=0; iter<NUM_ITERS; iter++) {
2       MPI_Request __req0, __req1;
3       MPI_Irecv(&A[0][0],COLS,MPI_DOUBLE,bottom,0,com,&__req0);
4       MPI_Irecv(&A[ROWS-1][0],COLS,MPI_DOUBLE,top,1,com,&__req1);
5       MPI_Send(&A[1][0],COLS,MPI_DOUBLE,bottom,1,com);
6       MPI_Send(&A[ROWS-2][0],COLS,MPI_DOUBLE,top,0,com);
7       // stencil loop after fission
8       for(unsigned i = 2; i<ROWS-2; ++i)
9           for(unsigned j = 1; j<COLS-1; ++j)
10              tmp[i][j] = A[i][j] + 1/4*(A[i+1][j]+A[i-1][j]+A[i][j-1]+A[i
                    ][j+1]);
11      MPI_Wait(&__req0, MPI_STATUS_IGNORE);
12      // first iteration of stencil
13      for(unsigned j = 1; j<COLS-1; ++j)
14          tmp[1][j] = A[1][j] + 1/4*(A[2][j]+A[0][j]+A[1][j-1]+A[1][j
                +1]);
15      MPI_Wait(&__req1, MPI_STATUS_IGNORE);
16      // last iteration of stencil loop
17      for(unsigned j = 1; j<COLS-1; ++j)
18          tmp[ROWS-2][j] = A[ROWS-2][j] + 1/4*(A[ROWS-1][j]+
19                              A[ROWS-3][j]+A[ROWS-2][j-1]+A[ROWS-2][j+1]);
20      double** ttemp=A; A=tmp; tmp=ttemp; // swap arrays
21  }
```

Listing 1.2. 5-points stencil code after code optimization

Handling of MPI Routine Semantics. Once the program is in normal form, we replace MPI statements with their semantically equivalent loops as described in Section 3.3. From this representation of the input program (which does not contain MPI statements anymore), we proceed with the extraction of the SCoP and the dependence polyhedron associated to it. In doing so we keep a link to the communication statement being replaced internally.

Code Transformation. Once the instance-based DDG is generated, we apply a sequence of transformations as described in Algorithm 1. The idea is to iterate through all the non loop-carried dependencies which have an MPI communication statement as the source and a loop body as sink. If the dependence applies to a subset of the instances of the sink then we split the loop, applying the loop fission transformation [10], at the range provided by the dependence analysis. In this way the iterations which are dependent on the MPI communication statement are isolated into a new loop statement. Notice that fission is possible as long as there are no dependencies in the loop body that conflict with the transformation being applied. The transformation framework in the Insieme Compiler implements a pre-condition analysis which determine whether a transformation can be safely applied.

The procedure repeats until a fix-point is reached where every dependence in the DDG applies to all the instances of the source and sink statement. The next step is to consider all dependencies between communication statements and computational loops based on the transformed code. For each of them, the source of the dependence – the communication statement – is removed from the code and the corresponding asynchronous version of the routine is scheduled in its earliest position (which is determined by constraints in the DDG). Listing 1.2 shows the transformed stencil code from Listing 1.1. The receive is scheduled at

Table 1. Evaluation of the transformed code on the VSC2 and LEO3 cluster, fixed problem size of 4Kx4K and NUM_ITERS=10

	VSC2				LEO3		
# of MPI	Original (in msecs.)	Transformed (in msecs.)	Improvement (in %)	# of MPI	Original (in msecs.)	Transformed (in msecs.)	Improvement (in %)
16	219	218	0.3	12	264.9	264.5	0.09
32	89.7	89.0	0.8	24	118.7	118.9	-0.01
64	35.1	32.0	9.5	48	37.4	37.0	0.9
128	20.1	17.9	12.6	96	21.0	20.2	4.0
256	13.1	11.5	13.5	192	11.3	9.8	15.3
512	12.0	9.3	27.9	384	7.6	6.4	19.1

the beginning of the loop body as shown in lines 3 and 4. The loop depending on the communication statement, i.e., the sink, is scheduled lazily prepending to it an MPI_Wait operation placed to preserve the semantics of the program, lines 11 – 19 of Listing 1.2. The remaining non-dependent loop iterations will be, by the end of the transformation, confined between the issuing of the asynchronous communication operations and the consumption of the received data (lines 8–10). Therefore maximizing the overlap window.

The transformation can be easily extended to take into account loop-carried dependencies, in that case the distance of the data dependence, d, defines the number of loop cycles which can be executed between the source and the sink of the dependence. This can be handled by automatically allocating an array of d requests objects for each communication routine where the MPI_Wait statement of a request generated by a communication statement at iteration i happens at iteration $i + d$. This transformation, also known as *software pipelining* [10], requires additional control code, therefore overhead, to be inserted by the compiler to correctly fill and unload the pipeline. A compiler can employ static heuristics in order to determine when software pipelining is beneficial for a given input code.

4.2   Evaluation

We tested the transformed 5-point stencil code, depicted in Listing 1.2, on two production clusters and compared its execution time with the original code shown in Listing 1.1. The (i) Vienna Supercomputing Cluster 2 (VSC2) is a HPC system which consists of 1,314 nodes, with 2 AMD 8-cores Opteron 6132 HE processors each; the (ii) LEO3 cluster which consists of 162 compute nodes, with 2 Intel 6-cores Xeon X5650 CPUs. Both clusters use InfiniBand 4x QDR high speed interconnect.

The code has been executed keeping the problem size constant, 4K by 4K elements, and varying the number of MPI processes, results for both architectures are shown in Table 1. We see that, as expected, the transformed code has overall a better performance. Additionally, the improvement increases with the number of cores since the smaller problem slice assigned to each processor is, the more dominant the communication overhead becomes. Since our transformation aims at hiding communication costs, its benefit grows as the computation/communication ratio diminishes.

5   Conclusions and Outlook

In this paper we showed a compiler optimization which leverages instance-based data dependence analysis, based on the polyhedral model, to isolate loop iterations which are dependent on MPI communication statements. Consecutive proper rescheduling of statements allows the communication/computation overlap to be maximized.

Differently from classic data dependence analysis results, which state dependence relationships at statement level, our approach finds overlap opportunities within loop iterations and therefore at a more finer grain level.

We implemented the entire approach in the Insieme source-to-source compiler [5] and showed how the transformed code has an improved performance, up to 28% faster with 512 cores, because of the increased overlap.

Acknowledgments. This work was supported by the Austrian Ministry of Science BMWF as part of the UniInfrastrukturprogramm of the Research Platform Scientific Computing at the University of Innsbruck. Furthermore, the computational results presented have been achieved in part using the Vienna Scientific Cluster (VSC).

References

1. Benabderrahmane, M.-W., Pouchet, L.-N., Cohen, A., Bastoul, C.: The Polyhedral Model Is More Widely Applicable Than You Think. In: Gupta, R. (ed.) CC 2010. LNCS, vol. 6011, pp. 283–303. Springer, Heidelberg (2010)
2. Danalis, A., Pollock, L., Swany, M.: Automatic MPI application transformation with ASPhALT. In: Par. and Distr. Proc. Symp., IPDPS 2007, pp. 1–8 (March 2007)
3. Danalis, A., Kim, K.Y., Pollock, L., Swany, M.: Transformations to parallel codes for communication-computation overlap. In: Proceedings of the 2005 ACM/IEEE Conference on Supercomputing, SC 2005, Washington, DC, USA, p. 58 (2005)
4. Danalis, A., Pollock, L., Swany, M., Cavazos, J.: MPI-aware compiler optimizations for improving communication-computation overlap. In: Proceedings of the 23rd International Conference on Supercomputing, ICS 2009, pp. 316–325 (2009)
5. Distributed and Parallel Systems Group, University of Innsbruck: Insieme Comiler and Runtime Infrastructure, http://insieme-compiler.org
6. Fahringer, T., Mehofer, E.: Buffer-Safe Communication Optimization Based on Data Flow Analysis and Performance Prediction. In: Malyshkin, V.E. (ed.) PaCT 1997. LNCS, vol. 1277, pp. 189–200. Springer, Heidelberg (1997)
7. Geimer, M., Wolf, F., Wylie, B.J.N., Ábrahám, E., Becker, D., Mohr, B.: The Scalasca performance toolset architecture. CCPE Journal 22(6), 702–719 (2010)
8. Girbal, S., et al.: Semi-automatic composition of loop transformations for deep parallelism and memory hierarchies. Intl. Journal of Par. Progr. 34(3), 261–317 (2006)
9. Gropp, W., Lusk, E., Skjellum, A.: Using MPI: portable parallel programming with the message-passing interface, 2nd edn. MIT Press, Cambridge (1999)

10. Kennedy, K., Allen, J.R.: Optimizing compilers for modern architectures: a dependence-based approach, San Francisco, CA, USA (2002)
11. Knüpfer, A., et al.: The vampir performance analysis tool-set. In: Tools for High Performance Computing, pp. 139–155 (2008)
12. MPI Forum: MPI: A Message-Passing Interface Standard. Version 2.2 (September 4, 2009), http://www.mpi-forum.org (December 2009)
13. Shende, S.S., Malony, A.D.: The Tau Parallel Performance System. Int. J. High Perform. Comput. Appl. 20(2), 287–311 (2006)
14. Thakur, R., Balaji, P., Buntinas, D., Goodell, D., Gropp, W., Hoefler, T., Kumar, S., Lusk, E., Traeff, J.L.: MPI at Exascale. In: Procceedings of SciDAC 2010 (June 2010)
15. Truong, H.-L., Fahringer, T.: SCALEA: A Performance Analysis Tool for Distributed and Parallel Programs. In: Monien, B., Feldmann, R.L. (eds.) Euro-Par 2002. LNCS, vol. 2400, pp. 41–55. Springer, Heidelberg (2002)
16. Vasilache, N., Cohen, A., Bastoul, C., Girbal, S.: Violated dependence analysis. In: ACM ICS (2006)
17. Verdoolaege, S.: isl: An Integer Set Library for the Polyhedral Model. In: Fukuda, K., van der Hoeven, J., Joswig, M., Takayama, N. (eds.) ICMS 2010. LNCS, vol. 6327, pp. 299–302. Springer, Heidelberg (2010)

mpicroscope: Towards an MPI Benchmark Tool for Performance Guideline Verification

Jesper Larsson Träff

Vienna University of Technology, Institute of Information Systems
Research Group Parallel Computing
Favoritenstrasse 16, 1040 Wien, Austria
`traff@par.tuwien.ac.at`

Abstract. We discuss a new, stand-alone MPI benchmark program (for now called mpicroscope) for assessing the performance of collective communication patterns, in particular of the standard MPI 2.2 collective operations. The benchmark is intended to facilitate comparisons between different ways of expressing the same functionality towards performing automatic detection of violations of self-consistent MPI performance guidelines. The benchmark can be used by MPI library developers for assessing the relative quality of new algorithms and implementations. It can also be used to make users aware of aspects of their MPI library where performance (portability) problems may lurk. The current version of the benchmark automatically detects, for any measured communication pattern, two universal, self-consistent guidelines that encourage *monotone* and *split-robust* performance.

The benchmark aims to employ sound benchmarking procedures and is controlled via command-line options. It covers the MPI 2.2 collective operations, and a number of alternative patterns that express MPI collective functionality. In contrast to many other benchmarks data can be structured as described by an MPI *derived datatype*. We present results from a small InfiniBand cluster with a vendor MPI library, showing performance guideline violations that were detected and highlighted with mpicroscope.

1 Introduction

Despite the ubiquitousness and universality of the Message-Passing Interface (MPI) standard [12], there seem to be no commonly agreed upon and broadly covering benchmark for thoroughly benchmarking the performance of given MPI libraries, although there have been many initiatives in this direction. Also, there are only few studies that compare quantitatively and qualitatively the many existing MPI benchmarks [8,11]. For an established and practically dominant interface as MPI is in the HPC domain, this is a curious state of affairs. It makes it difficult to compare MPI communication performance on different HPC systems on which application codes may run or have to be ported. It makes it difficult to assess whether the features of MPI that are exploited on one system will yield similarly good performance on another [19]. For MPI researchers it makes it

J.L. Träff, S. Benkner, and J. Dongarra (Eds.): EuroMPI 2012, LNCS 7490, pp. 100–109, 2012.

tedious to perform performance measurements; current practice unfortunately seems to be that each developer uses his own benchmark, which makes it difficult (depending on the degree to which details of the benchmark are known) to compare results. This is obviously detrimental to scientific work. An easy to use tool with community agreed functionality and solid benchmarking procedures would go along way towards remedying this situation.

Another important role of benchmarking is to assist in evaluating the internal performance consistency of MPI libraries. MPI provides many different ways to express the same functionality, often, however, with a clear, intended performance preference. A benchmark with which natural alternatives can be readily compared would be of help to check whether such implicit expectations – which we formalize as *self-consistent performance guidelines* [19] – are fulfilled. For all MPI communication operations there are unstated performance assumptions, for instance that communication time is non-decreasing with message length, and likewise a benchmark could easily validate (as will be shown) whether such expectations are fulfilled. Such meta-principles can all be defended by the argument that if they were violated, there would be an easy way for the MPI user to improve performance. This is undesirable, since such improvements per hand might not carry over to other systems and MPI libraries. MPI offers a huge number of possibilities to formulate performance expectations by relating different implementation alternatives, and as argued fulfillment of such expectations will support application performance portability [19]. The role of a benchmark tool would be to validate the expectations, formulated as self-consistent performance guidelines, and make the application programmer and MPI library developer aware of violations that could lead to performance portability problems.

Towards addressing these problems, we are developing yet another MPI benchmark with focus on assessing consistent performance of collective communication patterns. The benchmark first and foremost incorporates the 17 MPI 2.2 [12] collective operations, and supplements these with natural, alternative ways of expressing these patterns. This facilitates comparison with the implicit assumption that the specific MPI collective should be best. The benchmark is intended as a quick-and-dirty tool for the MPI library developer, and is controlled with commandline options with defaults that make it easy to selectively investigate any, some or all of the supported collective patterns. The same, sound (or at least: explicit) benchmarking procedures are used for all patterns under all circumstances. In contrast to many other benchmarks it covers also the derived datatype mechanism of MPI by providing a simple way of expressing hierarchical, regular data layouts with the different MPI datatype constructors [5]. For now we call this benchmark the mpicroscope.

1.1   Related Work

The mpicroscope benchmark has evolved from a handwritten benchmark used by the author over a number of years. As a proposal it is available to anyone interested for use, scrutiny and critical comment. Regarding benchmarking principles it is heavily inspired by mpptest as described in [4] and, of course, the

"Special Karlsruher MPI" benchmark, *SKaMPI*, as described in [1,2,13,14,15]. These benchmarks are fairly precise in stating their principles. Common pitfalls and problems with benchmarking collective operations are dealt with in [9], which among other things also introduces mechanisms for better synchronization. Some other, often used benchmarks (e.g, some versions of Intel's MPI Benchmark, IMB) apply unsound (pipelined rather than individual collective performance) or intransparent principles, and some are scantily documented (MPBench, MPIBench [7]). Other well-known benchmarking initiatives have other objectives, e.g., NetPIPE is rather for assessing network performance [20]. An interesting, recent benchmarking initiative that aims at providing library support for selective benchmarking from other tools or applications is described in [10]. The literature on comparing MPI benchmarks is unfortunately not extensive [8,11]. Self-consistent MPI performance guidelines as a means for ensuring performance portability of applications and MPI libraries were introduced in [18,19], and subsequently extended to other aspects of MPI [5,6].

2   Terminology and Methodology

In MPI all communication is wrt. a fixed set of processes represented by a *communicator*. Communication is out of/into *fixed buffers* allocated in user memory either by a standard memory allocator, e.g., `malloc`, or by the special MPI_Alloc_mem allocator. All communication operations can employ a *datatype* to describe the structure of the communicated data. Some collective patterns, e.g., MPI_Reduce, have a distinguished *root* process from which data originates or end up. Collective reduction operations employ a binary *reduction operator*. An mpiscope *experiment* fixes all these parameters. For each experiment the role of the benchmark is to measure, as accurately as possible and as detailed as desired, the communication performance for a selection of datasizes. The range and overall structure of the datasizes are given as experiment parameters (see Section 3). Each run of the benchmark goes through a set of selected collective patterns, per default all of the predefined patterns, and performs the experiment for each of these.

The datasize unit is bytes, and each datasize is translated to a corresponding, largest possible count of the experiment datatype. For each datasize all processes measures the execution time using MPI_Wtime. Processes are currently synchronized with MPI_Barrier [1,9]. The time for the slowest process is recorded as the *completion time* for that count. We call this an individual *measurement*. Measurements are performed in order of increasing count, that is for all counts c_i in an experiment $c_i < c_{i+1}$. Individual measurements are repeated until a stable, reproducible result is found. For this we use the notion of *tail*, a number of repetitions during which the minimum completion time is not supposed to change; if this is the case, this minimum completion time is taken as the "correct" time for the given count. If instead a better minimum completion time is found, the measurement is repeated for another tail of iterations. Over the course of the experiment the tail *decays* (linearly or exponentially), and when tail reaches one all measurements will terminate. The recorded completion time of the collective for count c_i is denoted by $T(c_i)$. We believe (and would like to prove) that this approach under reasonable assumptions ensures stable and reproducible measurements for each count. It is worth emphasizing that the mpicroscope benchmark measures the performance of individual collective patterns. The performance of repeated sequences of operations (e.g., several consecutive MPI_Bcast operations) is a different matter (there could be pipelining effects leading to entirely different results than a single, isolated call); if such behavior is of interest, a separate pattern capturing this must be added to the mpicroscope.

3   The Benchmark

The benchmark is written in C with macro support for implementing new communication patterns. It is controlled by command line options by which the experiment parameters (communicator, memory allocator, root process etc.) can be set and/or modified. Also data ranges and distributions can be set. A common benchmarking pitfall is to restrict sizes to only powers of two. To avoid this the mpicroscope offers exponential and linear distributions of measure points, with additional constant offsets. In an exponential distribution a base r is set together with the number of measure points in each interval $[r^k, r^{k+1}]$. In the linear distribution, upper limit and number of subdivisions is set. For each measure point c additional measure points $c-\epsilon$ and $c+\epsilon'$ can be requested. If options are repeated, either they have a cumulative effect, or the last one takes effect. For example, -range=0,10000 -exp=2,7 -exp=10,10 -range=10000,1000000 -lin=10 overlaps two exponential distributions in the range from 0 to 10,000 Bytes with a linear distribution with 10 measure points in the range from 10,000 to 1,000,000 Bytes.

The benchmark per default generates a file of raw completion times; there are options for splitting this into individual files for each pattern (as there is to select subsets of patterns) and to generate output with gnuplot commands for direct generation of plots (see Section7). There is also a simple "report generator" for taking these plots into a LaTeX document.

Correctness of the patterns is eminently important (no benchmarking of incorrect functionality!), but currently the benchmark offers no support for correctness checking. Likewise communication buffers are initialized only once; there is not support for controlling buffer placement and cache usage. This definitely needs to be included. To be detailed and accurate the benchmark is intended to do automatic refinement between counts where a linear interpolation shows unexpected change in performance. This has not been implemented yet, but SKaMPI and mpptest employ such mechanisms [4,14].

4   Meta-performance Guideline Verification

We use the semi-formal notation $MPI\_A(n) \preceq MPI\_B(n')$ to state performance guidelines. This expresses that execution of MPI function A with significant arguments (typically data sizes) of total size n is for almost all values of n not slower than MPI function B with arguments of size n', where n' is some function of n – *all other things being equal* (which they are of course not) [19]. The next sections introduce two universal guidelines with simple linear-time verification algorithms.

4.1   The Monotone Guideline

$$\text{MPI\_}A(n) \preceq \text{MPI\_}B(n + k) \tag{1}$$

The self-consistent, *monotone* performance guideline is applicable to all communication operations, and stipulates that the time for communicating n bytes be no larger than communicating $n + k$ bytes for any $k > 0$. Adherence to this guideline can easily be checked. Assume completion times are stored in order of increasing c. We scan backwards starting from the largest c. If a monotone violation $T(c_{i-1}) > T(c_i)$ is found, we scan backwards until a j with $T(c_{i-j}) \leq T(c_i)$ is found. The counts from c_{i-j} to c_i violate the monotone property.

4.2   The Split-Robust Guideline

$$\text{MPI\_}A(n) \preceq k\text{MPI\_}B(n/k) \tag{2}$$

The self-consistent *split-robust* performance guideline is likewise universally applicable [19]. It states that splitting data should not make a performance improvement, that is sending n bytes in k parts, $k > 1$, should not be faster than just sending the n bytes. We can partially check adherence to this principle in linear time. We scan forward, and for each c_i find the largest k for which $jT(c_i) < T(jc_i)$ for $1 < j \leq k$. If there is no measurement exactly for $T(ic_j)$ linear interpolation between $c_{j-1} < ic_i < c_j$ is applied to estimate the completion time.

5   Collective Patterns

The mpicroscope benchmark includes all 17 MPI 2.2 collective operations, and a number of additional patterns expressing the same functionality as native MPI collectives. For instance, the well-known algorithm for broadcast in terms of a scatter followed by an allgather operation [3] as used in some MPI libraries [16], allreduce expressed as reduce followed by broadcast, allgather in terms of gather and broadcast or simply multiple, concurrent broadcasts, alltoall communication expressed by one-sided communication, and so on, are included as collective patterns.

The mpicroscope has a common framework for writing patterns and provides some macro support which should make it possible for users to extend the benchmark with new patterns. The ambition is to provide a collection of sensible implementations for at least torus/mesh and fully connected architectures for each MPI collective. Benchmarking the native MPI collectives against these patterns would ensure a certain baseline performance, and guide against immediate performance portability problems.

A general expectation that can readily be checked with the benchmark is that each regular collective operation is not slower than the same pattern expressed by the corresponding, irregular (vector) operation, that is $\text{MPI\_}C(n) \preceq \text{MPI\_}Cv(n)$ where $C \in \{\text{MPI\_Gather, MPI\_Scatter, MPI\_Allgather, MPI\_Alltoall}\}$, similarly for MPI_Reduce_scatter_block. We list a number of more or less evident, self-consistent performance guidelines that can at the moment be checked with mpicroscope; this list is not exhaustive.

$$\text{MPI\_Bcast}(n) \preceq \text{MPI\_Scatter}(n) + \text{MPI\_Allgather}(n) \qquad (3)$$

$$\text{MPI\_Reduce}(n) \preceq \text{MPI\_Reduce\_scatter}(n) + \text{MPI\_Gather}(n) \qquad (4)$$

$$\text{MPI\_Allreduce}(n) \preceq \text{MPI\_Reduce\_scatter}(n) + \text{MPI\_Allgather}(n) \quad (5)$$

$$\text{MPI\_Allreduce}(n) \preceq \text{MPI\_Reduce}(n) + \text{MPI\_Bcast}(n) \qquad (6)$$

$$\text{MPI\_Reduce\_scatter}(n) \preceq \text{MPI\_Reduce}(n) + \text{MPI\_Scatterv}(n) \qquad (7)$$

$$\text{MPI\_Reduce\_scatter\_block}(n) \preceq \text{MPI\_Reduce}(n) + \text{MPI\_Scatter}(n) \qquad (8)$$

$$\text{MPI\_Scan}(n) \preceq \text{MPI\_Exscan}(n) + \text{MPI\_Reduce\_local}(n) \qquad (9)$$

$$\text{MPI\_Gather}(n) \preceq p\text{MPI\_Recv}(n/p) \qquad (10)$$

$$\text{MPI\_Scatter}(n) \preceq p\text{MPI\_Send}(n/p) \qquad (11)$$

$$\text{MPI\_Allgather}(n) \preceq \text{MPI\_Gather}(n) + \text{MPI\_Bcast}(n) \qquad (12)$$

$$\text{MPI\_Allgather}(n) \preceq \|_p\text{MPI\_Bcast}(n/p) \qquad (13)$$

$$\text{MPI\_Alltoall}(n) \preceq p\text{MPI\_Sendrecv}(n/p) \qquad (14)$$

$$\text{MPI\_Alltoall}(n) \preceq \text{MPI\_Win\_fence} + p\text{MPI\_Put}(n/p) +$$
$$\text{MPI\_Win\_fence} \qquad (15)$$

6   Datatypes

Per default all data are communicated as MPI_INT but other base datatypes are supported, e.g., MPI_CHAR, MPI_FLOAT, MPI_DOUBLE. Performance of collective patterns with structured data can also be assessed. The idea is to define a strided layout, much as can be captured with the MPI vector datatype constructor, in terms of a stride, a data block size (that must be no larger than the stride), and a number of repetitions. These three parameters can be given as options to the benchmark. Now, either of the MPI constructors can be selected as the way to describe this layout to the MPI library in order to make it possible to asses whether datatype performance guidelines as discussed in [5] are met. Hierarchical datatypes can be built up by repeating constructors, e.g., `-vector -index` would indicate that an indexed type is built over a vector, at each level using the given values of the three structural parameters. In addition there are patterns for benchmarking the performance of the MPI_Pack and MPI_Unpack routines. The supported binary operators for reductions operations are MPI_MAX, MPI_MIN, MPI_SUM, MPI_BAND; for derived datatypes a generic user-defined operation is used – we note that MPI support for defining such generic operators is severely lacking.

7   A Few Results

We give here two examples of how the mpicroscope can be used to investigate violations of performance guidelines and highlight potential performance (portability) problems with a specific MPI implementation on a specific system. Needless to say this should be followed by differential comparisons between different MPI libraries on the same system, and libraries on different systems.

The system at hand is a small InfiniBand based cluster with 36 nodes each equipped with two 8-core AMD Opteron 6134 "magny cours" processors (2.3GHz), and 32 GBytes of memory per node. The MPI library is the vendor library. All experiments used 30 nodes with 16 MPI processes on each. We ran the tool with the command mpirun [nodes, processes, pinning] mpicro -exp=2,5 -exp=10,10 -gnuplot-log which measures at powers of 2 with 5 measure points inbetween powers, and powers of 10, with 10 measure points inbetween. Per default the regular MPI_COMM_WORLD communicator is used, with communication buffers allocated with malloc. The run generates a stand-alone data file with gnuplot commands for doubly logarithmic time/datasize plots. The default tail is 10 repetitions with linear decay. The full run with all patterns required a number of repetitions ranging from 32 (Reducescatter+Gather, for Guideline 4) to 57 (Scatter+Allgather, for Guideline 3). Several executions were tried, and with a relatively unloaded but not exclusively reserved system, results seem reproducible.

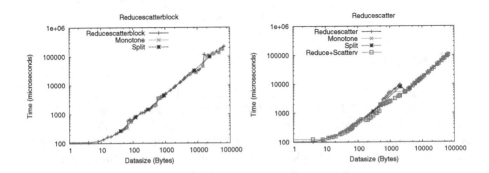

Fig. 1. Performance of MPI_Reduce_scatter_block vs. MPI_Reduce_scatter and the pattern MPI_Reduce+MPI_Scatterv (Guideline 7)

In Figure 1 we compare the regular MPI_Reduce_scatter_block (left) against the more general MPI_Reduce_scatter and an implementation of same in terms of MPI_Reduce and MPI_Scatterv (Guideline 7). In MPI_Reduce_scatter_block there are some violations of both monotone and split-robustness guidelines. More seriously, MPI_Reduce_scatter has a range around one KByte where the trivial implementation is significantly better. Also, better algorithms in terms of bandwidth [17] seems not to exploited; and especially for large data the regular MPI_Reduce_scatter_block operation is a factor of almost two slower than the more general MPI_Reduce_scatter collective.

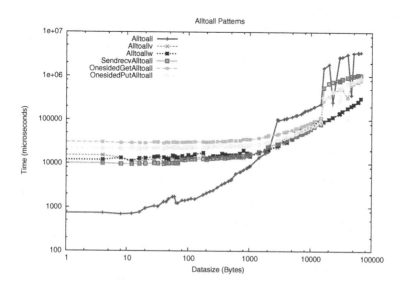

Fig. 2. Performance of MPI_Alltoall vs. MPI_Alltoallv vs. MPI_Alltoallw, vs. send-receive vs . one-sided put vs. one-sided get (Guidelines 14 and 15)

Finally, Figure 2 compares the current implementations of the alltoall communication pattern. The natural expectation is for MPI_Alltoall to be fastest, and this is indeed the case for messages up to about 2KBytes where there is an unfortunate switch point (this would also be seen in split-robustness violations) from which MPI_Alltoall performs the worst. Contrary to what the guidelines state, MPI_Alltoallw seems to fare the best. The send-receive pattern performs as well as the implementations in terms of one-sided puts and gets (these two are similar), with a curious decrease in performance around 20KBytes.

8   Summary and Outlook

The mpicroscope benchmark is a basis for a project that will continue over the next few years. The aim is to develop a fast, accurate, detailed performance microscope for use primarily by MPI developers. Interesting tradeoffs that will be explored are between speed and accuracy, in particular when automatic refinement is employed, as well as the reproducibility of the benchmark methodology. Also, we would like to put the methodology on a more firm statistical foundation. Other immediate issues concern the automatic refinement, outlier detection and elimination, and synchronization of timers.

The benchmark automatically detects violations of the monotone and split-robustness guidelines. Comparisons between different patterns were here done by hand. The idea is to augment the benchmark tool with scripts to facilitate these comparisons and possibly provide concise reports on violations. This will be more helpful to application programmers to avoid performance portability pitfalls.

Communication patterns have to be specified at compile time and explicitly programmed with the provided macro support. We envisage higher-level facilities for expressing performance guidelines that can be compiled directly into the required experiments.

References

1. Worsch, T., Reussner, R., Augustin, W.: On Benchmarking Collective MPI Operations. In: Kranzlmüller, D., Kacsuk, P., Dongarra, J., Volkert, J. (eds.) PVM/MPI 2002. LNCS, vol. 2474, pp. 271–279. Springer, Heidelberg (2002)
2. Augustin, W., Worsch, T.: Usefulness and Usage of SKaMPI-Bench. In: Dongarra, J., Laforenza, D., Orlando, S. (eds.) EuroPVM/MPI 2003. LNCS, vol. 2840, pp. 63–70. Springer, Heidelberg (2003)
3. Fox, G.C., et al.: Solving Problems on Concurrent Processors: General Techniques and Regular Problems. Prentice-Hall (1988)
4. Gropp, W.D., Lusk, E.: Reproducible Measurements of MPI Performance Characteristics. In: Margalef, T., Dongarra, J., Luque, E. (eds.) PVM/MPI 1999. LNCS, vol. 1697, pp. 11–18. Springer, Heidelberg (1999)
5. Gropp, W., Hoefler, T., Thakur, R., Träff, J.L.: Performance Expectations and Guidelines for MPI Derived Datatypes. In: Cotronis, Y., Danalis, A., Nikolopoulos, D.S., Dongarra, J. (eds.) EuroMPI 2011. LNCS, vol. 6960, pp. 150–159. Springer, Heidelberg (2011)
6. Gropp, W.D., Kimpe, D., Ross, R., Thakur, R., Träff, J.L.: Self-consistent MPI-IO Performance Requirements and Expectations. In: Lastovetsky, A., Kechadi, T., Dongarra, J. (eds.) EuroPVM/MPI 2008. LNCS, vol. 5205, pp. 167–176. Springer, Heidelberg (2008)
7. Grove, D., Coddington, P.: Precise MPI performance measurement using MPIBench. In: Proceedings of HPC Asia (2001)
8. Hamid, N.A.W.A., Coddington, P.D., Vaughan, F.: Comparison of MPI benchmark programs on shared memory and distributed memory machines (point-to-point communication). International Journal on High Performance Computing Applications 24(4), 469–483 (2010)
9. Hoefler, T., Schneider, T., Lumsdaine, A.: Accurately measuring collective operations at massive scale. In: 22nd IEEE International Symposium on Parallel and Distributed Processing (IPDPS), pp. 1–8 (2008)

10. Lastovetsky, A., Rychkov, V., O'Flynn, M.: MPIBlib: Benchmarking MPI Communications for Parallel Computing on Homogeneous and Heterogeneous Clusters. In: Lastovetsky, A., Kechadi, T., Dongarra, J. (eds.) EuroPVM/MPI 2008. LNCS, vol. 5205, pp. 227–238. Springer, Heidelberg (2008)
11. Mierendorff, H., Cassirer, K., Schwamborn, H.: Working with MPI Benchmarking Suites on ccNUMA Architectures. In: Dongarra, J., Kacsuk, P., Podhorszki, N. (eds.) PVM/MPI 2000. LNCS, vol. 1908, pp. 18–26. Springer, Heidelberg (2000)
12. MPI Forum. MPI: A Message-Passing Interface Standard. Version 2.2, September 4 (2009), http://www.mpi-forum.org
13. Reussner, R.: Using SKaMPI for developing high-performance MPI programs with performance portability. Future Generation Computer Systems 19(5), 749–759 (2003)
14. Reussner, R., Sanders, P., Prechelt, L., Müller, M.S.: SKaMPI: A Detailed, Accurate MPI Benchmark. In: Alexandrov, V.N., Dongarra, J. (eds.) PVM/MPI 1998. LNCS, vol. 1497, pp. 52–59. Springer, Heidelberg (1998)
15. Reussner, R., Sanders, P., Träff, J.L.: SKaMPI: A comprehensive benchmark for public benchmarking of MPI. Scientific Programming 10(1), 55–65 (2002)
16. Thakur, R., Gropp, W.D., Rabenseifner, R.: Improving the performance of collective operations in MPICH. International Journal on High Performance Computing Applications 19, 49–66 (2004)
17. Träff, J.L.: An Improved Algorithm for (Non-commutative) Reduce-Scatter with an Application. In: Di Martino, B., Kranzlmüller, D., Dongarra, J. (eds.) EuroPVM/MPI 2005. LNCS, vol. 3666, pp. 129–137. Springer, Heidelberg (2005)
18. Träff, J.L., Gropp, W.D., Thakur, R.: Self-consistent MPI Performance Requirements. In: Cappello, F., Herault, T., Dongarra, J. (eds.) PVM/MPI 2007. LNCS, vol. 4757, pp. 36–45. Springer, Heidelberg (2007)
19. Träff, J.L., Gropp, W.D., Thakur, R.: Self-consistent MPI performance guidelines. IEEE Transactions on Parallel and Distributed Systems 21(5), 698–709 (2010)
20. Turner, D., Oline, A., Chen, X., Benjegerdes, T.: Integrating New Capabilities into NetPIPE. In: Dongarra, J., Laforenza, D., Orlando, S. (eds.) EuroPVM/MPI 2003. LNCS, vol. 2840, pp. 37–44. Springer, Heidelberg (2003)

OMB-GPU: A Micro-Benchmark Suite
for Evaluating MPI Libraries on GPU Clusters

D. Bureddy, H. Wang, A. Venkatesh, S. Potluri, and D.K. Panda

Department of Computer Science and Engineering, The Ohio State University
{bureddy,wangh,akshay,potluri,panda}@cse.ohio-state.edu

Abstract. General-Purpose Graphics Processing Units (GPGPUs) are becoming a common component of modern supercomputing systems. Many MPI applications are being modified to take advantage of the superior compute potential offered by GPUs. To facilitate this process, many MPI libraries are being extended to support MPI communication from GPU device memory. However, there is lack of a standardized benchmark suite that helps users evaluate common communication models on GPU clusters and do a fair comparison for different MPI libraries. In this paper, we extend the widely used OSU Micro-Benchmarks (OMB) suite with benchmarks that evaluate performance of point-point, multi-pair and collective MPI communication for different GPU cluster configurations. Benefits of the proposed benchmarks for MVAPICH2 and OpenMPI libraries are illustrated.

Keywords: MPI, GPGPU, micro-benchmarks, clusters.

1 Introduction

General-purpose Graphics Processing Units (GPGPUs) are increasingly being used in the field of High End Computing. Many modern supercomputers are offering multiple GPUs per node to provide higher compute density and performance per watt. Taking advantage of this trend, many parallel scientific applications are being modified to take advantage of the GPGPUs offered by these modern systems.

MPI has been the most popular model for developing parallel scientific applications. The initial fact that GPGPUs had an independent memory address space complicated the process of porting MPI applications to these devices. The developers had to use multiple programming models for data movement: accelerator-specific programming models, such as CUDA or OpenCL, for CPU-GPU data movement and MPI for data transfer across nodes. Later versions of CUDA removed this restriction for NVIDIA GPUs, by providing a uniform virtual address space for both the GPU and host memory. This currently allows MPI libraries to support communication directly from device memory, without requiring any extensions to the MPI interface.

NVIDIA is one of the leading providers of GPU technology and CUDA is the most popular standard for programming their GPU devices. Currently, most of the popular open-source MPI libraries either have support for MPI communication from device memory of NVIDIA GPUs or efforts are underway to add such a support

J.L. Träff, S. Benkner, and J. Dongarra (Eds.): EuroMPI 2012, LNCS 7490, pp. 110–120, 2012.

[18,17,14,13,6,9]. However, a standard benchmark suite that allows end users to compare these different implementations and use the one that delivers the best performance for a given use-case does not exist. Modern node architectures allow multiple ways of configuring GPUs. For example, two GPUs on a system based on Intel architecture can be connected to the same PCIe interface, the same I/O hub or different I/O hubs. Different libraries make different design choices and deliver different performance based on the GPU configuration. The performance of GPU-GPU communication can also vary based on factors like buffer usage pattern, process to GPU binding among others. A standard benchmark suite should provide flexibility to compare the performance of different MPI libraries in these different scenarios.

The OSU Micro-benchmark (OMB) suite has been the most widely used set of benchmarks to compare the performance of different MPI libraries on modern clusters [10]. In this paper, we design and implement OMB-GPU, an extension to OMB that allows users to compare the performance of MPI libraries on GPU clusters. We make the following key contributions:

1. We design and implement OMB-GPU, a micro-benchmark suite to compare performance of MPI libraries on GPU clusters.
2. We provide benchmarks to measure performance of point-to-point, multi-pair and collective MPI communication from/to GPU devices.
3. We add infrastructure that displays the GPU configuration on a node and supports process-GPU mapping. This allows users to measure performance between different pairs of GPUs.
4. We provide different runtime options for buffer location and buffer reuse to emulate different communication patterns.

To the best of our knowledge, OMB-GPU is the first micro-benchmark suite that supports evaluation of communication performance using MPI libraries on GPU clusters.

2 Background and Related Work

In this section, we will discuss the necessary background and the related work. In this paper, we use CUDA as the accelerator-centric programming model, and we would like to note that the benchmarks can be easily extended to support OpenCL.

2.1 Programming on Heterogeneous Cluster with GPGPUs

In the heterogeneous cluster with GPGPUs, GPUs are connected to the local nodes as the peripherals via PCI express. The nodes are connected by the high performance network, such as InfiniBand. Using CUDA programming model, GPUs can read/write memory attached to the local node. But it is necessary to move the data from GPU device memory to the host memory before sending the data to the remote node. Usually, MPI is used to communicate the data across nodes. Multiple programming models for the data movement and management have increased the programming complexity. GPU-GPU MPI communication is proposed to use the standard MPI interfaces to unify the device memory and the host memory. It hides the GPU-CPU data movement and optimizes GPU-CPU data movement and management inside MPI library. The popular MPI libraries (MPICH2 [7], OpenMPI [9], and MVAPICH2 [8]) are adopting it in their open source libraries. But there is not a suite of benchmarks to evaluate the GPU-GPU MPI communication.

2.2 Related Work

Recently, many benchmarks have been proposed to evaluate the performance for GP-GPUs. Gbench [2] has been proposed to compare the GPU and CPU performance for the common Matlab computations. Parboil benchmark [11] and Rodinia benchmark [4] have the similar motivation as the Gbench, but include more diverse applications. OMB-GPU focuses on the common communication models in the applications instead of the computation. SHOC benchmark suite [5] has been proposed to test the performance and stability of the heterogeneous clusters with GPGPUs. It is a general benchmark suite using applications on the heterogeneous clusters. As illustrated in our previous research [17], the communication design and implementation will badly affect the entire application performance. It is necessary to provide a new benchmark focusing on the general communication models in these common applications.

In the existing benchmarks for MPI, such as Intel MPI Benchmarks [1], NAS Parallel Benchmarks [3], SPECMPI [16], both the source and the destination addresses are resided in the host memory. If programmers want to run these benchmarks on GPGPUs cluster, the additional CPU-GPU data movement and management have to be added. At the same time, since there are many factors to affect the data communication performance, such as the pinned or pageable host memory, the exclusive or shared usage for one GPU, the shared or not shared I/O Hub among GPUs and network NICs, and so on, it is hard to write the test programs and do a fair comparison on different MPI libraries in an ad-hoc manner. Moreover, it is necessary to identify these important architecture related parameters and understand how the benchmarks respond to changes of these parameters. In this paper, we will propose OMB-GPU to evaluate communication for the GPGPUs cluster.

3   Design Considerations

The performance of MPI communication from GPUs is influenced by a range of factors such as node configuration, process-to-GPU affinity, buffer usage pattern and others. We consider these aspects described below in designing the OMB-GPU benchmark suite.

GPU Configuration: It is becoming common for clusters to have multiple GPU devices installed per node. The way two GPUs are connected on a node decides the channels that are available for communication between these GPUs. Different channels have different performance as discussed in [15]. CUDA 4.1 makes it easier for processes using different GPUs to communicate with one another when the GPUs are connected to the same I/O Hub chip (on Intel architectures). It provides Inter-Process Communication (IPC) through which a process can directly read from or write to another process's buffer. The other communication channels available between GPUs on the same IOH are shared host memory and loop-back through the network adapter (Mellanox IB adapters, for example). Similar options are available when the GPUs are connected directly to an IOH or through a PCI-e switch. On the other hand, CUDA IPC mechanism is not supported when GPUs are connected to different I/O Hubs. The communication have to use the shared host memory or the network loop-back channels. Though the aforementioned channels are available between different pairs of GPUs, which of these channels are actually implemented depends on the MPI library. The user has to depend on commands/tools like lspci and nvidia-smi to get the configuration of GPUs on a give node. Tools like Portable Hardware Locality (hwloc) [12] are starting to provide this information but are not complete from our experience. We also observed that the system architecture itself may not give the idea if channels like IPC are available between two GPUs. For example, we have seen that CUDA IPC does not work on some AMD platforms though an IOH like limitation is not documented for AMD platforms. For this reason, we have added infrastructure as part of the OMB-GPU suite, to detect the availability of IPC between different GPUs on a node. Figure 1 depicts a multi-GPU configuration with two Intel nodes and the available communication channels between different pairs of GPUs.

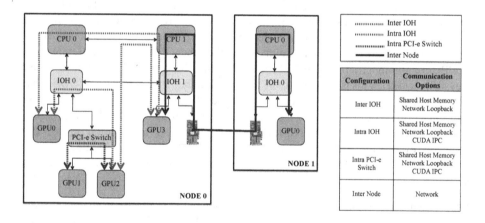

Fig. 1. A multi-GPU configuration and the available communication channels

GPU Context Creation: A CUDA context is analogous to a process on a CPU. All the resources allocated and actions performed by a process on a GPU are encapsulated inside a CUDA context. A context can be created using explicit context creation calls or is created when the first call to CUDA runtime happens. CUDA requires some of the device properties (selection of scheduling, availability of pinned host memory and others) to be set before the context is created. On the other hand, MPI libraries usually need to make some CUDA calls from inside MPI_Init for tasks like buffer allocation, buffer registration, IPC channel detection and others. Some of these calls will require a context to be created. To allow for this, applications normally set the required device properties and initialize the context before they call MPI_Init. MPI launchers provide information about MPI process rank (within a node and across the job) through an environment variable to allow application to take care of GPU binding during the context creation process. The benchmarks in OMB-GPU mimic the behavior of the application of selecting a device and creating a context before MPI_Init is called. The process-GPU affinity, as discussed later in this section, is done by reading the local MPI rank information provided by different MPI libraries.

Buffer Location: Some of the GPU clusters are truly heterogeneous in the sense that some nodes are equipped with GPUs while others are not. In such a case, some MPI processes might be using the GPUs while other run a purely host based code. Depending upon an application's necessities there may arise situations where the application needs to transfer data: a) from a GPU device buffer to a GPU device buffer, b) from a GPU device buffer to a host buffer, c) from a host buffer to a GPU device buffer and d) from a host buffer to another host buffer. To facilitate the characterization of performance of communication primitives under different circumstances we design OMB-GPU benchmark suite to allow for users to use simple parameters to indicate the location of buffers involved in the communication.

Affinity: As discussed earlier, the communication channels and hence the communication performance varies depending on how the GPUs are configured on the system. When there are several GPUs on the node, it will be important to understand the performance characteristics of communication within the same GPU, between different pairs of GPUs or among groups of GPUs. Processes incur context switching overheads when they share a GPU. This is expected to be alleviated in the future version of CUDA. Due to context creation requirements mentioned earlier, GPU device selection and context creation has to be taken care of by the application, or the benchmark in this case, before MPI_Init is called. Most MPI libraries expose the MPI rank information through the launchers, even before MPI_Init is called. We use this information to provide a process-GPU binding interface in OMB-GPU. We provide information about the interface in Section 4.

Buffer Reuse: The usage pattern of communication buffers can vary from one application to another. Also, the performance of several designs in MPI libraries can vary based on the communication buffers are reused or not. A popular example is the registration cache in the case of networks like IB. We can see similar cases with GPU communication. When IPC-based designs used for communication between GPUs connected to the same IOH, IPC handle caching can benefit performance when there is buffer reuse and when buffers are not freed until when the application exits. However such an optimization is not possible when communication buffers are not reused and are freed intermittently in applications or benchmarks. We provide an option to enable or disable buffer reuse in OMB-GPU, to enable study of these performance characteristics.

4   Benchmarks for GPU-GPU MPI Communication

We add a set of benchmarks to compare the performance of different MPI implementations for GPU clusters. The standard OSU point-to-point Latency, Bandwidth, Bidirectional and Multi-pair benchmarks are extended to evaluate the MPI communication performance with GPU devices. Each of these benchmarks takes two input parameters. The first parameter indicates the location of the buffers at rank 0 and the second parameter indicates the location of the buffers at rank 1. The value of each of these parameters can be either .H. or .D. to indicate if the buffers are to be on the Host or on the Device, respectively. When no parameters are specified, the buffers are allocated on the host.

OMB-GPU provides an option for users to set process-to-GPU affinity. The user can specify the GPUs to be used by each MPI process as a colon separated list, using the GPU_MAPPING parameter. For example, GPU_MAPPING=0:1 maps MPI process with local rank 0 (rank within a node) to GPU0 and MPI process with local rank 1 to GPU1. OMB-GPU currently uses launcher specific parameters to get local rank information of a process. OMB-GPU also provides information about GPU configuration on a node. Each of the benchmarks provides an option that displays IPC capabilities between every pair of GPUs on the node. This allows users to select the appropriate GPUs through process-to-GPU binding. Figure 2 shows the sample output on dual-socket Intel Westmere node with three GPUs where the first GPU is connected to one IOH chip and the other two GPUs are connected to another IOH chip.

```
---------------------------------------------
         CUDA IPC Access Matrix
---------------------------------------------
     GPU |   0      1      2
---------------------------------------------
      0  |  Yes    No     No
      1  |  No     Yes    Yes
      2  |  No     Yes    Yes
---------------------------------------------
```

Fig. 2. CUDA IPC access matrix as displayed by OMB-GPU on a dual-socket Intel Westmere node with 3 GPUs

4.1   Point-to-Point Communication

Latency: The latency benchmark is carried out in a ping-pong fashion. The sender sends a message with a certain data size to the receiver and waits for a reply from the receiver. The receiver receives the message from the sender and sends back a reply with the same data size. Many iterations of this ping-pong test are carried out and average one-way latency numbers are obtained. Blocking version of MPI functions (MPI_Send and MPI_Recv) with GPU device or host buffers are used in the benchmark.

Bandwidth: The bandwidth benchmark is carried out by having the sender sending out a fixed number of back-to-back messages to the receiver and then waiting for a reply from the receiver. The receiver sends a reply only after receiving all these messages.

This process is repeated for several iterations and the bandwidth is calculated based on the elapsed time. Non-blocking version of MPI functions (MPI_Isend and MPI_Irecv) with GPU device or host buffers are used in the benchmark.

Bidirectional Bandwidth: The bidirectional bandwidth benchmark is similar to the bandwidth test, except that both the nodes involved send out a fixed number of back-to-back messages and wait for the reply. This benchmark measures the maximum sustainable aggregate bandwidth between two processes.

4.2 Multi-pair Communication

Multiple Bandwidth (Message Rate Benchmark): The multi-pair bandwidth and message rate test evaluates the aggregate uni-directional bandwidth and message rate between multiple pairs of processes. Each of the sending processes sends a fixed number of messages back-to-back to the paired receiving process before waiting for a reply from the receiver. This process is repeated for several iterations. A process of rank r is paired with a process with rank (r + comm_size/2)%comm_size. This benchmark can be used to measure the aggregate bandwidth and message rate within a node or across nodes by arranging the host file accordingly.

Multi-pair Latency Benchmark: This test is very similar to the latency test. However, at the same instant multiple pairs are performing the same test simultaneously.

4.3 Collective Communication

The collective benchmarks for various MPI collective operations MPI_Allgather, MPI_Alltoall, MPI_Allreduce, MPI_Bcast, MPI_Gather, MPI_Reduce, MPI_Reduce_scatter, MPI_Scatter and vector collectives to measure the latency of collective operations in GPU device buffers. These benchmarks measure the min, max and the average latency of the collective operation across N processes, for various message lengths, over a large number of iterations. All the processes either use GPU device or host buffers for communication.

5 Experimental Results

5.1 Experimental Setup

We used a two node cluster for point-to-point benchmark evaluation. Each node is equipped with 12-core Intel Westmere CPUs with two NVIDIA Tesla C2075s. The CPUs are clocked at 2.40 GHz and the node has 24 GB host memory. The node runs Red Hat Linux 5.4, OFED 1.5.1, MVAPICH2-1.8, OpenMPI-trunk (r26442)and CUDA Toolkit 4.1. Each GPU has 6GB of memory and ECC is enabled. We also use a cluster with eight node GPU cluster for our collective benchmark evaluation. Each node is equipped with dual Intel Xeon Quad-core Westmere CPUs operating at 2.53 GHz,

12 GB host memory, and NVIDIA Tesla C2050 GPUs with 3 GB DRAM. The Infini-Band HCAs used on this cluster are Mellanox QDR MT26428. Each node has Red Hat Linux 5.4, OFED 1.5.1, MVAPICH2-1.8, OpenMPI-trunk (r26442) and CUDA Toolkit 4.1.

5.2   Impact of Design considerations

GPU Configuration: Figures 3(a) and 3(b) show the impact of GPU configuration on MPI latency and Bandwidth performance. An intra-IOH configuration offers better performance than an inter-IOH configuration. As it is explained in Section 3, this is due to the support for peer-to-peer memory copies, when two GPUs are connected to the same IOH chip. As illustrated in Figure 3(b), for the intra-IOH bandwidth, OpenMPI is better in large data size, while MVAPICH2 is better in others. It is due to the cached IPC handle used in OpenMPI design. Through the different performance results, our benchmarks provide the insights of different designs in MPI libraries.

Buffer Location: Figures 3(c) and 3(d) compare MPI latency performance with communication buffers located in 'Host' or 'Device' memory.

Affinity: Figure 3(e) shows the impact of process-to-GPU affinity on MPI latency performance. It compares the case where both processes are bound to the same GPU with the case where they are bound to different GPUs. As explained in Section 3, there is a high context switch overhead when both MPI ranks access the same GPU simultaneously. The effect of context switch is dominated by the copy latencies at larger message sizes.

Buffer Reuse: In Figure 3(f), we show that buffer reuse patterns have a significant impact on the intranode GPU-GPU performance in some MPI implementations. This impact is mostly because of caching mechanisms employed by MPI implementations when CUDA IPC is used.

5.3   Micro-Benchmark Results

Point-to-Point Benchmarks: We show the basic internode and intranode latency performance results with OMB-GPU in Figures 4(a) and 4(b). Figures 4(c), 4(d), 4(e) and 4(f) show internode and intranode bandwidth and bi-directional bandwidth performance results.

Multi-pair Benchmark: Figure 6(a) shows the bandwidth results with one pair and two pairs of processes between two nodes. The effective communication channel utilization is improved with multiple pairs.

Collective Benchmarks: In OMB-GPU, we provide a set of benchmarks to measure the performance of various MPI collective communication primitives on GPU device memory. Figures 5(a), 5(b) and 5(c) show results with some of the most frequently used collectives: AlltoAll, Scatter and Gather using OMB-GPU.

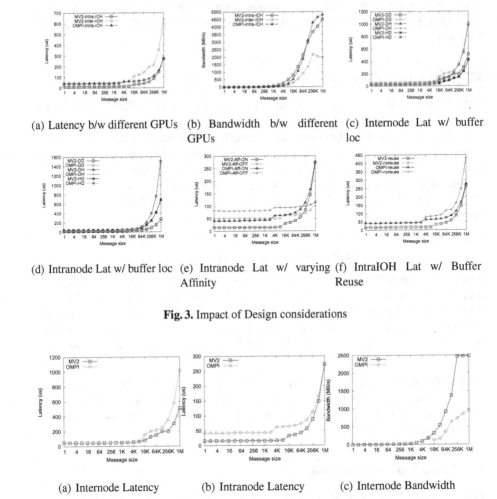

(a) Latency b/w different GPUs (b) Bandwidth b/w different (c) Internode Lat w/ buffer
                                    GPUs   loc

(d) Intranode Lat w/ buffer loc (e) Intranode Lat w/ varying (f) IntraIOH Lat w/ Buffer
                                     Affinity   Reuse

Fig. 3. Impact of Design considerations

(a) Internode Latency   (b) Intranode Latency   (c) Internode Bandwidth

(d) Intranode Bandwidth   (e) Internode Bidir Bandwidth (f) Intranode Bidir Bandwidth

Fig. 4. Point-to-Point Performance

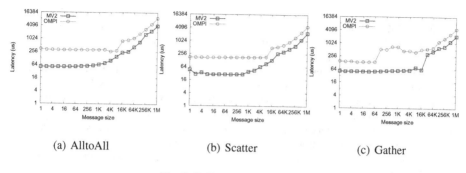

(a) AlltoAll   (b) Scatter   (c) Gather

Fig. 5. Collective Performance

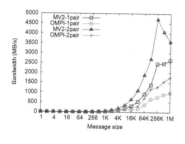

(a) Multi-Pair Bandwidth

Fig. 6. Multi-pair Bandwidth Performance

6   Conclusion

In this paper, we proposed extensions to the popular OSU Micro-Benchmark suite that will help in evaluating MPI libraries on GPU clusters. We provided benchmarks to measure latency, bandwidth, bidirectional bandwidth performance of point-to-point MPI communication. We also provided benchmarks to measure multi-pair and collective MPI communication. We designed a flexible benchmark infrastructure and provided runtime options to measure the impact of GPU configuration, GPU affinity, buffer location and buffer reuse on GPU-GPU MPI communication. To the best of our knowledge, this is the first micro-benchmark suite that helps MPI implementers and end users to compare performance of different MPI libraries on GPU clusters.

Some of the benchmarks introduced in this paper have been made available to the community through OMB-3.6 and MVAPICH2-1.8 releases. We plan to release the rest of the features and benchmarks in the future releases.

Acknowledgments. This research is supported in part by U.S. Department of Energy grant #DE-FC02-06ER25755; National Science Foundation grants #CCF-0916302, #OCI-0926691, #OCI-1148371 and #CCF-1213084.

References

1. Intel MPI Benchmark, http://www.intel.com/cd/software/products/
2. Jacket GBENCH, http://www.accelereyes.com/gbench
3. NAS Parallel Benchmarks, http://www.nas.nasa.gov
4. Che, S., Sheaffer, J.W., Boyer, M., Szafaryn, L.G., Wang, L., Skadron, K.: A Characterization of the Rodinia Benchmark Suite with Comparison to Contemporary CMP Workloads. In: Proceedings of the 2009 IEEE International Symposium on Workload Characterization, IISWC 2009 (2009)
5. Danalis, A., Marin, G., McCurdy, C., Meredith, J.S., Roth, P.C., Spafford, K., Tipparaju, V., Vetter, J.S.: The Scalable HeterOgeneous Computing (SHOC) Benchmark Suite. In: Proceedings of the 3rd Workshop on General Purpose Processing on Graphics Processing Units, GPGPU 2010 (2010)
6. Ji, F., Aji, A.M., Dinan, J., Buntinas, D., Balaji, P., Feng, W., Ma, X.: Efficient Intranode Communication in GPU-Accelerated Systems. In: Proceedings of AsHES, in conjunction with IPDPS 2012 (2012)
7. Argonne National Laboratory: MPICH2: High-performance and Widely Portable MPI, http://www.mcs.anl.gov/research/projects/mpich2/
8. Network-Based Computing Laboratory: MVAPICH: MPI over InfiniBand and 10GigE/iWARP, http://mvapich.cse.ohio-state.edu/
9. Open MPI: Open Source High Performance Computing, http://www.open-mpi.org
10. OSU Microbenchmarks, http://mvapich.cse.ohio-state.edu/benchmarks/
11. Parboil Benchmarks, http://impact.crhc.illinois.edu/parboil.aspx
12. Portable Hardware Locality (hwloc), http://www.open-mpi.org/projects/hwloc/
13. Potluri, S., Wang, H., Bureddy, D., Singh, A.K., Rosales, C., Panda, D.K.: Optimizaing MPI Communication on Multi-GPU Systems using CUDA Inter-Process Communication. In: Proceedings of the AsHES, in conjunction with IPDPS 2012 (2012)
14. Singh, A.K., Potluri, S., Wang, H., Kandalla, K., Sur, S., Panda, D.K.: MPI Alltoall Personalized Exchange on GPGPU Clusters: Design Alternatives and Benefits. In: Proceedings of the Workshop on Parallel Programming on Accelerator Clusters (PPAC), in conjunction with Cluster 2011 (2011)
15. Spafford, K., Meredith, J.S., Vetter, J.S.: Quantifying NUMA and Contention Effects in Multi-GPU systems. In: Proceedings of the Fourth Workshop on General Purpose Processing on Graphics Processing Units, GPGPU 2011 (2011)
16. SPEC MPI 2007, http://www.spec.org/mpi/
17. Wang, H., Potluri, S., Luo, M., Singh, A.K., Ouyang, X., Sur, S., Panda, D.K.: Optimized Non-contiguous MPI Datatype Communication for GPU Clusters: Design, Implementation and Evaluation with MVAPICH2. In: Proceedings of Cluster 2011 (2011)
18. Wang, H., Potluri, S., Luo, M., Singh, A.K., Sur, S., Panda, D.K.: MVAPICH2-GPU: Optimized GPU to GPU Communication for InfiniBand Clusters. In: Proceedings of the 2011 International Supercomputing Conference, ISC 2011 (2011)

Micro-applications for Communication Data Access Patterns and MPI Datatypes

Timo Schneider[1], Robert Gerstenberger[1], and Torsten Hoefler[1,2]

[1] University of Illinois at Urbana-Champaign, IL, USA
{timos,gerro,htor}@illinois.edu
[2] Department of Computer Science, ETH Zurich, Switzerland
htor@inf.ethz.ch

Abstract. Data is often communicated from different locations in application memory and is commonly serialized (copied) to send buffers or from receive buffers. MPI datatypes are a way to avoid such intermediate copies and optimize communications, however, it is often unclear which implementation and optimization choices are most useful in practice. We extracted the send/recv-buffer access pattern of a representative set of scientific applications into micro-applications that isolate their data access patterns. We also observed that the buffer-access patterns in applications can be categorized into three different groups. Our micro-applications show that up to 90% of the total communication time can be spent with local serialization and we found significant performance discrepancies between state-of-the-art MPI implementations. Our micro-applications aim to provide a standard benchmark for MPI datatype implementations to guide optimizations similarly to SPEC CPU and the Livermore loops do for compiler optimizations.

1 Introduction

The MPI (Message Passing Interface) Standard [14] has become the de-facto standard to write distributed high-performance scientific applications. The advantage of MPI is that it enables a user to write performance-portable codes. This is achieved by abstraction: Instead of expressing a communication step as a set of point-to-point communications in a low-level communication API it can be expressed in an abstract and platform independent way. MPI implementers can tune the implementation of these abstract communication patterns for specific machines. MPI plays a similar role in the development of performance portable codes than high-level languages: Instead of coding a loop in inline assembly and using SIMD instructions the same loop can be expressed in a high-level language, using auto-vectorization features of the compiler. The programmer does not have to understand the details of the target platform and possible optimization techniques to write efficient application kernels.

MPI Derived Datatypes (DDTs), allow the specification of arbitrary data layouts in all places where MPI functions accept a datatype argument (i.e., MPI_INT). We give an an example for the usage of DDTs to send/receive a

J.L. Träff, S. Benkner, and J. Dongarra (Eds.): EuroMPI 2012, LNCS 7490, pp. 121–131, 2012.

vector of integers in Figure 1. All elements with even indices are to replaced by the received data, elements with odd indices are to be sent. Without the usage of MPI DDTs one would have to allocate temporary buffers and manually pack-/unpack the data. The usage of MPI DDTs greatly simplifies this example. If the used interconnect supports non-contiguous transfers (such as Cray Gemini [2]) the two copies can be avoided completely. Therefore the usage of DDTs not only simplifies the code but also can improve the performance due to the zero-copy formulation.

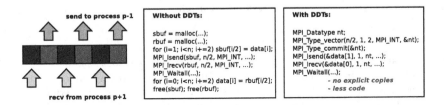

Fig. 1. An example use case for MPI derived datatypes

Not many scientific codes leverage MPI DDTs, even though their usage would be appropriate in many cases. One of the reasons might be that current MPI implementations in some cases still fail to deliver the expected performance, as shown by Gropp et al. in [9], even though a lot of work is done on improving DDT implementations [18, 6, 20]. Most of this work is guided by a small number of micro-benchmarks. This makes it hard to gauge the impact of a certain optimization on real scientific codes.

Coming back to the high-level language analogy made before and comparing this situation to the that of people developing new compiler optimizations techniques or microarchitecture extensions we see that, unlike for other fields, there is no application derived set of benchmarks to evaluate MPI datatype implementations. Benchmark suites such as SPEC [8] or the Livermore Loops [13] are used by many (e.g., [1]) to evaluate compilers and microarchitectures. To address this issue, we developed a set of micro applications[1] that represent access patterns of representative scientific applications as optimized pack loops as well as MPI datatypes. Micro applications are, similarly to mini-applications [3, 10, 5], kernels that represent real production level codes. However, unlike mini-applications that represent whole kernels, micro-applications focus on one particular aspect (or "slice") of the application, for example the I/O, the communication pattern, the computational loop structure, or, as in our case, the communication data access pattern.

1.1   Related Work

Previous work in the area of MPI derived datatypes focuses on improving its performance, either by improving the way derived datatypes are represented

---

[1] Which can be downloaded from http://unixer.de/research/datatypes/ddtbench

in MPI or by using more cache efficient strategies for packing and unpacking the datatype to and from a contiguous buffer [6]. Interconnect features such as RDMA Scatter/Gather operations [20] have also been considered. However, performance of current datatype implementations remains suboptimal and has not received as much attention as latency and bandwidth, probably due to the lack of a reasonable and simple benchmark. For example Gropp et al. found that several basic performance expectations are violated by MPI implementations in use today [9].

The performance of MPI Datatypes is often measured using micro-benchmarks such as those proposed by Reussner [16]. Several application studies demonstrate that MPI datatypes can outperform explicit packing in real-world application kernels [11, 12]. Those results are often either artificial (randomly chosen access patterns) or too complex to compare different implementations efficiently (part of a large application for which the performance is influenced by too many factors such as CPU speed). For example, many datatype optimization papers ignore the *unstructured access* class that we identify in this work completely even though this access pattern is found in many molecular dynamics and finite element codes.

However, the issue of preparing the communication buffer has received very little attention compared to tuning the communication itself. In this work, we show that the serialization parts of the communication can take a share of up to 90% of the total communication overheads because they happen at the sender *and* at the receiver.

Our micro-applications offer three important features: (1) they represent a comprehensive set of application use cases, (2) they are easy to compile and use on different architectures, and (3) they isolate the data access and communication performance parts and thus enable the direct comparison of different systems. They can be used as benchmarks for tuning MPI implementations as well as for hardware/software co-design of future (e.g., exascale) network hardware that supports scatter/gather access.

2   Representative Communication Data Access Patterns

We analyzed many parallel applications, miniapps and application benchmarks for their local access patterns to send and receive memory. Our analysis covers the domains of atmospheric sciences, quantum chromodynamics, molecular dynamics, material science, geophysical science, and fluid dynamics. We created 7 micro apps to span all application areas. Table 1 provides an overview of investigated application classes, their test cases, and a short description of the respective data access patterns. In detail, we analyzed the complex applications WRF [17], SPECFEM3D_GLOBE [7], MILC [4] and LAMMPS [15], representing the fields of weather simulation, seismic wave propagation, quantum chromodynamics and molecular dynamics. We also included existing parallel computing benchmarks and mini-apps, such as the NAS [19], the Sequoia benchmarks as well as the Mantevo mini apps [10].

Table 1. Overview of the Application Areas, Represented Scientific Applications, and Test Names for our Micro-Applications

Application Class	Testname	Access Pattern
Atmospheric Science	WRF_x_vec WRF_y_vec WRF_x_sa WRF_y_sa	struct of 2D/3D/4D face exchanges in different directions (x,y), using different (semantically equivalent) datatypes: nested vectors (_vec) and subarrays (_sa)
Quantum Chromodynamics	MILC_su3_zd	4D face exchange, z direction, nested vectors
Fluid Dynamics	NAS_MG_x NAS_MG_y NAS_MG_z	3D face exchange in each direction (x,y,z) with vectors (y,z) and nested vectors (x)
	NAS_LU_x NAS_LU_y	2D face exchange in x direction (contiguous) and y direction (vector)
Matrix Transpose	FFT	2D FFT, different vector types on send/recv side
	SPECFEM3D_mt	3D matrix transpose,
Molecular Dynamics	LAMMPS_full LAMMPS_atomic	unstructured exchange of different particle types (full/atomic), indexed datatypes
Geophysical Science	SPECFEM3D_oc SPECFEM3D_cm	unstructured exchange of acceleration data for different earth layers, indexed datatypes

We found that MPI derived datatypes (DDTs) are rarely used and thus we analyzed the data access patterns of the (pack and unpack) loops that are used to (de-)serialize data for sending and receiving. Interestingly, the data access patterns of all those applications can be categorized into three classes: *Cartesian Face Exchange*, *Unstructured Access* and *Interleaved Data*.

In the following we will describe each of the three classes in detail and give specific examples of codes that fit each category.

2.1   Face Exchange for n-dimensional Cartesian Grids

Many applications store their working set in n-dimensional arrays that are distributed across one or more dimensions. In a communication face, neighboring processes then exchange the "sides" of "faces" of their part of the working set. For this class of codes, it is possible to construct matching MPI DDTs using the subarray datatype or nested vectors. Some codes in this class, such as WRF, exchange faces of more than one array in each communication step. This can be done with MPI DDTs using a struct datatype to combine the sub-datatypes that each represents a single array.

The **Weather Research and Forecasting (WRF)** application uses a regular three-dimensional Cartesian grid to represent the atmosphere. Topographical land information and observational data are used to define initial conditions of forecasting simulations. WRF employs data decompositions in the two horizontal dimensions only. WRF does not store all information in a single data structure, therefore the halo exchange is performed for a number of similar arrays. The slices of these arrays that have to be communicated are packed into a single buffer. We create a struct of hvectors of vector datatypes or a struct of subarrays datatypes for the WRF tests, which are named WRF_{x,y}_{sa,vec}, one test for each direction, and each datatype choice (nested vectors or subarrays).

NAS MG communicates the faces of a 3d array in a 3d stencil where each process has six neighbors. The data access pattern for one direction is visualized in Figure 2(a). The pack function in MG could be replaced by constructing an appropriate subarray datatype or using vector datatypes. Our NAS_MG micro-app has one test for the exchange in each of the three directions NAS_MG_{x,y,z} using nested vector datatypes.

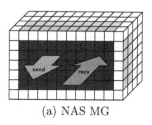
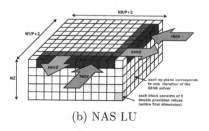

(a) NAS MG   (b) NAS LU

Fig. 2. Data Layout of the NAS LU and MG benchmark

The **NAS LU** application benchmark solves a three dimensional system of equations resulting from an unfactored implicit finite-difference discretization of the Navier-Stokes equations. In the dominant communication function, LU exchanges faces of a four-dimensional array. The first dimension of this array is of fixed size (5). The second (nx) and third (ny) dimension depend on the problem size and are distributed among a quadratic processor grid. The fourth (nz) dimension is equal to the third dimension of the problem size. Figure 2(b) visualizes the data layout. Our NAS_LU micro-app represents the communication in each of the two directions NAS_LU_{x,y}.

The **MIMD Lattice Computation (MILC)** Collaboration studies Quantum Chromodynamics (QCD), the theory of strong interaction, a fundamental force describing the interactions of quarks and gluons. The MILC code is publicly available for the study of lattice QCD. The su3_rmd application from that code suite is part of SPEC CPU2006 and SPEC MPI. Here we focus on the CG solver in su3_rmd. Lattice QCD represents space-time as a four-dimensional regular grid of points. The code is parallelized using domain decomposition and must be able to communicate with neighboring processes that contain off-node neighbors of the points in its local domain. MILC uses 48 different MPI DDTs [11] to accomplish its halo exchange in the 4 directions. The MILC_su3_zd micro-app performs the communication done for the −z direction.

An important observation we made from constructing datatypes for the applications in the face-exchange class is that the performance of the resulting datatype heavily depends on the data-layout of the underlying array. For example, if the exchanged face is contiguous in memory (e.g., for some directions in WRF and MG), using datatypes can essentially eliminate the packing overhead completely. That is the reason we included tests for each direction applicable.

2.2   Exchange of Unstructured Elements

The codes in this class maintain some form of scatter-gather lists which hold the indices of elements to be communicated. Molecular Dynamics applications (e.g., LAMMPS) simulate the interaction of particles. Particles are often distributed based on their spatial location and particles close to boundaries need to be communicated to neighboring processes. Since particles move over the course of the simulation each process keeps a vector of indices of local particles that need to be communicated in the next communication step. This access pattern can be captured by an indexed datatype. A similar access pattern occurs in Finite Element Method (FEM) codes (i.e., Mantevo MiniFE/HPCCG) and the Seismic Element Method (SEM) codes such as SPECFEM3D_GLOBE. Here each process keeps a mapping of mesh points in the local mesh defining an element and the global mesh. Before the simulation can advance in time the contributions from all elements which share a common global grid point need to be taken into account.

LAMMPS is a molecular dynamics simulation framework which is capable of simulating many different kinds of particles (i.e., atoms, molecules, polymers, etc.) and the forces between them. Similar to other molecular dynamics codes it uses a spatial decomposition approach for parallelization. Particles are moving during the simulation and may have to be communicated if they cross a process boundary. The properties of local particles are stored in vectors and the indices of the particles that have to be exchanged are not known a priori. Thus, we use an indexed datatype to represent this access. We created two tests, LAMMPS_{full,atomic}, that differ in the number of properties associated with each particle.

SPECFEM3D_GLOBE is a spectral-element application that allows the simulation of global seismic wave propagation through high resolution earth models. It is used on some of the biggest HPC systems available [7]. Grid points that lie on the sides, edges or corners of an element are shared between neighboring elements. The contribution for each global grid point needs to be collected, potentially from neighboring processes. Our micro-app representing SPECFEM3D has two tests, SPECFEM3D_{oc,cm}, which differ in the amount of data communicated per index.

Our results show that current derived datatype implementations are often unable to improve such unstructured access over packing loops. Furthermore, the overheads of creating datatypes for this kind of access (indexed datatypes) are high.

2.3   Interleaved Data or Transpose

Fast Fourier Transforms (FFTs) are used in many scientific applications and are among the most important algorithms in use today. For example, a two-dimensional FFT can be computed by performing 1d-FFTs along both dimensions. If the input matrix is distributed among MPI processes along the first dimension, each process can compute one a 1d-FFT without communication. After this step the matrix has to be redistributed, such that each process now holds complete vectors of the other dimension, which effectively transposes the distributed matrix. After the second 1d-FFT has been computed locally the matrix is transposed again to regain the original data layout. In MPI the matrix transpose is naturally done with an MPI_Alltoall operation. Hoefler and Gottlieb presented a zero-copy implementation of a 2d-FFT using MPI DDTs to eliminate the pack and unpack loops in [11] and demonstrated performance improvements up to a factor of 1.5 over manual packing. The FFT micro-app captures the communication behavior of a two-dimensional FFT.

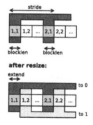

Fig. 3. Datatype for 2D-FFT

SPECFEM3D_GLOBE exhibits a similar pattern, which is used to transpose a distributed 3D array. We used Fortran's COMPLEX datatype as the base datatype for the FFT case in our benchmark and a single precision floating point value for the SPECFEM3D_MT case. The MPI DDTs used in those cases are vectors of the base datatypes where the stride is the matrix size in one dimension. To interleave the data this type is resized to the size of one base datatype. An example for this technique is given in Figure 3.

3   Micro-applications for Benchmarking MPI Datatypes

We implemented all data access schemes that we discussed above as micro applications with the various tests. For this, we use the original data layout and pack loops whenever possible to retain the access pattern of the applications. We also choose array sizes that are representing real input cases. The micro-applications are implemented in Fortran (the language of most presented applications) and compiled with highest optimization.

We then perform a ping-pong-like benchmark between two hosts using MPI_Send() and MPI_Recv() utilizing the original pack loop and our datatype as shown in Figure 4. We also perform packing with MPI using MPI_Pack() and MPI_Unpack(), cf. Figure 4(c). For comparison we also perform a traditional ping-pong of the same data size as the MPI DDTs type size.

The procedure runs two nested loops: the outer loop creates a new datatype in each iteration and measures the overhead incurred by type creation and commit; the inner loop uses the committed datatype a configurable number of times. Time for each phase (rectangles in Figure 4) is recorded to a result file and is analyzed with statistical software packages such as GNU R, for which we provide some example scripts. Measurements are done only on the client side, so the benchmark does not depend on synchronized clocks.

Let t_{pp} be the time for a round-trip including all packing operations (implicit or explicit) and t_{pack} the time to perform explicit packing (manual loop or pack/unpack). In the DDT case is $t_{pack} = 0$. The network communication part can then be expressed as $t_{net} = t_{pp} - t_{pack}$ and is equivalent to a traditional normal

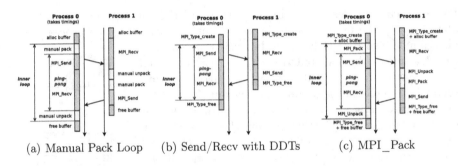

(a) Manual Pack Loop   (b) Send/Recv with DDTs   (c) MPI_Pack

Fig. 4. Measurement Loops for the Micro-Applications

ping-pong result. The overhead for packing relative to the communication time can be expressed as $ovh = \frac{t_{pp}-t_{net}}{t_{pp}}$.

The serial communication time t_{net} was practically identical for the tested MPI implementations ($< 5\%$ variation). This enables us to plot the relative overheads for different libraries into a single diagram for a direct comparison. Figure 5 shows those relative pack overheads for some representative micro-application tests performed with Open MPI 1.6 as well as MVAPICH 1.8 on a cluster with AMD Opteron 270 HE dual core CPUs and an SDR Infiniband interconnect; we always ran one process per node to isolate the off-node communication. We observe that the datatype engine of Open MPI performs better than MVAPICH's implementation. We also see that the dimensions/direction in which face exchanges occur have a significant impact on their performance (cf. WRF tests where the y direction has a much smaller packing overhead). This can be explained if we consider the memory layout of the underlying array - for some dimensions contiguous "strips" of data can be sent, while for others each element to be sent has a large stride. The SPECFEM3D tests show that unordered accesses with indexed datatypes are not implemented efficiently by both Open MPI and MVAPICH. This benchmark shows the importance of optimizing communication memory accesses: up to 80% of the communication time of the WRF_x_vec test case are spend with packing/unpacking data, which can be reduced to 70% with MPI DDTs. In the NAS_LU_x case, which sends a contiguous buffer, using MPI DDTs reduce the packing overhead from 40% to 15%.

Note that the overhead for the creation of the datatype was not included in the calculations of the packing overheads in Figure 5. We show the creation overheads and the absolute times for small number of tests in Figure 6 (the available space does not allow for presenting all collected results). We plot t_{net} as the communication time for the manual packing case. We note that the explicit packing numbers in the plot were doubled for a comparison with DDTs because DDTs implicitly pack at the sender and unpack at the receiver. Our results indicate that Open MPI's DDT engine is faster than manual packing for WRF, even if the datatypes were created for each communication (which is unnecessary

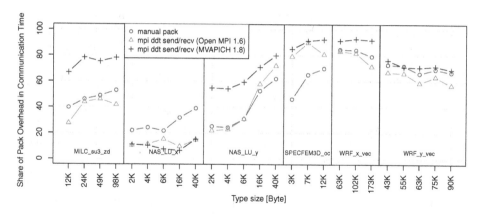

Fig. 5. Packing overheads (relative to communication time) for different micro-apps and datasizes

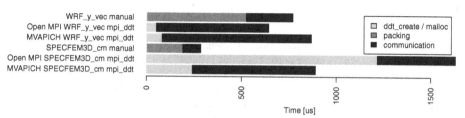

Fig. 6. Representative absolute benchmark results for comparing datatype creation and commit overheads, manual packing, and datatype communication overheads

in this case). But we also see that Open MPI has a much higher overhead for creating indexed datatypes, as used in SPECFEM3D, than MVAPICH.

4   Conclusions and Future Work

We analyzed a set of scientific applications for their communication buffer access patterns and isolated those patterns in micro-applications to experiment with MPI datatypes. In this study, we found three major classes of data access patterns: Face exchanges in n-dimensional Cartesian grids, irregular access of datastructures of varying complexity based on neighbor-lists in FEM, SEM and molecular dynamics codes as well as access of interleaved data in order to redistribute data elements in the case of matrix transpositions. In some cases (such as WRF) several similar accesses to datastructures can be fused into a single communication operation through the usage of a struct datatype. We provide the micro-applications to guide MPI implementers in optimizing datatype implementations and to aid hardware-software co-design decisions for future interconnection networks.

We demonstrated that the optimization of data packing (implicit or explicit) is crucial, as packing can make up up to 90% of the communication time with the data access patterns of real world applications. We showed that in some cases zero-copy formulations can help to mitigate this problem.

In the future we plan to extend our benchmark to allow for assessment of the overlap potential of different datatype engines. Another interesting possibility is studying how well different MPI DDT implementations make use of the available cache hierarchy. Of course the benchmark can also be extended by incorporating more application derived access patterns, for example by investigating parallel graph algorithms and codes.

Acknowledgments This work was supported by the DOE Office of Science, Advanced Scientific Computing Research, under award number DE-FC02-10ER26011, program manager Sonia Sachs.

References

1. Aiken, A., Nicolau, A.: Optimal loop parallelization. SIGPLAN Not. 23(7), 308–317 (1988), http://doi.acm.org/10.1145/960116.54021
2. Alverson, R., Roweth, D., Kaplan, L.: The Gemini System Interconnect. In: 18th IEEE Symp. on High Performance Interconnects, pp. 83–87 (2010)
3. Barrett, R.F., Heroux, M.A., et al.: Poster: mini-applications: vehicles for co-design. In: Proceedings of the 2011 Companion on High Performance Computing Networking, Storage and Analysis Companion, SC 2011 Companion, pp. 1–2. ACM (2011)
4. Bernard, C., Ogilvie, M.C., DeGrand, T.A., et al.: Studying quarks and gluons on MIMD parallel computers. High Performance Computing Applications (1991)
5. Brunner, T.A.: Mulard: A multigroup thermal radiation diffusion mini-application. Tech. rep., DOE Exascale Research Conference (2012)
6. Byna, S., Gropp, W., Sun, X.H., Thakur, R.: Improving the performance of MPI derived datatypes by optimizing memory-access cost. In: Cluster Computing (2003)
7. Carrington, L., Komatitsch, D., et al.: High-frequency simulations of global seismic wave propagation using SPECFEM3D_GLOBE on 62K processors. In: ACM/IEEE Conference on Supercomputing (2008)
8. Dixit, K.M.: The SPEC benchmarks. Parallel Computing 17 (1991)
9. Gropp, W., Hoefler, T., Thakur, R., Träff, J.L.: Performance Expectations and Guidelines for MPI Derived Datatypes. In: Cotronis, Y., Danalis, A., Nikolopoulos, D.S., Dongarra, J. (eds.) EuroMPI 2011. LNCS, vol. 6960, pp. 150–159. Springer, Heidelberg (2011)
10. Heroux, M.A., Doerfler, D.W., et al.: Improving performance via mini-applications. Tech. rep., Sandia National Laboratories, SAND 2009-5574 (2009)
11. Hoefler, T., Gottlieb, S.: Parallel Zero-Copy Algorithms for Fast Fourier Transform and Conjugate Gradient Using MPI Datatypes. In: Keller, R., Gabriel, E., Resch, M., Dongarra, J. (eds.) EuroMPI 2010. LNCS, vol. 6305, pp. 132–141. Springer, Heidelberg (2010)
12. Lu, Q., Wu, J., Panda, D., Sadayappan, P.: Applying MPI derived datatypes to the NAS benchmarks: A case study. In: Intl. Conf. on Parallel Processing (2004)

13. McMahon, F.H.: The Livermore Fortran Kernels: A computer test of the numerical performance range. Tech. rep., Lawrence Livermore National Laboratory, UCRL-53745 (1986)
14. MPI Forum: MPI: A Message-Passing Interface Standard. Version 2.2 (2009)
15. Plimpton, S.: Fast parallel algorithms for short-range molecular dynamics. Computational Physics 117(1) (1995)
16. Reussner, R., Träff, J.L., Hunzelmann, G.: A Benchmark for MPI Derived Datatypes. In: Dongarra, J., Kacsuk, P., Podhorszki, N. (eds.) PVM/MPI 2000. LNCS, vol. 1908, pp. 10–17. Springer, Heidelberg (2000)
17. Skamarock, W.C., Klemp, J.B.: A time-split nonhydrostatic atmospheric model for weather research and forecasting applications. J. Comput. Phys. 227(7), 3465–3485 (2008), http://dx.doi.org/10.1016/j.jcp.2007.01.037
18. Träff, J.L., Hempel, R., Ritzdorf, H., Zimmermann, F.: Flattening on the Fly: Efficient Handling of MPI Derived Datatypes. In: Margalef, T., Dongarra, J., Luque, E. (eds.) PVM/MPI 1999. LNCS, vol. 1697, pp. 109–116. Springer, Heidelberg (1999)
19. der Wijngaart, R.F.V., Wong, P.: NAS parallel benchmarks version 2.4. Tech. rep., NAS Technical Report NAS-02-007 (2002)
20. Wu, J., Wyckoff, P., Panda, D.: High performance implementation of MPI derived datatype communication over infiniband. In: Parallel and Distributed Processing Symposium (2004)

Leveraging MPI's One-Sided Communication Interface for Shared-Memory Programming

Torsten Hoefler[1,2], James Dinan[3], Darius Buntinas[3],
Pavan Balaji[3], Brian W. Barrett[4], Ron Brightwell[4],
William Gropp[1], Vivek Kale[1], and Rajeev Thakur[3]

[1] University of Illinois, Urbana, IL, USA
{htor,wgropp,vivek}@illinois.edu
[2] Department of Computer Science, ETH Zurich, Switzerland
htor@inf.ethz.ch
[3] Argonne National Laboratory, Argonne, IL, USA
{dinan,buntinas,balaji,thakur}@mcs.anl.gov
[4] Sandia National Laboratories, Albuquerque, NM, USA
{bwbarre,rbbrigh}@sandia.gov

Abstract. Hybrid parallel programming with MPI for internode communication in conjunction with a shared-memory programming model to manage intranode parallelism has become a dominant approach to scalable parallel programming. While this model provides a great deal of flexibility and performance potential, it saddles programmers with the complexity of utilizing two parallel programming systems in the same application. We introduce an MPI-integrated shared-memory programming model that is incorporated into MPI through a small extension to the one-sided communication interface. We discuss the integration of this interface with the upcoming MPI 3.0 one-sided semantics and describe solutions for providing portable and efficient data sharing, atomic operations, and memory consistency. We describe an implementation of the new interface in the MPICH2 and Open MPI implementations and demonstrate an average performance improvement of 40% to the communication component of a five-point stencil solver.

1 Introduction

MPI [1] has been the dominant parallel programming model since the mid-1990s. One important reason for this dominance has been its ability to deliver portable performance on large, distributed-memory massively parallel processing (MPP) platforms, large symmetric multiprocessing (SMP) machines with shared memory, and hybrid systems with tightly coupled SMP nodes. For the majority of these systems, applications written with MPI were able to achieve acceptable performance and scalability. However, recent trends in commodity processors, memory, and networks have created the need for alternative approaches. The number of cores per chip in commodity processors is rapidly increasing, and memory capacity and network performance are not able to keep up the same

J.L. Träff, S. Benkner, and J. Dongarra (Eds.): EuroMPI 2012, LNCS 7490, pp. 132–141, 2012.

pace. Because memory capacity per core is decreasing, mapping a single operating system process to an MPI rank and assigning a rank per core severely limit the problem size per rank. In addition, MPI's single-copy model for both message passing and one-sided communication exacerbate the memory bandwidth problem by using intranode memory-to-memory copies to share data between ranks. Moreover, network interfaces are struggling to support the ability for all cores on a node to use the network effectively. As a result, applications are moving toward a hybrid model mixing MPI with shared-memory models that attempt to overcome these limitations [2, 3].

A relatively straightforward and incremental approach to extending MPI to support shared memory has recently been approved by the MPI Forum. Several functions were added, which enable MPI ranks within a shared memory domain to allocate shared memory for direct load/store access. The ability to directly access a region of memory shared between ranks is more efficient than copying and reduces stress on the memory subsystem. Sharing a region of memory between ranks also overcomes the per core memory capacity issue and provides more flexibility in how the problem domain is decomposed. This approach reduces the amount of memory consumed for some data structures such as read-only databases that replicate state across all ranks. From a programming standpoint, providing shared memory supports structured programming, where data is private until it is explicitly shared. The alternative, where data is shared and must be explicitly made private, introduces more complexity into an existing MPI application and the associated MPI implementation. Shared memory is also nearly ubiquitous, given the prevalence of multicore processors.

This paper describes these recent extensions to the MPI Standard to support shared memory, discusses implementation options, and demonstrates the performance advantages of shared memory for a stencil benchmark.

Motivation and Related Work

Support for shared memory in MPI has been considered before, but a number of factors have made such support increasingly compelling. In particular, although POSIX shared memory can be used independently from MPI, the POSIX shared-memory model has several limitations that can be overcome by exposing it through MPI. First, POSIX shared-memory allocation is not a collective operation. One process creates a region of memory and allows other processes to attach to it. Making shared-memory creation collective offers an opportunity to optimize the layout of the memory based on the layout of the ranks. Since the MPI implementation has knowledge of the layout of the shared-memory region, it may be able to make message-passing operations using this region more efficient. For example, MPI may be able to stripe messages over multiple network interfaces, choosing the interface that is closest to the memory being sent. Integration between the MPI runtime system and shared memory simplifies shared-memory allocation and cleanup. Relying on an application using POSIX shared memory directly to clean up after abnormal termination has been problematic. Having the MPI implementation be responsible for allocating and freeing shared memory is a better solution. Knowledge of shared memory inside the MPI implementation also provides better support and integration with MPI tools, such as correctness and performance debuggers. Furthermore, nearly all MPI implementations already have the infrastructure for allocating and managing shared memory since it is used for intranode data movement, so the burden on existing implementations is light.

Previous work on efficiently supporting MPI on shared-memory systems has concentrated mostly on mapping an MPI rank to a system-level or user-level thread [4–7]. This approach allows MPI ranks to share memory inside an operating system process, but it requires program transformation or knowledge on the part of the programmer to handle global and static variables appropriately. Systems specifically aimed at mixing MPI and shared memory have been developed, effectively augmenting MPI with shared-memory capabilities as the new extensions do. LIBSM [8] and the Unified Parallel System [9] are two such systems developed to support the ability for applications to use both MPI and shared memory efficiently. However, neither of these systems actually made internal changes to the MPI implementation; rather, they provided an application-level interface that abstracted the capabilities of message passing and shared memory.

The need for shared memory in MPI was brought up at the Forum by R. Brightwell, who proposed a malloc/free interface which did not define synchronization semantics. T. Hoefler later proposed to merge this functionality into the newly revamped one-sided communication interface. Hoefler and J. Dinan brought forward a concrete proposal, which the Forum eventually voted for inclusion in MPI-3. The interface described in this paper is what will be included in MPI-3.

2   Extending MPI with Integrated Shared Memory

MPI's remote memory access (RMA) interface defines one-sided communication operations, data consistency, and synchronization models for accessing memory regions that are exposed through MPI windows. The MPI-2 standard defined conservative, but highly portable semantics that would still guarantee correct execution on systems without a coherent memory subsystem. In this model, the programmer reasons about the data consistency and visibility in terms of separate private (load/store access) and public (RMA access) copies of data exposed in the window.

The MPI-3 RMA interface extends MPI-2's *separate* memory model with a new *unified* model, which provides relaxed semantics that can reduce synchronization overheads and allow greater concurrency in interacting with data exposed in the window. The unified model was added in MPI-3 RMA to enable more efficient one-sided data access in systems with coherent memory subsystems. In this model, the public and private copies of the window are logically identical, and updates to either "copy" automatically propagate. Explicit synchronization operations can be used to ensure completion of individual or groups of operations.

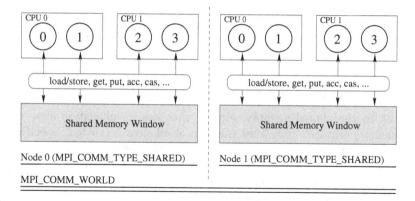

Fig. 1. Interprocess shared-memory extension using MPI RMA; an execution with two nodes is shown, and a shared memory window is allocated within each node

The unified memory model defines an efficient and portable mechanism for one-sided data access, including the needed synchronization and consistency operations. We observe that this infrastructure already provides several important pieces of functionality needed to define a portable, interprocess shared-memory interface. We now discuss the additional functionality, illustrated in Figure 1, that is needed to extend the RMA model in order to support load/store accesses originating from multiple origin processes to data exposed in a window. In addition, we discuss new functionality that is needed to allow the user to query system topology in order to identify groups of processes that communicate through shared memory.

2.1   Using the RMA Interface for Shared Memory

In the MPI-2 one-sided communication interface, the user first allocates memory and then exposes it in a window. This model of window creation is not compatible with the interprocess shared-memory support provided by most operating systems, which require the use of special routines to allocate and map shared memory into a process's address space. Therefore, we have created a new routine, MPI_Win_allocate_shared, that collectively allocates and maps shared memory across all processes in the given communicator.

CPU load and store instructions are similar to one-sided get and put operations. In contrast with get/put, however, load/store operations do not pass through the MPI library; and, as a result, MPI is unaware of which locations were accessed and whether data was updated. Therefore, the separate memory model conservatively defines store operations as updating to full window in order to prevent data corruption on systems whose memory subsystem is not coherent. However, an overwhelming majority of parallel computing systems do provide coherent memory, and on these systems this semantic is unnecessarily restrictive. Therefore, MPI-3 defines a unified memory model where store operations do not conflict with accesses to other locations in the window. This model closely matches the shared-memory programming model used on most systems, and windows allocated by using MPI_Win_allocate_shared are defined to use the unified memory model.

2.2   Mapping of Inter-process Shared Memory

Each rank in the shared-memory window provides an allocation size, and a shared memory segment of at least the sum of all sizes is created. Specifying a per rank size rather than a single, global size allows implementations to optimize data locality in nonuniform memory architectures. By default, the allocated shared-memory region is required to be contiguous. That is, the memory region associated with rank N in a given window must be directly before the memory region associated with rank $N + 1$. The info key alloc_shared_noncontig allows the user to relax this allocation constraint. When this key is given, MPI can map the segments belonging to each process into noncontiguous locations. This can enable better performance by allowing MPI to map each segment on a page boundary, potentially eliminating negative cache and NUMA effects.

Many operating systems make it difficult to ensure that shared memory is allocated at the same virtual address across multiple processes. The MPI one-sided interface, which encourages the dynamic creation of shared-memory regions throughout an application's life, exacerbates this problem. MPI_Win_allocate_shared does not guarantee the same virtual address across ranks, and it returns only the address of the shared-memory region for the local rank. MPI_Win_shared_query provides a query mechanism for determining the base address in the current process and size of another process's region in the shared-memory segment. The address of the absolute beginning of the window can be queried by providing MPI_PROC_NULL as the rank argument to this function.

2.3   Querying Machine Topology

The MPI_Win_allocate_shared function expects the user to pass a communicator on which a shared-memory region can be created. Passing a communicator where this is not possible is erroneous. In order to facilitate the creation of such a "shared memory capable" communicator, MPI-3 provides a new routine, MPI_Comm_split_type. This function is an extension of the MPI_Comm_split functionality, with the primary difference being that the user passes a type for splitting the communicator instead of a color. Specifically, the MPI-3 standard defines the type MPI_COMM_TYPE_SHARED, which splits a communicator into subcommunicators on which it is possible to create a shared-memory region.

The MPI_Comm_split_type functionality also provides an info argument that allows the user to request for architecture-specific information that can be used to restrict the communicator to span only a NUMA socket or a shared cache level, for example. While the MPI-3 standard does not define specific info keys, most implementations are expected to provide NUMA and cache management capabilities through these info keys.

3   Implementation of Shared-Memory RMA

The shared-memory RMA interface has been implemented in both MPICH and Open MPI by using similar techniques. In this section we describe the steps required for the MPI library to allocate a shared window; we also provide implementation details.

The *root* (typically the process with rank 0 in the associated communicator) allocates a shared-memory region that is large enough to contain all of the window segments of all processes sharing the window. Once the shared-memory region has been created, information identifying the shared-memory region is broadcast to the member processes, which then attach to it. At any process, the base pointer of a window segment can be computed by knowing the size and base pointer of the previous window segment: the base pointer of the first window segment, segment 0, is the address of where the shared-memory segment was attached; and the base pointer of segment i is $base\_ptr_i = base\_ptr_{i-1} + seg\_size_{i-1}$.

Scalability needs to be addressed for two implementation issues: (1) computing the sum of the shared window segments in order to determine the size of the shared-memory segment and (2) computing the base pointer of a window segment. For windows with a relatively small number of processes, an array of the segment size of each process can be stored locally at each process by using an all-gather operation. From this array, the root process can compute the size of the shared-memory segment, and each process can compute the base pointer of any other segment. For windows with a large number of processes, however, the offsets may be stored in a shared-memory segment, with scalable collectives (reduce, broadcast, exscan) used to compute sizes and offsets.

When the alloc_shared_noncontig info key is set to "true," the implementation is not constrained to allocate the window segments contiguously; instead, it can allocate each window segment so that its base pointer is aligned to optimize memory access. Individual shared-memory regions may be exposed by each rank, an approach that can be used to provide optimal alignment and addressing but requires more state. An alternative implementation would be to allocate the window as though it was allocated contiguously, except that the size of each window segment is rounded up to a page boundary. In this way each window segment is aligned on a page boundary, and shared state can be used to minimize resource utilization. Both MPICH and Open MPI use the latter approach.

Figure 2 shows the three shared-memory allocation strategies discussed above. In Figure 2(a) we see the contiguous memory allocation method. The figure shows four processes each of which has the entire memory region attached. The shared-memory region contains four window segments of different sizes. Figures 2(b) and 2(c) show noncontiguous allocations. In Figure 2(b) each window segment is allocated in a separate shared-memory region. Each process attaches all the memory regions. In Figure 2(c) a single shared-memory region is attached by each process. Each window segment is padded out to a window boundary. The first and third segments do not end on a page boundary; thus, we see that those segments are padded so that the next window segment starts on a page boundary.

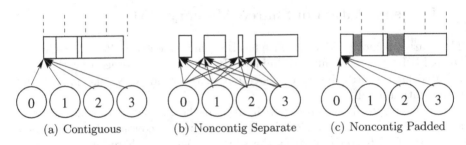

(a) Contiguous   (b) Noncontig Separate   (c) Noncontig Padded

Fig. 2. Shared-memory window allocation strategies. Dotted lines in (a) and (c) represent page boundaries. In (b) each window segment is allocated in a separate shared-memory region and is page aligned.

Synchronization operations must provide processor memory barriers to ensure consistency semantics but otherwise are straightforward to implement. Because of the direct memory access available for all target operations, communication calls may be implemented as memory copies performed during the communication call itself. While an implementation could choose to implement the accumulate operations by using processor atomics, locks and memory copies can also provide the required semantics. Both MPICH and Open MPI use a spinlock per target memory region to implement accumulate operations, because of the simplicity of implementation and greater portability.

4   Use Cases and Evaluation

Shared-memory windows in MPI programs have multiple effects on future parallel programming techniques. Current scientific applications often use OpenMP to enable sharing of large data structures (e.g., hash tables or lookup tables/databases) among cores inside a compute node. This approach requires using two different models of parallelization: MPI and a carefully crafted OpenMP layer that enables scalability to the large core counts (32–64) in today's architectures. This often requires an "MPI-style" domain decomposition of the OpenMP parts, effectively leading to a complex two-stage parallelization of the program. Shared-memory windows allow a structured approach to this issue in that OpenMP can be used where it is most efficient (e.g., at the loop level) and shared memory can be shared across different MPI processes with a single level of domain decomposition.

A second use-case is to use shared-memory windows for fast intranode communications. Here, the user employs a two-level parallelization in order to achieve the highest possible performance using true zero-copy mechanisms (as opposed to MPI's mandated single-copy from send buffer to receive buffer). This has the advantage over a purely threaded approach that memory is explicitly shared and heap corruptions due to program bugs are less likely (cf. [10]). An example of this benefit explored with an early prototype of the shared-memory extensions can be found in [11]. This work demonstrates the incremental approach of incorporating shared memory into an MPI application in order to reduce the iteration count of the linear solver portion of an application. The rest of the application, which performs and scales well, can remain unchanged and largely unaware of the use of shared memory.

Shared-memory regions can also help better support the use of accelerators within an MPI application. For example, if an application is running with one MPI rank per core and all ranks wish to transfer data to a GPU, it can be challenging to coordinate the transfer of data between the host memory of each rank and GPU memory. Using shared memory, one rank can be responsible for transferring data between the host and the device, reducing the amount of coordination among ranks.

Five-Point Stencil Kernel Evaluation

We will now evaluate the performance improvements that can be achieved with shared-memory windows using an application kernel benchmark. We prefer not to show the usual ping-pong benchmarks because they would simply show the MPI overhead versus the performance of the memory subsystem while hiding important effects caused by the memory allocation strategy. Instead, we use a simple, two-dimensional Poisson solver, which computes a heat propagation problem using a five-point stencil. The $N \times N$ input grid is decomposed in both dimensions by using MPI_Dims_create and MPI_Cart_create. The code adds one-element-deep halo zones for the communication. The benchmark utilizes nonblocking communication of $8 \cdot N$ Bytes in each direction to update the halo zones and MPI_Waitall to complete the communication. It then updates all local grid points before it proceeds to the next iteration.

The shared-memory implementation utilizes MPI_Comm_split_type to create a shared-memory communicator and allocates the entire work array in shared memory. Optionally, it provides the alloc_shared_noncontig info argument to allow the allocation of localized memory. The communication part of the original code is simply changed to MPI_Win_fence in order to ensure memory consistency and direct memory copies from remote to local halo zones. To simplify the example code, we assume that all communications are in shared memory only. The following listing shows the relevant parts of the code (variable declarations and array swapping are omitted for brevity).

```
MPI_Comm_split_type(comm, MPI_COMM_TYPE_SHARED, 0, MPI_INFO_NULL, &shmcomm);

MPI_Win_allocate_shared(size*sizeof(double), info, shmcomm, &mem, &win);
MPI_Win_shared_query(win, north, &sz, &northptr);
// ... south, east, west directions

for(iter=0; iter<niters; ++iter) {
  MPI_Win_fence(0, win); // start new access and exposure epoch
  if(north != MPI_PROC_NULL) // the "communication"
    for(int i=0; i<bx; ++i) a2[ind(i+1,0)] = northptr[ind(i+1,by)];
  // ... south, east, west directions
  update_grid(&a1, &a2); // apply operator and swap arrays
}
```

We ran the benchmark on a six-core 2.2 GHz AMD Opteron CPU with two MPI processes and recorded communication and computation times separately. Open MPI and MPICH perform similarly because of the similar implementations; we focus on experimentation with the MPICH implementation.

Figure 3(a) shows the communication times of the send/recv version (red line with dots) and the shared-memory window versions (green line with triangles), as well as the communication time improvement of the shared-memory window version (blue crosses). In general, we show that the communication overhead for shared-memory window version is 30-60% lower than for the traditional message-passing approach. This is due to the direct memory access and avoided matching queue and function call costs.

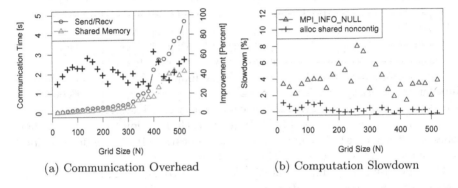

(a) Communication Overhead   (b) Computation Slowdown

Fig. 3. Communication and computation performance for the five-point stencil kernel

Figure 3(b) shows the computation time of the shared-memory window version, that is, the time to update the inner grid cells relative to the computation time of the send/recv version. We observe a significant slowdown (up to 8%) of the computation without the alloc_shared_noncontig argument. This is partially due to false sharing and the fact that the memory is local to rank 0. Indeed, the slowdown of the computation eliminated any benefit of the faster communication and made the parallel code slower. Specifying alloc_shared_noncontig eliminates the overhead down to the noise ($< 1.7\%$) and leads to an improvement of the overall runtime.

5   Conclusions and Outlook

In this work, we described an MPI standard extension to integrate shared memory functionality into MPI-3.0 through the remote memory access interface. We motivated this new interface through several use-cases where shared memory windows can result in improved performance, scaling, and capabilities. We discussed the design space for this new functionality and provided implementations in two major MPI implementations which will both be available shortly in the official releases.

To evaluate the application-level impact of shared memory windows, we performed a performance study using a heat-propagation 5-point stencil benchmark. The benchmark illustrated two important aspects: (1) an average 40% reduction in data movement time compared with a traditional send/recv formulation and (2) the potentially detrimental slowdown of computation if false sharing and NUMA effects are ignored. By allowing the MPI implementation to automatically adjust the shared memory mapping, we showed that these negative performance effects can be eliminated.

For future work, we plan to further investigate NUMA-aware allocation strategies, direct mapping of shared memory (e.g., XPMEM), and the effective use of the info argument to MPI_Comm_split_type to expand this routines topology querying capabilities. We also plan to apply the shared memory extensions to incomplete factorization codes, as well as to a human heartbeat simulation code.

Acknowledgments. This work was supported by the Office of Advanced Scientific Computing Research, Office of Science, U.S. Department of Energy, under Contract DE-AC02-06CH11357, under award number DE-FC02-10ER26011 with program manager Sonia Sachs, under award number DE-FG02-08ER25835, and as part of the Extreme-scale Algorithms and Software Institute (EASI) by the Department of Energy, Office of Science, U.S. DOE award DE-SC0004131. Sandia is a multiprogram laboratory operated by Sandia Corporation, a Lockheed Martin Company, for the United States Department of Energys National Nuclear Security Administration, under contract DE-AC-94AL85000.

References

1. MPI Forum: MPI: A Message-Passing Interface Standard. Version 2.2 (September 4, 2009), http://www.mpi-forum.org/docs/mpi-2.2/mpi22-report.pdf
2. Smith, L., Bull, M.: Development of mixed mode MPI / OpenMP applications. Scientific Programming 9(2,3), 83–98 (2001)
3. Rabenseifner, R., Hager, G., Jost, G.: Hybrid MPI/OpenMP parallel programming on clusters of multi-core SMP nodes. In: Proc. of the 17th Euromicro Intl. Conf. on Parallel, Distributed and Network-Based Processing (February 2009)
4. Demaine, E.: A threads-only MPI implementation for the development of parallel programs. In: Proceedings of the 11th Intl. Symp. on HPC Systems, pp. 153–163 (1997)
5. Bhargava, P.: MPI-LITE: Multithreading Support for MPI (1997), http://pcl.cs.ucla.edu/projects/sesame/mpi_lite/mpi_lite.html
6. Shen, K., Tang, H., Yang, T.: Adaptive two-level thread management for fast MPI execution on shared memory machines. In: Proceedings of the ACM/IEEE Conference on Supercomputing (1999)
7. Tang, H., Shen, K., Yang, T.: Program transformation and runtime support for threaded MPI execution on shared memory machines. ACM Transactions on Programming Languages and Systems 22, 673–700 (2000)
8. Shirley, D.: Enhancing MPI applications through selective use of shared memory on SMPs. In: Proc. of the 1st SIAM Conference on CSE (September 2000)
9. Los Alamos National Laboratory: Unified Parallel Software Users' Guide and Reference Manual (2001)
10. Lee, E.A.: The problem with threads. Computer 39(5), 33–42 (2006)
11. Heroux, M.A., Brightwell, R., Wolf, M.M.: Bi-modal MPI and MPI+threads computing on scalable multicore systems. IJHPCA (2011) (submitted)

Wait-Free Message Passing Protocol for Non-coherent Shared Memory Architectures*,**

Isaías A. Comprés Ureña, Michael Gerndt, and Carsten Trinitis

Technical University of Munich (TUM), Institute of Informatics,
Boltzmannstr. 3, 85748 Garching, Germany
{Isaias.Compres,Michael.Gerndt,Carsten.Trinitis}@tum.de

Abstract. The number of cores in future CPUs is expected to increase steadily. Balanced CPU designs scale hardware cache coherency functionality according to the number of cores, in order to minimize bottlenecks in parallel applications. An alternative approach is to do away with hardware coherence entirely; the Single-chip Cloud Computer (SCC), a 48 core experimental processor from Intel labs, does exactly that. A wait-free protocol for message passing on non-coherent buffers was introduced with the RCKMPI library, in order to support MPI on the SCC. In this work, the message passing performance of the protocol is modeled. Additionally, a port for symmetric multi-processors is introduced and used for comparison with MPICH2-Nemesis and Open MPI. Performance is analyzed based on statistics collected on a 4-dimensional space composed of source rank, target rank, message size and frequency.

Keywords: MPI, message passing, communication protocol, non-coherent shared memory, non-blocking, wait-free.

1 Introduction

Parallelism has been steadily increasing in CPUs. Embedded, desktop and server CPUs today contain multiple cores, and in some cases two or more hardware threads per core. As a consequence, application performance today is closely related to the available parallelism of the algorithms used. When implementing parallel software, several programming models are available. The message passing parallel programming model can be used to develop for both shared and distributed memory systems. The Message Passing Interface (MPI) is a standard for message passing that is widely used in industry and academia.

Most multi- and many-core CPUs today offer a shared and coherent memory address space to the programmer. The Single-chip Cloud Computer (SCC) [17]

---

* The communication protocol presented here was developed in cooperation with Intel Labs Braunschweig for the RCKMPI library. RCKMPI is provided by Intel under an open-source license at the MARC community [1].
** Support for this work was provided by the Transregional Collaborative Research Centre 89: Invasive Computing (InvasIC) [7].

J.L. Träff, S. Benkner, and J. Dongarra (Eds.): EuroMPI 2012, LNCS 7490, pp. 142–152, 2012.

is one exception: it offers a separate memory address space per each core and some shared memory that is not kept coherent by the hardware. In that sense, the SCC can be seen as a distributed memory system on a chip. In addition, 384KB (8KB per core) of on-die directly addressable SRAM is available; this memory is referred to as the Message Passing Buffer(MPB) and can be used for low-latency and high-bandwidth communication. The SCC cores are based on the P54C design and can reach frequencies of 800MHz. The number of transistors required for each P54C core allows the SCC to integrate 48 cores, a relatively large number when compared to currently available commercial CPUs. Because of the moderate performance of these cores, results of parallel applications on the SCC are better evaluated in terms of scaling rather than absolute performance.

In order to efficiently support MPI, Intel Labs introduced a customized MPI library for the SCC: RCKMPI [14]; it is an MPICH2 [4] implementation extended with SCC specific channels. RCKMPI provides protocol implementations that rely on the MPB only, shared memory only, and a combination on both. When using SCC Linux, a single OS image with a private address space is run per core. Current shared memory MPI implementations, that require a single OS image across the participating cores, do not work on the SCC. In order to measure how the protocols of the RCKMPI library compare to existing MPICH2 and Open MPI [6] implementations, a port to symmetric multi-processors is necessary.

In this work, a detailed description of the protocol used in the recently released RCKMPI2 is presented and its message passing performance is modeled. Furthermore, a port to X86 symmetric multi-processors is used to evaluate the effectiveness of the design when compared to Open MPI and MPICH2-Nemesis. Performance results are presented and analyzed based on statistics collected in a 4-dimensional space composed of: source rank, target rank, message size and frequency.

2   Related Work

The SCC maps naturally to message passing programming models. There are standard and non-standard message passing libraries available for it. The first non-standard library available for the platform is called RCCE [18] and there is a non-blocking version of it (iRCCE [12] from RTWH Aachen). Additionally, other projects have implemented their own message passing based communication protocols, like the TACO [19] and X10 [9] ports to the SCC.

There are currently two MPI projects for the SCC: the RCKMPI [14] and the SCC-MPICH [11] libraries. Christgau [10] et al. presented improvements to RCKMPI, by the addition of topology-awareness to the library. An improved communication protocol was recently released with RCKMPI2 [13], which is the focus of this paper, as a result of cooperation between the Technical University of Munich (TUM) and Intel Labs Braunschweig.

3   Communication Protocol

The protocol originally developed for the SCC in RCKMPI2 [13] is presented in this section. The main goal of the design is to avoid the use of operating system managed locks. As a secondary goal, the protocol should be light in computational requirements, given the modest performance of the SCC cores. The protocol consists of 2 simple sub-protocols. In this section, both sub-protocols and their interaction are described in detail.

3.1   Base Sub-Protocol

The base sub-protocol utilizes buffers that are statically allocated at initialization and are placed at the receiver (labeled internally as Exclusive Write Sections). One is allocated for each hardware thread in the node; this allows for efficient support for MPI-2 dynamic processes, since no allocations are necessary for extra processes when they are spawned (important for resource aware applications based on the invasive programming model [15]). These buffers have a single writer (remote sender) and a single reader (local receiver); this setup allows for a non-blocking design that consists of a set of single-writer single-reader pairs per process. Progress is achieved through polling of metadata found in these dedicated buffers. The metadata consist of:

- **Extended Sub-Protocol Bit-Field:**Used to control access to the general-purpose EWS (gEWS) used by the extended sub-protocol.
- **Extended Sub-Protocol control:**Used to control the extended sub-protocol mode of operation (normal, serialized or spin-buffer).
- **Message Size:** Bytes of payload currently available.
- **Packet Size:** Total bytes of the MPICH2 packet in transit.
- **Receive Sequence:** Receive acknowledge sequence.
- **Send Sequence:** Sequence number of the message in the payload area.

The only requirement for this protocol is that all memory operations are done before the metadata is updated. In the SCC, this is trivial since all memory operations are serialized. In SMPs, a store fence needs to be issued before updating the metadata. There are no other hardware requirements to ensure consistency and no OS managed locks are necessary. The base sub-protocol is wait-less, since the number of steps required to transmit a message is bounded by the size of the dedicated buffers. In a real-time system, the size of EWSs can be adjusted to meet timing constraints.

3.2   Extended Sub-Protocol

The extended sub-protocol uses a dedicated buffer that is located at the sender, and labeled internally as the general-purpose EWS (gEWS). It can be used to send messages to several receivers at the same time. This buffer can be locked for use in optimized collectives (or even process management operations as described in [15]). Progress based on the base sub-protocol is not interrupted when the gEWS is explicitly locked or when not available due to a late receiver.

The bit-field and mode of operation are specified through the base sub-protocol. Set bits indicate that a chunk of the gEWS is used for the current message. The gEWS is owned by the sender, and the bit-field is therefore specified by the sender alone. In the SCC, this has the advantage that the sender can keep the global state of the bit-field in its private memory space, and is therefore not subject to races.

4   Protocol Characterization

The original release of RCKMPI [14] used only the base sub-protocol (although with dedicated buffers larger than 64 bytes, based on the number of processes in an MPI job). The time required to transfer an MPICH2 packet with the original protocol can be approximated with the following equation:

$$T_x(B, n) = [t_{sp}(n) + t_w(b(n)) + t_{rp}(n) + t_r(b(n))] \left\lceil \frac{B}{b(n)} \right\rceil + t_h(B) \qquad (1)$$

where B is the size of the MPICH2 packet to send and n is the number of processes of the MPI job. The size of the EWS (in bytes), dependent on the number of processes, is represented by $b(n)$. To send a packet, the sender needs to poll the receive flag for the target process; this time is represented by t_{sp}. After the target EWS is available for writing, the bytes are written in t_w seconds. At the receiver, the progress engine polls the metadata to detect new messages; t_{rp} seconds are spent in doing this and t_r seconds of CPU time are used reading the available payload. Polling operations are done in round-robin fashion and therefore their time depends on the number of processes n. These operations are done for each round trip of the communication protocol. The handling time t_h is done only once when the packet is complete at the receiver; handling of a packet depends on its type and number of bytes (only the number of bytes are taken into account in this model).

The number of round trips required is the ceiling of the size of the packet B divided by the size of the EWS $b(n)$ (the $\left\lceil \frac{B}{b(n)} \right\rceil$ factor in formula 1). The time required to write at the sender and to read at the receiver is the same: $t_w(b(n)) = t_r(b(n))$. These are *memcpy* operations and their aggregated time $t_{rw}(B)$ is assumed to depend on the total number of bytes to transfer, independently of the number of round trips. The time required for polling (in an n process MPI job) at the sender and receiver can be represented by a single variable for their combined time as $t_p(n)$. With these observations, 1 can be simplified as:

$$T_x(B, n) = t_{rw}(B) + t_p(n) \left\lceil \frac{B}{b(n)} \right\rceil + t_h(B) \qquad (2)$$

The term $t_p(n) \left\lceil \frac{B}{b(n)} \right\rceil$ scales poorly with the number of processes, since it multiplies two expressions that increase with the number of processes. The polling

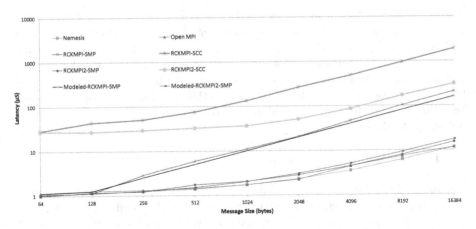

Fig. 1. OSU multi-latency test results and model predictions (40 processes)

overhead t_p depends on the process count and increases linearly with it. The number of round trips $\left\lceil \frac{B}{b(n)} \right\rceil$ depends on the process count as well, since the size of $b(n)$ is determined at initialization based on the MPI job size.

The new design can be modeled similarly to the original one. The effect of the gEWS in the protocol, is that depending on its available bytes, the round trips required to transfer a packet are greatly reduced:

$$T_x(B, n, t) = t_{rw}(B) + t_p(n)\left\lceil \frac{B}{b_s(t) + b_d} \right\rceil + t_h(B) \tag{3}$$

where $b_s(t)$ is the amount of available bytes in the shared buffer at a particular instant in time and is application dependent, while b_d is the size of the dedicated buffer.

It can be observed that in both the new and older design, communication between a pair or processes is never stopped. If the gEWS is not available due to a late receiver, performance is just degraded based on the size of the dedicated receive buffer b_d.

5   Performance Evaluation

A port of the RCKMPI2 channel to SMPs was developed. This allows for the comparison with mature message passing solutions: MPICH2-Nemesis and Open MPI. All applications and libraries were compiled with GCC version 4.5 and the -O3 flag. The SuperMUC's fat nodes [3] were used for evaluation, which consist of four Intel Xeon E7-4870 10-core CPUs attached to 256GBs of RAM; this limits our experiments on shared memory to 40 cores or less. RCKMPI2 was configured with 32KB shared buffers for the extended sub-protocol and 256B dedicated buffers for the base sub-protocol. The SCC was configured with 800MHz for the cores, 1600MHz for the mesh and 1066MHz for the DDR3 memory. MPICH2 version 1.4.1p1 was configured with –enable-fast=all, while Open MPI 1.6 had the –with-mpi-param-check=never flag set.

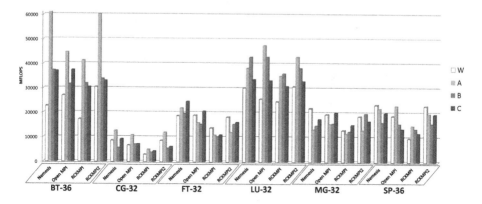

Fig. 2. NPB performance for sizes W, A, B and C (name and process count)

5.1 Synthetic Benchmarks and Model Verification

Point-to-point performance data collected with the OSU [5] micro-benchmarks' multi-latency test are presented in figure 1, together with the predicted values from the model presented in section 4. For the model, the following values were plugged in (based on zero byte and large message latency): $t_{rw}(B) + t_h(B) = B * 10^{-3}$ μS and $t_p(40) = 1$ μS. The buffers $b_s(t)$ and b_d were set at 32KB and 256B respectively; $b_s(t)$ was assumed to be fully available at all times (which is indeed the case for the multi-latency test).

Performance is comparable for all SMP implementations (except RCKMPI) for small messages. Nemesis and Open MPI lead for larger messages since both utilize KNEM [2,8]. It can be observed that the model predicts the general behavior of both the old RCKMPI and new RCKMPI2 implementations.

5.2 NAS Parallel Benchmarks

The NAS parallel benchmarks[20] are useful for evaluating parallel computers. The algorithms used by it are found very often in scientific applications. Results for the NAS parallel benchmarks are presented here. In addition to the results, message passing statistics are introduced to understand the effect of the workloads on the new protocol design.

The statistical method for message passing traffic analysis was done in the library, at the channel interface of MPICH2. This provides insight into the actual traffic generated by the CH3 device, in contrast to tools that collect data at the PMPI layer such as IPM [16]. The analysis requires low computational overhead,

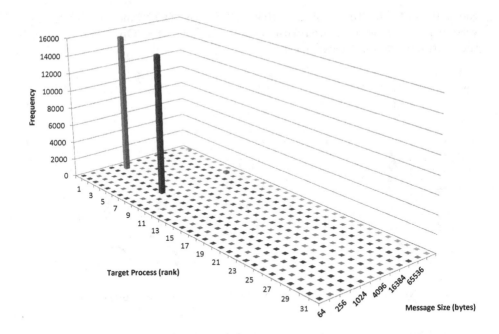

Fig. 3. Outgoing packet statistics at rank 0 for LU size C (32 processes)

and could be used in the future to adjust buffer sizes at run-time. Additionally, the sparse patterns in communication can be used to compute optimal topologies that may be passed to process managers.

Figure 2 presents results for different NPB benchmarks (with maximum process counts given our nodes). It can be observed that the RCKMPI2 protocol is competitive with Nemesis in LU. To gain insight as to why this is the case, the communication pattern of the application is analyzed in terms of outgoing messages per rank and message size combinations. Figure 3 shows the results for LU size C with 32 processes at rank 0. The actual bytes transfered can be seen in figure 4. Both of these figures (as well as the following BT ones) contain little information, but are still purposely presented to illustrate the sparseness in these spaces. In the case of the NPB's LU and BT benchmarks discussed here, the spaces tend to become more sparse as process counts are increased. For LU, the probability of the shared buffer being available was recorded to be 100% for each run, which indicates zero contention.

Performance results of the BT benchmark for 36 processes are also presented in figure 2. As can be seen, the new channel implementation is outperformed by Nemesis and Open MPI for size C. The reason behind this can be determined by doing the same statistical analysis introduced previously. Figure 5 presents the frequency of outgoing messages and figure 6 the total amount of bytes. It can be seen that MPI traffic is less sparse than in the LU case. The probability of the shared buffer being available was measured per size as: 100% for W; 24.52% for

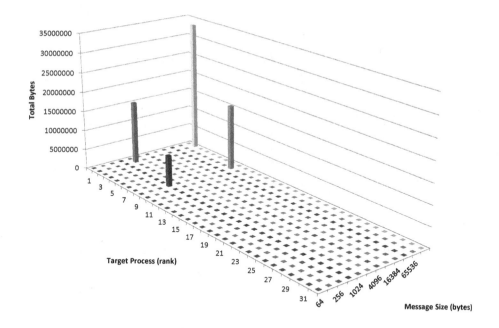

Fig. 4. Outgoing traffic in bytes at rank 0 for LU size C (32 processes)

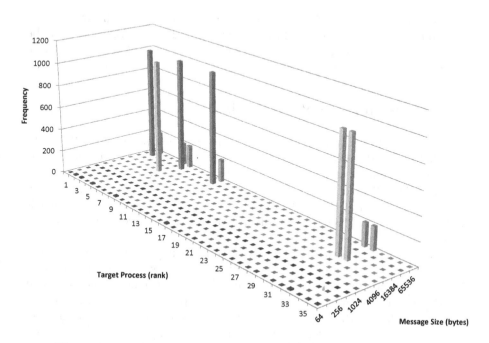

Fig. 5. Outgoing packet statistics at rank 0 for BT size C (36 processes)

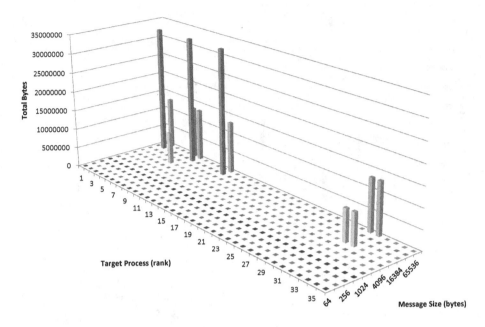

Fig. 6. Outgoing traffic in bytes at rank 0 for BT size C (36 processes)

A; 19.21% for B; and 13.57% for C. These measurements have high variance, but are useful to identify contention of the shared buffer. Time information would be expensive in terms of storage, but correlation data of events related to congestion can be of interest for future analyses.

6   Conclusion and Future Work

A description and analysis of the latest communication protocol of RCKMPI, an MPICH2 based implementation that targets the SCC, was presented. The protocol is composed of 2 sub-protocols that operate together; the first sub-protocol uses dedicated buffers placed at the receiver while the second utilizes a shared buffer placed at the sender. The main advantage of the design is that it can be easily mapped to hardware buffers that are non-coherent (as in the case of the SCC).

A port of the scheme was done to symmetric multi-processors through the use of shared memory segments, in order to compare its performance to other MPI implementations. Performance results of the OSU multi-latency test and the NAS parallel benchmarks were presented. The protocol has comparable performance to Open MPI and MPICH2-Nemesis for small messages, with a small performance advantage under certain circumstances. Large message performance is clearly more efficient on MPICH2-Nemesis and Open MPI, due in part to the use of KNEM (not useable in the SCC due to lack of a DMA controller).

To better explain the performance of the different benchmarks, a statistical method was presented that is based on 4 dimensions: source rank, target rank, message size and frequency. It was shown that the vast majority of the MPI traffic (generated by the applications tested) goes to a few target ranks and under a few message sizes. This indicates that buffer sizes for communication between particular ranks in an application can be a target for optimization.

References

1. Intel's Many-core Applications Research Community,
   http://communities.intel.com/community/marc
2. KNEM: High-Performance Intra-Node MPI Communication,
   http://runtime.bordeaux.inria.fr/knem/
3. Leibniz-Rechenzentrum (LRZ): SuperMUC Petascale System,
   http://www.lrz.de/services/compute/supermuc/systemdescription/
4. MPICH2, http://www.mcs.anl.gov/research/projects/mpich2/
5. Ohio State University (OSU) Micro-Benchmarks,
   http://mvapich.cse.ohio-state.edu/benchmarks/
6. Open MPI, http://www.open-mpi.org/
7. Transregional Research Center InvasIC, http://www.invasic.de
8. Buntinas, D., Goglin, B., Goodell, D., Mercier, G., Moreaud, S.: Cache-Efficient, Intranode, Large-Message MPI Communication with MPICH2-Nemesis. In: Parallel Processing, ICPP 2009 (2009)
9. Chapman, K., Hussein, A., Hosking, A.L.: X10 on the Single-chip Cloud Computer: Porting and Preliminary Performance. In: Proceedings of the ACM SIGPLAN X10 Workshop (2011)
10. Christgau, S., Kiertscher, S., Schnor, B.: The Benefit of Topology Awareness of MPI Applications on the SCC. In: 3rd Many-core Applications Research Community (MARC) Symposium (2011)
11. Clauss, C., Lankes, S., Bemmerl, T.: Performance Tuning of SCC-MPICH by Means of the Proposed MPI-3.0 Tool Interface. In: Cotronis, Y., Danalis, A., Nikolopoulos, D.S., Dongarra, J. (eds.) EuroMPI 2011. LNCS, vol. 6960, pp. 318–320. Springer, Heidelberg (2011)
12. Clauss, C., Lankes, S., Reble, P., Bemmerl, T.: Recent Advances and Future Prospects in iRCCE and SCC-MPICH. In: 3rd Many-core Applications Research Community (MARC) Symposium (2011)
13. Comprés Ureña, I.A., Gerndt, M.: Improved RCKMPI's SCCMPB Channel: Scaling and Dynamic Processes Support. In: 4th Many-core Applications Research Community (MARC) Symposium (2011)
14. Comprés Ureña, I.A., Riepen, M., Konow, M.: RCKMPI – Lightweight MPI Implementation for Intel's Single-chip Cloud Computer (SCC). In: Cotronis, Y., Danalis, A., Nikolopoulos, D.S., Dongarra, J. (eds.) EuroMPI 2011. LNCS, vol. 6960, pp. 208–217. Springer, Heidelberg (2011)
15. Comprés Ureña, I.A., Riepen, M., Konow, M., Gerndt, M.: Invasive MPI on intel's single-chip cloud computer. In: Proceedings of the 25th International Conference on Architecture of Computing Systems (2012)
16. Fuerlinger, K., Wright, N.J., Skinner, D.: Effective Performance Measurement at Petascale Using IPM. In: International Conference on Parallel and Distributed Systems, ICPADS (2010)

17. Held, J.: Single-chip Cloud Computer, an IA Tera-scale Research Processor. In: Guarracino, M.R., Vivien, F., Träff, J.L., Cannatoro, M., Danelutto, M., Hast, A., Perla, F., Knüpfer, A., Di Martino, B., Alexander, M. (eds.) Euro-Par-Workshop 2010. LNCS, vol. 6586, p. 85. Springer, Heidelberg (2011)
18. Mattson, T.G., Riepen, M., Lehnig, T., Brett, P., Haas, W., Kennedy, P., Howard, J., Vangal, S., Borkar, N., Ruhl, G., Dighe, S.: The 48-core SCC Processor: the Programmer's View. In: Proceedings of the International Conference for High Performance Computing, Networking, Storage and Analysis (2010)
19. Rotta, R.: On Efficient Message Passing on the Intel SCC. In: 3rd Many-core Applications Research Community (MARC) Symposium (2011)
20. Wong, F.C., Martin, R.P., Arpaci-Dusseau, R.H., Culler, D.E.: Architectural requirements and scalability of the nas parallel benchmarks. In: Proceedings of the Conference on Supercomputing (1999)

An Efficient Kernel-Level Blocking
MPI Implementation

Atsushi Hori[1], Toyohisa Kameyama[1], Yuichi Tsujita[2],
Mitaro Namiki[3], and Yutaka Ishikawa[1,4]

[1] RIKEN AICS, 7-1-26 Minatojima, Chuo-ku, Kobe, Hyogo 650-0047, Japan
[2] Kinki Unversity, 1 Takaya Umenobe, Higashi-Hiroshima,
Hiroshima 739-2116, Japan
[3] Tokyo University of Agriculture and Technology, 3-8-1 Harumi-cho, Fuchu,
Tokyo 183-8538, Japan
[4] The University of Tokyo, 7-3-1 Hongo, Bunkyo-ku, Tokyo 113-0033, Japan

Abstract. The technique of user-level communication, where incoming messages wait in a busy loop, is used in most MPI implementations to achieve high communication performance. However, in some cases a kernel-level blocking receive is preferred. Some MPI implementations have an option to switch from user-level to kernel-level blocking with the sacrifice of communication performance. This paper identifies the problems when implementing kernel-level blocking receiving and proposes several techniques to avoid these problems. Evaluations show that the proposed kernel-level blocking techniques may achieve comparable performance with user-level communication.

Keywords: user-level communication, kernel-level blocking, MVAPICH, two-phase wait, NAS parallel benchmark.

1   Background

In MPI, a blocking function call means the function call only returns when the goal of the function has been reached. The `MPI_Recv()` function, for example, is a blocking function that waits inside the function until the matching message is received. When the TCP protocol is used for the underlying communication layer, incoming messages are first received in the OS kernel, then passed to the user program by a system call. When no message is received, the receiving system call blocks in the kernel and the receiving process relinquishes its processor. This is called *kernel-level blocking*. Eventually, another process eligible to run may be scheduled, or the processor falls into a sleep when no other processes are eligible to run. An alternative way to implement the blocking receive is to wait for an incoming message in a tight loop of calls to a low-level, non-blocking receive function in the process. This is called *user-level blocking*. In this way, the receiving process keeps running. This paper discusses kernel-level blocking and user-level blocking.

The user-level communication technique, first proposed by von Eicken[1], has generated a wide variety of user-level communication libraries[2,3,4]. In user-level

J.L. Träff, S. Benkner, and J. Dongarra (Eds.): EuroMPI 2012, LNCS 7490, pp. 153–162, 2012.

communication, the significant overheads of handling interrupts and system calls, which are mandatory for kernel-level blocking, are eliminated and thus its communication performance can be better than that of kernel-level communication.

Busy-waiting in user-level blocking can be problematic for two reasons. 1) If the number of running processes and/or threads is larger than the number of cores, then the other processes or threads eligible to run cannot be scheduled until the time slice of the currently running process is exhausted. 2) Busy-waiting consumes significant electric power while the processing core is doing nothing meaningful but is waiting for incoming messages.

This paper shows that the kernel-level blocking receive can be implemented with performance comparable to that of the user-level busy-wait receive, if the MPI implementation is right. A naive kernel-level blocking implementation, even with two-phase blocking[5], where a short busy-wait loop is followed by a blocking system call, can result in poor parallel application performance. The key to avoiding this poor application performance is in the progress routine of the MPI implementation. This paper proposes several techniques to improve the performance of the kernel-level blocking MPI.

In the following sections, evaluations were done on a 16-node cluster. Each node has two Nehalem processors (2.67 GHz), 2 sockets with 4 cores each for a total of 8 cores, and is connected with the QDR Infiniband network. In the following sections, two MPI implementations are used. One is MVAPICH2 (v1.7)[6] and the other is SCore MPI[7] based on MPICH2-1.2.1. Both MPI implementations support the kernel-level blocking receive. In SCore MPI, PMX[8] is used as a multiprotocol, low-level communication library supporting Shmem, Ethernet, Myrinet (Myri10G), and Infiniband. PMX also supports the kernel-level blocking receive. The evaluations are done with 16 nodes and 4 processes on each node. The bindings between the CPU core and the process are the same in all cases of MVAPICH2 and SCore MPI. Unfortunately, MVAPICH2 with the blocking option has a problem when running a parallel program having more than 64 processes.

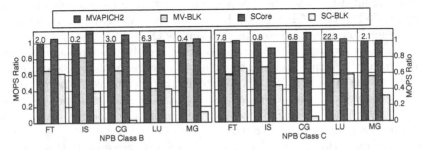

Fig. 1. Comparison of User-Level and Naive Kernel-Level Blocking

2   Kernel Level Blocking

Figure 1 shows the performance graphs of NAS parallel benchmark (NPB) programs, FT, IS, CG, LU, and MG[9], with class B (left graph) and class C (right graph). These programs were chosen because they can run on the same number of processes and thus be compared in a fair manner. In NPB, a problem size can be chosen for running the benchmark program. Class C is a larger problem size than is Class B. In the legend of the graphs, *MVAPICH2* denotes the NPB programs run with the MVAPICH2 library, and *SCore* denotes the NPB program runs with SCore MPI. *MV-BLK* denotes using MVAPICH2 with the MV2_USE_BLOCKING option [10] enabled, and *SC-BLK* denotes using SCore MPI with a blocking option. The numbers above the top of the MVAPICH2 bars are the execution times in seconds measured by the NPB programs. The Y-axes represent the relative performance to the MVAPICH2 (user-level blocking) cases.

As easily seen in Figure 1, the kernel-level blocking receive can severely degrade the application performance. The blocking performance of SCore MPI appears to have higher sensitivity with applications, since its performance numbers diverge. The possible reason for this phenomenon is discussed in Section 2.2.

In the following subsections, several techniques to avoid this performance degradation in the kernel-level blocking receive are proposed. Eventually, it is shown that, by combining the proposed techniques and applying them to the SCore MPI, the NPB application performance with the kernel-level blocking MPI becomes comparable with the performance of the non-blocking MPI.

2.1   Two-Phase Blocking

A two-phase technique[5] was previously proposed to avoid the high overhead of kernel-level blocking. In the two-phase technique, first, the user-level busy-wait is used to wait a while for an event, and then a system call sets a block in the kernel. Figure 2 shows the NPB results using the SCore MPI with the two-phase technique. The threshold values, which are the number of iterations in the busy loop until calling the blocking system call for receiving, are as follows: *immediate* (0), *1,000, 10,000, 100,000*, and *1,000,000*. The performance numbers of the *immediate* cases, which are equivalent to the threshold value of zero, in this graph are the same as those in the SCore MPI naive blocking cases in Figure 1. The Y-axis is the relative performance to the user-level blocking cases.

In the cases of IS and MG, the performance is improved, especially with the threshold value of 10^5. However, the performance is worse when the threshold value is set to 10^6. This is unexpected, since the number of non-blocking iterations can be considered to be an infinite value. In user-level blocking, the larger the threshold value, the closer the performance is to the corresponding performance of the non-blocking case.

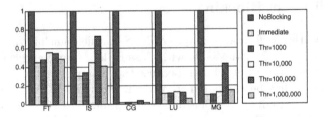

Fig. 2. Two-Phase Blocking (Class B - SCore MPI)

2.2   The Progress Routine

The phenomenon in Figure 2 can be explained as follows. Figure 3 is the pseudo-code of a typical MPI progress routine in an MPI library. This function is basically called at least once every time an MPI function is called so that communicating processes can progress.

```
MPID_progress_function( ... ) {
    try_recv_message( recv_queue );
    if( send_queue ) send_message( send_queue );
}
```

Fig. 3. An example of an MPI progress routine

An MPICH implementation has a send queue and a receive queue. The send queue holds pending message send requests, and the receive queue hold the receive requests.

A naive implementation of kernel-level blocking can be carried out by a simple replacement of the user-level `try_recv_message()` function with the kernel-blocking `blocking_recv_message()` function. When the process can be blocked in the `blocking_recv_message()` function, even if some entries are present in the `send_queue`, the message send in the `send_queue` is postponed until the blocking receive returns. This also postpones the execution of the other process waiting for a message in the send queue. This message sending delay due to the two-phase technique can spread to the entire parallel program execution. Putting the `send_message()` function before calling the `blocking_recv_message()` function does not help much, because the progress function is called repeatedly in the context of a blocking function, such as the `MPI_Waitall()` function, until the conditions are met to return. Thus, the phenomenon in Figure 2 can be explained. The smaller threshold value can decrease the frequency of calling the kernel-blocking receiving, and the larger threshold value can increase the latency of message sending.

In general, the blocking receive function must not be called when something is to be done as soon as possible in the progress routine. Figure 4 shows the modified version of the progress routine. Here, the blocking receive function is called only when the `nothing_todo_but_receiving()` predicate returns true.

```
MPID_progress_function( ... ) {
    if( !nothing_todo_but_receiving() ) {
        send_message( send_queue );
        try_recv_message( recv_queue );
    } else {
        blocking_recv_message( recv_queue );
    }
}
```

Fig. 4. Modified Blocking MPI Progress Routine

In an MPICH implementation, the progress routine is an interface function called the Abstract Device Interface (ADI) between the MPI body and a low-level communication layer. Remember that the progress routine is typically called every time an MPI function is called by a user program. However, in some cases the progress routine must return immediately without calling the blocking receive function. The above nothing_todo_but_receiving() predicate comes from two sources. One is originated in the software layer above the progress routine, and the other is originated in the ADI itself.

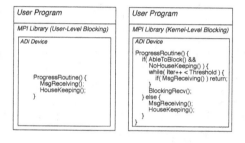

Fig. 5. MPICH Progress Routine Implemenation

When the MPI_Irecv() function is called, for example, the progress routine does not block. In contrast, when the MPI_Wait() function is called, the progress routine may block. The information to determine whether the progress routine can block comes from the context in which the MPI function is called by a user program. In MVAPICH2, no such send queue exists because MVAPICH2 mostly uses RDMA and the send queue is not needed. In the MVAPICH2 progress routine, clean-up of the Completion Queue[11] is still required as the post processing of RDMA. In the SCore MPI, in some cases message sending cannot take place immediately and therefore the send queue is required.

Thus, this "housekeeping" process in the progress routine depends on the low-level communication device to be used. The implementation difference between MVAPICH2 and SCore MPI can be explained by the effect of the kernel-level blocking on the application performance, as shown in Figure 1.

Another point to implementing an efficient kernel-level blocking receive is the handling of multiple protocols. Recent clusters consist of nodes having multi-core CPUs and multiple MPI processes can run simultaneously in the node. Most MPI implementations support multiple protocols of intra-node communication and inter-node communication. The kernel-level blocking progress routine must wait for incoming messages in a single system call. Cascading calls of the blocking system calls for each low-level communication device can cause a large delay of message receiving or even a deadlock.

As already mentioned, SCore MPI uses the PMX low-level communication library that supports multiple protocols. The Shmem PMX device is used for intra-node communication and the Infiniband PMX device is used for inter-node communication in the evaluations in this paper. PMX has a routing table to select the appropriate device according to the index of the destination node, and thus multiple protocols are combined as one abstracted PMX device. By enabling the kernel-level blocking receive, the PMX can return a set of file descriptors (FD_SET) with which the user program can block the point of calling the (p)select() system call and then wait for incoming messages coming through various PMX devices. In this way, the cascaded blocking problem can be avoided.

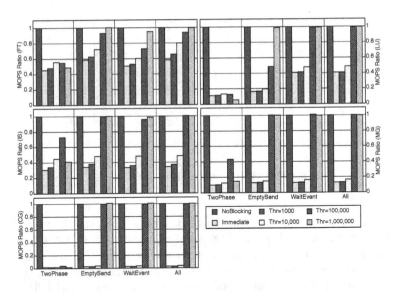

Fig. 6. Comparison of Blocking Techniques (Class B, NP=64)

2.3 Improved Blocking Receive

By considering all the techniques (right-hand side of Figure 5), Figure 6 shows the graphs of the NPB programs running with the SCore MPI. On the X-axes, *TwoPhase* means that the bars show the relative performance to the non-blocking performance with only the two-phase technique, as already shown in Figure 2. *EmptySend* means that kernel-level blocking takes place when the send queue is empty in the progress routine, in addition to the two-phase technique. *WaitEvent* means that blocking takes place if the upper MPI layer allows blocking receive, in addition to the two-phase technique. The right-most *All* means that the bars show the performance of the cases using all of the above techniques.

```
 PID USER      PR  NI  VIRT  RES  SHR S %CPU %MEM    TIME+  COMMAND
28233 hori      20   0  654m 398m 3644 R 99.4  1.6  0:08.39 is.D.64
28234 hori      20   0  656m 399m 3636 R 96.4  1.7  0:08.19 is.D.64
28235 hori      20   0  656m 397m 3660 R 95.4  1.6  0:08.17 is.D.64
28236 hori      20   0  654m 399m 3644 R 95.4  1.7  0:08.15 is.D.64
```

Fig. 7. Screenshot of the `top` Command in the is.D.64 Program

The phenomenon where the performance drops with the threshold value of 10^6 in *TwoPhase* disappears in the cases with the other techniques. In many cases, except FT and IS, *WaitEvent* performs better than does *EmptySend*, and *All* performs as well as does *WaitEvent*. *All* performs better than does *WaitEvent* in the FT and IS cases, when the threshold value is larger than 10^5. The blocking performance with *All* is almost equal to the performance of non-blocking cases when the threshold value is 10^5, except in the FT case. With the threshold value of 10^6, the performance is almost equal to the non-blocking performance.

A micro benchmark, which measured the time of 10^6 busy-wait iterations in the blocking receive routine with the same configuration as the evaluations in this section, took 89 msec. This seems too long and does not have any possibility of calling the kernel-level blocking system call. Figure 7 shows a screenshot of the Linux `top` command while running the `is.D.64` benchmark program of the NPB with the threshold value of 10^6. Class D was chosen because the execution times of the smaller classes are too short to take a screenshot. The CPU percentage number is always greater than 99% when the user-level communication takes place. However, some of the percentage numbers of the screenshot indicate 95.4% in this figure. This means that kernel-level blocking takes place on those processes having a lower CPU percentage.

Figure 8 shows the graphs of the number of blocking times in the left column and the graphs of the accumulated time of blocking in the right column for each threshold while running with 128 processes (16 nodes, 8 processes). The X-axes and Y-axes are log scales and the zero values are not shown in these graphs. The number of blocking times and the accumulated time of blocking are the average numbers of each process in a single run. As expected, the larger the threshold value, the less the number of blocking times and the shorter the accumulated time of blocking. The larger the problem size, the higher the possibility of blocking.

The number of blocking times decreases drastically from some (ten) thousands to some tens or less, when the threshold value gets higher. The overhead of kernel-level blocking is very high. Thus, the key point to achieving negligible overhead of kernel-level blocking is when to block while waiting for messages having large latencies. The two-phase blocking is not optimal, although it is easy to implement. As shown in Figure 8, the optimal threshold value depends on the communication pattern, the problem size, and possibly the number of processes.

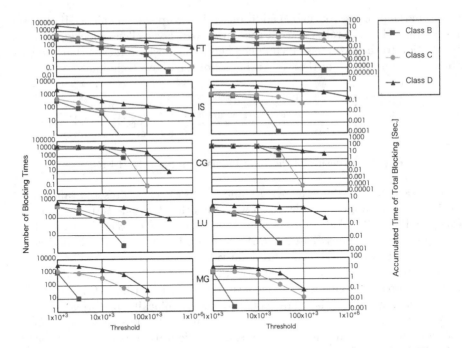

Fig. 8. Number of Blocking Times and Accumulated Time of Blocking for Each Threshold (NP=128)

3 Related Work

Damianakis et al. investigated various blocking techniques in a cluster environment and reported that the two-phase spin-block technique was the best[12]. Their evaluation was done on a distributed file system.

Vishnu et al. investigated the relation of performance and energy consumption by comparing kernel-level communication and user-level communication[13]. They developed their own software layer on top of the one-sided communication library, ARMCI[14]. They reported the case where two-phase kernel-level receiving is more power efficient than is user-level communication.

In contrast to the above two papers, this paper notes the problems of when to implement kernel-level blocking in the MPI. It is shown that a carefully designed MPI may avoid the performance degradation due to kernel-level blocking.

4 Discussion

One may argue that kernel-level blocking may not be needed if the performance of the kernel-level blocking MPI is no better than that of the user-level blocking MPI. From MPI specification version 2[15], `MPI_Spawn()` functions are introduced and an MPI program may spawn additional processes. When the newly created process is eligible to run on the same core where an existing MPI process is already running, then user-level blocking can cause significant overhead. Or, when an MPI process creates a new thread and when the number of threads on a node exceeds the number of CPU cores, then user-level blocking can result in low performance. Modern operating systems can handle the situation that the number of processes and/or threads eligible to run exceeds the number of cores on a node. However, most of the current HPC programming environments ignore this situation and utilize user-level communication. In this sense, kernel-level blocking is the correct procedure.

Recent Intel CPUs support the `MONITOR` and `MWAIT` instructions[16] to wait for hardware events in a deeper sleep mode and thus power consumption can be reduced. Recent Linux kernels also support these instruction pairs and have successfully reduced the idling power. Kernel-level blocking can fall into a deeper sleep mode. According to the IESP roadmap[17], the power wall can be a major obstacle to implement exa-scale machines. Thus, kernel-level blocking may help save power, while the busy loop of user-level blocking simply wastes power.

5   Summary

The user-level blocking communication technique, currently used in most MPI implementations, can be problematic when spawning new process(es) or thread(s), and can needlessly consume electric power. In contrast, the kernel-level blocking communication may run processes and/or threads in a more efficient way, and thus may save electric power. However, the kernel-level blocking communication has been said to have low communication performance due to its interrupt handling and system call overhead.

This paper shows that if an MPI implementation is designed carefully, then the kernel-level blocking communication may result in a comparable performance with that using the user-level communication. It is shown that the widely used two-phase blocking technique can be of some help; however, it can also lead to other overhead. The progress routine in the MPI library must be re-designed so that kernel-level blocking does not interfere with other functions in an MPI implementation.

The proposed techniques to implement an efficient kernel-level blocking MPI were implemented in SCore MPI and evaluated by using NAS parallel benchmark programs. The results show that the performances of the benchmark programs using kernel-level communication are almost the same as those using user-level communication.

Acknowledgment. This research is partially supported by the CREST project of JST (Japan Science and Technology Agency).

References

1. von Eicken, T., Basu, A., Buch, V., Vogels, W.: U-net: a user-level network interface for parallel and distributed computing. SIGOPS Oper. Syst. Rev. 29, 40–53 (1995)
2. von Eicken, T., Culler, D.E., Goldstein, S.C., Schauser, K.E.: Active messages: a mechanism for integrated communication and computation. In: Proceedings of the 19th Annual International Symposium on Computer Architecture, ISCA 1992, pp. 256–266. ACM, New York (1992)
3. Pakin, S., Karamcheti, V., Chien, A.A.: Fast messages: Efficient, portable communication for workstation clusters and mpps. IEEE Parallel Distrib. Technol. 5, 60–73 (1997)
4. Tezuka, H., Hori, A., Ishikawa, Y., Sato, M.: Pm: An Operating System Coordinated High Performance Communication Library. In: Hertzberger, B., Sloot, P.M.A. (eds.) HPCN-Europe 1997. LNCS, vol. 1225, pp. 708–717. Springer, Heidelberg (1997)
5. Ousterhout, J.: Scheduling techniques for concurrent systems. In: 3rd International Conference on Distributed Computing Systems, pp. 22–30. IEEE (1982)
6. Liu, J., Wu, J., Kini, S.P., Wyckoff, P., Panda, D.K.: High performance RDMA-based MPI implementation over InfiniBand. In: Proceedings of the 17th Annual International Conference on Supercomputing, ICS 2003, pp. 295–304. ACM, New York (2003)
7. PC Cluster Consortium: SCore, http://www.pccluster.org/
8. Hori, A.: PMX Specification –DRAFT–, http://www.pccluster.org/score_doc/score-7.0.2/pdf/PMX-spec.pdf
9. NASA: NAS Parallel Benchmarks, http://www.nas.nasa.gov/Resources/Software/npb.html
10. MVAPICH Team: MVAPICH2 1.7 User Guide (2012)
11. OpenFabrics Alliance: OFED, http://www.openfabrics.org/
12. Damianakis, S., Chen, Y., Felten, E.W.: Reducing waiting costs in user-level communication. In: 11th International Parallel Processing Symposium, pp. 381–387. IEEE Computer Society Press (1997)
13. Vishnu, A., Song, S., Marquez, A., Barker, K., Kerbyson, D., Cameron, K., Balaji, P.: Designing energy efficient communication runtime systems for data centric programming models. In: Proceedings of the 2010 IEEE/ACM Int'l Conference on Green Computing and Communications & Int'l Conference on Cyber, Physical and Social Computing, GREENCOM-CPSCOM 2010, pp. 229–236. IEEE Computer Society, Washington, DC (2010)
14. Nieplocha, J., Tipparaj, V., Krishnan, M., Panda, D.K.: High performance remote memory access communication: The armci approach. Int. J. High Perform. Comput. Appl. 20(2), 233–253 (2006)
15. Message Passing Interface Forum: MPI-2: Extensions to the Message-Passing Interface (2003), http://www.mpi-forum.org/docs/mpi2-report.pdf
16. Intel Corporation: Intel 64 and IA-32 Architectures Software Developer's Manual (2011)
17. Dongarra, J., Choudhary, A., Kale, S., et al.: The International Exascale Software Project Roadmap. White paper, Argonne National Laboratory (October 2010)

Automatic Resource-Centric Process Migration for MPI

Amnon Barak, Alexander Margolin, and Amnon Shiloh

The Hebrew University of Jerusalem, Department of Computer Science, 91904, Israel
{amnon,alexam02,amnons}@cs.huji.ac.il

Abstract. Process migration refers to the ability to move a running process from one node and make it continue on another. The MPI standard prescribes support for process migration, but so far it was implemented mostly via checkpoint-restart. This paper presents an automatic and transparent process migration framework that can be used for MPI processes. This framework is advantageous when migration of individual processes for purposes such as load-balancing is more adequate than checkpointing the whole job. The paper describes this framework for process migration in clusters and multi-clusters, how it was tuned for Open MPI and the performance of migrated MPI processes.

Keywords: Cluster, MPI, process migration, load-balancing, checkpoint.

1 Introduction

The term "process migration" refers to the ability to stop a running process on one node and make it continue from the same point on another. The main advantage of process migration is run-time flexibility. This includes redistribution of processes for improved performance and resource utilization, e.g., for load-balancing; and flexible cluster configuration, including orderly shutdown, addition of nodes and inclusion in a multi-cluster. In spite of the advantages, the main drawbacks of process migration are the complexity of maintaining migrated processes seamlessly and the need for an adequate policy to decide when, where and which process(es) to migrate.

The MPI standard [1] prescribes support for process migration, but so far direct support was implemented mostly via Checkpoint-Restart (CR) of a whole job, using a package such as the Berkeley Lab BLCR [2]. In the CR approach, all the processes of a job are stopped and their images are saved to persistent storage. The CR approach is reasonable when the demand for resources is relatively stable, but inadequate when resources and/or demand for resources change frequently, such as when running processes with uneven loads; when processes change their demand for resources (cores, GPUs, memory); when temporarily oversubscribing; when nodes are reclaimed by users with higher priority; and when CPUs slow down due to overheating. In such cases, direct migration of individual processes is lighter and more adequate because it does not stop the whole job. This is the main contribution of the current paper.

J.L. Träff, S. Benkner, and J. Dongarra (Eds.): EuroMPI 2012, LNCS 7490, pp. 163–172, 2012.

As an example where process migration can benefit queued MPI jobs, consider a situation where a job is scheduled to start on a given time, but few of its designated nodes are not available at that time, either because they are down or because they are used by overdue jobs. When process migration is available and memory is sufficient, the processes of the scheduled job can be temporarily assigned to nodes that are already available, despite oversubscribing, and later be migrated to additional nodes as they become available. This avoids situations where jobs are queued while nodes are available but remain idle.

This paper presents a transparent (proactive) process migration framework for MPI based on features of MOSIX [3], a management system targeted for HPC on Linux clusters and multi-clusters. Its relevant features include a decentralized gossip algorithm that provides each node with information about cluster-wide resources [4]; a set of online algorithms that use this information to assign and actively reassign (migrate) processes to nodes, to optimize the performance [5]; and the actual process migration software.

The paper is organized as follows: Sec. 2 describes our process migration framework, including the run-time environment and the algorithms for initiating and managing process migrations in clusters and multi-clusters. Sec. 3 describes how our framework runs migratable Open MPI jobs, including allocation of resources and direct communication between migrated MPI processes. Sec. 4 presents various performance aspects of our process migration using standard benchmarks. Related works are described in Sec. 5 and our conclusion in Sec. 6.

2   A Framework for Process Migration

Process migration refers to the ability to stop a running process on one node, preserve all its important elements and then make it continue from the same point on another node. The elements to be preserved depend on the interface between the process and its immediate run-time environment. In a previous project, we developed a process migration framework for general Linux processes [3]. Since MPI processes run on Linux, we used that framework for migration of MPI processes.

This section presents relevant features of our process migration framework, including the run-time environment, the algorithms for initiating and managing migrations and support of multi-clusters.

2.1   Our Run-Time Environment

In order to support generic Linux processes, it is important that a process sees the same environment, including files, sockets, process IDs, etc., regardless where it runs or is migrated to. To achieve that, we developed a virtual environment (sandbox) in which each migrated process seem to run as if it is still in its original "home-node", where it was created. This is accomplished by intercepting all the system-calls of the process, then forwarding most of them to the home-node, performing them there and returning the results to the migrated process.

This approach, which isolates the process from the node in which it is currently running, provides maximal file and data consistency, as well as support of nearly all traditional IPC mechanisms such as messages, semaphores pipes, sockets and signals (with process-IDs kept intact), excluding only shared-memory. The drawback of this approach is that the maintenance of migrated processes requires increased management and network overheads.

To reduce the network overhead incurred by the use of home-nodes, we developed a peer-to-peer "postal" protocol for direct communication between migrated processes, bypassing their respective home-nodes. This OSI layer 4 protocol guarantees that data always arrives in order and is never lost even when the senders and receivers migrate several times and even while they are in mid-migration, all transparent to the program. This is especially efficient for processes that migrated to the same node.

2.2   Initiating and Managing Process Migration

In our framework, process migration can be triggered either automatically or manually, including by the process itself. Automatic migrations are supervised by competitive on-line algorithms that attempt to improve the performance using a gossip-based information collection and process profiling [4]. Process profiling is performed by continuously collecting information about each process' characteristics, such as size, rates of system-calls and volume of I/O. This result in determining the best location for each process, taking into account the respective speed, current load, available memory in the nodes and the migration cost. As resources and the profile of the process change, and subject to threshold values to avoid over migrations, processes may be reassigned and migrated to better locations - which is particularly useful for jobs with unpredictable or changing resource requirements and when several users run simultaneously. The objective are:

- Load balancing.
- Assigning processes to faster nodes.
- Assigning processes to nodes with sufficient memory.
- Sharing the cluster resources among several users.

While a process can be migrated by the framework at any time, processes can also explicitly request to be migrated to any desired node. This way, if a process is expecting to do a significant amount of communication with another process, it can request to be migrated to the location of that other process, or it can "invite" another process (of the same user) to migrate to its current node. Either way, the goal is to reduce the communication latency and the network overhead. Obviously, this option is limited by the fact that only a limited number of processes can run efficiently on each node.

2.3   Multi-clusters

A multi-cluster is a collection of private clusters that are configured to work together. Each cluster may belong to a different group that is willing to share its computing resources so long as it is allowed to disconnect its cluster at any time, especially when they are needed by its local users.

The automatic migration algorithms of the previous section also manage multi-clusters, with only minor adjustments. Note that all migrated processes still run in the environment of their own home-cluster. Thus, from the user's perspective, it does not matter whether their applications run in their own cluster or out on a different cluster.

To allow a flexible use of nodes within and among different groups, we developed a priority scheme, whereby local processes and processes with a higher priority can always move in and push out processes with a lower priority. By proper setting of the priority, private clusters can be shared among users. Public clusters can also be set to be shared among all users.

3   Running Migratable Open MPI Jobs

This section describes an adaptation of our framework for Open MPI jobs.

3.1   Initial Assignment

The standard practice in Open MPI is to rely for resource discovery on an XML input file provided by each user. This file usually includes the list of nodes and their resources, e.g., number of cores and total memory. Using this information, Open MPI usually assigns processes to nodes in a round-robin fashion, regardless of the current status and availability of these resources.

Our framework provides a dynamic resource discovery system. The simplest approach is to start all the MPI processes in the same node and let our framework migrate them automatically to different available nodes. A variation of this approach is to start an equal number of processes on a fixed (small) subset of nodes and then allow those processes to migrate. Another approach is to find a set of best-available nodes, then launch the MPI processes on that list of nodes. We developed a new Resource Allocation Subsystem (RAS) module which does that. We also added a module under the Open MPI ORTE Daemon's Local Launch Subsystem (ODLS) component, which intercepts the process launch and modifies the arguments so that it uses our framework to launch the Open MPI processes. The launch command line may include three new flags:

- Disallow automatic migration.
- Allow migration to other clusters - in a multi-cluster configuration.
- Start the process on the best available node, not necessarily its home-node.

3.2   Direct Communication between Open MPI Processes

The main difference between migrating independent processes and MPI processes is the extensive use of the point-to-point Inter-Process Communication (IPC).

MPI usually carries its IPC via TCP/IP sockets, which are critical to the performance of the entire job. This section presents an emulation of TCP/IP sockets using Direct COMmunication (DiCOM) between migrated MPI processes.

Since our postal protocol provides a different API based on unidirectional, per-process mailboxes and not on TCP/IP, translation is therefore required.

The following features of DiCOM are designed to assist this translation:

- A process's mailbox can accumulate data packets from multiple sources, which are then read by the process, usually sequentially. However, an optional feature allows reading mailbox data out-of-order according to specified conditions, such as the PID of the sender process.
- Reading a mailbox can be either blocking or non-blocking.
- Asynchronous notification of message-arrival.

The Byte-Transfer Layer (BTL) component of Open MPI consists of independent modules that provide lower level communication, i.e., sending and receiving raw data for the use of higher layers. Examples of such modules are low-latency interconnections such as OpenIB (Infiniband); communication over shared memory; and the fall-back module - TCP/IP. Note that BTL modules are unaware which MPI function they serve, since this is included in the data itself.

We added a new BTL module for emulating TCP communication using DiCOM. This OSI layer 5 module is responsible to establish a link to the current location of the target MPI process and to transfer data to this process. The module implements a series of functions which are registered and called by the MPI run-time components. The module functions are called in different phases of running each MPI process as follows:

- **Registration Phase:** The module receives low-level communication parameters.
- **Initialization Phase:** The module detects whether it runs under our framework, and if so, receives the necessary details to contact other processes within that framework (otherwise this module is not used). This is also where DiCOM's asynchronous notification of message arrival is turned on.
- **Progress Phase:** The MPI run-time system informs the module that new message(s) have arrived. The module then uses DiCOM's out-of-order and non-blocking message reading functionalities to direct incoming messages to those layers of MPI that are waiting to receive the corresponding messages.
- **Message Send Phase:** Outgoing messages are converted and sent using the DiCOM API.
- **Message Receive Phase:** The MPI higher layers register their interest in receiving incoming messages.
- **Finalization Phase:** Connections are closed and resources are released.

3.3   Oversubscribing

Oversubscribing is an allocation policy that assigns more than one process per core [8]. Traditionally, oversubscribing was discouraged for MPI processes, but process migration provides a greater incentive to use it. Temporary oversubscribing with process migration can be beneficial in certain situations, including the following:

- Allowing a job to start on schedule, even if some designated nodes are not available, making use of other idle nodes.
- When it is necessary to shut down few nodes, e.g., due to overheating or for maintenance, without stopping the whole job.
- When CPU speeds are not uniform, new jobs can begin on slower nodes, then migrate to faster ones as they become available. Also, jobs that are past their allocated time can be migrated to slower nodes rather then killed.
- When running jobs with processes of uneven CPU demands, including when CPU usage is unknown in advance.

4   Performance of Process Migration

This section presents various performance aspects of our process migration using standard benchmarks. The tests were done on a symmetric cluster of Intel's Quad-core i7 (2.67 GHz) and 6GB memory nodes, connected by QDR Infiniband. Each test was performed 5 times and the average of the results is shown.

4.1   IPC between Migrated MPI Processes

To evaluate the performance of our BTL module, described in Sec.3.2, we used the OSU benchmark [6]. Two MPI processes were migrated to different nodes and communicated with and without the module. The left and right sides of Fig. 1 show the respective (log scale) latency and bandwidth for message sizes up to 131KB. The measurements show that the latency with DiCOM was up to 7.5 times less than without DiCOM while the bandwidth was up to 2.3 times higher. This is due to DiCOM's success in avoiding the overhead of communicating via home-nodes.

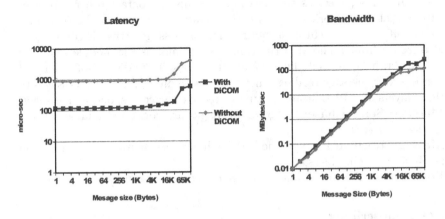

Fig. 1. Latency and bandwidth between migrated MPI processes

4.2 Overhead of Migrated Processes

We used the NPB benchmark suite [7] to compare the run-time of class C applications, initially starting all the processes in different idle nodes, then immediately migrating away some processes to other idle nodes, from none to all 4.

The results are shown in Table 1. For each application, the "None" column shows the run-time (in Sec.) of the applications without migrating, while the remaining columns show the corresponding run-times with 1–4 migrations. Accordingly, both applications with large memory and applications with higher IPC volumes incur higher overhead, consisting of migration plus communication.

Table 1. Run-times of NPB applications with different number of migrated processes

Application	Number of migrated processes				
name	None	1	2	3	4
MG	39.3	39.9	39.9	40.1	40.1
LU	313.3	317.1	317.5	315.2	315.1
BT	336.5	342.2	342.7	342.2	343.3
CG	72.8	76.1	75.8	75.9	77.3
SP	352.9	365.1	364.8	365.7	365.9
EP	93.4	93.3	93.1	92.4	92.8

4.3 Migration Speeds

We repeated the previous test, this time migrating only one process 10 times back and forth, resulting in Table 2. Column 2 shows the run-time (in Sec.) without migrating, Columns 3, the run-time with 10x2 migrations, then Column 4 shows the average time per migration. Column 5 gives the size of migrated processes, then the last column shows the migration speeds. It can be seen that larger processes migrate relatively faster for their size. This is explained by the fixed cost of initiating and managing a migration.

Table 2. Migration time and speed of NPB applications

Application name	Run-time without migration	With 10 x 2 migrations	Average migration time	Process size MB	Migration speed MB/Sec.
MG	39.2	59.4	1.01	618.2	612.1
LU	313.3	320.4	0.36	196.6	546.1
BT	338.3	355.9	0.88	413.1	469.4
CG	72.8	83.8	0.59	260.6	441.7
SP	353.0	374.9	1.10	352.3	320.3
EP	92.2	93.4	0.06	17.0	283.3

4.4   Benefiting from Oversubscribing

To show how jobs with non-uniform workload distribution can benefit from over-subscribing, we ran an application that simulated processes with uneven run-time. A fixed problem was divided into a variable number of processes, some short and some long, thus leaving room for improvement by combining over-subscribing with load balancing. Processes that migrate from a node where all other processes are active to a node where some processes are idle can get more CPU cycles, both for themselves and for the processes on their former node, thus reducing the overall run-time of the job.

We initially ran 4 long ($\sim$1800 Sec.) processes in one 4-core node and 4 short ($\sim$360 Sec.) processes in the remaining 4-core nodes. We then applied oversub-scribing by dividing each process into 2 processes of equal time (1800 Sec. to 2x900 Sec. processes and 360 Sec. to 2x180 Sec. processes). We repeated the test, further dividing the 1800 Sec. processes into 3, 4 and 6 processes of equal time. Table 3 shows the average run-time (in Sec.) of the application with and without process migration. For reference, Column 4 shows the optimal (theoretical) run-time with migration (excluding migration overheads).

Table 3. Run-times of a job with non-uniform workload with and without migration

Number of processes per core	Without migration	With migration	Optimal run-time
1	1798	1799	1798
2	1797	1079	1079
3	1796	839	839
4	1796	722	719
6	1797	608	599

From the table it can be seen that process migration improves performance and that nearly-optimal run-times were achieved.

4.5   Resolving Memory Pressure

This test demonstrates how process migration can improve the performance by better utilization of memory resources. In a cluster of multi-cores, although only one process at most is assigned per core, it is quite possible to arrive at "memory-oversubscribing" resulting in memory thrashing.

We enforced memory-oversubscribing in an application that simulated processes with unpredictable memory demands, initially with one process per core. As a result, the memory of some 4-core nodes was exhausted, causing them to thrash. We ran the application twice. Without process migration the average run-time was 590 Sec. and with process migration it was 369 Sec., an improvement of 37.5%.

5   Related Work

The migration of processes has been shown to improve the run-time of MPI jobs [9]. So far, the majority of work was based on Checkpoint-Restart (CR) of a whole job [10, 11, 12], which was accomplished by user-level or kernel-level libraries [13], such as BLCR [2]. Using RDMA over Infiniband was shown to improve the performance of the above [14, 15].

An alternative form of CR is available in Java-MPI [16] using JVMs. In this approach the process state is captured in one JVM and can then be restored on another.

Adaptive MPI (AMPI) supports transparent process migration [17], based on the CHARM++ framework that provides load-balancing through user-level migratable threads. AMPI requires the applications to be rewritten in the CHARM++ object oriented language.

A feature that allows an Open MPI process to restart communication over a different network after a checkpoint was presented in [18]. This feature can improve the communication between MPI processes that were moved to a common node.

For better load-balancing and other optimizations of MPI process placement, it was shown that processes can hint the underlying MPI implementation about their expected load, thus allowing the implementation to achieve a better placement [19].

6   Conclusions

Traditionally, process migration has been associated both with improved performance, by load-balancing and with flexibility, by dynamic reallocation of resources. These two properties seem even more important for the next generation's medium/large (Peta/Exa) scale systems that will include thousands of nodes with diverse resources, where node failures are expected to be quite common. In large systems, gossip algorithms about the state of the nodes are necessary to support process migration. This paper presented a proactive process migration framework for running Open MPI processes in clusters and multi-clusters. The performance penalty of our framework is reasonable.

One way to reduce the dependency of MPI jobs on our "Archimedes stand"[1] home-node, is to start all the processes of a job on a few home-nodes, then distribute processes to the remaining nodes. A more challenging project would be to develop a process migration scheme that does not use home-nodes at all.

Acknowledgments. The authors wish to thank E. Levy for his help. This research was supported in part by grants from the Council for Higher Education and from Dr. and Mrs. Silverston, Cambridge, UK.

References

[1] The Message Passing Interface (MPI) standard, http://www.mcs.anl.gov/mpi/
[2] Berkeley Lab Checkpoint/Restart, http://ftg.lbl.gov/checkpoint

---

[1] Give me a place to stand and I will move the whole world, Archimedes 287 BC.

[3] Barak, A., Shiloh, A.: The MOSIX cluster operating system for high-performance computing on Linux cluster, multi-clusters and clouds (2012), http://www.MOSIX.org/pub/MOSIX_wp.pdf

[4] Amar, L., Barak, A., Drezner, Z., Okun, M.: Randomized gossip algorithms for maintaining a distributed bulletin board with guaranteed age properties. Concurrency and Computation: Practice and Experience 21, 1907–1927 (2009)

[5] Amir, Y., Awerbuch, B., Barak, A., Borgstrom, R.S., Keren, A.: An opportunity cost approach for job assignment in a scalable computing cluster. IEEE Tran. Parallel and Dist. Systems 11(7), 760–768 (2000)

[6] Liu, J., Chandrasekaran, B., Yu, W., Wu, J., Buntinas, D., Kini, S.P., Wyckoff, P., Panda, D.K.: Micro-benchmark level performance comparison of high-speed cluster interconnects. Hot Interconnect 11 (2003), http://nowlab.cse.ohio-state.edu/publications/conf-papers/2003/liuj-hoti03.pdf

[7] Bailey, D., Barszcz, E., Barton, J., Browning, D., Carter, R., Dagum, L., Fatoohi, R., Fineberg, S., Frederickson, P., Lasinski, T., Schreiber, R., Simon, H., Venkatakrishnan, V., Weeratunga, S.: The NAS parallel benchmarks. Tech. Report RNR-94-007, NASA (1994)

[8] Iancu, C., Hofmeyr, S., Blagojevic, F., Zheng, Y.: Oversubscription on multicore processors. In: Proc. 2010 IEEE Int'l Sym. on Parallel and Dist. Processing (2010)

[9] Corbal, J., Duran, A., Labarta, J.: Dynamic load balancing of MPI+OpenMP applications. In: Proc. Int'l Conf. on Parallel Processing (ICPP), pp. 195–202 (2004)

[10] Hursey, J., Squyres, J.M., Mattox, T.I., Lumsdaine, A.: The design and implementation of checkpoint/restart process fault tolerance for Open MPI. In: Proc. 21st IEEE Int'l Parallel and Dist. Processing Sym. (IPDPS), pp. 1–8 (2007)

[11] Liu, T., Ma, Z., Ou, Z.: A novel process migration method for MPI applications. In: Proc. 15th IEEE Pacific Rim Int'l Sym. on Dependable Computing, pp. 247–251 (2009)

[12] Wang, C., Mueller, F., Engelmann, C., Scott, S.: Proactive process-level live migration in HPC environments. In: Proc. 2008 ACM/IEEE Conf. on Supercomputing, SC (2008)

[13] Roman, E.: A Survey of Checkpoint/Restart implementations. Tech. Report LBNL-54942C, Berkeley Lab. (2002)

[14] Gao, Q., Yu, W., Huang, W., Panda, D.K.: Application-transparent checkpoint/restart for MPI programs over Infiniband. In: Proc. 35th Int'l Conf. on Parallel Processing (ICPP), pp. 471–478 (2006)

[15] Ouyang, X., Rajachandrasekar, R., Besseron, X., Panda, D.K.: RDMA-based job migration framework for MPI over Infiniband. In: Proc. 2010 IEEE Int'l Conf. on Cluster Computing (CLUSTER), pp. 116–125 (2010)

[16] Ma, R.K.K., Wang, C., Lau, F.C.M.: M-JavaMPI: A Java-MPI binding with process migration support. In: Proc. 2nd IEEE Int'l Sym. on Cluster Computing and the Grid (CCGRID), p. 255 (2002)

[17] Huang, C., Zheng, G., Kale, L., Kumar, S.: Performance evaluation of Adaptive MPI. In: Proc. 11th ACM SIGPLAN Sym. on Principles and Practice of Parallel Programming (PPoPP), pp. 12–21 (2006)

[18] Hursey, J., Mattox, T.I., Lumsdaine, A.: Interconnect agnostic checkpoint/restart in Open MPI. In: Proc. 18th ACM Int'l Sym. on High Performance Dist. Computing (HPDC), pp. 49–58 (2009)

[19] Keller, J., Majeed, M., Kessler, C.W.: Balancing CPU load for irregular MPI applications. In: Proc. Int'l Conf. on Parallel Computing, ParCo (2011)

An Integrated Runtime Scheduler for MPI

Humaira Kamal and Alan Wagner

Dept. of Computer Science, University of British Columbia, Vancouver, Canada
{kamal,wagner}@cs.ubc.ca

Abstract. Fine-Grain MPI (FG-MPI) supports function-level parallelism while staying within the MPI process model. It provides a runtime that is directly integrated into the MPICH2 middleware and uses lightweight coroutines to implement an MPI-aware scheduler. Our key observation is that having multiple MPI processes per OS-process, with a runtime scheduler can be used to simplify MPI programming and achieve performance without adding complexity to the program. The performance part of the program is now outside of the specification of the program in the runtime where performance can be tuned with few, if any, changes to the code.

Keywords: MPICH2, Function-level Parallelism, Fine-Grain, MPI-aware Scheduler, MPI Runtime.

1 Introduction

MPI has the reputation of being difficult to program [6]. Although some of the difficulties may be inherent to message passing, many of the popular parallel languages used on multicore processors also use message-passing. However, one notable difference between MPI and these parallel languages is the granularity of MPI processes. Processes in MPI are coarse grain and programmed to make it easy to match the number of processes to the available hardware, whereas many parallel languages support finer grain to match processes to the structure of the program. By fine grain we mean function-level parallelism where processes may have tens of instructions rather than the thousands of instructions in coarse grain program-level parallelism. One can have function-size programs in MPI but it is not done because over-subscribing processes to nodes is inefficient due to the context switch time between OS-level processes and because the OS scheduler is unaware of the cooperative nature of the processes. There are also OS limitations, even with lighter-weight OS processes, when there are too many processes on a node.

We introduced Fine-Grain MPI (FG-MPI) to investigate the extent to which function-level parallelism can be supported while staying within the MPI process model [8,9]. To this end, FG-MPI augments the MPI middleware inside each OS-process with a runtime that supports hundreds and thousands of finer-grain MPI processes inside an OS-process. There are more MPI processes than cores and we still can match the number of OS-processes to number of cores to

J.L. Träff, S. Benkner, and J. Dongarra (Eds.): EuroMPI 2012, LNCS 7490, pp. 173–182, 2012.

maximize the parallelism, but now we can map multiple MPI processes to each OS-process. There is still "over-subscription", but it is now the FG-MPI runtime and scheduler that is managing the MPI processes inside each OS-process. This makes it possible to support the added concurrency that results when functions are processes.

When writing FG-MPI programs we noticed that we did not need to rely as much on non-blocking communication. Non-blocking communication makes it possible to have multiple outstanding messages that increases asynchrony and allows one to overlap communication with computation. This can reduce the idle time that results when processes are stuck waiting for a message to arrive. To avoid idle time the programmer tries to post messages as soon as possible, overlap that with some computation while periodically checking for new messages to process as well as posting new ones. Optimizing the messaging in this manner to reduce idle time and increase "slackness" breaks the cohesion of the program structure, adds complexity, and is less portable with respect to performance. Our key observation is that having multiple processes per OS-process with an MPI-aware scheduler provides an alternative way to achieve the performance without the complications to the program. The runtime scheduler acts as an abstraction device that the programmer can use to replace the hand-coded message scheduling parts of their program. As a result, the program is easier to understand and the performance-oriented aspect is outside of the specification of the program in the runtime where performance can be tuned with few, if any, changes to the code.

In the paper we describe two main design issues in FG-MPI that made it possible to support this MPI runtime model: (a) the use of coroutines and non-preemptive threads, (b) the integration of FG-MPI into existing middleware (MPICH2) rather than a layer running on top of MPI (Section 2). In Section 3, we describe the design of the scheduler and how it interacts with the MPI progress engine. Finally in Section 4, we give an example of using FG-MPI to re-structure a typical use of non-blocking communication and also compare the performance of the scheduler one to the hand-coded one.

Our hope is that the FG-MPI design and its proof of concept in a working system may provide a way for other MPI implementations to augment MPI to support this fine-grain model. Secondly we hope, by way of illustration in this paper, that extending MPI's runtime model to fine-grain can make MPI programming easier and a better overall solution that can seamlessly scale from multicore inside the box to multiple machines and cores outside of the box.

2   FG-MPI Runtime

One major decision in the design of FG-MPI and the support of multiple MPI processes within an OS-process was the use of coroutines as a basis for non-preemptive scheduling of the processes.[1] Our system uses a modular approach and is capable of making use of different coroutine libraries through a configuration option. We currently support Toernig's coroutine library, and PCL

---

[1] MPI processes sharing the same address space are referred to as *collocated* processes.

(Portable Coroutine Library). Capriccio [13] and other systems had shown that coroutine-based threads have fast context-switching time, low communication and synchronization overhead and scale to support large numbers of threads. The benefits of coroutines at the language level are well-known and they are supported in many languages (Python, Lua) including parallel languages used on multicore (Erlang, Go Language). Cooperative multithreading can be difficult in general but for MPI the messaging-passing and calls to the middleware provide a natural yield point.

With regards to implementation, having non-preemptive processes was crucial. Since only one collocated process is active, it was possible to share the middleware without using locks and ensure that the middleware is in a consistent state between scheduling points. There have been previous attempts at pre-emptive thread-based MPI implementations [5,11], but they have remained largely incomplete due to the complexity of managing synchronization primitives and challenges in scaling. The challenges and overheads of thread-safety of MPI middleware are well known [2,12] and it is an important problem but the use of coroutines circumvents the need for locks to support multitasking and the guaranteed atomicity made it easier to reason about the state of the middleware.

The second major design decision was integration of FG-MPI directly into MPI rather than an attempt to design a new implementation of MPI or to use coroutines and layer it on top of MPI. Adaptive MPI is an implementation of MPI that supports fine-grain processes, however, AMPI [7] implements the MPI library on top of Charm++ rather than directly into an existing MPI. This requires their own implementation of MPI and the Charm++ runtime also needs a communication layer. This can result in an MPI sandwich, with MPI running on top of Charm++ which in turn runs over MPI. In FG-MPI, all MPI communication directly invokes the corresponding lower level MPI implementation of the call in the middleware, whereas in the layered approach only a subset of the MPI communication in the lowest layer is used. More importantly, a scheduler layered on top of MPI would be MPI-aware but operates independently from the lower level MPI progress engine. The result is multiple independent control loops and schedulers, where it is difficult to coordinate their activities with regards to the scheduling of asynchronous and synchronous messages.

We integrated FG-MPI into MPI by extending the MPICH2 middleware. Figure 1 shows the integration of FG-MPI in the layered modular architecture of MPICH2. The MPICH2 ADI3 layer represents the data structures and functions that are provided by an implementation. Representation in this layer is in terms of MPI requests/messages and the functions for manipulating those requests. One of the main considerations in FG-MPI was to support large amounts of concurrency through scalable sharing of MPI structures among the coroutines. To this end, a large number of MPI storage structures such as posted receive queues, unexpected messages queues, communicator and request pools are shared by the coroutines (see Figure 2). Other structures that are integral to MPI are communicators and groups and their scalability and sharing is essential to FG-MPI. In past work [8] we discuss in detail how we share these structures and

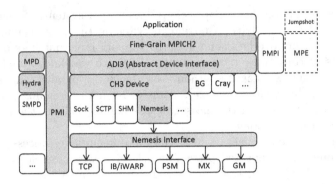

Fig. 1. FG-MPI Architecture. Shading shows the layers of MPICH2 that were augmented in the FG-MPI implementation. Figure adapted from [1].

scale to hundreds and thousands of MPI processes. FG-MPI uses the Nemesis CH3 channel, which is a highly optimized communication subsystem that provides multi-network support [3] including fast shared memory communication between processes on the same node.

MPICH2 is optimized for OS-process level communication, and one interesting problem that arose as a result was that the message match header did not need to contain the rank of the destination process, as it is implicit from the OS-process identifier. In FG-MPI, since there may be multiple MPI processes inside the OS-process, the destination rank of the process is necessary to de-multiplex the message from the OS-process network point of attachment to the MPI process. As a result we had to extend the message match header as well as increase the packet header size to include the destination rank. Communication in Nemesis is tuned for better cache performance and although we have not done a low-level comparison we have not noticed any performance differences at the application layer as a result of our extension.

Inside the middleware we maintain two separate tables: (a) connection routing table (point of attachments) and (b) process name table (MPI_COMM_WORLD ranks).[2] This separates the namespace of the point of attachment from that of the ranks. We emphasize the separation of these two namespaces because it is an example of the importance of naming in a distributed system [10]. Separating the namespace for the point of attachment and ranks is required to de-couple MPI processes from the hardware. Although we have not yet considered process mobility, it greatly simplifies that as well. The issue of naming also arises with respect to mapping where it is easier to map processes when the rank is used as a semantically pure identifier rather than an integer range from 0 to $N - 1$.

Based on this experience we believe this type of integration is possible with other implementations of MPI. Finally note that FG-MPI extends MPICH2 and the FG-MPI runtime is only set-up when there is more than one MPI process in an OS-process.

---

[2] We do not support MPI-2 dynamics.

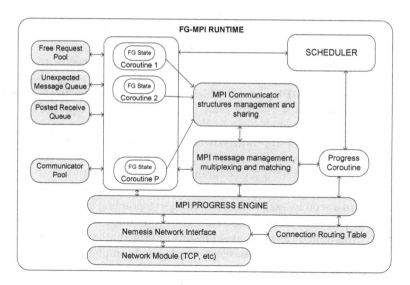

Fig. 2. FG-MPI Runtime System. Shaded regions show the middleware structures shared among the collocated MPI processes.

3 Integrated MPI Scheduler

We maintain a run queue and a blocked queue for collocated MPI processes inside each OS-process. Scheduling events inside the middleware invoke the scheduler, which according to the scheduling policy, blocks the current process or adds it back onto the run queue, and chooses the next process to resume. We provide a scheduler framework that allows us to add new policies as the need may arise. The selection of the scheduler is provided as a command line option to mpiexec. The most interesting aspect of the scheduler is its integration into the MPI middleware and interaction with events occurring inside the progress engine.

As Figure 2 shows, many of the key data structures in the middleware, such as the message queues, request pools and communicator pool, are shared among all of the collocated MPI processes. In FG-MPI, communication can be both internal (among collocated processes) and external (between non-collocated processes) and supports the different types of MPI calls such as blocking, non-blocking etc. When a process makes an MPI call it will progress its request as far as possible. For example, if it is a send request, it may match a pre-posted receive from another collocated process and complete its call, or it may initiate a communication transfer over the external link to a receiver in another address space. A message arriving at the message matching layer may complete a pending request or this may be an unexpected message, which will be queued until a matching receive request arrives. Most importantly, however, since the state of the progress engine is shared, MPI processes can cooperatively progress pending messages for other collocated processes and notify the scheduler. The scheduler, based on the notification may add processes to the run queue.

Another example of cooperation is that of a pre-posted receive request for which a ready-to-send (RTS) arrives to initiate the long message handshake. It is possible that the MPI process, which posted that receive request, is not currently executing, but a clear-to-send (CTS) can be sent by the currently executing process on its behalf.

Internal communication is optimized to take advantage of a single address space, as well it is an opportunity for the scheduler, depending on the type of communication, to block one process until the communication can be completed after which both processes can proceed. For collocated processes, the scheduler follows a natural order where a send message schedules the corresponding receive process that can continue to progress the message chain. The communication among collocated processes involves a single `memcpy`, avoiding any intermediate system copies. Similarly for external events, once a message is received and completed the corresponding MPI process is scheduled to continue advancing the computation. As well, for collectives such as barrier, that last collocated process completing the barrier can gang-schedule all of the processes in the barrier since they can all proceed.

In many cases we have found that even a very basic round-robin (RR) scheduler which keeps all the processes on the run queue is adequate [9]. Because the scheduling overhead is relatively small, as long as the collocated processes are easy to keep busy, the RR scheduler works well. One more additional advantage of the RR scheduler is that it is deterministic and gives more predictable executions. This is one of the nice properties of introducing a scheduler over preemptive threads (either pthreads or OS-threads) where the programmer has less control on when processes are de-scheduled. The deterministic property of RR has also proven useful as a tool for debugging programs.

It is not sufficient to have only RR since there are simple cases where RR does extremely poorly. For example, consider the simple ring program, the forward communication of messages works well when it is the same order as the scheduling order, however, communication in the reverse direction is slow due to re-scheduling delay of all of the processes on the run queue. This was our motivation for introducing a scheduling framework rather than one or more fixed policies. The policy ultimately depends on the application where ideally processes on the critical execution path are scheduled first. Finally, note that the scheduling policy is local to an OS-process and does not have to be global.

One interesting problem that arises with the scheduler, that allows blocking of MPI processes, is deadlock. Deadlock can occur, for instance, when all of the collocated processes are blocked waiting for a external event. One alternative is simply not to block all processes or to simply keep one or more processes on the queue. Deciding on whether or not to block a process depending on the state of other collocated processes is complicated. There are a large number of MPI calls and different scenarios that would need to be considered and analyzed. However, there is a simple very scalable solution to this problem.

We introduced a progress coroutine in our runtime that comes into existence the first time an MPI process blocks on a receive. Once created, the progress coroutine remains on the run queue. When called, this coroutine executes the progress-loop in the middleware and progresses pending incoming and outgoing messages. Whenever there is a receive that could be matched by a message from a remote process it ensures that we poll the external link for more data and on arrival of such a message wakes up the blocked process. As well, as discussed above, a clear-to-send (CTS) may be sent by the progress coroutine for a pre-posted receive. A progress coroutine avoids the checking that would have been necessary when blocking processes and also provides an easy way to measure the idle time and "slackness" during runtime.

4   Programmability and Non-blocking Communication

As mentioned in Section 1, non-blocking communication adds to the programming complexity of MPI programs. Consider the program in Listing 1.1 showing a simple use of non-blocking communication, which tries to post as many messages as possible to keep the process busy.

```
int main( int argc, char *argv[] )
{  ...
  MPI_Irecv(..., recvRequests(2));
  do {
    compute_local(...);
    MPI_Waitany(2, recvRequests, ..., recvStatus);
    switch(recvStatus->tag) {
    case tag1:
      compute_A();
      MPI_Send(...);
      MPI_Irecv(..., recvRequests(1));
    case tag2:
      compute_B();
      MPI_Send(...);
      MPI_Irecv(..., recvRequests(1));
    }
  } while(...);
  ...
}
```

Listing 1.1. Scheduling communication and computation by non-blocking operations

As previously described there are three main parts to the program: (a) allocating and managing message request buffers, (b) checking for message completions and then processing the messages, (c) a compute part that may or may not depend on the messages send and received. What are complexities in the above listing:

(i) The compute and communication parts of the code are interleaved and the programmer needs to balance the computation with the polling of the link via the middleware.

(ii) The user needs to manage the request buffers for the multiple outstanding messages. The programmer also needs to be aware of all the different types of outstanding messages and how messages are matched. This often results in the use of MPI_ANY_SOURCE and MPI_ANY_TAG.

As shown in Listing 1.2 with FG-MPI we can re-organize the program into three smaller processes: compute_local(), process_A() and process_B(). The FGmpiexec call binds the MPI process ranks to concurrent functions through a user-specified binding_func and initiates the runtime.

```
int main( int argc, char *argv[] ){
    FGmpiexec(&argc, &argv, &binding_func);
    return (0);
}
int process_A( int argc, char** argv ){
    do{
        MPI_Recv(..., tag1,...);
        compute_A();
        MPI_Send(...);
    }while(...);
}
int process_B( int argc, char** argv ){
    do{
        MPI_Recv(..., tag2,...);
        compute_B();
        MPI_Send(...);
    }while(..);
}
int compute_local( int argc, char** argv ){
    do{
        ...
        if (...) MPIX_Yield();
    }while(...);
}
```

Listing 1.2. Defining MPI processes as concurrent functions all mapped to the same OS-process. Each MPI process also calls MPI_Init and MPI_Finalize.

As opposed to Listing 1.1, there are no non-blocking requests and associated structures in Listing 1.2 and no need to remember that the posted requests have to be checked for completion. Listing 1.1 has requests that are global over the entire program and no clear demarcation between different types of requests. FG-MPI places all of corresponding computation and communication code pertaining to one activity into one process. This makes it easier to read and easier to change the code.

The purpose of the control loop in Listing 1.1 is to schedule different parts of the code based on the message events from MPI_Waitany(). In the FG-MPI version of the code there is no MPI_Waitany(). The control loop is now handled by the FG-MPI scheduler rather than having to be hand-coded into the program. In Listing 1.2, should process_A() now require we receive two messages rather than one, we only need to add another MPI_Recv(), however, for Listing 1.1 there are questions as to whether we need to introduce another case and tag and how it might be matched.

In both listings it is important that the compute_local() code invoke the progress engine sufficiently often to not unduly delay the remaining computation and communication. In Listing 1.2, MPIX_Yield() can be appropriately placed when needed to provide an explicit de-scheduling point that automatically resumes at the proper place. Changing the rate at which the network is polled in Listing 1.1 requires reorganizing the computation, which is not as easy.

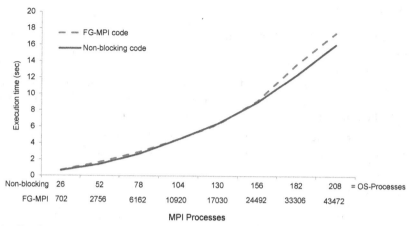

Fig. 3. Performance comparison of non-blocking code using `MPI_Waitany` with functional-level concurrency in FG-MPI. Number of OS-Processes is same in both cases. In FG-MPI, the MPI processes are evenly distributed across the OS-Processes.

Expressing additional concurrency in the program gives us the opportunity to exploit it, however, it does require structuring the code and mapping MPI processes to functions as we now have the MPMD (Multiple Program Multiple Data) process model. We have two levels of mapping in FG-MPI. The first level specifies how OS-processes are mapped to the cores and nodes and the number of MPI processes mapped to each OS-process. This is done through an `nfg` (number of fine-grain) flag to the standard `mpiexec` command. The second level defines MPI processes as functions and this is done through a call to `FGmpiexec` in `main()`. Although we have an extra-level of mapping, this is outside of the application code and gives us more flexibility in mapping to OS-processes and nodes. As well, we can match the OS-processes to the cores to minimize the effect of OS-noise and not rely on the OS scheduler, which introduces yet another control loop that is unaware of the cooperative nature of MPI processes. Finally, FG-MPI extends MPI so the programmer can manage as little or as much of the non-blocking communication as they wish.

We created a benchmark program, similar to the codes in Listings 1.1 and 1.2, to evaluate the overhead of introducing more MPI processes in FG-MPI. This benchmark introduced asynchrony on a much larger scale than shown in the two listings and the total amount of computation and communication increased with the number of OS-processes. In Figure 3, we compare the FG-MPI code with multiple MPI processes per OS-process with the non-blocking MPI code. Our results show that even with the introduction of more than 24,000 fine-grain MPI processes compared to 156 coarse-grain processes, the performance remains the same. As we increase beyond this to more than 43,000 processes, there is a small overhead of 8.7%. A real-world example from the CoSMoS [4] project that uses FG-MPI and models emergent behaviour through thousands of MPI processes was presented in past work [9].

5   Conclusions

Our runtime scheduler, through direct integration in MPICH2, is reactive to MPI events occurring inside the progress engine and its light-weight design enables definition of MPI processes as functions that can be flexibly mapped to OS-processes, cores and nodes. This relieves the programmer from scheduling computation and communication inside the application and focus on "what" needs to be scheduled rather than "how" to manage it.

Acknowledgements. This work was supported in part by the Institute for Computing, Information and Cognitive Systems (ICICS) at UBC.

References

1. Argonne National Laboratory. MPICH2: Performance and portability. In: SC 2007 Flyer (2007)
2. Balaji, P., Buntinas, D., Goodell, D., Gropp, W.D., Thakur, R.: Toward Efficient Support for Multithreaded MPI Communication. In: Lastovetsky, A., Kechadi, T., Dongarra, J. (eds.) EuroPVM/MPI 2008. LNCS, vol. 5205, pp. 120–129. Springer, Heidelberg (2008)
3. Buntinas, D., Gropp, W., Mercier, G.: Design and evaluation of Nemesis, a scalable, low-latency, message-passing communication subsystem. In: Proc. of the 6th IEEE Intl. Symp. on Cluster Computing and the Grid, pp. 521–530. IEEE Computer Society, Washington, DC (2006)
4. CoSMoS. Complex systems modelling and simulation infrastructutre, http://www.cosmos-research.org/
5. Demaine, E.: A threads-only MPI implementation for the development of parallel programs. In: Proceedings of the 11th International Symposium on High Performance Computing Systems, pp. 153–163 (1997)
6. Gropp, W.D.: Learning from the Success of MPI. In: Monien, B., Prasanna, V.K., Vajapeyam, S. (eds.) HiPC 2001. LNCS, vol. 2228, pp. 81–94. Springer, Heidelberg (2001)
7. Huang, C., Lawlor, O.S., Kal, L.V.: Adaptive MPI. In: Rauchwerger, L. (ed.) LCPC 2003. LNCS, vol. 2958, pp. 306–322. Springer, Heidelberg (2004)
8. Kamal, H., Mirtaheri, S.M., Wagner, A.: Scalability of communicators and groups in MPI. In: Proc. of the 19th ACM Intl. Symposium on High Performance Distributed Computing, HPDC 2010, pp. 264–275. ACM, New York (2010)
9. Kamal, H., Wagner, A.: FG-MPI: Fine-Grain MPI for multicore and clusters. In: 11th IEEE Intl. Workshop on Parallel and Distributed Scientific and Engineering Computing (PDSEC) held in conjunction with IPDPS-24, pp. 1–8 (April 2010)
10. Saltzer, J.: On the naming and binding of network destinations. Network Working Group (1993), http://tools.ietf.org/html/rfc1498
11. Tang, H., Yang, T.: Optimizing threaded MPI execution on SMP clusters. In: ICS 2001: Proc. of 15th Intl. Conf. on Supercomputing, pp. 381–392. ACM, New York (2001)
12. Thakur, R., Gropp, W.: Test Suite for Evaluating Performance of MPI Implementations That Support MPI_THREAD_MULTIPLE. In: Cappello, F., Herault, T., Dongarra, J. (eds.) PVM/MPI 2007. LNCS, vol. 4757, pp. 46–55. Springer, Heidelberg (2007)
13. von Behren, R., Condit, J., Zhou, F., Necula, G., Brewer, E.: Capriccio: scalable threads for internet services. In: SOSP 19, pp. 268–281. ACM, New York (2003)

High Performance Checksum Computation for Fault-Tolerant MPI over Infiniband

Alexandre Denis[1], Francois Trahay[2], and Yutaka Ishikawa[3]

[1] INRIA Bordeaux – Sud-Ouest / LaBRI, France
alexandre.denis@inria.fr
[2] Institut Mines-Telecom, Telecom SudParis, 91011 Evry, France
francois.trahay@it-sudparis.eu
[3] University of Tokyo, Japan
ishikawa@il.is.s.u-tokyo.ac.jp

Abstract. With the increase of the number of nodes in clusters, the probability of failures and unusual events increases. In this paper, we present checksum mechanisms to detect data corruption. We study the impact of checksums on network communication performance and we propose a mechanism to amortize their cost on InfiniBand. We have implemented our mechanisms in the NEWMADELEINE communication library. Our evaluation shows that our mechanisms to ensure message integrity do not impact noticeably the application performance, which is an improvement over the state of the art MPI implementations.

Keywords: Checksum, Fault-Tolerance, High-performance networks, Infini-Band.

1 Introduction

Since the development of large scale supercomputers have led to systems composed of hundreds of thousands of components, the likelihood of hardware or software failure becomes embarrassing. The design of future supercomputers foreshadows an increasing number of components, decreasing the mean time between failure [4]. Multiple causes of failures exists — software bugs, hardware failures, failed switch, electromagnetic perturbation, faulty cable shielding — leading to various types of failures — crashed nodes, lost packets, data corruption. Communication libraries implement a variety of mechanisms to detect and survive these failures.

We focus in this paper on the detection of data corruption in MPI network communication through the use of checksums.

On their way from the sender memory through the receiver memory, messages may be corrupted with some bits flipped. It may occur on the wire, in the NIC, or on the PCIe bus. Most network hardware use checksums internally to ensure message integrity on the wire, but corruption may occur at any other given point [7]. To ensure end-to-end message integrity from sender memory through receiver memory, communication libraries use *checksums*: the sender computes a checksum of the message to be sent and its headers and sends it with the message headers. The receiver computes the checksum on the received messages; if it doesn't match the one received alongside the data,

J.L. Träff, S. Benkner, and J. Dongarra (Eds.): EuroMPI 2012, LNCS 7490, pp. 183–192, 2012.

it means corruption occurred: either the data, the headers, or the checksum itself have been corrupted during the transfer. In this case, the message is considered as lost and the communication library retransmits the packet.

In this paper, we study the impact of checksuming on communication performance and propose mechanisms to amortize their cost on InfiniBand.

The remainder of this paper is organized as follows: Section 2 presents related work. In Section 3, we analyze the cost of checksum on communication performance. Section 4 presents the technique we propose to amortize the cost of checksum computation on InfiniBand. Results are discussed in Section 5 and we draw a conclusion in Section 6.

2   Related Work

Some works have focused on the effectiveness [13,12] of error detection for various checksums algorithms, or on the performance [8,9] of checksum computation. To our knowledge, these works have not been integrated into any MPI implementation.

Failure detection in MPI relies usually on heart beat technique [2] or on sender-based logging [16] that consist in detecting remote activity through the network. Such techniques detect node or link failures, not data corruption.

LA-MPI [11] and OPENMPI [15] ensure the integrity of messages by computing checksums. This allows to detect corrupted fragments and to retransmit them, but this technique suffers from a large overhead that significantly impacts the performance of applications. Since LA-MPI has been superseded by OPENMPI, in this paper we compare our approach against OPENMPI only.

We have implemented our proposed checksum mechanisms in NEWMADELEINE [1] since it was more convenient for us to work in our own communication library. However, these mechanisms are intended to be generic and not specific to NEWMADELEINE, thus they could probably be implemented in any other MPI implementation.

3   Checksum Cost Analysis

In this Section, we study the cost of various checksum algorithms and their impact on communication performance.

Computing checksums has a cost that may lower the available bandwidth. The precise cost depends on the checksum algorithm, the compiler, and the CPU. In this paper, we consider the following algorithms: *sum*– plain sum of 32 bits words; *XOR*– XOR all 32 bits words; *Adler-32, Fletcher-64* [9], *Jenkins One-at-a-time* [12], *FNV1a* [10], *Knuth hashing, MurmurHash2a, Paul Hsieh Superfast*– a collection of well-known fast hashing functions that can be used as error-detection (non-cryptographic) checksum; *CRC*– 32 bits CRC computed with SSE 4.2 (non-accelerated CRC is too slow to be considered here). Algorithms *sum* and *XOR* are given as performance reference only, but are not suitable [13] to detect reliably errors on more than one bit; *CRC* is expected to be slow but offers the best error detection; other algorithms are expected to be a good compromise [8].

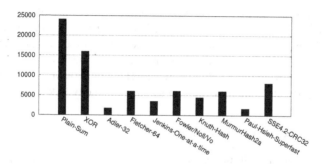

Fig. 1. Bandwidth of some checksum algorithms on 32 kB blocks

Figure 1 shows the bandwidth of these checksums on our `jack` cluster, equipped with dual-core Xeon X5650 at 2.67 GHz, on 32 kB blocks that fit the L1 cache. The plain *sum* and *XOR* are the fastest, and will likely always be on any hardware. However, it cannot reliably detect corruption beyond a single bit. For a better error detection, *Fletcher-64*, *FNV1a*, *MurmurHash2a* and *SSE4.2 CRC* are good candidates on this particular machine and compiler. They perform around 6 GB/s which makes 1.5 ns/word, *i.e.* 4 cycles per 32-bit word.

We have observed a huge performance discrepancy from one CPU to another, and from one compiler to another, e.g. *Fletcher-64* is 60 % faster with `icc` than with `clang` on Nehalem, and with `gcc` *Fletcher-64* is slower than *FNV1a* on Nehalem but the reverse is true on Dunnington. Therefore we use auto-tuning [3] to choose dynamically the best performing checksum algorithm.

Even when selecting the fastest checksum algorithm, checksum computation has a huge impact on network performance. Let L be the length of a given message, we model the checksum time as a linear function in the form $T_{csum}(L) = \frac{L}{B_{csum}}$, and the network as $T_{net}(L) = \lambda_{net} + \frac{L}{B_{net}}$ with λ_{net} and B_{net} the latency and bandwidth of the network. Both sender and receiver must compute the checksum to ensure data integrity. For a naive approach — the sender computes the checksum, then sends data, then the receiver computes the checksum — the total transfer time is: $T(L) = \frac{L}{B_{csum}} + \lambda_{net} + \frac{L}{B_{net}} + \frac{L}{B_{csum}}$. The apparent bandwidth converges asymptotically towards $\frac{1}{\frac{1}{B_{net}} + \frac{2}{B_{csum}}}$. On the `jack` cluster, we have $B_{net} = 3\,GB/s$ and $B_{csum} = 6\,GB/s$ for *Fletcher-64*, thus the apparent bandwidth of the naive approach is $1.5\,GB/s$ which is 50 % of the network bandwidth. We get results in this order of magnitude on most contemporary hardware.

4 Amortizing the Cost of Checksum Computation

In this Section, we present our approach which consists in amortizing the cost of checksum computation by combining the checksum and the memory copy wherever it happens, and in overlapping computation and network transfer.

We have implemented our mechanisms in the NEWMADELEINE communication library, which decouples upper layers communication requests from network interface.

It applies optimization strategies inbetween in order to use more efficiently the network [1]. For instance, multiple small messages from the application may be aggregated and sent as a single packet on the network. Another optimization consists in using simultaneously multiple links by splitting large messages. To survive network failures, a sender-based logging mechanism [16] was implemented in NEWMADELEINE. When a data corruption is detected, the message sent through the faulty link is retransmitted.

4.1 Combining Checksum and Memory Copy

On the `jack` machine used in the previous Section, the memory bandwidth for reading is 9700 MB/s and the copy bandwidth is 4530 MB/s. Thus, the simplest checksum algorithms are memory-bound and the others are in the same order of magnitude as memory bandwidth. It is then expected that a large part of the cost of a naive approach for checksums will be actually memory access. For multiplexing and to apply optimization strategies, NEWMADELEINE always copies small packets. Even large packets sent with *rendez-vous* over InfiniBand go through a super-pipelined protocol [6] using a copy.

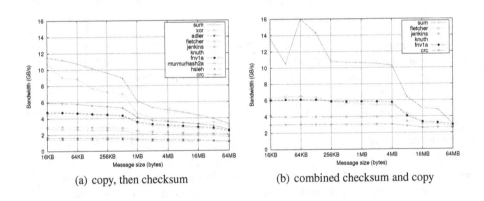

(a) copy, then checksum   (b) combined checksum and copy

Fig. 2. Performance of copy and checksum on cluster `jack`

We propose to take benefit from these copies to amortize the cost of checksum, *i.e.* reduce the memory accesses needed for checksuming by combining copy and checksum, and overlap memory accesses and checksum computation thanks to CPU being superscalar. We propose to compute the checksum on the fly at every place where data is copied in NEWMADELEINE. Two approaches are possible: copy data then compute checksum, relying on data having been fetched in cache by the copy; combine checksum computation and memory copy, *i.e.* for each word fetch from memory, compute checksum, store at destination.

We have implemented the first approach with the full collection of checksum functions; the benchmarks results are presented in Figure 2(a). We have implemented the second approach with a selection of checksums; the benchmarks results are depicted in

Figure 2(b). We observe that combining the checksum and the memory copy is always beneficial, except for SSE 4.2 CRC where the checksum-only implementation is optimized in assembly where the combined version is written in C with compiler intrinsics for SSE. Once again, we rely on auto-tuning to dynamically decide which version to use.

4.2 Checksums for Small Messages (Eager Send)

In NEWMADELEINE, small packets are sent with an eager protocol: data is copied to add the headers and to apply optimization strategies such as aggregation of multiple messages into one packet. To add checksuming, we simply change this copy into the combined checksum and copy. On the receiver side, NEWMADELEINE receives packets in its internals buffers, then parses headers, performs matching, and unpacks data to its final destination in the user buffers. Here again we change the copy into a combined checksum and copy.

Let λ_{net} and B_{net} be the latency and bandwidth of the network; $B_{csum+copy}$ the bandwidth of the combined memory copy and checksum computation, then the total transfer time for a message of length L sent with eager mode is $T(L) = \frac{2 \times L}{B_{csum+copy}} + \lambda_{net} + \frac{L}{B_{net}}$

On the jack cluster, equipped with ConnectX2 InfiniBand QDR HCA, we have $\lambda_{net} = 1.4\,\mu s$; $B_{net} = 3\,GB/s$; $B_{csum+copy} = 6\,GB/s$. Then we can compute the expected overhead of checksums to be 34 % on 4 kB messages. This cost is quite high, but lower than the asymptotic cost since network latency cannot be neglected for small packets. A pipeline to overlap checksum computation and network transfers wouldn't be beneficial since fragmentation overhead would not compensate for the checksum cost on such small packets.

4.3 Checksums for Large Messages (*rendez-vous*)

Large messages are sent through a *rendez-vous* protocol in NEWMADELEINE. On InfiniBand, we use a variable depth super-pipeline [6] to fetch data into registered memory. We propose to combine the checksum computation with the copy performed by the super-pipeline on both sender and receiver sides. We expect it would amortize the memory transfers needed for checksum, and overlap checksum computation and network transfers.

As depicted in Figure 3, this protocol overlaps copy and RDMA. The chunk size $C_n = q^n$ is growing from chunk to chunk, as a geometric series with a ratio q being equal to the bandwidth ratio between network and copy. The size of the first chunk C_0 is determined so as its copy perfectly overlaps the *rendez-vous* round-trip ($\frac{C_0}{B_{copy}} = 2\lambda_{net}$ computed by auto-tuning). A sub-blocking mechanism amortizes the cost of the copy of the last chunk.

We have shown [6] that the total transfer time of the superpipeline protocol is:

$$T_{superpipeline}(L) = \frac{b}{B_{copy}(L)} + g \times n + \lambda_{net} + \frac{L}{B_{net}}$$

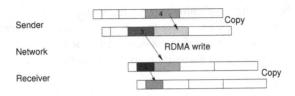

Fig. 3. Super-pipeline for memory copy: a pipeline with a variable chunk size

with the number of gaps:

$$n = \log_q \left(1 + \frac{L}{C_0} (q - 1) \right)$$

and L is the message length, λ_{net} the network latency, B_{net} the network bandwidth, g the gap as in the LogP model [5], q the ratio of the finite geometric series of chunk size, and b the sub-block size. The overhead of this protocol compared to the raw network performance is comprised of: the copy of the first sub-block of size b; the n gaps between packets.

The addition of checksum to the copy has an impact on the first term (copy of the first sub-block) and on q. The impact on the first term consists in the checksum of a 4 KB sub-block, which is half a micro-second on our jack cluster with *FNV1a*. The impact on q used as the base of a logarithm is limited, e.g. with the parameters of the jack cluster for a 1 MB message, it adds an overhead of one gap, *i.e.* 300 ns. The total overhead of checksuming on this example is less than 1 % according to the theoretical model.

5   Evaluation

In this Section, we present the experimental results obtained by comparing the checksum-enabled NEWMADELEINE with the original NEWMADELEINE and OPEN-MPI (ob1 and csum). We used MPICH2-nmad [14] as an MPI interface over NEW-MADELEINE, and compared against latest stable release OPENMPI 1.4.5. We evaluate the raw overhead of checksums computation as well as their impact on NAS Parallel Benchmarks.

The results we present were obtained on the jack and graphene clusters. Cluster jack is equipped with dual-core Xeon X5650 at 2.67 GHz and ConnectX2 QDR (MT26428) InfiniBand; compiler is icc 12.1. Cluster graphene features ConnectX DDR (MT26418) InfiniBand cards on quad-core nodes equipped with Intel Xeon X3440; compiler is gcc 4.4.

5.1   Raw Checksum Overhead

We used Netpipe to measure the raw MPI performance on InfiniBand on both clusters. Bandwidth results for NEWMADELEINE with various checksum algorithms are

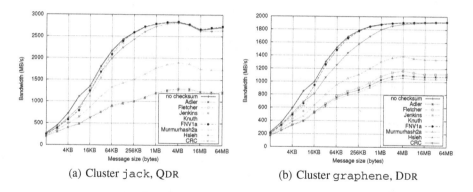

Fig. 4. NEWMADELEINE bandwidth with various checksums algorithms

depicted in Figure 5.1. On both clusters, for small packets before the *rendez-vous* threshold (16 KB), the impact of checksums is quite high, around 30 %, which is consistent with our model in Section 4. For these packet sizes, there is no pipelining nor any mechanism to amortize the cost of checksuming except the combination of copy and checksum. The performance of these combined operations cannot be higher than the peak checksum performance, which is much lower than copy for such packet size that fit the cache.

For messages larger than 16 KB, the bandwidth overhead ranges from 3 % for 64 KB to less than 0.5 % asymptotically for the fastest checksum algorithms. *FNV1a* is a sensible default choice on most machines and compilers if auto-tuning has not been performed yet, but auto-tuning may still improve performance by a few percents, e.g. *Fletcher* is 2 % faster than *FNV1a* on cluster jack (but *Fletcher* is 40 % slower on graphene).

We compared our checksum-enabled MPI implementation against OPENMPI. The bandwidth results are depicted in Figure 5 and 6. On cluster jack (Figure 5), NEW-MADELEINE and OPENMPI get roughly the same bandwidth without checksums. When checksums are enabled, the bandwidth is lowered by 20 % for OPENMPI, and by at most 3 % for NEWMADELEINE, thanks to the super-pipeline protocol. On cluster graphene (Figure 6), OPENMPI is slightly faster than NEWMADELEINE when checksums are disabled. When checksums are enabled, OPENMPI suffers a performance drop of 60 % while the overhead is below 2 % for NEWMADELEINE.

5.2   NAS Parallel Benchmarks

We also run the NAS Parallel Benchmarks on the graphene cluster. Table 1 reports results for class B on 16 nodes. We report raw performance results (median time from 10 runs) as well as time differences as percentage.

The results show that OPENMPI is slightly faster than MPICH2-nmad when checksums are disabled. This can be explained by NEWMADELEINE optimization strategies causing a longer software stack, thus a higher latency, with no gain when there is a single communication flow as in the NAS Parallel Benchmarks.

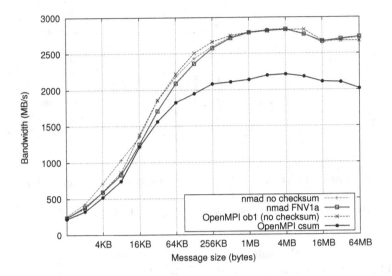

Fig. 5. Bandwidth over QDR InfiniBand on cluster `jack`

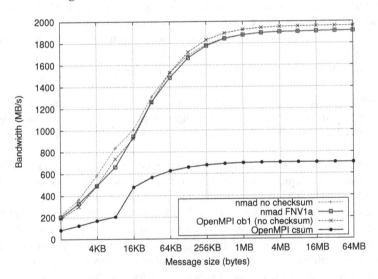

Fig. 6. Bandwidth over DDR InfiniBand on cluster `graphene`

Table 1. NAS results on cluster `graphene`

	is.B.16	lu.B.16	ft.B.16	cg.B.16	mg.B.16
MPICH2-nmad (no checksum)	0.37 s	18.54 s	5.06 s	5.72 s	0.71 s
MPICH2-nmad *FNV1a*	0.37 s	18.57 s	5.05 s	5.69 s	0.72 s
OPENMPI ob1	0.35 s	17.89 s	4.89 s	5.60 s	0.71 s
OPENMPI csum	0.43 s	19.30 s	5.45 s	6.59 s	0.79 s
OPENMPI csum / OPENMPI ob1	+22.86%	+7.88%	+11.45%	+17.68%	+11.27%
MPICH2-nmad *FNV1a* / MPICH2-nmad no checksum	+0%	+0.16%	-0.20%	-0.52%	+1.41%
MPICH2-nmad *FNV1a* / OPENMPI csum	-13.95%	-3.78%	-7.34%	-13.66%	-8.86%

When checksums are enabled, OPENMPI suffers a performance penalty from 7 % to more than 22 %. On the other hand, enabling checksums in MPICH2-nmad (*FNV1a* is selected by auto-tuning here) has a negligible impact on performance.

When comparing both checksum-enabled OPENMPI and MPICH2-nmad, MPICH2-nmad is faster by 3 % to 14 %. This demonstrates that our approach to amortize the cost of checksum computation is competitive.

6   Conclusion and Future Work

The advent of large scale supercomputers composed of hundreds of thousands of components have raised reliability issues. Beside node failures, the interconnection system may suffer from errors leading to data corruption. The classical solution to detect such errors is the use of checksums, which have an impact on network performance.

In this paper, we have proposed a mechanism that amortizes the cost of checksum computation in MPI implementations for InfiniBand. We have implemented and evaluated this mechanism. Our evaluation shows that it causes a performance degradation of at most a few percents in the worst case for micro-benchmarks, and the difference is negligible on NAS benchmarks. This is a huge improvement over the state of the art.

In the future, we plan to study the integration of these techniques in upper layers of the software stack. For instance, parallel file systems – such as PVFS – that need reliable communication subsystems may also benefit from the message integrity mechanism we proposed.

Acknowledgments. This work was supported in part by the ANR-JST project FP3C.

Experiments presented in this paper were carried out using the Grid'5000 experimental testbed, being developed under the INRIA ALADDIN development action with support from CNRS, RENATER and several Universities as well as other funding bodies (see https://www.grid5000.fr).

References

1. Aumage, O., Brunet, E., Furmento, N., Namyst, R.: NewMadeleine: a Fast Communication Scheduling Engine for High Performance Networks. In: CAC 2007: Workshop on Communication Architecture for Clusters, held in conjunction with IPDPS 2007 (2007),
   http://hal.inria.fr/inria-00127356
2. Bertier, M., Marin, O., Sens, P.: Implementation and performance evaluation of an adaptable failure detector. In: International Conference on Dependable Systems and Networks (2002)
3. Brunet, E., Trahay, F., Denis, A., Namyst, R.: A sampling-based approach for communication libraries auto-tuning. In: International Conference on Cluster Computing (IEEE Cluster), pp. 299–307. IEEE Computer Society Press, Austin (2011),
   http://hal.inria.fr/inria-00605735/
4. Cappello, F., Geist, A., Gropp, B., Kale, L., Kramer, B., Snir, M.: Toward exascale resilience. International Journal of High Performance Computing Applications 23(4) (2009)
5. Culler, D., Karp, R., Patterson, D., Sahay, A., Schauser, K.E., Santos, E., Subramonian, R., von Eicken, T.: Logp: towards a realistic model of parallel computation. In: ACM SIGPLAN Symposium on Principles and Practice of Parallel Programming, PPOPP 1993, pp. 1–12. ACM, New York (1993), http://doi.acm.org/10.1145/155332.155333

6. Denis, A.: A High Performance Superpipeline Protocol for InfiniBand. In: Jeannot, E., Namyst, R., Roman, J. (eds.) Euro-Par 2011, Part II. LNCS, vol. 6853, pp. 276–287. Springer, Heidelberg (2011), http://hal.inria.fr/inria-00586015/

7. Dinaburg, A.: Bitsquatting, DNS hijacking without exploitation. In: Black Hat Conference (July 2011)

8. Feldmeier, D.C.: Fast software implementation of error detection codes. IEEE/ACM Trans. Netw. 3(6), 640–651 (1995), http://dx.doi.org/10.1109/90.477710

9. Fletcher, J.: An arithmetic checksum for serial transmissions. IEEE Transactions on Communications 30(1), 247–252 (1982)

10. Fowler, G., Noll, L.C., Vo, K.P., Eastlake, D.: The FNV non-cryptographic hash algorithm. IETF Internet-draft (March 2012)

11. Graham, R., Choi, S., Daniel, D., Desai, N., Minnich, R., Rasmussen, C., Risinger, L., Sukalski, M.: A network-failure-tolerant message-passing system for terascale clusters. International Journal of Parallel Programming 31(4) (2003)

12. Jenkins, B.: Hash functions. Dr Dobb's Journal (September 1997)

13. Maxino, T.C., Koopman, P.J.: The effectiveness of checksums for embedded control networks. IEEE Transactions on Dependable and Secure Computing 6(1) (January 2009)

14. Mercier, G., Trahay, F., Buntinas, D., Brunet, É.: NewMadeleine: An Efficient Support for High-Performance Networks in MPICH2. In: Proceedings of 23rd IEEE International Parallel and Distributed Processing Symposium (IPDPS 2009). IEEE Computer Society Press, Rome (2009), http://hal.archives-ouvertes.fr/hal-00360275

15. Shipman, G.M., Graham, R.L., Bosilca, G.: Network Fault Tolerance in Open MPI. In: Kermarrec, A.-M., Bougé, L., Priol, T. (eds.) Euro-Par 2007. LNCS, vol. 4641, pp. 868–878. Springer, Heidelberg (2007)

16. Zwaenepoel, D., Johnson, D.: Sender-based message logging. In: 17th International Symposium on Fault-Tolerant Computing

An Evaluation of User-Level Failure Mitigation Support in MPI

Wesley Bland[1], Aurelien Bouteiller[1], Thomas Herault[1], Joshua Hursey[2], George Bosilca[1], and Jack J. Dongarra[1]

[1] Innovative Computing Laboratory, University of Tennessee
{bland,bouteill,herault,bosilca,dongarra}@eecs.utk.edu
[2] Oak Ridge National Laboratory
hurseyjj@ornl.gov

Abstract. As the scale of computing platforms becomes increasingly extreme, the requirements for application fault tolerance are increasing as well. Techniques to address this problem by improving the resilience of algorithms have been developed, but they currently receive no support from the programming model, and without such support, they are bound to fail. This paper discusses the failure-free overhead and recovery impact aspects of the User-Level Failure Mitigation proposal presented in the MPI Forum. Experiments demonstrate that fault-aware MPI has little or no impact on performance for a range of applications, and produces satisfactory recovery times when there are failures.

1 Introduction

In a constant effort to deliver steady performance improvements, the size of High Performance Computing (HPC) systems, as observed by the Top 500 ranking[1], has grown tremendously over the last decade. This trend is unlikely to stop, as outlined by the International Exascale Software Project (IESP) [9] projection of the Exaflop platform, a milestone that should be reached as soon as 2019. Based on the foreseeable limits of the infrastructure costs, an Exaflop capable machine is expected to be built from gigahertz processing cores, with thousands of cores per computing node, thus requiring millions of computing cores to reach the mark. Even under the most optimistic assumptions about the individual components' reliability, probabilistic amplification from using millions of nodes has a dramatic impact on the Mean Time Between Failure (MTBF) of the entire platform. The probability of a failure happening *during the next hour* on an Exascale platform is disturbingly close to 1; thereby many computing nodes will inevitably fail during the execution of an application [7]. It is even more alarming that most popular fault tolerant approaches see their efficiency plummet at Exascale [3,4], calling for application centric failure mitigation strategies [15].

The prevalence of distributed memory machines promotes the use of the message passing model. An extensive and varied spectrum of domain science

---

[1] http://www.top500.org/

J.L. Träff, S. Benkner, and J. Dongarra (Eds.): EuroMPI 2012, LNCS 7490, pp. 193–203, 2012.
© Springer-Verlag Berlin Heidelberg 2012

applications depend on libraries compliant with the MPI standard[2]. Although unconventional programming paradigms are emerging [18,20], most delegate their data movements to MPI and it is widely acknowledged that MPI is here to stay. However, MPI has to evolve to effectively support the demanding requirements imposed by novel architectures, programing approaches, and dynamic runtime systems. In particular, its support for fault tolerance has always been inadequate [13]. To address the growing interest in fault-aware MPI, a working group has been formed in the context of the MPI Forum. Their User-Level Failure Mitigation (ULFM) [1] proposal features the basic interface and new semantics to enable applications and libraries to repair the state of MPI and tolerate failures. The purpose of this paper is to evaluate the tradeoffs that are needed for the integration of this fault mitigation specification and its impact (or lack thereof) on MPI performance and scalability. The contributions of this work are to evaluate the difficulties faced by MPI implementors, and demonstrate the feasibility of a low-impact implementation on the failure-free performance as well as an estimate of the recovery time of the MPI state after a failure.

The remainder of this paper is organized as follows: the next section introduces a short history of fault tolerance in MPI; Section 3 presents the constructs introduced by the proposal; Section 4 discusses the challenges faced by MPI implementors; then the performance impact of the implementation in Open MPI is discussed in Section 5 before we conclude in Section 6.

2   Related Work

Efforts toward fault tolerance in MPI have previously been attempted. Automatic fault tolerance [5,6] is a compelling approach for users, as failures are completely masked and handled internally by the MPI library, which requires no new interfaces to MPI or application code changes. Unfortunately, many recent studies point out that automatic approaches, either based on checkpoints or replication, will exhibit poor efficiency on Exaflop platforms [3,4].

Application Based Fault Tolerance (ABFT) [8,10,15] is another approach that promises better scalability, at the cost of significant algorithm and application code changes. Despite some limited successes [2,13], MPI interfaces need to be extended to effectively support ABFT. The most notable past effort is FT-MPI [11]. Several recovery modes were available to the user. In the *Blank* mode, failed processes were replaced by MPI_PROC_NULL; messages to and from them were silently ignored and collective algorithms had to be significantly modified. In the *Replace* mode, faulty processes were replaced with new processes. In all cases, only MPI_COMM_WORLD would be repaired and the application was in charge of rebuilding any other communicators, leading to difficult library composition. No standardization effort was pursued, and it was mostly used as a playground for understanding the fundamental concepts.

A more recent effort to introduce failure handling mechanisms was the Run-Through Stabilization proposal [16]. This proposal introduced many new

---

[2] http://mpi-forum.org/docs/mpi-2.2/mpi22-report.pdf

constructs for MPI including the ability to "validate" communicators as a way of marking failure as recognized and allowing the application to continue using the communicator. It included other new ideas such as Failure Handlers for uniform failure notification. Because of the implementation complexity imposed by resuming operations on failed communicators, this proposal was eventually unsuccessful in its introduction to the MPI Standard.

3   New MPI Constructs

This section succinctly presents the prominent interfaces proposed to enable effective support of User-Level Failure Mitigation for MPI applications. The interested reader can refer to the technical document for a complete description of the interfaces [1] and to the amended standard draft[3].

Designing the mechanism that users would use to manage failures was built around three concepts: 1) simplicity, the API should be easy to understand and use in most common scenarios; 2) flexibility, the API should allow varied fault tolerant models to be built as external libraries and; 3) absence of deadlock, no MPI call (point-to-point or collective) can block indefinitely after a failure, but must either succeed or raise an MPI error. Two major pitfalls must be avoided: jitter prone, permanent monitoring of the health of peers a process is not actively communicating with, and expensive consensus required for returning consistent errors at all ranks. The operative principle is then that errors (`MPI_ERR_PROC_-FAILED`) are not indicative of the return status on remote processes, but are raised only at a particular rank, when a particular operation cannot complete because a participating peer has failed. The following functions provide the basic blocks for maintaining consistency and enabling recovery of the state of MPI.

`MPI_COMM_FAILURE_ACK` & `MPI_COMM_FAILURE_GET_ACKED`: These two calls allow the application to determine which processes within a communicator have failed. The acknowledgement function serves to mark a point in time which will be used as a reference. The function to get the acknowledged failures refers back to this reference point and returns the group of processes which were locally known to have failed. After acknowledging failures, the application can resume `MPI_ANY_SOURCE` point-to-point operations between non-failed processes, but operations involving failed processes (such as collective operations) will likely continue to raise errors.

`MPI_COMM_REVOKE`: Because failure detection is not global to the communicator, some processes may raise an error for an operation, while others do not. This inconsistency in error reporting may result in some processes continuing their normal, failure-free execution path, while others have diverged to the recovery execution path. As an example, if a process, unaware of the failure, posts a reception from another process that has switched to the recovery path, the matching send will never be posted. Yet no failed process participates in the operation

---

[3] http://svn.mpi-forum.org/trac/mpi-forum-web/ticket/323

and it should not raise an error. The receive operation is effectively deadlocked. The revoke operation provides a mechanism for the application to resolve such situations before entering the recovery path. A revoked communicator becomes improper for further communication, and all future or pending communications on this communicator will be interrupted and completed with the new error code MPI_ERR_REVOKED. It is notable that although this operation is not collective (a process can enter it alone), it affects remote ranks without a matching call.

MPI_COMM_SHRINK: The shrink operation allows the application to create a new communicator by eliminating all failed processes from a revoked communicator. The operation is collective and performs a consensus algorithm to ensure that all participating processes complete the operation with equivalent groups in the new communicator. This function cannot return an error due to process failure. Instead, such errors are absorbed as part of the consensus algorithms and will be excluded from the resulting communicator.

MPI_COMM_AGREE: This operation provides an agreement algorithm which can be used to determine a consistent state between processes when such strong consistency is necessary. The function is collective and forms an agreement over a boolean value, even when failures have happened or the communicator has been revoked. The agreement can be used to resolve a number of consistency issues after a failure, such as uniform completion of an algorithmic phase or collective operation, or as a key building block for strongly consistent failure handling approaches (such as transactions).

4   Implementation Issues

In this section, we detail the challenges and advantages of the aforementioned MPI constructs. They unfold along three main axes, the amount of supplementary state and memory to be kept within the MPI library, the additional operations to be executed on the critical path of communication routines, and the algorithmic cost of failure recovery routines. We discuss, in general, options available to implementors, and highlight issues with insight from a prototype implementation in Open MPI [12].

4.1   Impact on Communication Routines

Memory: Because a communicator cannot be repaired, tracking the state of failed processes imposes a minimal memory overhead. From a practical perspective each node needs a global list of detected failures, shared by all communicators; its size grows linearly with the number of failures, and it is empty as long as no failures occur. Within each communicator, the supplementary state is limited to two values: whether the communicator is revoked or not, and an index in the global list of failures denoting the last acknowledged failure (with MPI_COMM_FAILURE_ACK). For efficiency reasons, an implementation may decide to cache the fact that some failures have happened in the communicator so that collective operations and `MPI_ANY_SOURCE` receptions can bail out quickly. Overall, the supplementary memory consumption from fault tolerant constructs is small, independent of the total number of nodes, and unlikely to affect the cache and TLB hit rates.

Conditionals: Another concern is the number of supplementary conditions on the latency critical path. Indeed, most completion operations require a supplementary conditional statement to handle the case where the underlying communication context has been revoked. However, the prediction branching logic of the processor can be hinted to favor the failure free outcome, resulting in a single load of a cached value and a single, mostly well-predicted, branching instruction, unlikely to affect the instruction pipeline. It is notable that non-blocking operations raise errors related to process failure only during the completion step, and thus do not need to check for revocation before the latency critical section.

Matching Logic: `MPI_COMM_REVOKE` does not have a matching call on other processes on which it has an effect. As such, it might add detrimental complexity to the matching logic. However, any MPI implementation needs to handle unexpected messages. The order of revocation message delivery is loose enough that the handling of revocation notices can be integrated within the existing unexpected message matching logic. In our implementation in Open MPI, we leverage the active message low level transport layer to introduce revocation as a new active message tag, without a single change to the matching logic.

Collective Operations: A typical MPI implementation supports a large number of collective algorithms, which are dynamically selected depending on criteria such as communicator or message size and hardware topology. The loose requirements of the proposal concerning error reporting of process failures in collective operations limits the impact it has on collective operations. Typically, the collective communication algorithms and selection logic are left unchanged. The only new requirement is that failures happening at any rank of the communicator cause all processes to exit the collective (successfully for some, with an error for others). Due to the underlying loosely-connected topologies used by some algorithms, a point-to-point based implementation of a collective communication is unlikely to detect all process failures. Fortunately, a practical implementation exists that does not require modifying any of the collective operations: when a rank raises an error because of a process failure, it can revoke an internal, temporary communication context associated with the collective operation. As the revocation notice propagates on the internal communicator, it interrupts the point-to-point operations of the collective. An error code is returned to the high level MPI wrapper, which in turn raises the appropriate error on the user's communicator.

4.2   Recovery Routines

Some of the recovery routines described in Section 3 are unique in their ability to deliver a valid result despite the occurrence of failures. This specification of correct behavior across failures calls for resilient, more complex algorithms. In most cases, these functions are intended to be called sparingly by users, only after actual failures have happened, as a means of recovering a consistent state across all processes. The remainder of this section describes the algorithms that can be used to deliver this specification and their cost.

Agreement: The agreement can be conceptualized as a failure-resilient reduction on a boolean value. Many agreement algorithms have been proposed in the literature; the log-scaling two-phase consensus algorithm used by the ULFM prototype is one of many possible implementations of `MPI_COMM_AGREE` operation based upon prior work in the field. Specifically, this algorithm is a variation of the multi-level two-phase commit algorithms [19]. The algorithm first performs a reduction of the input values to an elected coordinator in the communicator. The coordinator then makes a decision on the output value and broadcasts that value back to all of the alive processes in the communicator. The complexity of the agreement algorithm appears when adapting to an emerging process failure of the coordinator and/or participants. A more extensive discussion of the algorithmic complexity has been published by Hursey, et.al. [17]. The algorithmic complexity of this implementation is $O(log(n))$ for the failure free case, matching that of an `MPI_ALLREDUCE` operation over the alive processes in the communicator.

Revoke: Although the revoke operation is not collective, the revocation notification needs to be propagated to all alive processes in the specified communicator, even when new failures happen during the revoke propagation. These requirements are not without recalling those from the *reliable broadcast* [14]. Among the four defining qualities of a reliable broadcast (*Termination, Validity, Integrity, Agreement*), the termination and integrity criteria can be relaxed in the context of the revoke algorithm. If a failure during the Revoke algorithm kills the initiator as well as all the already notified processes, the Revoke notification is indeed lost, but the observed behavior, from the view of the application, is indiscernible from a failure at the initiator before the propagation started. As the algorithm still ensures agreement, there are no opportunities for inconsistent views.

In the ULFM implementation, we used a naive flooding algorithm for simplicity. The initiator marks the communicator as revoked and sends a Revoke message to every processes in the groups (local and remote) of the communicator. Upon reception of a revoke message, if the communicator is not already revoked, it is revoked and the process acts as a new initiator. Better algorithms exist, but even this naive approach provides reasonable performance (see Section 5) considering it is called only in response to an actual failure.

Shrink: The Shrink operation is, algorithmically, an agreement on which the consensus is done on the group of failed processes. Hence, the two operations have the same algorithmic complexity. Indeed, in the prototype implementation, `MPI_COMM_AGREE` and `MPI_COMM_SHRINK` share the same internal implementation of the agreement.

5 Performance Analysis

The following analysis used a prototype of the ULFM proposal based on the development trunk of Open MPI [12] (r26237). The test results presented were gathered from the Smoky system at Oak Ridge National Laboratory. Each node contains four quad-core 2.0 GHz AMD Opteron processors with 2 GB of memory per compute core. Compute nodes are connected with gigabit Ethernet and InfiniBand. Some shared-memory benchmarks were conducted on Romulus, a 6×8-core AMD Opteron 6180 SE with 256GB of memory (32GB per socket) at the University of Tennessee.

The NetPIPE benchmark (v3.7) was used to assess the 1-byte latency and bandwidth impact of the modifications necessary for the ULFM support in Open MPI. We compare the vanilla version of Open MPI (r26237) with the ULFM enabled version on Smoky. Table 1 highlights the fact that the differences in performance are well below the noise limit, and that the standard deviation is negligible proving the performance stability and lack of impact.

Table 1. NetPIPE results on Smoky

1-byte Latency (microseconds) (cache hot)					
Interconnect	Vanilla	Std. Dev.	Enabled	Std. Dev.	Difference
Shared Memory	0.8008	0.0093	0.8016	0.0161	0.0008
TCP	10.2564	0.0946	10.2776	0.1065	0.0212
OpenIB	4.9637	0.0018	4.9650	0.0022	0.0013

Bandwidth (Mbps) (cache hot)					
Interconnect	Vanilla	Std. Dev.	Enabled	Std. Dev.	Difference
Shared Memory	10,625.92	23.46	10,602.68	30.73	-23.24
TCP	6,311.38	14.42	6,302.75	10.72	-8.63
OpenIB	9,688.85	3.29	9,689.13	3.77	0.28

The impact on shared memory systems, which are sensitive even to small modifications of the MPI library, has been further assessed on the Romulus machine – a large shared memory machine – using the IMB benchmark suite (v3.2.3). As shown in Figure 1, the duration difference of all the benchmarks (point-to-point and collective) remains below 5%, thus within the standard deviation of the implementation on that machine.

To measure the impact of the prototype on a real application, we used the Sequoia AMG benchmark[4]. This MPI intensive benchmark is an Algebraic Mult-Grid (AMG) linear system solver for unstructured mesh physics. A weak scaling study was conducted up to 512 processes following the problem *Set 5*. In Figure 2, we compare the time slicing of three main phases (Solve, Setup, and SStruct) of the benchmark, with, side by side, the vanilla version of the Open MPI implementation, and the ULFM enabled one. The application itself is not fault tolerant and does not use the features proposed in ULFM. The goal of this benchmark is to demonstrate that a careful implementation of the proposed semantic does not impact the performance of the MPI implementation, and ultimately leaves the behavior and performance of legacy applications unchanged. The results show that the performance difference is negligible.

---

[4] https://asc.llnl.gov/sequoia/benchmarks/#amg

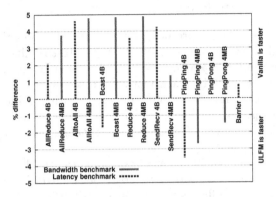

Fig. 1. The Intel MPI Benchmarks: relative difference between ULFM and the vanilla Open MPI on shared memory (Romulus). Standard deviation ≈5% on 1,000 runs.

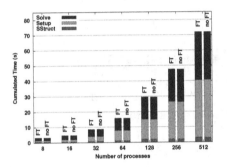
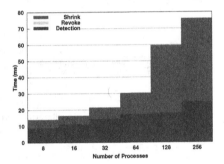

Fig. 2. Comparison of the vanilla and ULFM versions of Open MPI running Sequoia-AMG at different scales (Smoky)

Fig. 3. Evaluation of the Fault Injection Benchmark with full recovery at different scales (Smoky)

To assess the overheads of recovery constructs, we developed a synthetic benchmark that mimics the behavior of a typical fixed-size tightly-coupled fault-tolerant application. Unlike a normal application it performs an infinite loop, where each iteration contains a failure and the corresponding recovery procedure. Each iteration consists of 5 phases: in the first phase (*Detection*), all processes but a designated victim enter a Barrier on the intracommunicator. The victim dies, and the failure detection mechanism makes all surviving processes exit the Barrier, some with an error code. In Phase 2 (*Revoke*), the surviving processes that detected a process-failure related error during the previous phase invoke the new construct `MPI_COMM_REVOKE`. Then they proceed to Phase 3 (*Shrink*) where the intracommunicator is shrunk using `MPI_COMM_SHRINK`. The two other phases serve to repair a full-size intracommunicator using spawn and intercommunicator merge operations to allow the benchmark to proceed to the next round.

In Figure 3, we present the timing of each phase, averaged upon 50 iterations of the benchmark loop, for a varying number of processes on the Smoky machine. We focus on the three points related to ULFM: failure detection, revoke and shrink. The failure detection is mildly impacted by the scale. In the prototype implementation, the detection happens at two levels, either in the runtime system or in the MPI library (when it occurs on an active link). Between the two detectors, all ranks get notified within 30ms of the failure (this compares to the 1s timeout at the link level). Although the revoke call will inject a linear number of messages (at each rank) in the network to implement the level of reliability required for this operation, the duration of this call itself is under $50\mu s$ and is not visible in the figure. The network is disturbed for a longer period, due to the processing of the messages, but this disturbance will appear in the network only after a failure occurred. The last call shown in the figure is the shrink operation. Although its duration increases linearly with the number of processes (the figure has a logarithmic scale on the x-axis), this cost must only be paid after a failure, in order to continue using collective operations. In its current implementation, shrink requires an agreement, the allocation of a new communicator identifier, and the creation of the communicator (with `MPI_COMM_SPLIT`). Most of the time spent in the shrink operation is not in the agreement (which scales logarithmically), but in the underlying implementation of the communicator creation.

6   Conclusion

Many responsible voices agree that sharp increases in the volatility of future, extreme scale computing platforms are likely to imperil our ability to use them for advanced applications that deliver meaningful scientific results and maximize research productivity. Moreover, it is clear that any techniques developed to address this volatility must be supported in the programming and execution model. Since MPI is currently, and will likely continue to be – in the medium-term – both the de-facto programming model for distributed applications and the default execution model for large scale platforms running at the bleeding edge, MPI is the place in the software infrastructure where semantic and run-time support for application faults needs to be provided.

The ULFM proposal is a careful but important step forward toward accomplishing this goal. It not only delivers support for a number of new and innovative resilience techniques, it provides this support through a simple, straightforward and familiar API that requires minimal modifications of the underlying MPI implementation. Moreover, it is backward compatible with previous versions of the MPI standard, so that non fault-tolerant applications (legacy or otherwise) are supported without any changes to the code. Perhaps most significantly, applications can use ULFM-enabled MPI without experiencing any degradation in their performance, as we demonstrate in this paper.

Several applications, ranging from Master-Worker to tightly coupled, are currently being refactored to take advantage of the semantics in this proposal. Beyond applications, the expressivity of this proposal is investigated in the context of providing extended fault tolerance models as convenience, portable libraries.

References

1. Bland, W., Bosilca, G., Bouteiller, A., Herault, T., Dongarra, J.: A proposal for User-Level Failure Mitigation in the MPI-3 standard. Tech. rep., Department of Electrical Engineering and Computer Science, University of Tennessee (2012)
2. Bland, W., Du, P., Bouteiller, A., Herault, T., Bosilca, G., Dongarra, J.: A Checkpoint-on-Failure Protocol for Algorithm-Based Recovery in Standard MPI. In: Kaklamanis, C., Papatheodorou, P., Spirakis, P.G. (eds.) Euro-Par 2012. LNCS, vol. 7484, pp. 477–488. Springer, Heidelberg (2012)
3. Bosilca, G., Bouteiller, A., Brunet, É., Cappello, F., Dongarra, J., Guermouche, A., Hérault, T., Robert, Y., Vivien, F., Zaidouni, D.: Unified Model for Assessing Checkpointing Protocols at Extreme-Scale. Tech. report RR-7950, INRIA (2012)
4. Bougeret, M., Casanova, H., Robert, Y., Vivien, F., Zaidouni, D.: Using group replication for resilience on exascale systems. Tech. Rep. 265, LAWNs (2012)
5. Bouteiller, A., Bosilca, G., Dongarra, J.: Redesigning the message logging model for high performance. CCPE 22(16), 2196–2211 (2010)
6. Buntinas, D., Coti, C., Herault, T., Lemarinier, P., Pilard, L., Rezmerita, A., Rodriguez, E., Cappello, F.: Blocking vs. non-blocking coordinated checkpointing for large-scale fault tolerant MPI protocols. FGCS 24(1), 73–84 (2008)
7. Cappello, F., Geist, A., Gropp, B., Kalé, L.V., Kramer, B., Snir, M.: Toward exascale resilience. IJHPCA 23(4), 374–388 (2009)
8. Davies, T., Karlsson, C., Liu, H., Ding, C., Chen, Z.: High Performance Linpack Benchmark: A Fault Tolerant Implementation without Checkpointing. In: 25th ICS, pp. 162–171. ACM (2011)
9. Dongarra, J., Beckman, P., et al.: The international exascale software roadmap. IJHPCA 25(11), 3–60 (2011)
10. Du, P., Bouteiller, A., et al.: Algorithm-based fault tolerance for dense matrix factorizations. In: 17th SIGPLAN PPoPP, pp. 225–234. ACM (2012)
11. Fagg, G.E., Dongarra, J.J.: FT-MPI: Fault Tolerant MPI, Supporting Dynamic Applications in a Dynamic World. In: Dongarra, J., Kacsuk, P., Podhorszki, N. (eds.) EuroPVM/MPI 2000. LNCS, vol. 1908, pp. 346–353. Springer, Heidelberg (2000)
12. Gabriel, E., Fagg, G.E., Bosilca, G., Angskun, T., Dongarra, J., Squyres, J.M., Sahay, V., Kambadur, P., Barrett, B.W., Lumsdaine, A., Castain, R.H., Daniel, D.J., Graham, R.L., Woodall, T.S.: Open MPI: Goals, Concept, and Design of a Next Generation MPI Implementation. In: Kranzlmüller, D., Kacsuk, P., Dongarra, J. (eds.) EuroPVM/MPI 2004. LNCS, vol. 3241, pp. 97–104. Springer, Heidelberg (2004)
13. Gropp, W., Lusk, E.: Fault tolerance in message passing interface programs. IJHPCA 18, 363–372 (2004)
14. Hadzilacos, V., Toueg, S.: Fault-tolerant broadcasts and related problems. In: Distributed Systems, 2nd edn., pp. 97–145. ACM/Addison-Wesley (1993)
15. Huang, K., Abraham, J.: Algorithm-based fault tolerance for matrix operations. IEEE Transactions on Computers 100(6), 518–528 (1984)
16. Hursey, J., Graham, R.L., Bronevetsky, G., Buntinas, D., Pritchard, H., Solt, D.G.: Run-Through Stabilization: An MPI Proposal for Process Fault Tolerance. In: Cotronis, Y., Danalis, A., Nikolopoulos, D.S., Dongarra, J. (eds.) EuroMPI 2011. LNCS, vol. 6960, pp. 329–332. Springer, Heidelberg (2011)

17. Hursey, J., Naughton, T., Vallee, G., Graham, R.L.: A Log-Scaling Fault Tolerant Agreement Algorithm for a Fault Tolerant MPI. In: Cotronis, Y., Danalis, A., Nikolopoulos, D.S., Dongarra, J. (eds.) EuroMPI 2011. LNCS, vol. 6960, pp. 255–263. Springer, Heidelberg (2011)

18. Lusk, E., Chan, A.: Early Experiments with the OpenMP/MPI Hybrid Programming Model. In: Eigenmann, R., de Supinski, B.R. (eds.) IWOMP 2008. LNCS, vol. 5004, pp. 36–47. Springer, Heidelberg (2008)

19. Mohan, C., Lindsay, B.: Efficient commit protocols for the tree of processes model of distributed transactions. In: SIGOPS OSR, vol. 19, pp. 40–52. ACM (1985)

20. Sterling, T.: HPC in Phase Change: Towards a New Execution Model. In: Palma, J.M.L.M., Daydé, M., Marques, O., Lopes, J.C. (eds.) VECPAR 2010. LNCS, vol. 6449, p. 31. Springer, Heidelberg (2011)

Efficient MPI Implementation
of a Parallel, Stable Merge Algorithm

Christian Siebert[1] and Jesper Larsson Träff[2]

[1] RWTH Aachen University and German Research School
for Simulation Sciences GmbH
Schinkelstrasse 2a, 52062 Aachen, Germany
`c.siebert@grs-sim.de`
[2] Vienna University of Technology, Institute of Information Systems
Research Group Parallel Computing
Favoritenstrasse 16, 1040 Wien, Austria
`traff@par.tuwien.ac.at`

Abstract. We study different approaches to implement an optimal, stable two-way merge algorithm for distributed-memory parallel architectures. The algorithm takes as input two ordered sequences, which are distributed blockwise across all available processes such that each process owns a block of elements of each sequence. The task for each process is to produce an ordered block of elements from the stable merge of the input sequences. We present an optimal, perfectly load-balanced, stable parallel algorithm that accomplishes this task. We describe three different implementation alternatives using one-sided communication of the Message-Passing Interface (MPI). Further, we discuss problematic issues with the current MPI 2.2 one-sided interface and enabling features that may be found in future versions of the MPI standard. Experimental results on a large IBM Blue Gene/P supercomputer show perfect scalability of our implementation: with a fixed input size per process the running time remains (almost) constant with increasing number of processes, and with a fixed total problem size our implementation improves the time to solution for up to 32,768 MPI processes.

1   Introduction

Merging of ordered sequences is a fundamental operation in many applications and a key ingredient for many parallel, notably sorting algorithms. As such it has been studied intensively. However, most parallel merging algorithms are designed for shared-memory architectures [1–3, 5, 6, 10, 11], and only few algorithms have been described [4] and fewer implemented for distributed-memory architectures. For instance, the latter BSP algorithm builds on shared-memory algorithms that are both unnecessarily complicated and potentially inefficient, in terms of both non-dominant splitting overhead and achieved load balance. Although this algorithm could be implemented in MPI, we are not aware of any such implementation. In this paper we describe an algorithm that is both simpler to implement and better in terms of load balance and overhead. Although

J.L. Träff, S. Benkner, and J. Dongarra (Eds.): EuroMPI 2012, LNCS 7490, pp. 204–213, 2012.

similar in nature to the algorithm presented in [2], our algorithm was discovered independently. A specific improvement is that our algorithm is stable, a desirable property for inputs with duplicate elements. The algorithm employs a logarithmic time preprocessing step, very similar to binary search, which can be naturally expressed with one-sided communication. The specific contribution for the MPI community is that we analyze and experimentally compare implementation alternatives with the one-sided communication model of MPI 2.2 [7]; and show that some of the resulting problems can be resolved with the one-sided model proposed for the upcoming MPI 3.0 standard (see www.mpi-forum.org).

2   Distributed, Stable Two-Way Merging

Let stable_merge(A, B) denote the stable merge of two ordered arrays A and B. Stability means that elements of A that are equal to elements of B are placed before the elements of B in the output, and that the relative order of any sequence of equal elements in either A or B is preserved in the output. The distributed, stable merging problem is the following. The two ordered arrays A and B with m and n elements, respectively, are distributed blockwise across the available p processes, such that process r for $0 \leq r < p$ has a block of m_r consecutive elements $A[s_r^A, \ldots, s_r^A + m_r - 1]$ and a block of n_r consecutive elements $B[s_r^B, \ldots, s_r^B + n_r - 1]$ with start indices $s_r^A = \sum_{i=0}^{r-1} m_i$ and $s_r^B = \sum_{i=0}^{r-1} n_i$, respectively. Each process r produces a block $C[s_r^A + s_r^B, \ldots, s_r^A + s_r^B + m_r + n_r - 1]$ of consecutive elements of $C = $ stable_merge(A, B).

All parallel merge algorithms divide the input sequences into smaller, disjoint, consecutive sequences, that can be merged pairwise in parallel into the corresponding positions of the output array. Our algorithm accomplishes this by using the following idea: given an index i (say the start index $s_r^A + s_r^B$ in C for process r) in the output array C, determine the two indices j and k in the input arrays A and B, such that stably merging the prefixes $A[0, \ldots, j-1]$ and $B[0, \ldots, k-1]$ will produce exactly the prefix $C[0, \ldots, i-1]$ of the stably merged result $C = $ stable_merge(A, B). We call j and k the *co-ranks* of i. Put differently, j and k index the first elements of A and B that are *not* among the first i elements of the stably merged output C. For any process r the co-ranks of the start indices $i_r = s_r^A + s_r^B$ and $i_{r+1} = s_{r+1}^A + s_{r+1}^B$ will determine exactly the blocks of A and B needed to produce the output sequence of C for process r. Based on these co-ranks, process r can also determine from which processes to get the input blocks, and perform a local merge on them to produce the final result. All that is needed is an efficient algorithm for computing the co-ranks for any given index i in C. We present and discuss such an algorithm below.

The sequential co-ranking algorithm is given as a C program fragment in Figure 1. It maintains the invariant that $i = j + k$. For both j and k indices lower bound indices are also maintained. For any given input index i with $0 \leq i < m + n$ it chooses the largest possible j index in A, and starts out with the assumption that $A[j-1] \leq B[k]$, meaning that all elements of A up to j have to come before the B elements in stable_merge(A, B). If this is not the case,

```
// initialize start indices, invariant i = j+k, j as large as possible
j = min(i,m); k = i-j; j_low = max(0,i-n); // k_low set in first iteration
active = 1;
do {
    // converge indices to the co-ranks
    if (j>0&&k<n&&A[j-1]>B[k]) {
        delta = (1+j-j_low)/2;
        k_low = k;
        j -= delta; k += delta;
    } else if (k>0&&j<m&&B[k-1]>=A[j]) {
        delta = (1+k-k_low)/2;
        j_low = j;
        k -= delta; j += delta;
    } else active = 0; // co-ranks found
} while (active);
```

Fig. 1. Algorithm to find the co-ranks j and k for an index i in the output array C

the index j in A is decreased by halving the interval between j and its lower index j_low. Should it turn out that $B[k-1] \geq A[j]$ then instead the k index in B is decreased. To maintain the invariant, whenever either index is halved, the other index is increased by the same amount. The lower bound indices are chosen such that the array bounds m and n cannot be exceeded when an index is increased. Note that the lower index k_low for k does not need to be initialized separately, since at the beginning only the first if condition may be true, which will cause this index to be initialized properly.

Analysis shows that the algorithm takes at most $\lceil \log_2(\min(m,n)) \rceil + 1$ iterations, since the value delta is halved in each iteration, regardless of which branch is taken, and delta is initially at most $\min(m,n)$. For brevity, we omit the proof that the co-ranks indeed correspond to the indices for the prefixes needed to produce a stable merge here, although it is not difficult to see.

The distributed version of the algorithm has the input arrays A and B distributed over all processes. The accesses to the array fields therefore potentially entail remote accesses to the memory of other processes. The fully distributed, stable merge algorithm for each process r can be stated as follows:

1. Let $i_r = s_r^A + s_r^B$ be the start index for process r in the output array C. Compute the co-ranks j_r and k_r via a distributed version of Algorithm 1.
2. Get the co-ranks j_{r+1} and k_{r+1} from process $r+1$ (the last process $r = p-1$ sets $j_{r+1} = j_r + m_r = m$ and $k_{r+1} = k_r + n_r = n$).
3. Get $A[j_r \ldots j_{r+1}-1]$ and $B[k_r \ldots k_{r+1}-1]$ from the processes that own these array blocks via communication.
4. Locally compute stable_merge($A[j_r \ldots j_{r+1}-1], B[k_r \ldots k_{r+1}-1]$) to produce the final result $C[i_r \ldots i_{r+1} - 1]$.

Theorem 1. *Let $m_r + n_r$ be the maximum number of elements for some process. The above algorithm merges two sequences in time $\mathcal{O}(\log(\min(m,n)) + m_r + n_r)$.*

Proof. We assume the co-ranking algorithm used in Step 1 is correct. It completes in $\mathcal{O}(\log(\min(m,n)))$ iterations with at most 4 single-element remote memory accesses per iteration. Step 2 requires a communication of only two values. The data exchange in step 3 communicates a total volume of $m_k + n_k$ elements. With a balanced distribution of the arrays, each array block $A[j_r,\ldots,j_{r+1}-1]$ spans a constant number of processes, so getting the block takes a constant number of communication steps with a total volume of $m_k + n_k$ elements. The local stable merge in Step 4 takes $\mathcal{O}(m_k + n_k)$ operations. In total, our distributed merge algorithm therefore completes in time $\mathcal{O}(\log(\min(m,n)) + m_r + n_r)$. $\square$

The proof assumes that any concurrent read accesses that may occur during Step 1 and Step 3 can be handled efficiently.

3   Implementation Alternatives

The distributed merge algorithm has a straight-forward implementation with any communication interface that supports one-sided communication. Indeed, the MPI 2.2 one-sided communication model [7, Chapter 11] should in principle enable an efficient, highly portable implementation. It offers different implementation alternatives, which we evaluate for our algorithm. The algorithm consists of two main communication phases: first, the co-ranking algorithm requires $\mathcal{O}(\log(\min(m,n)))$ potentially remote single-word accesses per process. The binary search like pattern is data dependent, therefore irregular, and in each iteration only the source process knows which data elements to assess on which processes. This phase is thus a paradigmatic case for one-sided communication. We note that a standard binary search follows much the same pattern, which makes our implementation alternatives also relevant for distributed binary searches in general. During the other main communication phase in Step 3, each process copies the array blocks needed for the local merge. This step can also be expressed conveniently with one-sided communication.

For the implementation alternatives that use the MPI 2.2 one-sided model, we assume that the input arrays A and B are exposed in (two disjoint) *communication windows*. The alternatives differ in how accesses to the windows are synchronized. We assume that for any global array index i each process r can efficiently (that is, in constant time) compute both: the rank of the target process that owns the corresponding block of A and B, and the local index in the block. This can easily be done for regular distributions of the A and B arrays. Note, however that the correctness of our implementations does not require any specific distribution. Each iteration in Step 1 performs up to four MPI_Get operations, namely to access array elements $A[j-1]$, $B[k]$ and $A[j]$, $B[k-1]$. This can be optimized further by aggregating two or more accesses, if they are located on the same process. For ease of exposition, we do not discuss such (minor) improvements.

3.1 Active Target Synchronization with an Upper Bound of Fences

The first implementation variant uses active target synchronization via a collective *fence* operations. Each iteration of Algorithm 1 becomes a global access epoch, which is surrounded by MPI_Win_fence for each window. In an epoch, each process performs up to four remote memory accesses with MPI_Get. The actual number of iterations that is needed to determine the co-ranks is data-dependent. Therefore, the processes do not necessarily perform the same number of iterations. This is a problem because the collective MPI_Win_fence operation must be called by all processes. One solution is shown in Algorithm 2: it imposes a worst-case upper bound on the number of epochs. Processes that complete the co-ranking procedure early, perform empty epochs to keep in sync with the remaining, potentially still active, processes. An upper bound on the number of iterations is $\lceil \log_2(\min(m,n)) \rceil + 1$.

```
j = min(i,m); k = i-j; j_low = max(0,i-n);
upper = ceil(log2(min(m,n)))+1; active = 1;
do {
    MPI_Win_fence(MODE_NOPUT|MODE_NOPRECEDE);    // (1) start access epoch
    // on both A and B window (not shown)
    if (j>0) a1=GET(A[j-1]); if (k<n) b1=GET(B[k]);
    if (k>0) b2=GET(B[k-1]); if (j<m) a2=GET(A[j]);
    MPI_Win_fence(MODE_NOSTORE|MODE_NOSUCCEED); // (2) end access epoch
    if (j>0&&k<n&&a1>b1) {
        delta = (1+j-j_low)/2;
        k_low = k;
        j -= delta; k += delta;
    } else if (k>0&&j<m&&b2>=a2) {
        delta = (1+k-k_low)/2;
        j_low = j;
        k -= delta; j += delta;
    } else active = 0;
    upper--;
} while (active);
// execute epochs until upper bound is reached
while (upper-- > 0) {
    MPI_Win_fence(MODE_NOPUT|MODE_NOPRECEDE);    // mimic (1)
    MPI_Win_fence(MODE_NOSTORE|MODE_NOSUCCEED);  // mimic (2)
}
```

Fig. 2. Co-ranking using collective fences and an upper bound on number of iterations

The GET functionality determines both the target process and the local index on that process for a given global index. It calls MPI_Get to remotely access this element. Since all (local and remote) accesses to the input arrays are read-only, we use the MPI assertions MPI_MODE_NOPUT and MPI_MODE_NOSTORE as optimization hints to the MPI library. The additional MPI_MODE_NOPRECEDE and MPI_MODE_NOSUCCEED assertions indicate that there is no active epoch before the opening and after the closing fence. An optimization not considered here would use only a single fence between iterations, but the last assertion pair could be expected to ensure this behavior. With the Blue Gene/P MPI implementation however, there was no performance difference whether these assertions were used or not, which suggests some room for improvement within the MPI library.

3.2   Active Target Synchronization with Global Reduction

Our first implementation variant uses a precalculated upper bound on the number of iterations. However, this is a theoretical worst case and might in practice be too large. If all processes find their co-ranks faster, all extraneous fences consume unnecessary time. To avoid these superfluous fences, we determine at the end of each epoch whether all processes have finished co-ranking. This is accomplished by an MPI_Allreduce at the end of each iteration. Each process contributes its local active flag. Local flag values are combined with a logical "or", and the result tells every process whether there are still active processes. This variant is shown in Algorithm 3. Everything in [...] is as in Algorithm 2.

```
[...]
active = 1;
do {
    MPI_Win_fence(MODE_NOPUT|MODE_NOPRECEDE);    // (1) start access epoch
    if (j>0) a1=GET(A[j-1]); if (k<n) b1=GET(B[k]);
    if (k>0) b2=GET(B[k-1]); if (j<m) a2=GET(A[j]);
    MPI_Win_fence(MODE_NOSTORE|MODE_NOSUCCEED);  // (2) end access epoch
    [...]
    MPI_Allreduce(MPI_IN_PLACE,&active,1,MPI_INT,MPI_LOR,MPI_COMM_WORLD);
} while (active);
```

Fig. 3. Active one-sided variant with MPI_Allreduce to determine termination

This variant can never use more iterations than the first implementation. However, whenever the number of iterations of some rank is close to the upper bound, the extra MPI_Allreduce calls are "pure overhead". Unfortunately, without doing the actual co-ranking, there is no way to tell in advance whether Algorithm 2 or 3 is preferable. The MPI standard might be able to help with the general problem exposed by this example, namely to detect epochs where there is no communication activity. A fence operation could report back whether the epoch had any one-sided communication activity – in many cases, the MPI library implementation would have to detect this internally anyway.

Both variants so far have the drawback of adding a collective call to each iteration of the co-ranking algorithm, thus increasing the worst-case complexity by a factor reflecting the time for a collective fence and global reduction operation.

3.3   Passive Target Synchronization with Shared Locks

The third implementation variant uses passive target synchronization. The advantage here is that no collective operations as in the previous variants are required. Since we need the actual data directly after the GET call, each MPI_Get is encapsulated by MPI_Win_lock() and MPI_Win_unlock() operations. All remote accesses are read operations, thus we can allow concurrent accesses by specifying the lock to be shared. Although this implementation involves lock overhead, the processes can now work and terminate independently. The optional assertion MPI_MODE_NOCHECK indicates to the MPI library that accesses are not conflicting (shared and exclusive). On the Jugene system (see Section 4), this assertion improves the performance of the co-ranking by up to 640% at $32k$ MPI processes.

```
double GET(global_pos, window)
{
    target_rank = ...global_pos...; // compute rank from global index
    local_pos = ...global_pos...;   // compute local index
    MPI_Win_lock(MPI_LOCK_SHARED,target_rank,MPI_MODE_NOCHECK,window);
    MPI_Get(result,1,MPI_DOUBLE,target_rank,local_pos,1,MPI_DOUBLE,window);
    MPI_Win_unlock(target_rank,window);
    return result;
}
```

Fig. 4. The GET functionality for the lock variant implementation

The MPI 2.2 one-sided model allows to perform the lock on only one process at a time, which limits concurrency between MPI_Get calls within each iteration. A different interface might potentially yield better performance. One-sided communication interfaces such as ARMCI [8] or SHMEM [9] define their one-sided communication operations to be explicitly blocking or nonblocking, which gives further opportunities to increase concurrency as discussed in the next section.

3.4   MPI 3.0

The proposed MPI 3.0 standard (available at www.mpi-forum.org) considerably extends the MPI 2.2 one-sided communication model and does address some of the problems discussed above. In particular, it introduces new MPI_Rget and MPI_Rput one-sided communication operations, which return a request object. Inside the epoch it is possible to complete such operations by issuing an MPI_Wait on this request. With this feature, the whole merge algorithm could be performed in a single MPI_Win_fence epoch. Each process would independently iterate, and enforce completion of the MPI_Rget calls in each iteration.

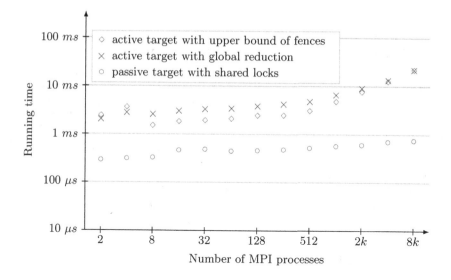

Fig. 5. Co-ranking performance with the three implementation variants, weak scaling

4   Experimental Results

We have implemented the distributed, stable merging algorithm with all three alternatives for the co-ranking step. The implementations have been evaluated on a large distributed-memory supercomputer: the "Jugene" IBM Blue Gene/P installation in Jülich/Germany with 73,728 nodes, each equipped with a 4-way PowerPC processor (850 MHz) and 2 GiB memory.

All experiments used double-precision floating-point elements with sorted random inputs, and were conducted in SMP mode with one MPI process per node. We performed both strong and weak scaling experiments. Figure 5 shows weak scaling results for the three co-ranking implementation variants. The two input arrays have 10 and 20 million elements per process, respectively. Therefore, the total number of elements is p times these local sizes. Since the number of iterations of the co-ranking algorithm is logarithmic in the minimum number of elements, we would expect its running time for an increasing number of processes to grow with at least $\mathcal{O}(\log p)$. The passive target variant seems to achieve this slow growth while the curves for the two active target variants show a steeper ascent. Both variants with the collective fence synchronization are by far slower than the lock variant, reaching a factor of 29 difference at 8,192 processes. We therefore choose the lock variant as our implementation for the co-ranking step.

In Figures 6 and 7, we present the individual times for the three main steps of the complete merge algorithm: co-ranking, copying of remote data, and local merge. We determined the running time of the local merge $T_{\text{seqmerge}}(n, m)$ to be $0.0484 \cdot (n + m)$ μsec. We use this sequential time to calculate the parallel efficiency of our merge implementation $E(n, m, p)$ as $T_{\text{seqmerge}}(n, m)/(p \cdot T_{\text{parmerge}})$, which is given as a percentage above the total running time.

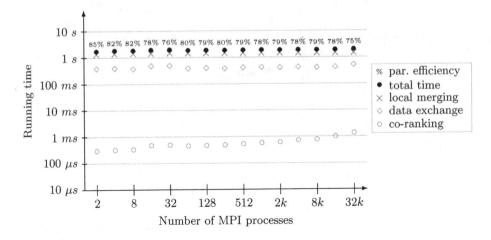

Fig. 6. Merging performance on Jugene, weak scaling

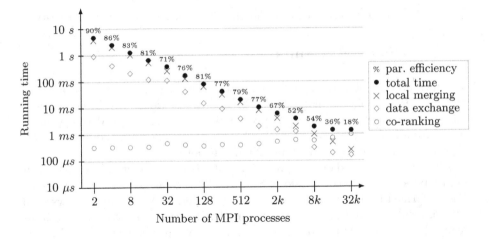

Fig. 7. Merging performance on Jugene, strong scaling

Figure 6 shows the weak-scaling behavior for the individual steps of the parallel merge algorithm, including its total running time. Note that the co-ranking step is indeed about a thousand times faster than the data copy and local merge. With a fixed input size per process, we would expect the running time for the data copy and local merge to remain constant, which is indeed the case. Only the time of the co-rank step increases very slowly with p. The overall parallel efficiency stays at around 80%.

Figure 7 presents results from a strong scaling experiment. The total number of elements for the two input arrays are $32 \cdot 2^{20}$ and $48 \cdot 2^{20}$, respectively. This means that we always use only 640 MiB of input data and distribute this over an increasing number of processes. Even with such a relatively small amount of data (note that this Blue Gene/P system has only 2 GiB of memory available per node), our lock-based co-ranking implementation scales up to 32,768 processes, where only a few thousand input elements exists per process, albeit with decreasing efficiency from around $2k$ processes.

5 Summary and Outlook

We presented a stable, distributed-memory parallel merge algorithm, and in particular discussed implementation alternatives in the MPI 2.2 and MPI 3.0 one-sided communication models. The alternatives have been implemented and we reported on initial experiments on a Blue Gene/P system. To our surprise, the lock-based variant used for the co-ranking preprocessing step showed considerably better performance than the other possibilities considered. However, this still needs stronger experimental support, and we are continuing the experimental work with the distributed merge algorithm.

Acknowledgments. The authors want to thank the anonymous reviewers for the valuable comments, Harald Klimach for his input on the manuscript, and Marc-André Hermanns for his ideas concerning the one-sided implementations.

References

1. Akl, S.G., Santoro, N.: Optimal parallel merging and sorting without memory conflicts. IEEE Transactions on Computers C-36(11), 1367–1369 (1987)
2. Deo, N., Jain, A., Medidi, M.: An optimal parallel algorithm for merging using multiselection. Information Processing Letters 50(2), 81–87 (1994)
3. Deo, N., Sarkar, D.: Parallel algorithms for merging and sorting. Information Sciences 56(1-3), 151–161 (1991)
4. Gerbessiotis, A.V., Siniolakis, C.J.: Merging on the BSP model. Parallel Computing 27(6), 809–822 (2001)
5. Hagerup, T., Rüb, C.: Optimal merging and sorting on the EREW PRAM. Information Processing Letters 33, 181–185 (1989)
6. Katajainen, J., Levcopoulos, C., Petersson, O.: Space-efficient parallel merging. Informatique Théoretique et Applications 27(4), 295–310 (1993)
7. MPI Forum. MPI: A Message-Passing Interface Standard. Version 2.2 (September 4, 2009), www.mpi-forum.org
8. Nieplocha, J., Tipparaju, V., Krishnan, M., Panda, D.K.: High performance remote memory access communication: The ARMCI approach. International Journal on High Performance Computing Applications 20(2), 233–253 (2006)
9. Poole, S.W., Hernandez, O., Kuehn, J.A., Shipman, G.M., Curtis, A., Feind, K.: OpenSHMEM - toward a unified RMA model. In: Padua, D.A. (ed.) Encyclopedia of Parallel Computing, pp. 1379–1391. Springer (2011)
10. Shiloach, Y., Vishkin, U.: Finding the maximum, merging and sorting in a parallel computation model. Journal of Algorithms 2, 88–102 (1981)
11. Varman, P.J., Iyer, B.R., Haderle, D.J., Dunn, S.M.: Parallel merging: algorithm and implementation results. Parallel Computing 15(1-3), 165–177 (1990)

Efficient Distributed Computation
of Maximal Exact Matches

Mohamed Abouelhoda[1,2] and Sondos Seif[2]

[1] Faculty of Engineering, Cairo University, Giza, Egypt
mabouelhoda@yahoo.com
[2] Center for Informatics Sciences, Nile University, Giza, Egypt
sondosseif@gmail.com

Abstract. Given two long strings S and T, representing two genomic sequences, and given a user defined threshold ℓ, the problem of computing maximal exact matches (*MEMs*) is to find each triple (p_1, p_2, l) specifying two matching substrings $S[p_1..p_1 + l - 1] = T[p_2..p_2 + l - 1]$, such that $l \geq \ell$ and $S[p_1 - 1] \neq T[p_2 - 1]$ and $S[p_1 + l] \neq T[p_2 + l]$. Computing *MEMs* is a major problem in bioinformitcs, because it is a primary step in identifying regions of common similarity among genomic sequences. Faster solutions to this problem are still demanded to overcome the ever increasing amount of genomic sequences to be compared to each other. In this paper, we present a parallel version of the *MEM* algorithm running on a computer cluster. Our experimental results show that our algorithm is efficient and scalable.

Keywords: Maximal Exact Matches, Bioinformatics, Computer Cluster, MPI.

1 Introduction

Genomes are made up of DNA and they are represented as strings over an alphabet of four characters, where each character refers to a chemical unit called nucleotide. Genome comparison is the task of identifying the regions of similarity between two or multiple genomes. This task is the next logical step after the raw genomic sequence data become available, because it helps in annotating genomic regions and elucidating their functions. The idea is that the common regions are likely of common functions and the unique regions refer to genetic traits unique to each genome. This task is a computationally challenging due to the following main reasons:

1. The large size of individual genomes deposited in public databases. To take one example, the size of the human genome is three Gbp (i.e., three Giga base pairs, which means three Giga characters), divided into 23 strings called chromosomes. The mouse genome is of similar size and it is divided into 21 chromosomes. Comparing the two multi-chromosomal genomes requires running 483 pairwise comparisons. This will take several days using the best sequential algorithm [3].
2. The ever increasing amount of genomic data. To date (April 2012), there are 3173 complete genomes in addition to other 10479 genome projects that are still ongoing [4]. The current challenge therefore is no longer in data acquisition but in the analysis step to turn this overwhelming amount of data into useful knowledge.

J.L. Träff, S. Benkner, and J. Dongarra (Eds.): EuroMPI 2012, LNCS 7490, pp. 214–223, 2012.
© Springer-Verlag Berlin Heidelberg 2012

Genome comparison software tools have depended on the computation of *maximal exact matches (MEMs)* as a first step to identify regions of similarity [6, 8, 13, 14]. The idea is that regions without *MEMs* are not similar and can be excluded from consideration, while regions including *MEMs* are candidate regions of similarity. The *MEMs* in these regions are further clustered and processed to verify that each region is of enough similarity. The final output is an alignment of these regions, where the *MEMs* are among the parts that exactly match. To speed up the computation of *MEMs*, the comparison tools resort to linear-space indexing data structures such as the suffix tree or the suffix array [1, 2, 7]. Based on these data structures, the running time for computing all *MEMs* for two strings S and T with lengths n_s and n_t, respectively, is $O(n_s + n_t + z)$, where z is the number of reported *MEMs*.

The sequential algorithms for computing the *MEMs* already reached the optimal time complexity. The only way to cope with the increasing data size is the use of parallel and distributed architecture. In this paper, we present a parallel algorithm to compute *MEMs* using a computer cluster, based on MPI. Our algorithm is based on (compressed) indexing data structures to achieve the optimal running time within each node. Our algorithm is also suitable when the amount of memory in each node is limited, which holds true for massively parallel architectures, like some versions of Blue Gene. Furthermore, we introduce an interesting theoretical result in which there will be no need for indexing data structures when the number of processors is high enough.

2   Review of Sequential *MEMs* Algorithm

2.1   Basic Notions and Definitions

Let S denote a string with length $n = |S|$ over a finite alphabet Σ. We write $S[i]$ to denote the ith character of S, and we write $S[i..j]$ to denote the substring starting at position i and ending at position j in S, $0 \le i \le j < n$. The ith suffix of S, denoted by $S(i)$, is the substring $S[i..n-1]$.

Let S and T be two strings over the same alphabet and of lengths n_s and n_t, respectively. A match of length l is a substring that occurs in both S and T. An occurrence of this match is defined by the triple (p_1, p_2, l), which specifies the l-length substring $S[p_1..p_1 + l - 1]$ in S that matches the l-length substring $T[p_2..p_2 + l - 1]$ in T.

Definition 1. *A maximal exact match, MEM, is a match (p_1, p_2, l) such that $S[p_1-1] \ne T[p_2 - 1]$ and $S[p_1 + l] \ne T[p_2 + l]$; i.e., there are no further matching characters on the left and on the right side of the MEM.*

Property 1. Assume a 2D space and assume that string S is aligned to the x-axis and T is aligned to the y-axis. A *MEM* defined by (p_1, p_2, l) can be specified in this space by the two points (p_1, p_2) and $(p_1 + l - 1, p_2 + l - 1)$. The line connecting these two points has a slope of 45 degree and is parallel to the diagonal of this space. Figure 1 shows some *MEMs* plotted in a 2D space.

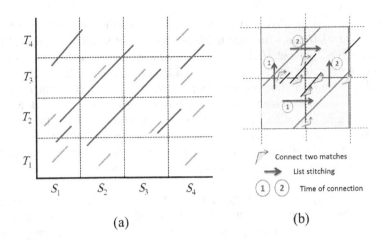

(a)   (b)

Fig. 1. (A) Maximal exact matches in a two dimensional space. The x and y axes refer to the input strings and the *MEMs* are specified by lines with a slope of 45 degree. The grid defines the partitioning of this space, where each grid cell includes the matches between the segments S_i of S and T_j of T. Each node in the computer cluster is responsible for one grid cell. Some *MEMs* can be distributed over multiple nodes and these should be stitched together. (B) Stitching a *MEM* within a **2x2** sub-grid. The gray matches touch the borders of the outer grid boundaries.

2.2 Sequential Computation of *MEMs*

Definition 2. *Given two strings S and T and a threshold ℓ, the problem of computing MEMs is to identify all triples (p_1, p_2, l) representing the MEMs such that $l \geq \ell$.*

Computing *MEMs* is a well studied problem and there are many sequential algorithms for solving it [1,2,5,7,9–11]. Assuming that T is shorter than S, a space efficient algorithm for computing *MEMs* works as follows: First, an index data structure (suffix tree, suffix array, or compressed versions of them) is constructed for T. Then S is streamed against the index of T to match each suffix $S(i)$ against the index and to report *MEMs* if exist. To avoid repeating computation when moving to suffix $S(i+1)$, some links are kept to use the matching information obtained at position i. The construction of the index takes $O(n_t)$ time and space. The matching algorithm takes $O(n_s + z)$, where z is the number of output *MEMs*. That is, the complexity of this algorithm is $O(n_s + n_t + z)$. Note that z is very large with theoretical bound of $O(n_s n_t)$.

3 Parallelization of the *MEMs* Algorithm

Our strategy for parallelizing the computation of *MEM* is to partition the input string S and T into $N \geq 1$ and $M \geq 1$ segments, respectively. Then each pair of segments is processed by one processor. At first glance, this strategy seems to be straightforward. But, as we shall see, there is a challenge in handling the *MEMs* that cross the boundary between the segments to guarantee that no match will be missing in the output.

Algorithm 1 (ParallelMEM)

   1. Arrange the processing nodes logically into a 2D $N \times M$ grid, each node is denoted by $P_{x,y}$

   2. Divide S into N partitions (segments) and T into M partitions (segments)

   3. Copy the ith segment of S (denoted by S_i) to all the $P_{i,y}$, $y \in [1..M]$

   4. Copy the jth segment of T (denoted by T_j) to all the $P_{x,j}$, $x \in [1..N]$

   5. In each processor, ComputeMEM(S_i, T_j, ℓ)

   6. Store each match that lies on the boundary of S_i or T_j (call these matches Boundary Matches) and output the others

   7. StitchBoundaryMatches()

Figure 1 shows an example of the general partitioning and some of the matches distributed over more than one segment. The step of collecting border matches into *MEMs* and further implementation details will be the focus of the coming sections.

Algorithm 1 describes our strategy for computing the *MEMs* in parallel. In this algorithm, *ComputeMEM(S', S'')* specifies a function of computing *MEMs* with minimum length ℓ between two strings S' and S'', using any of the algorithms cited in Section 2. Steps 1-4 of this algorithm for partitioning the data and distributing it on the cluster nodes will be handled in the following subsection. Step 7 defined by the function *StitchBoundaryMatches()* will be handled in detail in the subsequent subsections.

3.1 Cluster Topology and Data Partitioning

We logically arrange the given processors in an $N \times M$ 2D grid. In our implementation, N and M are specified by the user according to the infrastructure at hand. Each processor in this grid is denoted by $P_{x,y}$, $x \in [1..N]$ and $y \in [1..M]$. We assume that the sequences S and T are aligned with the x- and y-axis of the grid, respectively. There are two strategies to run Steps 2-4 in Algorithm 1 in parallel. In the first, each processor can fetch its data from the storage. With a parallel file system and suitable infrastructure, this step will take $O(\frac{n_s}{N} + \frac{n_t}{M})$ time. In the second strategy, where the storage access is a bottleneck, the processors of the first row of the grid read the respective segments from the file storing the sequence S. Then each processor $P_{1,y}$ broadcasts its segments to the M processors in its column, $y \in [1..M]$. Similarly, the processors of the first column read the respective segments from the file storing the sequence T. Then each processor $P_{x,1}$ broadcasts its segments to the N processors in its row, $x \in [1..N]$. The broadcast operation takes $O(n \log P)$, where n is the data size and P is the number of processors. Hence, Steps 2-4 in this algorithm takes $O(\frac{n_s}{N} + \frac{n_t}{M})$ using the former strategy, and $O(n_s + \frac{n_s}{N} \log N + n_t + \frac{n_t}{M} \log M)$ using the latter one. In our complexity analysis, we will assume that the first strategy is the one in use.

3.2 Stitching the Matches: *Collect_on_Quartets*

If the overall number of the matches touching the grid boundaries is not so large, then one processor can simply gather all these matches and process them to produce the final set of *MEMs*. Otherwise, a more sophisticated strategy is needed. In this subsection, we introduce an optimal method, which we call *Collect_on_Quartets*.

In each node, we arrange the boundary matches in four lists L_l, L_r, L_u, and L_d to store the border matches touching the left, right, upper, and lower boundary, respectively. For ease of presentation and to avoid tedious mathematical details, we assume that the grid size is a power of two and the segments in each node are of equal length. First, we will consider the general case in which $N > 1$ and $M > 1$. Then, we will discuss the case in which $N = 1$ or $M = 1$.

Algorithm 2 includes the major steps of the *Collect_on_Quartet* method. Here, we explain how the algorithm works and clarify the communication pattern among the cluster nodes. The algorithm iteratively processes matches in sub-grids of increasing sizes such that the sub-grid size is a power of four. In the first iteration, matches in each sub-grid of size 2×2 are processed. In the second iteration, remaining matches in each sub-grid of size 4×4 are processed. This goes on until there is just one single large grid including all the processors. Figure 2 shows the sub-grids of increasing sizes.

The tagging step (Line 5) specifies that the processors only on the boundary of these sub-grids will take part in the computation. That is, these processors will be involved in stitching the matches with the processors lying in the boundaries of the contiguous sub-grids. In this step, each processor identifies itself and its position in the grid. This can be done using simple arithmetic operations. The tagged processors are highlighted in the right part of Figure 2. Once the processors are tagged, the matches can be stitched into *MEMs* as explained in the following paragraphs.

To ease the presentation, we will start with explaining the first iteration of the algorithm, where matches within sub-grids of size 2×2 are processed. Let P_{ll}, P_{lr}, P_{ul}, P_{ur} denote the lower-left, lower-right, and upper-left, and upper-right processors of a sub-grid of size 2×2. An example of such sub-grid is illustrated in Figure 2. This part of the algorithm is composed of three major phases: 1) Connecting matches between P_{ll}, P_{lr}, and P_{ul}, 2) connecting matches between P_{lr}, P_{ul}, and P_{ur}, and 3) updating information of matches ending in both P_{ll} and P_{ur}. The three phases collectively correspond to Lines 6 and 7 of the algorithm, and they are illustrated in the right part of Figure 1. The details of these phases are explained in the following paragraphs.

Phase 1: Consider the three processors P_{ll}, P_{lr}, and P_{ul}. We conduct the following two steps in parallel: 1) The matches in the lists L_r of P_{ll} are stitched with the matches in L_l of P_{lr}. 2) The matches in the lists L_u of P_{ll} are stitched with the matches in L_d of P_{ul}. Stitching the matches between two processors does not involve establishment of pointers but just the identification of the corresponding matches and updating the respective match lengths. This is achieved by the following steps:

1. Update the lengths of the corresponding matches in L_r of P_{ll} and in L_l of P_{lr}. This step is achieved in linear time using an algorithm similar to the merge algorithm.
2. If a match occurs also in L_u of P_{lr}, then it is identified in this L_u and its length is updated. In this case, we say (for a certain reason that will be made clear below) that the processor communicates with itself to update the information in L_u. Similarly, if a match occurs in L_d of P_{ll}, we update its length in this list.
3. Update the lengths of the corresponding matches in L_d of P_{ul} and L_u of P_{ll}. This step is also achieved in linear time as in Step 1 above.
4. If a match occurs also in L_r of P_{ul}, then it is identified in this L_l and its length is updated. Similarly, if a match occurs in L_l of P_{ll}, we update its length in this list.

Algorithm 2 (StitchBoundaryMatches: *Collect_on_Quartets*)
1. *In each node P_{ij}, $i \in [1..N]$ and $j \in [1..M]$, create four lists L_l, L_r, L_u, L_d*
   to store border matches of the left, right, up, and down borders, respectively.
2. $k = 2$
3. **while** *($k \leq M$)*
4.   *Set sub-grid size to $k \times k$*
5.   *Tag the processors on the borders of each sub-grid*
6.   *Connect matches (in tagged processors) among sub-grids*
7.   *Update match length for all matches in all lists*
8   *Report all matches touching none of the sub-grid borders*
9. $k = 2k$

Phase 2: We conduct other two analogous steps to that in Phase 1: 1) The matches in the lists L_l of P_{ur} are stitched with the matches in L_r of P_{ul}. 2) The matches in the lists L_d of P_{ur} are stitched with the matches in L_u of P_{lr}. After finishing these steps, the following lists can be deleted: L_r of P_{ll} and P_{ul}, L_l of P_{lr} and P_{ur}, L_u of P_{ll} and P_{lr}, and L_d of P_{ul} and P_{ur}.

Phase 3: Consider the two gray matches in Figure 1(b). These gray matches touch the outer boundaries of the sub-grid. The match length in L_u and L_r of P_{ur} is updated by the steps of the previous two phases. But this information is not yet up-to-date in L_d and L_l of P_{ll}. This means that P_{ll} and P_{ur} should communicate together to update the match length in L_d of P_{ll}, and this is important for subsequent iterations of the algorithm.

Now, consider the step of processing 4×4 sub-grids and consider the *MEM* in Figure 2 that extends from processor $P_{3,1}$ to processor $P_{8,8}$, passing through the tagged processors $P_{4,2}$, $P_{5,2}$, $P_{6,4}$, and $P_{6,5}$. In Phase 1 of connecting and updating the match, $P_{4,2}$ communicates with $P_{5,2}$ to update match lengths in L_r of the former and L_l of the latter. Then $P_{4,2}$ communicates with $P_{3,1}$ to update the match length in L_d of $P_{3,1}$. Finally, $P_{5,2}$ communicates with $P_{6,4}$ to update match length in L_u of $P_{6,4}$. In phase 2, $P_{6,4}$, and $P_{6,5}$ communicate with each other to update L_u of the former and L_d of the latter. Then $P_{6,5}$ communicates with $P_{8,8}$ to update L_r of $P_{8,8}$. In phase 3, $P_{8,8}$ communicates with $P_{3,1}$ to update L_d of $P_{3,1}$. Grids of size larger than 4×4 are processed in an analogous way.

As we have seen, not all messaging steps take place between contiguous processors, which could make a problem in identifying the messaging partner. To solve this problem, we make use of the property that the *MEMs* are specified in this space by lines with 45 degree slope, and we identify the communication partner of a node in constant time using some geometric-based arithmetic operations. For example, in Phase 1 and for sub-grids of size 4×4, the processor $P_{4,y}$ on the same column including $P_{4,2}$ communicates with the processor $P_{y,1}$.

3.3 The Case of $M = 1$ or $N = 1$

Without loss of generality, assume that $M = 1$. In this case, the whole T is matched against segments of S. This simplifies the processing, because it is enough to have

Processing sub-grids of size 4   Processing sub-grids of size 16

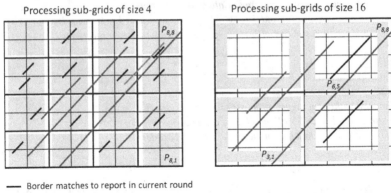

—— Border matches to report in current round
—— Border matches kept to next round

Fig. 2. Connecting matches over a set of 64 processors. Highlighted cells refer to the respective tagged processors, which take part in computation at the respective iteration. In the first iteration (left), matches in sub-grids of size 2×2 are stitched. In the second iteration (right), matches in sub-grids of size 4×4 are stitched. In the third iteration (not shown), the remaining matches are reported.

just two lists L_l and L_r in each node. The communication pattern involves contiguous and non-contiguous processors to connect matches touching the boundaries at each iteration. More details about this case will be given in an extended version of this work.

3.4   Shorter *MEMs* on the Boundary

The function *ComputeMEM*(S_i, T_j, ℓ) in Algorithm 1 computes matches with minimum length ℓ, where in practice $\ell \ll |S|$ and $\ell \ll |T|$. This can lead to the problem that the *MEMs*, which are distributed on two processors and the length of their matches in each processor is $l < \ell$, will be missing. To overcome this bottleneck, we use overlapping partitions (segments) and run the *ComputeMEM* function on the concatenated strings $S_i' + S_i + S_i''$ and $T_j' + T_j + T_j''$, where S_i' and S_i'' are two ℓ-length strings contiguous to S_i, and T_j' and T_j'' are two ℓ-length strings contiguous to T_j. The matches in the four lists L_l, L_r, L_u, and L_d in each processor still store the matches with respect to the boundaries of S_i and T_j, as discussed before.

3.5   Algorithm Complexity

As we mentioned in Subsection 2.2, the time for computing *MEMs* in each processor is $O(\frac{S}{N} + \frac{T}{M} + z')$, where z' is the number of matches in a partition (node). In practice, z' is a fraction of the whole number of matches z; a rough assumption of it for large datasets and shorter ℓ is that $z' \to O(\frac{z}{N \times M})$.

Table 1. The string datasets used in our experiments and their sizes in million characters. The first 5 datasets are real and the last two ones are artificial. The alphabet size in all datasets is 4.

Dataset	Description	Size
$hchrx$	Human Chromosome X	49 M
$cchrx$	Chimpanzee Chromosome X	42 M
$hchr2$	Human Chromosome 2	76 M
$mchr1$	Mouse Chromosome 1	62 M

Dataset	Description	Size
$rchr9$	Rodent Chromosome 9	34 M
$art1$	Artificial Data 1	616 M
$art2$	Artificial Data 2	616 M

The time complexity of function *StitchBoundaryMatches* in Algorithm 2 is derived as follows: Connecting the match set between two lists in (two contiguous or non-contiguous) processors requires $O(z')$ time. Because the number of iterations in this algorithm is $O(\max\{\log_4 N, \log_4 M\})$, the total time complexity of the *StitchBoundaryMatches* function is $O(z'(\max\{\log_4 N, \log_4 M\}))$. Adding the complexity of partitioning and distributing the segments on the grid nodes to the above two complexities, the overall complexity of computing the *MEMs* in parallel is $O(\frac{S}{N} + \frac{T}{M} + z' + z' \max\{\log_4 N, \log_4 M\})$.

4 The Case for Large Number of Processors

Consider the case in which the number of processors available is in the order of $O(\frac{n_s \times n_t}{\ell^2})$ or when $\ell \geq \min\{\frac{|S|}{N}, \frac{|T|}{M}\}$. In this case, all *MEMs* will be distributed over more than one processor or at least touch the boundaries of the node. In this case, there will be no need to use an indexing data structure and it will be enough to use a string matching algorithm where we find the substrings of a given string that matches a prefix of the other. For example, the L_l list of a processor is filled with matches computed between the prefix of S_i and all substrings of T_j. To find these matches in linear time, one can use the Z-algorithm [7] over the concatenated string $S_i T_j$.

5 Implementation and Experimental Results

We conducted some experiments over real and artificial data to evaluate the performance of our algorithm. Our algorithm in this paper is implemented using MPICH2 and runs on a computer cluster of 64 nodes connected through 1G Ethernet switches. Each node includes a 2.3GHz AMD CPU and 64 GB RAM. The datasets used in our experiments are described in Table 1. The function *ComputeMEM* is based on the suffix array and it is implemented as described in [2].

Table 2 summarizes the results of our experiments for computing the *MEMs* between different pairs of the strings in Table 1. The minimum length parameter $\ell = 10$, which leads to large number of matches. The experiment were conducted over a varying number of nodes and different grid configurations. The resulting *MEMs* are kept in the nodes and not collected in a central location. Also the time for transferring the genomic segments was not included as it is negligible compared to the computation time.

Table 2. Running times in minutes for comparing different pairwise strings on different cluster sizes and configurations. The column "SeqTime" includes the sequential running times. The column "GridSize" includes the size of the cluster and its configuration in a 2D grid. The columns "CompTime", "ComTime", "TotalTime" include the computation, communication, and total time of the experiment, respectively. The column titled "Speedup" includes the achieved speed up. Finally, the columns titled "Border-Matches" and "TotalMatches" include the number of matches lying on the border of the grid and the number of all *MEMs*, respectively; ('M'="million").

S	T	SeqTime	Grid Size	CompTime	ComTime	TotalTime	Speedup	Border Matches	Total Matches
$hchrx$	$cchrx$	214.91	4x4	13.06	6.34	19.4	11	7705	6565M
$hchrx$	$cchrx$	214.91	8x4	8.21	8.37	16.58	12.6	6899	6565M
$hchrx$	$cchrx$	214.91	6x6	6.3	4.77	11.1	19.5	11959	6565M
$hchrx$	$cchrx$	214.91	8x6	4.33	4.38	8.7	24.4	16854	6565M
$hchrx$	$cchrx$	214.91	8x8	2.05	2.48	4.5	43.1	25694	6565M
$hchr2$	$mchr1$	385.47	4x4	20.99	16.48	37.5	10.1	34276	1193M
$hchr2$	$mchr1$	385.47	8x4	13.67	14.36	28.1	14.5	19243	1193M
$hchr2$	$mchr1$	385.47	6x6	9.84	10.68	20.2	19.5	21119	1193M
$hchr2$	$mchr1$	385.47	8x6	6.63	6.16	12.8	29.6	25941	1193M
$hchr2$	$mchr1$	385.47	8x8	5.57	5.65	11.1	35	35041	1193M
$mchr1$	$rchr9$	191.04	4x4	15.89	16.06	32.0	5.2	27024	5760M
$mchr1$	$rchr9$	191.04	8x4	9.78	9.47	19.1	10.1	9933	5760M
$mchr1$	$rchr9$	191.04	6x6	6.75	6.94	13.6	13.6	66915	5760M
$mchr1$	$rchr9$	191.04	8x6	4.15	5.14	9.3	20.5	32422	5760M
$mchr1$	$rchr9$	191.04	8x8	3.02	3.35	6.4	29.8	78620	5760M
$art1$	$art2$	283.72	4x4	17.44	96.76	114.1	2.5	2939742	7900M
$art1$	$art2$	283.72	8x4	11.37	56.57	68.9	5.1	2939696	7900M
$art1$	$art2$	283.72	6x6	7.94	39.64	47.4	6.0	4239662	7900M
$art1$	$art2$	283.72	8x6	4.94	29.81	35.0	6.5	4239726	7900M
$art1$	$art2$	283.72	8x8	1.90	19.81	21.7	13.5	8537736	7900M

From the results we observe good scalability of our algorithm, especially with real datasets. We also observe that the number of border matches increases with the number of nodes, which leads to higher communication time. In some cases, we observe super-linear speedup in the computation time compared to the sequential time. This is because the index data structure is built for only segments of T and we match segments of S against them, which leads to better cache performance and faster matching.

6   Conclusions

In this paper, we have presented a parallel distributed algorithm for computing maximal exact matches. Over a grid of $N \times M$ processors, our algorithm takes $O(\frac{S}{N} + \frac{T}{M} + z' + z' \max\{\log_4 N, \log_4 M\})$ time and linear space.

Our algorithm is suitable for the case in which the amount of memory in each node is limited. This makes it a good choice for massively parallel architectures, like some versions of Blue Gene. The current version of our implementation is based on the suffix array. In a future version, we will integrate compressed versions of this data structure to further reduce the space. This space reduction will affect the running time, but could solve a memory problem at the user's infrastructure.

Our parallel algorithm presented here can also be used with other variations of *MEMs* such as rare *MEMs* and maximal unique matches [2, 12], provided that the function *ComputeMEM* is modified to produce these matches.

Acknowledgment. This work was partially funded by a grant from IBM. We thank Hisham Mohamed for help in primary investigation. Author names are in alphabetical order.

References

1. Abouelhoda, M.I., Kurtz, S., Ohlebusch, E.: The Enhanced Suffix Array and Its Applications to Genome Analysis. In: Guigó, R., Gusfield, D. (eds.) WABI 2002. LNCS, vol. 2452, pp. 449–463. Springer, Heidelberg (2002)
2. Abouelhoda, M.I., Kurtz, S., Ohlebusch, E.: Replacing suffix trees with enhanced suffix arrays. J. Discrete Algorithms 2(1), 53–86 (2004)
3. Abouelhoda, M.I., Kurtz, S., Ohlebusch, E.: CoCoNUT: An efficient system for the comparison and analysis of genomes. BMC Bioinformatics 9, 476 (2008)
4. Bernal, A., Ear, U., Kyrpide, N.: Genomes OnLine Database (GOLD): A monitor of genome projects world-wide. Nucleic Acids Research 29(1), 126–127 (2001)
5. Delcher, A.L., Phillippy, A., Carlton, J., Salzberg, S.L.: Fast algorithms for large-scale genome alignment and comparison. Genome Research 30(11), 2478–2483 (2002)
6. Deogen, J.S., Yang, J., Ma, F.: EMAGEN: An efficient approach to multiple genome alignment. In: Proc. of Asia-Pacific Bioinf. Conf., pp. 113–122 (2004)
7. Gusfield, D.: Algorithms on Strings, Trees, and Sequences. Cambridge University Press, New York (1997)
8. Höhl, M., Kurtz, S., Ohlebusch, E.: Efficient multiple genome alignment. Bioinformatics 18(suppl. 1), S312–S320 (2002)
9. Khan, Z., Bloom, J.S., Kruglyak, L., Singh, M.: A practical algorithm for finding maximal exact matches in large sequence datasets using sparse suffix arrays. Bioinformatics 25(13), 1609–1616 (2009)
10. Kurtz, S., Phillippy, A., Delcher, A.L., et al.: Versatile and open software for comparing large genomes. Genome Biology 5(2), R12+ (2004)
11. Ohlebusch, E., Gog, S.: Space-efficient genome comparisons with compressed full-text indexes. In: BICoB, pp. 19–24 (2010)
12. Ohlebusch, E., Kurtz, S.: Space efficient computation of rare maximal exact matches between multiple sequences. J. Comp. Biol. 15(4) (2008)
13. Shibuya, T., Kurochkin, I.: Match Chaining Algorithms for cDNA Mapping. In: Benson, G., Page, R.D.M. (eds.) WABI 2003. LNCS (LNBI), vol. 2812, pp. 462–475. Springer, Heidelberg (2003)
14. Treangen, T.J., Messeguer, X.: M-GCAT: Interactively and efficiently constructing large-scale multiple genome comparison frameworks. BMC Bioinformatics 7, 433 (2006)

Scalable Algorithms
for Constructing Balanced Spanning Trees
on System-Ranked Process Groups

Akhil Langer, Ramprasad Venkataraman, and Laxmikant Kale

Department of Computer Science
University of Illinois at Urbana-Champaign
{alanger,ramv,kale}@illinois.edu

Abstract. Current implementations of process groups (subcommunicators) have non-scalable (O(group size)) memory footprints and even worse time complexities for setting up communication. We propose *system-ranked process groups,* where member ranks are picked by the runtime system, as a cheaper and faster alternative for a subset of collective operations (barrier, broadcast, reduction, allreduce).

This paper presents two distributed algorithms for balanced, k-ary spanning tree construction over system-ranked process groups obtained by splitting a parent group. Our schemes have much smaller memory footprints and also perform better, even at modest process counts. We demonstrate performance results up to $131,072$ cores of BlueGene/P.

Keywords: distributed algorithms, exascale, spanning trees, process groups, sub-communicators.

1 Introduction

Process Groups are subsets of processes (ranks) in a parallel program that participate in specific portions of the parallel execution and are addressable as a unified entity. Most parallel programming models provide entities equivalent to process groups (communicators in MPI) and mechanisms to create, store and manage these entities. Several existing parallel runtime implementations require $O(n)$ storage and $O(n \log n)$ computation per process to create and manage a process group with n members [5,6]. They will consume prohibitive amounts of memory and reach scalability limits on current and future extreme-scale architectures. Parallel programs typically compound this problem by creating and using many such groups. Trends in high performance system architecture point to a slower growth in the available memory than in the number of threads of execution [12]. Thus, it is imperative that runtime software adopt leaner, resource-conserving algorithms and book-keeping mechanisms to manage process groups.

The work presented in this paper is motivated by these realizations, and focuses on mechanisms for the creation of process groups. In order to remain relevant to multiple parallel programming systems, we do not consider MPI-specific

J.L. Träff, S. Benkner, and J. Dongarra (Eds.): EuroMPI 2012, LNCS 7490, pp. 224–234, 2012.

solutions, nor do we bind ourselves to the current standard. We preface our work by making a case for *system-ranked process groups* with a reduced feature set that can be realized by simply constructing spanning trees over the group (Section 2). We then explore distributed algorithms for the creation of communication trees spanning new groups obtained by enrolling a subset of members from a parent group. To ensure support for nested (or recursive) partitioning of a parent group, we assume that initial communication for spawning a new process group will occur over the spanning tree of the parent. We base our algorithms on the assumption that memory is a constrained resource, and impose limits on its transient and final consumption.

Our efforts have resulted in two distributed tree construction algorithms: a Shrink-and-Balance algorithm (Section 4), and a Rank-and-Hash algorithm (Section 5). They consume just $O(\log n)$, $O(1)$ memory per process and $O(\log^2 n)$, $O(\log n)$ time respectively. To corroborate our analysis with actual measurements, we implement our algorithms and compare their performance (Section 6) with a reference "centralized" implementation (Section 3) that exhibits $O(m)$ space and $O(m + \log n)$ time complexity; and with a comm_split from a vendor-tuned MPI implementation. Our algorithms scale well to large supercomputers and exhibit competitive performance at large process counts.

2 System-Ranked Process Groups

We propose that unranked or system-ranked process groups be supported in parallel programming systems as they will satisfy a portion of use-cases for process groups at a much lower resource cost.

Motivations. Our stance germinates from the observation that user-assigned ranks within a process group are not always necessary to express parallel algorithms. This is especially true of a subset of collective operations: *barrier, broadcast, reduce and allreduce*. The results of these collectives are independent of the ranks from which the individual data contributions arise (assuming commutative operations). There is also evidence that a sizable fraction of collective communication in applications involve these operations [1,13,15]. We enumerate a few examples of algorithms and applications that use just these collectives:

Parallel Linear Algebra: Several algorithms for manipulating linear systems of equations use block or compressed representations of matrices. The algorithms

---

Terminology

- **n** Number of processes in parent process group.
- **m** Number of processes participating in the new process group.
- **k** Branching factor (degree) of the spanning tree.
- $d_{i,k}$ Depth of a rank i process in a balanced spanning tree of branching factor k.
- **f** fraction of members of original process group participating in new group.

are then expressed by collectively addressing processes that own a row or column of matrix elements/blocks. For eg, recent work has demonstrated a high performance dense LU factorization using only the aforementioned collectives on non-trivially defined groups of processes, in a parallel programming paradigm that supports unranked and system-ranked process groups [10].

Master-Worker Algorithms: A master-worker expression of several parallel algorithms primarily use broadcasts and reductions during their execution. Many of these have use for process groups in efficiently expressing parallel logic. Some examples include: *a*) Map-Reduce *b*) Histogram sorting *c*) some Divide-and-Conquer algorithms, and *d*) Monte Carlo computations.

Ab-initio Quantum Chemistry: OpenAtom is a massively parallel quantum chemistry application with several phases of computation in a step. A description of the parallel structure [3] demonstrates the use of multiple process groups just for performing broadcasts, reductions and allreduces among members.

Approach. Since the collectives of interest can be expressed as operations over a communication tree spanning the members of the group, we chose a tree-based representation of groups and cast the problem of efficient group construction into the *efficient construction of trees spanning the members of a new group*.

Possible Functionality. System-ranked process groups are primarily for supporting the aforementioned collectives. User-specified roots for the collectives can be supported by: *a*) forwarding data from the tree root to the user-specified root *b*) tolerating some imbalance by using any vertex in the tree as a broadcast root *c*) constructing multiple (but a small number of) trees with different roots. Point-to-point messaging can be supported by discovering and caching the ids of the (typically) small number of frequent communication partners. Finally, in keeping with a pay-only-for-use policy, user-supplied ranks can be supported atop system-ranked groups by performing the sort as an additional step.

Benefits. Letting the runtime system assign ranks to processes enrolling in a group liberates it from having to sort user-supplied keys to identify ranks. Avoiding this $O(m \log m)$ computation can result in significant speedups of group creation mechanisms. Tailoring the communicators (groups) to subsets of use-cases will permit implementations that are less resource-intensive and faster. It may also permit optimization of the communication operations themselves.

3   The Reference Centralized Algorithm

Group creation in MPI typically performs an allgather followed by a sort. Removing support for user-assigned ranks eliminates the sorting, but still requires an allgather which takes $O(m)$ storage on each process. Our reference "centralized" implementation replaces this allgather with a gatherv-scatter that only has an $O(m + \log n)$ time and $O(m)$ transient memory footprint. We believe this represents a conservative baseline for comparing our distributed algorithms.

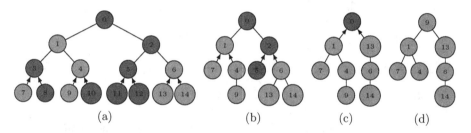

Fig. 1. Tree shrinking in the Shrink-and-Balance scheme using leaves as fillers. Red: non-participating process (hole); Green: participating process.

The implementation performs an *upward* pass (gatherv) over the original spanning tree in which only members of the new group contribute their process ids. The resulting list is sent to the root process of the new group (picked from the list). This is followed by a *downward* pass (scatter) over the spanning tree under construction. A vertex's immediate children are picked from the list of members and the remaining list partitioned among them to populate their sub-trees.

4 The Shrink-and-Balance Algorithm

Upward Pass. The Centralized scheme collects enrollment information, but does not act on it until it reaches the root of the parent spanning tree. Because we'd like to avoid gathering $O(n)$ enrollment data, we base our first algorithm on the idea of using information earlier. The Shrink-and-Balance scheme immediately uses enrollment data during the upward pass to shrink the original spanning tree by excluding non-participating processes. This results in *holes* at the vertices of the original tree where processes choose to drop out of the new group. In order to maintain a contiguous tree structure, these holes are "filled" with processes that are members in the new group. Fillers are either a participating leaf process (Figure 1) or a participating immediate child process. Using leaf vertices as fillers requires a process v with rank i to send $\min(subtree(v), d_{i,k})$ leaves as candidate fillers to its parent; to potentially fill holes at each of its $d_{i,k}$ (1) direct ancestors. Since at most $\log n$ vertices may be sent, the space and time complexity of the upward pass is $O(\log n)$ and $O(\log^2 n)$, respectively. Space constraints prevent a description of using immediate children as fillers.

Downward Pass. Although the upward pass yields a contiguous, participants-only spanning tree, there are no guarantees on its quality. To obtain a balanced tree with the desired branching factor, the algorithm continues into a downward pass. All further communication now occurs over the newly constructed tree.

In the downward pass, the scheme balances the tree while minimizing the number of vertex migrations. The size of the new group is used to compute the ideal height h ($d_{m-1,k} + 1$) of a perfectly balanced tree spanning tree (1).

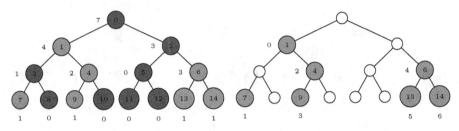

(a) Subtree sizes after the upward pass   (b) Ranks after the downward pass

Fig. 2. Assignment of ranks in the Rank-and-Hash scheme

This target height yields the maximum size of each of the subtrees of the root (2). If the size of a subtree is greater than its maximum capacity, some vertices must move out of it in order to limit its height to $h-1$. All such subtrees (i.e. their roots) are marked as vertex *suppliers*. Similarly, child vertices whose subtrees are smaller than their maximum permitted sizes, are marked as potential *consumers*.

$$d_{i,k} = \lfloor \log_k (i(k-1)+1) \rfloor \tag{1}$$

$$max\_size = \frac{k^h - 1}{k - 1} \tag{2}$$

Each vertex V (starting with the root), performs a "matchmaking" step, ensuring that each of its supplier subtrees is assigned one or more consumers that can absorb the excess vertices of the supplier within their subtrees. If V has missing children, it requests vertices from supplier(s) for itself. Once these supplier vertices are assigned, each subtree is within its size limits. The vertex V concludes its role by invoking a balancing step on each of its subtrees. The downward pass thus recurses down the tree, ensuring a tree that is as shallow as possible. By checking the current height of a subtree against its maximum permissible height, the algorithm avoids striving unnecessarily for perfect balance.

Our experiments show that the memory footprint of the downward pass is very small, although a theoretical upper bound is yet to be established. For e.g., on $128K$ cores of BG/P, there were at most 13 suppliers for process groups of sizes ranging from 0.1% to 99% of the parent group. Identifying (and moving) an excess vertex may take $O(\log n)$ time in the worst case. Since this can happen at every level of the shrunk tree, the time complexity of the scheme is $O(\log^2 n)$.

5   The Rank-and-Hash Algorithm

The Rank-and-Hash scheme works by assigning ranks to the participating processes in the downward pass, and then enabling the discovery of the process ids corresponding to any rank via a hash function.

Upward Pass. The upward pass is a simple reduction up the original spanning tree. Each vertex receives participation information from its children, stores this information and passes a reduced count (including its participation decision) up the spanning tree. This leaves each vertex with the size of each of its subtrees.

Downward Pass. The size of the tree determines the available ranks $[0, m)$. This range is split among the subtrees based on their sizes. Splitting continues down the original spanning tree until all the available ranks are divided among all the participating processes. Non-participating processes are not assigned any ranks. Figures 2a and 2b show the subtree size and rank information after the upward and the downward passes respectively.

Identifying Tree Neighbors. A process of rank i in the new group can compute the ranks of its parent p (3), and children (4) in the tree. However, the process ids of these ranks are still unknown. The discovery of ids is done via *intermediary* processes that mediate an exchange of ids between a parent and its children. The id of an intermediary process (H_i) representing rank i, is computed via a function that hashes rank i to id H_i. Each rank i, sends its id to the intermediaries H_i and H_p, representing the rank i and its parent p. In return, it receives two messages: one each from H_p and H_i with the ids of its parent and children, respectively.

$$p = \begin{cases} 0, & i = 0 \\ \lfloor \frac{i-1}{k} \rfloor, & otherwise \end{cases} \tag{3}$$

$$C_i = \begin{cases} [k*i+1, k*(i+1)] & k*(i+1) < m \\ [k*i+1, m) & k*i+1 < m \le k*(i+1) \\ \phi & otherwise \end{cases} \tag{4}$$

Memory consumption for each of these phases is small and is independent of group size ($O(1)$). The overall time complexity is $O(\log n)$ each for the upward and downward phases, and $O(1)$ for the hashing phase.

6 Results

Experimental Setup. We bracket our algorithms between a broadcast on the original spanning tree and a reduction on the newly constructed tree and time the whole phase. The size of the new group is specified via a participation fraction f. All processes sample from a uniform distribution $u(0, 1)$ and use f to determine their participation in the new group. For fair comparisons, we use repeatable seeds to ensure identical groups across multiple runs. We also apply the same sequential optimizations to all implementations. The runs were performed on "Intrepid", an IBM BlueGene/P supercomputer at Argonne National Laboratory. These algorithms were implemented using the Charm++ [7] parallel programming framework. We report results only for spanning trees with branching factor 3 but similar patterns were observed with other branching factors.

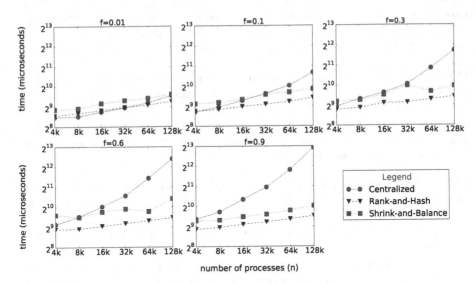

Fig. 3. Scaling behavior of the three algorithms on IBM BG/P at various participation fractions (f) with n ranging from $4,096$ to $131,072K$ processes

Performance. Figure 3 compares the scalability of the two algorithms with the baseline centralized scheme for process groups of different sizes. The results show that except at very low participation fractions (e.g. at $f = 0.01$), the distributed schemes outperform the baseline even at modest process counts. The Shrink-and-Balance scheme is slower than the Rank-and-Hash scheme because of a longer critical path. However, both attain the goal of reduced memory footprint.

Message Counts. The total number of messages for a reduce or gather over the original spanning tree is $n-1$; for a broadcast or scatter over the new tree is $m-1$. Hence, the centralized scheme sends $O(n + m)$ messages. The Rank-and-Hash scheme has an additional phase for id exchange. All m vertices send 2 messages to intermediary processes and receive 1 message with parent information. The $\frac{m}{k}$ non-leaf vertices also receive a message with child information. The total message count is hence $n+4m+\frac{m}{k} = O(n+m)$. The Shrink-and-Balance scheme requires additional messages to fill holes during the upward pass, and to identify and move excess vertices during the downward pass. An upper bound on message counts is elusive because it depends on the location of the holes and the quality of the shrunk tree. Our experiments show that counts are far fewer than the Rank-and-Hash scheme. At $128K$ processes and $f = 0.6$ the number of messages sent by the Centralized, Shrink-and-Balance and the Rank-and-Hash scheme were 2.1, 2.6 and 4.9×10^5, respectively. Figure 4 compares message counts in both schemes with the reference. We expect that at extreme scales, when multiple groups are being formed simultaneously, or when group formation occurs concurrently with other communication in the application, the Shrink-and-Balance scheme may have an advantage over the Rank-and-Hash scheme.

Comparison with MPI_Comm_split. In the two widely-used open-source MPI implementations: MPICH and OpenMPI, MPI_Comm_split is implemented as an $O(n)$ allgather followed by $O(\frac{n}{c} \log \frac{n}{c})$ sort, where c is the number of colors (assuming splits of equal size). To compare, we implemented a multi-color version of the Rank-and-Hash scheme. During the upward-pass member counts of each color are gathered at the root, which takes $O(\min(c \log n, n))$. If the original tree is shrunk into c pieces, dissemination in the downward pass can be accomplished in $O(\log n)$, totaling to a time complexity of $O(\min(c \log n, n))$. As the number of colors approaches n, time complexity of the Rank-and-Hash scheme approaches that of MPI_Comm_split. In Table 1, we compare the performance of MPI_Comm_split with Rank-and-Hash scheme on $32,768$ cores of BG/P.

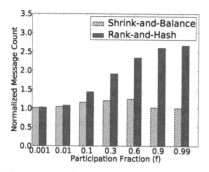

Fig. 4. Message counts, normalized against centralized scheme at same f, for $n = 128K$ on IBM BG/P

Table 1. Execution times (ms) of the Rank-and-Hash scheme and MPI_Comm_split from vendor's implementation on $32K$ cores of BG/P

splits (c)	MPI Comm-split	Rank-and-Hash
1	134.968	0.708
2	106.573	0.713
4	96.989	0.760
8	93.536	0.785

7   Related Work

Balaji et al [2] discuss the memory overheads of subcommunicator storage in MPI and note that memory usage increases with process count, significantly affecting the number of subcommunicators that can be created. They report that, on BlueGene/P, the number of new communicators that can be created at $128K$ processes drops to as low as 264 from 8189 at $1K$ processes. Their findings strengthen the argument for cheap process groups.

Sack et al [14] propose a distributed algorithm for ordered subcommunicator construction that uses $O(n/p)$ memory and $O(p \log n + \log^2 n + \frac{n}{p} \log p)$ time where p is the number of processes used for parallel key sorting. They reduce storage requirements to $O(n/p)$ by using distributed tables for storing the ranks.

Recent work by Moody et al [11] mentions a generalized MPI_Comm_split They propose creating and storing process groups as chains in $O(1)$ memory and $O(\log n)$ construction time. They perform collectives by exchanging appropriate process ids during the operation. Our work exhibits several differences. First, we avoid the extra $O(n)$ messaging required to exchange process ids during every collective call. This also results in lesser dependencies on remote information for the progress of the collective, which should lead to lesser wait times and faster completion of the operation. We believe this benefit will become more prominent for implementations that exploit one-sided data transfer calls provided by some network messaging APIs [4,9]. Second, our schemes can construct and use communication trees of arbitrary branching factors. Achieving this using chains will be difficult, and will effectively amount to constructing a spanning tree. This is of practical consequence for collectives on many architectures as binary trees do not always perform as well as other k-ary trees.

Other work [8,16] describes several techniques for the compact representation of MPI groups. They are quite effective in the presence of exploitable patterns in the member ranks. In contrast, we do not design specific data structures or compaction mechanisms, nor do we provide a complete solution for the current MPI standard. We believe several use cases can be met by the altered functionality we propose; and our work explicitly targets relevance beyond MPI.

8   Summary and Future Work

In this paper, we have motivated support for system-ranked process groups and discussed how they are suited to a subset of collectives. We have developed two algorithms, Shrink-and-Balance and Rank-and-Hash, for creating balanced, k-ary tree based process groups while consuming small amounts of memory. We discovered that our algorithms are also faster than a reference implementation even on 128K processes of a terascale supercomputer[1]; and significantly faster than the comm_split implementation of the native MPI library. We summarize our analysis in Table 2.

Table 2. Space and time complexities for different group creation schemes

	MPI(typical)	Centralized	Shrink-and-Balance	Rank-and-Hash
Space	$O(n)$	$O(m)$	$O(\log n)$	$O(1)$
Time	$O(n + m\log m)$	$O(m + \log n)$	$O(\log^2 n)$	$O(\log n)$
Msg Count	$n\log n$	$n + m$	$\Omega(n + m)$	$n + 4m + \frac{m}{k}$
Max Msg Size	$O(n)$	$O(m)$	$O(\log n)$	$O(1)$

There are several immediate extensions to the work described here. The Shrink-and-Balance scheme sends fewer messages despite having a longer critical path than the Rank-and-Hash scheme. We intend to evaluate performance in the presence of other communication and computation akin to real application execution scenarios. We also plan further experiments with larger numbers of

[1] ALCF compute resources were used under DOE contract DE-AC02-06CH11357.

splits. We believe these experiments will throw more light on the relative merits of the two algorithms discussed here, and possibly lead to further improvements.

Another planned direction is to account for network-topology. The algorithms described here can be executed hierarchically, such that each subtree is restricted to a small neighborhood of the network. This can reduce the number of network links traversed along the tree and improve performance of the targeted collectives. The complexity will be very similar to the current schemes.

Acknowledgement. This work was supported in part by DOE DE-SC0001845 and NSF ITR-0833188.

References

1. Antypas, K., Shalf, J., Wasserman, H.: NERSC6 Workload Analysis and Benchmark Selection Process. Tech. Rep. LBNL-1014E, Lawrence Berkeley National Lab. (2008)
2. Balaji, P., Chan, A., Thakur, R., Gropp, W., Lusk, E.: Toward Message Passing for a Million Processes: Characterizing MPI on a Massive Scale Blue Gene/P. Computer Science-Research and Development 24(1), 11–19 (2009)
3. Bohm, E., Bhatele, A., Kale, L.V., Tuckerman, M.E., Kumar, S., Gunnels, J.A., Martyna, G.J.: Fine Grained Parallelization of the Car-Parrinello ab initio MD Method on Blue Gene/L. IBM Journal of Research and Development: Applications of Massively Parallel Systems 52(1/2), 159–174 (2008)
4. Cray Inc.: Using the GNI and DMAPP APIs (2010), http://docs.cray.com/books/S-2446-3103/S-2446-3103.pdf
5. Gabriel, E., Fagg, G.E., Bosilca, G., Angskun, T., Dongarra, J., Squyres, J.M., Sahay, V., Kambadur, P., Barrett, B., Lumsdaine, A., Castain, R.H., Daniel, D.J., Graham, R.L., Woodall, T.S.: Open MPI: Goals, Concept, and Design of a Next Generation MPI Implementation. In: Kranzlmüller, D., Kacsuk, P., Dongarra, J. (eds.) EuroPVM/MPI 2004. LNCS, vol. 3241, pp. 97–104. Springer, Heidelberg (2004)
6. Gropp, W., Lusk, E.: Users Guide for Mpich, a Portable Implementation of Mpi. Mathematics and Computer Science Division, Argonne National Laboratory. Tech. rep., ANL-96/6 (1996)
7. Kale, L., Arya, A., Bhatele, A., Gupta, A., Jain, N., Jetley, P., Lifflander, J., Miller, P., Sun, Y., Venkataraman, R., Wesolowski, L., Zheng, G.: Charm++ for Productivity and Performance: A Submission to the 2011 HPC Class II Challenge. Tech. Rep. 11-49, Parallel Programming Laboratory (November 2011)
8. Kamal, H., Mirtaheri, S.M., Wagner, A.: Scalability of Communicators and Groups in Mpi. In: Proceedings of the 19th ACM International Symposium on High Performance Distributed Computing, HPDC 2010, pp. 264–275. ACM (2010)
9. Kumar, S., Mamidala, A., Faraj, D., Smith, B., Blocksome, M., Cernohous, B., Miller, D., Parker, J., Ratterman, J., Heidelberger, P., Chen, D., Steinmacher-Burow, B.: Pami: A Parallel Active Message Interface for the Bluegene/q Supercomputer. In: Proceedings of 26th IEEE International Parallel and Distributed Processing Symposium (IPDPS), Shanghai, China (May 2012)

10. Lifflander, J., Miller, P., Venkataraman, R., Arya, A., Jones, T., Kale, L.: Mapping Dense Lu Factorization on Multicore Supercomputer Nodes. In: Proceedings of IEEE International Parallel and Distributed Processing Symposium 2012 (May 2012)
11. Moody, A., Ahn, D.H., de Supinski, B.R.: Exascale Algorithms for Generalized MPI_Comm_split. In: Cotronis, Y., Danalis, A., Nikolopoulos, D.S., Dongarra, J. (eds.) EuroMPI 2011. LNCS, vol. 6960, pp. 9–18. Springer, Heidelberg (2011)
12. Peter Kogge, E.: ExaScale Computing Study: Technology Challenges in Achieving Exascale Systems. Tech. rep. (2009)
13. Rabenseifner, R.: Automatic MPI Counter Profiling. In: 42nd CUG Conference (2000)
14. Sack, P., Gropp, W.: A Scalable MPI_Comm_split Algorithm for Exascale Computing. In: Keller, R., Gabriel, E., Resch, M., Dongarra, J. (eds.) EuroMPI 2010. LNCS, vol. 6305, pp. 1–10. Springer, Heidelberg (2010)
15. Skinner, D., Verdier, F., Anand, H., Carter, J., Durst, M., Gerber, R.: Parallel Scaling Characteristics of Selected NERSC User Project Codes. Tech. Rep. LBNL/PUB-904, Lawrence Berkeley National Lab. (2005)
16. Träff, J.L.: Compact and Efficient Implementation of the MPI Group Operations. In: Keller, R., Gabriel, E., Resch, M., Dongarra, J. (eds.) EuroMPI 2010. LNCS, vol. 6305, pp. 170–178. Springer, Heidelberg (2010)

A Hybrid Parallelization
of Air Quality Model with MPI and OpenMP

Gian Franco Marras[1], Camillo Silibello[2], and Giuseppe Calori[2]

[1] CINECA - SuperComputing Applications and Innovation Department - SCAI,
Via Magnanelli 6/3, 40033 Casalecchio di Reno, Bologna (Bo)
g.marras@cineca.it

[2] Arianet S.r.l., Via Gilino 9, 20128 Milano (Mi)
{c.silibello,g.calori}@aria-net.it

Abstract. This paper presents the parallelization of FARM, a 3D Eulerian chemical-transport model on structured and nested grids. The parallelization has been developed using the MPI library and OpenMP directives implementing a Master-Worker strategy. Benchmarking in different architectures is also discussed.

Keywords: Hybrid Parallelization, Derived Datatypes, Multigrid, Scalability.

1 Introduction

European Directives [1] for air quality impose increasingly strict control of the air pollutant concentrations. To develop efficient plans to control the emissions and achieve meaningful abatements of air concentrations, the use of Air Quality Models (AQMs) is highly recommended. While AQMs allow to model and forecast the behaviour of chemical constituents that have an impact on the air pollutant concentrations, they are computationally intensive applications. Incorporation of detailed chemistry and physics significantly increase the computing time, as do the need to describe the phenomena with sufficient resolution over a given domain or the need to perform long-term and/or multiple runs for scenario analyses. With this work we show that the computing time of an AQM can be considerably reduced with an efficiently parallelization of the code.

The paper is organized as follows: in Section 2 we describe the AQM that we have used; in Sections 3 and 3.2 we describe parallelizations within MPI and OpenMP; in Section 3.3 we describe a parallelization mode implemented with both schemes, the hybrid parallelization. In Section 4 we give our main results and conclusions.

2 Flexible AiR Quality Model

Flexible AiR quality Model (FARM) is a 3D Eulerian chemical-transport model (CTM) written in Fortran 77/90 used to study the transport, chemical conversion

J.L. Träff, S. Benkner, and J. Dongarra (Eds.): EuroMPI 2012, LNCS 7490, pp. 235–245, 2012.

and deposition of atmospheric pollutants. The code can be configured to be used in a variety of applications, according to specific problem features, computational resources and data availability. FARM allows management of multiple grids with different resolution. Each grid is structured, that is to say that they are logically mapped onto a parallelepiped lattice with $N_x \cdot N_y \cdot N_z$ points. For convenience we denote the three spatial dimensions by x, y, z but the grids do not have to be aligned with the geographic coordinate system. For each simulation grid, a set of input files must be provided in form of regularly time-varying data archives (e.g.: hourly based). As output, FARM produces NetCDF-files[1] containing 2D and 3D gas- and aerosol phase time-dependent concentrations of selected species, a restart file, which is usually used for long-term applications, and a log file.

2.1   Model Formulation

Within FARM, physical and chemical processes influencing the concentration field within the modelling domain are described by a system of partial differential equations (PDE). Each equation describes the time dependency of the i-th chemical species average concentration, c_i, within each grid cell volume as the sum of the contributions given by all the chemical and physical processes in that volume. For a single-phase atmosphere (e.g. gas) this system has the form:

$$\frac{\partial c_i}{\partial t} = -u\frac{\partial c_i}{\partial x} - v\frac{\partial c_i}{\partial y} - w\frac{\partial c_i}{\partial z} + K_{xx}\frac{\partial^2 c_i}{\partial x} + K_{yy}\frac{\partial^2 c_i}{\partial y} + \frac{\partial}{\partial z}\left(K_{zz}\frac{\partial c_i}{\partial z}\right) + S_i + C_i + R_i \quad (1)$$

where u, v and w are the components of the wind velocity vector K_{xx}, K_{yy} and K_{zz} are the diagonal terms of the diffusivity tensor S_i is the source term, C_i the gas phase reaction term and R_i is the removal term due to dry and wet deposition processes. The lateral diffusivities are assumed to be space independent and coherent ($K_{xx} = K_{yy} = K_H$; $K_{zz} = K_V$).

Numerical integration is performed following *operator splitting*, a method that subdivides the multidimensional problem into time-dependent one-dimensional problems, which are then solved sequentially over the time step Δt. According to this technique the time evolution of the i-th chemical species over the time is computed as follows:

$$c_i(\boldsymbol{x}, t + \Delta t) = L_x(\Delta t)L_y(\Delta t)L_z(\Delta t)L_c(\Delta t)c_i(\boldsymbol{x}, t) \quad (2)$$

where L_x, L_y are advection-diffusion operators along the two horizontal axes, L_z is the vertical operator taking into account transport, diffusion, source injection and dry deposition processes in the adopted coordinates system, and L_c the operator containing all chemical conversion terms.

---

[1] NetCDF is a set of software libraries and self-describing, machine-independent data formats that support the creation, access, and sharing of array-oriented scientific data (http://www.unidata.ucar.edu/software/netcdf/).

2.2 Numerical Algorithms

PDE involved in horizontal and vertical advection-diffusion operators are solved using finite elements schemes [2]. In horizontal directions a method based on Blackman cubic polynomials [3] is used, while the numerical integration of the vertical equation is performed using a hybrid method employing a hybrid semi-implicit Crank-Nicolson/fully implicit scheme [3]. The equations describing the chemical mechanism are generally highly complex and nonlinear, forming a stiff system of ordinary differential equations (ODEs). Starting from a formal description of the involved reactions and rates, Kinetic Pre-Processor [4] (KPP), is used to generate the production and destruction terms which are the included into the model. These resulting equations are solved in FARM by means of Rosenbrock [5] and LSODE [6] integrators, also provided by KPP.

2.3 Nesting

FARM allows one-way and two-way grid nesting. In the one-way mode, at each given calculation, time interval concentrations calculated on a coarse domain feed the fine domain through the assignment of lateral boundary conditions. In the two-way mode, at the end of each time interval, concentrations values of the fine grid are used to update the concentrations values of the parent grid over the region of overlap. The number of nested grids is not limited, although there are restrictions and constraints:

- nesting can be applied only in the horizontal directions, therefore all grids must share the same vertical levels;
- each grid must be nested completely within its parent coarser grid;
- the horizontal spacing of a fine grid must be a finite interval of the coarser grid within which is embedded;
- the edges of a given fine grid domain must correspond to a coarse grid cell edge;
- fine grids inside a given parent grid cannot overlap each other.

3 Parallelization

The first version of FARM was a serial code. Afterwards, the growth of the computational time, due to the increasing complexity of the equations describing the chemical mechanisms, but even more to the expanding need of longer and multiple runs, required a parallelization phase to reduce execution time and permit efficiently production runs. In a first phase OpenMP [7] directives were added to quickly exploit shared memory systems. To overcome node limit and scale to cluster architectures a complete parallelization with Message Passing Interface [8] (MPI) was successively implemented. So currently, FARM can be run in four different modes: serial, MPI, OpenMP and Hybrid mode. This work has furthermore improved the flexibility of FARM allowing the porting on different platforms (Linux, Windows and AIX systems) and the possibility to use it in many architectures. Here we will describe the parallelization with MPI, OpenMP and Hybrid modes and the advantages of the latter.

3.1   MPI Implementation

Master-Worker Strategy. For every grid we use a Master-Worker strategy [9] where the Master process reads the input files, scatters data along the workers, collects the results and writes the output files. The Master is the same task for all the nested grids that may be employed in a given run. Worker processes can be either H-workers (horizontal operators) and/or V-workers (vertical operator) of the *i-th* nesting level grid. This strategy allows the overlapping of input/output time with computations. Master process, H- and V-workers are defined at the start-up of the computation time and depend on the number of points of each grid along x, y and z directions.

Domain Decomposition. The domain cannot be decomposed in one or more directions in a static way over the whole time step because the operator used for the transport along the considered direction requires the whole data set. Instead, we have decomposed the domain in two ways. Each grid is partitioned among the available processes along z (H-decomposition), and along x and y (V-decomposition) directions. In the H-decomposition the H-workers compute the transport along x and y. In a serial code this takes about 20% of the computational time. In the V-decomposition the V-workers compute the transport along z and the chemistry. At each time step a shuffling of the data from H- to V-decomposition and vice-versa is needed. In H-decomposition the scalability is limited by the number of grid points along the direction z, while in V-decomposition it is limited by the product of number of points along x and y directions. This decomposition ensures scalability for large number of processors, because the computational time of the chemistry and transport along z direction takes more than 70% of the total CPU time. This decomposition is called HV-partitioning [9]. Fig. 1 shows the partitioning along the workers processes. Currently the partitioning is automatically determined by the code during its startup phase, and cannot be changed by the user, while in the future alternative strategies will be also explored. The phases of a single time step of a parallel computation are listed in Table 1.

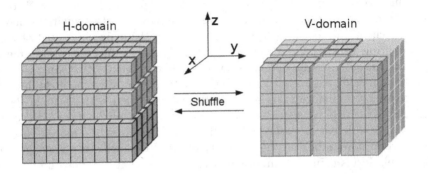

Fig. 1. Domain decomposition for HV-partitioning

Table 1. Phases of a single step of a parallel computation

Step	Processes	Mpi routine	Description	Domain
1.	Master H- & V-Workers	Distribution or scattering	The Master reads the input files and distributes data to the workers. Workers receive data from the Master.	H
2.	H-workers		Workers compute x and y transport.	H
3.	H- & V-Workers	Shuffling	Workers redistribute data from H-domain to V-domain.	H to V
4.	V-Worker		Workers compute z transport and chemistry.	V
5.	V- & H-Workers	Shuffling	Workers redistribute data from V-domain to H-domain.	V to H
6.	V-workers Master	Gathering	Workers send data to the Master. The Master collects all the data and write them in output files.	V

Communication Routines. For each MPI routine we have used derived datatypes (DDT) to specify arbitrary memory layouts for sending and receiving messages using a *zero-copy* mechanism [10]. Since the data are non-contiguous, the specification of DDT is needed in order to avoid manual copying of non-contiguous data in a buffer or the use of pack/unpack MPI routines. Therefore non-contiguous data with different size and different type can be transferred without additional copies using a single MPI message. Next we describe the communication routines written to distribute, scatter, gather and shuffle the arrays (see Table 1).

Distribution Routine. At the beginning the master process reads from files all the input data which are then scattered among the worker processes. In a single non-blocking MPI *send* routine, the Master send all the input data to all the H- and V- workers of the *i-th* grid. The workers wait for the message with a blocking MPI *receive* routine (Step 1).

Scattering Routine. At regular time steps, the Master sends to the H- and V-workers specific data fields. This routine is similar to the distribution routine, except that the Master process sends only one input data field to the workers, so it is called only when a specific field needs to be updated (Step 1).

Gathering Routine. At regular time steps, the Master must write the output files, usually concentration fields of the chemical species of interest for the user. In a single non-blocking MPI *receive*, the master process waits for the output data while all the workers send the field with a blocking MPI *send* routine (Step 6).

Shuffling Routine. From the H- to the V- domain the concentration fields must be sent and ordered from H- to V-worker processes (see Fig. 1). This routine is performed by a specific MPI *alltoall* routine (*MPI_Alltoallw*). We need this routine because it has the possibility to send and receive data of different DDT for all the workers. At each time step this routine is called two times: the first to send and reorder the concentration fields from the H- to the V-domains (Step 3), the second to send and reorder the same data in the reverse mode (Step 5).

3.2 OpenMP Implementation

In this implementation we have added parallel constructs and workshare directives to distribute the work among the threads.

The transport and the chemistry equations are divided among the threads in the following way:

- transport along x: iterations of the DO loop in the y direction are distributed among the threads through loop constructs;
- transport along y: iterations of the DO loop in the x direction are distributed among the threads through loop constructs;
- transport along z and chemistry: iterations of the DO loop in the y direction are distributed among the threads through loop constructs.

The scalability is limited only by the number of the available threads, which in shared memory systems or inside a single cluster's node is limited by the number of available cores.

3.3 Hybrid Implementation

The fusion of MPI with OpenMP implementation has been realized without further changes in the source code. The two implementations have been written in a way that the OpenMP directives and the MPI routines are completely separated.

The transport and the chemistry equation are therefore partitioned in the following way:

- In the H-domain:
    - transport along x: the z direction is partitioned among the H-workers processes while the y direction is distributed among the threads through OpenMP loop constructs;
    - transport along y: the z direction is partitioned among the H-workers processes while the x direction is distributed among the threads through OpenMP loop constructs;
- In the V-domain:
    - transport along z and chemistry: the x and y directions are partitioned among V-workers processes while the y direction is distributed among the threads through OpenMP loop constructs;

MPI implementation   Hybrid implementation

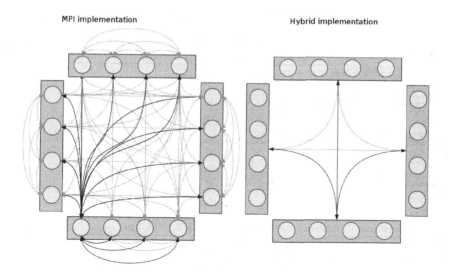

Fig. 2. Difference of number of messages for an *alltoall* routine between MPI and Hybrid implementation on four nodes (cyan rectangles) each one with four cores (yellow circles). Black lines represent all the messages related to a single core.

This implementation is useful to decrease the number of the processes, inherent synchronizations and exchange data size involved in the MPI *alltoall* routine (see Fig. 2).

4   Results

We have tested the scalability of a simulation with three nested grids on two different clusters (Tab. 2). The first grid has $61 \times 56 \times 12$ points, the second $102 \times 84 \times 12$, the third one $64 \times 56 \times 12$. The code has been compiled with *Open MPI* [11] (Version 1.4.4 compiled with *Intel* 12.1). In the MPI mode the number of mpi task is equal to the number of the available cores; in the hybrid mode the number of mpi task is equal to the number of the available nodes, and for each node the number of threads is equal to the number of the available cores. In Fig. 3 and 4 we report the simulation times and the speedup[2] in MPI and Hybrid mode for an increasing number of cores. Figures show that on both clusters FARM has a better scalability in the hybrid mode. In this mode the scalability improves mainly because the number of sent messages in an *alltoall* routine decreases by a factor of approximately n^2, with n being the number of threads inside each node. Another reason that contributes to the improvement of the scalability is that in the hybrid mode a higher number of cores can be

---

[2] Speedup is defined as T_s/T_p where T_s and T_p are respectively the computational time of the serial and parallel code.

Table 2. Clusters description

PLX

Processors Type:	2 six-cores Intel Xeon (Esa-Core Westmere) E5645 2.4 GHz
Number of nodes:	274
Number of cores:	3288
Internal Network:	Infiniband with 4x QDR switches (40 Gbps)
RAM:	14 TB (48 GB/Compute node)
Operating System:	Red Hat 4.1.2-50

ARPAP

Processors Type:	2 quad-cores Intel Xeon (Nehalem) E5520 2.27 GHz
Number of nodes:	32
Number of cores:	256
Internal Network:	Infiniband with 4x DDR switches (20 Gbps)
RAM:	160 GB (4 GB/Compute node)
Operating System:	Red Hat 4.1.2-44

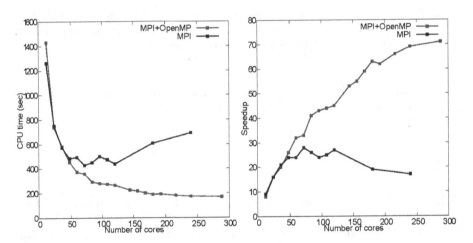

Fig. 3. CPU time and Speedup for an increasing number of workers on cluster PLX. MPI configuration is started with 12 MPI process for node while hybrid configuration is started with one MPI process and 12 threads for node.

available in the h-domain. While in the MPI mode the scalability in the h-domain is limited by the number of grid points along the direction z, in the hybrid mode the scalability is limited by the number of grid points along z times the number of the available threads for each node, and therefore the performance improves by a factor equal to the number of threads; in modern architectures this is an order of magnitude (see Sect. 3.3). Furthermore, in the hybrid mode the OpenMP directives improve the load balancing within the MPI tasks because the workload is redistributed at runtime among the threads. These results are also confirmed by profiling measures.

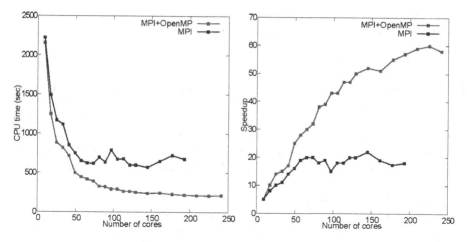

Fig. 4. CPU time and Speedup for an increasing number of workers on cluster ARPAP. MPI configuration is started with 8 MPI process for node while hybrid configuration is started with one MPI process and 8 threads for node.

Currently, we are testing particular configurations where we measure a significant performance improvement: by using the same number of CPU but different configurations on the node (e.g. on PLX, one mpi task and twelve threads versus two mpi tasks and six threads each) we find that the performance improves of $\sim 20\%$. This is likely to be caused by memory affinity effects on the NUMA[3] node. Namely on PLX, in case of one mpi task and twelve threads, the threads have different access times to different regions of memory; while in case of two mpi tasks, each with six threads, and each task working in a specific socket, the threads have only access directly to the local memory of the socket. These are however preliminary results since further testing is currently being carried out.

5   Conclusions and Future Work

In this work we have described the parallelization of FARM with MPI, OpenMP and Hybrid (MPI+OpenMP) paradigms. The Hybrid parallelization resulted in a better scalability because the number of sent messages in an *alltoall* routine decreases by a factor of n^2, with n equal to the number of threads inside each node. With the hybrid parallelization the scalability improves also because the number of available cores in the H-domain can be significantly higher than with the MPI parallelization.

In the future we will implement the possibility of modifying the domain decomposition parameters in order to choose alternative configurations to possibly

---

[3] Non Uniform Memory Access.

reach better performances. Furthermore, to decrease the number of all2all routines for time step, Eq. 2 will be transformed as follows:

$$c_i(\boldsymbol{x}, t + 2\Delta t) = L_x(\Delta t)L_y(\Delta t)L_z(\Delta t)L_c(2\Delta t)c_iL_z(\Delta t)L_y(\Delta t)L_x(\Delta t)(\boldsymbol{x}, t) \quad (3)$$

In the above equation the splitting operator is symmetric; the different operators are calculated first in direct, then in reverse order. In this way, for two time steps $(2\Delta t)$ the all2all routines are called two times, opposite to Eq. 2 where they are called two times for single time integration (Δt). This will possibly reduce the computational time up to the 15%, according to the CPU time for MPI tests performed with 120 workers[4]. The envisaged feature is suitable for both parallelizations, MPI and Hybrid.

A further improvement can be obtained by rearranging the access to the input and output files. By using the most recent versions of netCDF libraries (e.g netCDF 4.0 or higher) with parallel I/O, each worker can directly read or write its own domain region. With this feature all the MPI calls between the master and the workers are avoided. However in order to implement this feature a parallel filesystem is needed. In our case this would only be possible on PLX since ARPAP does not have a parallel filesystem.

Acknowledgements. The whole parallelization has been carried out within a collaboration between Arianet and ArpaPiemonte with Cineca[5]. The authors want to thank Massimo Muraro (ArpaPiemonte), Cineca and Arianet for this opportunity. It is a great pleasure to thank anonymous reviewers for their many constructive suggestions.

References

1. The European Parlament, Directive 2008/50/EC of the European Parliament and of the Council of 21 May 2008 on ambient air quality and cleaner air for Europe (2008)
2. Yamartino, R.J., Scire, J.S., Hanna, S.R., Carmichael, G.R., Chang, Y.S.: The calgrid mesoscale photochemical grid model. Atmospheric Environment 26A(8), 1493–1512 (1992)
3. Yamartino, R.: Nonnegative, conserved scalar transport using grid-cell-centered, spectrally constrained blackman cubics for application on a variable-thickness mesh. Monthly Weather Review 121, 753–763 (1992)
4. Damian, V., Sandu, A., Damian, M., Potra, F., Carmichael, G.R.: The kinetic preprocessor kpp – a software environment for solving chemical kinetics. Computers and Chemical Engineering (2002)
5. Sandu, A., Daescu, D., Carmichael, G.R.: Direct and adjoint sensitivity analysis of chemical kinetic system with kpp. Atmospheric Environment 37, 5083–5096 (2003)
6. Radhakrishnan, K., Hindmarsh, A.: Description and use of lsode, the livermore solver for differential equations. NASA Reference Pubblication, vol. 1327 (1993)

---

[4] Measurements performed with Scalasca - www.scalasca.org

[5] www.aria-net.it, www.arpa.piemonte.it, www.cineca.it

7. OpenMP Architecture Review Board, Openmp application program interface. Specification (2011)
8. Message Passing Interface Forum, MPI: A Message-Passing Interface Standard, Version 2.2. High Performance Computing Center Stuttgart (HLRS) (2009)
9. Miehe, P., Sandu, A., Carmichael, G.R., Tang, Y., Daescu, D.: A communication library for the parallelization of air quality model on structured grids. Atmospheric Environment 36(24), 3917–3930 (2002)
10. Hoefler, T., Gottlieb, S.: Parallel Zero-Copy Algorithms for Fast Fourier Transform and Conjugate Gradient Using MPI Datatypes. In: Keller, R., Gabriel, E., Resch, M., Dongarra, J. (eds.) EuroMPI 2010. LNCS, vol. 6305, pp. 132–141. Springer, Heidelberg (2010)
11. Gabriel, E., Fagg, G.E., Bosilca, G., Angskun, T., Dongarra, J.J., Squyres, J.M., Sahay, V., Kambadur, P., Barrett, B.W., Lumsdaine, A., Castain, R.H., Daniel, D.J., Graham, R.L., Woodall, T.S.: Open MPI: Goals, Concept, and Design of a Next Generation MPI Implementation. In: Kranzlmüller, D., Kacsuk, P., Dongarra, J. (eds.) EuroPVM/MPI 2004. LNCS, vol. 3241, pp. 97–104. Springer, Heidelberg (2004)

2nd Special Session on Improving MPI User and Developer Interaction (IMUDI 2012)

Dries Kimpe[1,2] and Jason Cope[3]

[1] Argonne National Laboratory, Argonne, IL 60439
dkimpe@mcs.anl.gov
[2] University of Chicago, Chicago, IL 60637
[3] DataDirect Networks, Inc., Columbia, MD 21046
jcope@ddn.com

While for many researchers MPI itself remains an active research topic, for many others it has become an invaluable tool to extract useful science from some of the most powerful machines available. Unfortunately these MPI application developers – and their highly valued experience and use cases – do not always find their way to the EuroMPI conference. The 2nd Special Session on Improving MPI User and Developer Interaction (IMUDI 2012) once again aims to improve the balance by actively reaching out to the application developer communities. By evaluating the MPI standard from the perspective of the MPI end-user (application and library developers) we hope to provide application developers the opportunity to highlight MPI issues that might not be immediately obvious to the developers of the various MPI implementations, while at the same time enabling the MPI developers to solicit feedback regarding future MPI development, such as the MPI-3 standardization effort.

This year's keynote speaker, Prof. Matthias Troyer (ETH Zurich), gracefully accepted to share his experiences in developing Boost.MPI. We peer-reviewed and selected four papers from the six papers submitted to the IMUDI 2012 session. These papers cover several topics that address software development challenges associated with the MPI standard: a discussion of MPI support for multi-application interaction, a study on the usability of the MPI shared file pointer routines, communication algorithms for data analysis and an analysis of efficient adjoints of one-sided MPI communication. We believe that the discussion of these topics in the IMUDI 2012 session will bring together MPI developers and MPI end-users, and help MPI users and implementors understand the challenges in developing MPI-based software and how to effectively use MPI in parallel software products.

We are grateful for the support and help provided by our colleagues for this event. While we cannot list them all, we especially thank the EuroMPI 2012 conference organizers, including Jack Dongarra (University of Tennessee - Knoxville), Siegfried Benkner (University of Vienna) and Jesper Larsson Träff (Vienna University of Technology) for their invaluable feedback. We also thank the members of the IMUDI 2012 program committee for reviewing the session

J.L. Träff, S. Benkner, and J. Dongarra (Eds.): EuroMPI 2012, LNCS 7490, pp. 246–247, 2012.

papers and their help in organizing the session. The program committee for this year's session included Andreas Knuepfer (ZIH, TU Dresden), Chris Carothers (RPI), Jack Poulson (UTexas), Jay Lofstead (Sandia National Laboratories), Quincey Koziol (The HDF Group), Sreeram Potluri (The Ohio State University), Terry Jones (Oak Ridge National Laboratory), Theron Voran (University of Colorado at Boulder) and Jeff Hammond (Argonne National Laboratory).

A Wish List for Efficient Adjoints
of One-Sided MPI Communication*

Michel Schanen and Uwe Naumann

LuFG Informatik 12: Software and Tools for Computational Engineering
RWTH Aachen University, Germany
{schanen,nauman}@stce.rwth-aachen.de
http://www.stce.rwth-aachen.de

Abstract. We present a generic approach to transforming one-sided
MPI communication in the context of adjoint code. The adjoint allows
us to compute gradients of multivariate function implementations at a
computational cost that is independent of the size of these gradients. In
this paper, we apply the adjoint model to codes containing one-side MPI
communication. The Partitioned Global Address Space notation is used
to derive the corresponding adjoint code. Our adjoint solutions rely on
certain workarounds due to limited adjoint support in the current MPI
standard. To avoid these, we provide a wish list for future MPI standards
that potentially lead to a more efficient adjoint communication.

Keywords: Algorithmic Differentiation, adjoint, gradient, one-sided
communication.

1 Introduction and Review of Related Work

The motivation for *adjoining* or reversing MPI communication arises in Algorithmic Differentiation (AD) where derivatives are computed by transforming or
overloading source code of an original function implementation F. Without loss
of generality we assume F to be a multivariate scalar vector function $y = F(\mathbf{x})$,
$\mathbb{R}^n \to \mathbb{R}$, where the *inputs* $\mathbf{x}$ and the *output* y are of size n and 1, respectively.
By exploiting the associativity of the chain rule of differential calculus, adjoints
are computed according to the *adjoint model*

$$\bar{\mathbf{x}} = \bar{\mathbf{x}} + \nabla F\left(\mathbf{x}\right)^{\mathsf{T}} \cdot \bar{y}, \tag{1}$$

where $\bar{\mathbf{x}}$ and $\bar{y}$ are the adjoints of $\mathbf{x}$ and y. ∇F denotes the gradient that contains
the partial derivatives of the output with respect to all inputs. Without going
into the details, it is crucial to understand that we can compute the gradient in
one sweep whereas for finite difference we need to rerun the entire code n times
while each time perturbing one input x_i. In terms of time complexity, this is an
improvement to $\mathcal{O}(1) \cdot cost(F)$ compared to $\mathcal{O}(n) \cdot cost(F)$ [3,8].

---

* This work was supported by the Fond National de la Recherche of Luxembourg
under grant PHD-09-145.

J.L. Träff, S. Benkner, and J. Dongarra (Eds.): EuroMPI 2012, LNCS 7490, pp. 248–257, 2012.

The downside of the adjoint model is its higher complexity reflected by a higher constant overhead in $\mathcal{O}(1)$. The reason is that the evaluation of the adjoints is in reverse order to the computation of the values (see (1)). We illustrate this with an example implementing the adjoint model applied to the function $y = F(\mathbf{x}) = sin(x_1 \cdot x_2)$, $\mathbb{R}^2 \to \mathbb{R}$ in Table 1. The values t and y are evaluated in the *forward section*. In the *reverse section* the adjoint incremental assignments are executed in reverse order to the value assignments in the forward section, amounting to a control flow reversal. In terms of MPI this implies a tracing of all communications. Additionally, the variables of the right hand side of each value assignment (e.g. $x[0]$, $x[1]$ in line 1) each become a left hand side of one incremental adjoint assignment ($\bar{x}[0]$ and $\bar{x}[1]$ in line 2 and 3). This represents a complete data flow reversal implying a reversal of all MPI communications in our code. Finally, the values of $x[0]$, $x[1]$ and t need to be recorded in the forward section since they are required for computation of the adjoints in the reverse section. Setting $\bar{y}$ to 1 results in a gradient computation with the partial derivatives of $\frac{d\mathbf{x}}{dy}$ contained in $\bar{x}[0]$ and $\bar{x}[1]$.

Table 1. Adjoint implementation of $y = F(\mathbf{x}) = sin(x_1 \cdot x_2)$

forward section $y = F(\mathbf{x})$	reverse section $\bar{\mathbf{x}} = \bar{\mathbf{x}} + \nabla F(\mathbf{x})^{\mathsf{T}} \cdot \bar{y}$
1 $t=x[0]*x[1]$ 2 $y=sin(t)$	1 $\bar{t}+=cos(t)*\bar{y}$ 2 $\bar{x}[0]+=x[1]*\bar{t}$ 3 $\bar{x}[1]+=x[0]*\bar{t}$

The adjoint code may be written by hand. However, from a non trivial code size onwards, this tends to be very error prone and difficult to maintain. Tools for AD aim at differentiating code semi-automatically, avoiding the tedious and mechanical application of the adjoint code generation rules. This may be achieved using a derivative code compiler [10,11,15] or by linking overloaded operator libraries [2,1,6]. Either way, the same logic of reversing the original program in order to compute adjoints, also applies to the MPI communication. There has been a steady effort to efficiently adjoin MPI communication. First attempts involved manual differentiation, transforming MPI calls by hand [5]. Later this was achieved automatically by source transformation or overloading [14,13] up to second-order derivatives [12].

In this paper, we specifically cover the adjoining of one-sided communication as described by the MPI 2.2 standard [4]. Although MPI is a symmetric interface and therefore allows a more or less efficient reversal of all communication, this does not imply that the interface allows an efficient reversal with respect to the chain rule of differential calculus. The reason is the incremental nature of the adjoint model which transforms assignments into reversed incremental assignments. This will pose some problems if applied to one-sided MPI communication. We try to expose those shortcomings of MPI with regard to incremental reversal and formulate a wish list to remedy the current situation.

2   Method

There are three one-sided communication calls MPI_Put, MPI_Get and MPI_Accumulate. We refer to these functions as Put, Get and Accumulate.

Put(Variable , Target , Displacement, Window)
Get(Variable , Target , Displacement, Window)
Accumulate(Variable, Operation, Target , Displacement, Window)
Fence

Additionally, we use reduced signatures to solely focus on the adjoining of a given communication. Put, Get and Accumulate are used on the origin's Variable (e.g. $x[i], \dots$) with the target process id Target (P1,P2,...), target window displacement Displacement (0,1,...) and the target window Window. Accumulate has the MPI operation as an additional argument (MPI_PROD, MPI_SUM,...). All fences are assumed to be global and have no arguments or options.

A prerequisite for this paper is a basic knowledge on one-sided MPI communication. We do not cover all three synchronization methods put forward by the MPI 2.2 standard. These are *Fence, Lock* and *Expose*. They are all brought down to a Fence. All solutions presented in this paper will work by analogy with all three synchronization methods.

To validate our proposed adjoint communication we rely on the PGAS (Partitioned Global Address Space) notation. Therein, each communication amounts to an assignment of variables with distinct prefixes. Sending the value of a variable x on process P1 to the variable y on process P2 is equivalent to the assignment $P2.y=P1.x$. Note that the nature of a communication is hidden. It may be blocking, non blocking or one-sided. In this paper, we will only cover the latter. Consider the following MPI program in Table 2 running on two processes P1 and P2.

Table 2. Pseudocode of the value of k being sent from process P1 to P2 and saved in l and its corresponding PGAS code

P1	P2	PGAS code
1 Win_create(NULL,win)	1 Win_create(y,win)	1 P1.x[0]=P1.k
2 x[0]=k	2 Fence	2 Fence
3 Fence	3 Fence	3 P2.y[0]=P1.x[0]
4 Put(x[0],P2,0,win)	4 $l=y$[0]	4 Fence
5 Fence	5 Win_free(win)	5 P2.l=P2.y[0]
6 Win_free(win)		

It describes a common use case where a buffer array element x[0] is filled with the value k on process P1. The value of x[0] is then sent over to process P2 using a Put. There it is received inside the window win mapped to array y. Finally, it is read by an assignment to variable l.

We convert this code into PGAS as shown in Table 2. The two codes of both processes are actually merged into one code. All variables are prefixed by their residing process id (here P1, P2). All statements involving no parallel communication remain unchanged, except for the prefix. As defined by the MPI standard, the period between two synchronizations (Fence) is an *access epoch*. We want to keep the notion of an access epoch in PGAS and therefore take the synchronization routines over to the PGAS code. The Put in pseudocode of P1 in Table 2 line 4 has become an assignment in the PGAS code of Table 2 line 3. There are multiple possible outcomes for the PGAS notation. The order of the PGAS statements is defined by the following rules:

- The order of execution of statements on one process stays the same. If statement s_i is executed before statement s_j ($s_i < s_j$), the same holds true in PGAS notation.
- The order of execution of two statements involving two or more processes is undefined in PGAS notation inside of access epochs.
- The access epochs are synchronized by the synchronization routine Fence. Matching synchronizations in pseudocode are merged into one synchronization call in PGAS code (e.g. in the pseudocode of Table 2 line 3 for P1 and line 2 for P2 are merged to line 2 of the PGAS code).

The only difference to standard PGAS code is the synchronization routine Fence, restricting the reordering of the statements in PGAS notation and thus illustrating the effect of synchronization on the possible outcome of the code. The one-sided communication assignment (line 3) is actually only executed on the origin (here P1).

Our robustness goal is that a deterministic program yields deterministic adjoints after it has been differentiated using AD [9]. If the adjoint computation is deterministic it is enough to prove that the program yields correct adjoints for one instance of its PGAS code.

In Sect. 3 we develop the adjoints to the Put and Get communication routines while in Sect. 4 we deal with the Accumulate call. In both sections we elaborate potential performance losses due to the incremental nature of the adjoint communication and suggest solutions to address these issues.

3   Adjoining Put and Get

The MPI standard specifically states that no overlapping local access and Remote Memory Access (RMA) *store* operation is allowed during an access epoch. Furthermore, no more than one store RMA operation is allowed on one memory location in one access epoch, with the exception of Accumulate. These two rules are essentially rules on the deterministic behaviour of a program. Nondeterministic behaviour is only possible if the order of two overlapping store operations on a memory location is unclear [9]. The MPI standard states:

"It is erroneous to have concurrent conflicting accesses to the same memory location in a window; if a location is updated by a put or accumulate operation, then this location cannot be accessed by a load or another RMA operation until the updating operation has completed at the target." [7]

Therefore we assume that any correct one-sided MPI code, restricted to Put and Get, is guaranteed to be deterministic. Furthermore, we assume that inside of an access epoch, a variable is at most read once. This breaks down to no overlapping RMA at all.

The only required prior knowledge about adjoint differentiation is that a communication via Put and Get amounts to an assignment in PGAS, with its adjoint being an incremental assignment according the adjoint model (see (1)). We take the code of Table 2 as a code base. It only has one single access to each memory location inside an access epoch. Any deterministic RMA MPI program, with no overlapping local access or RMA is a decomposition and concatenation of this code. In essence, each variable is only accessed at most once during an access epoch. Hence, there are at most one of such code snippets for each variable. The PGAS notation of the forward section matches Table 2.

Table 3.

forward section	reverse section
$y=x$	$\bar{x}+=\bar{y}$

(a) Adjoint mode rule for an assignment.

forward section	reverse section
1 $P1.x[0]=P1.k$	1 $P2.\bar{y}[0]+=P2.\bar{l}$
2 Fence	2 Fence
3 $P2.y[0]=P1.x[0]$	3 $P1.\bar{x}[0]+=P2.\bar{y}[0]$
4 Fence	4 Fence
5 $P2.l=P2.y[0]$	5 $P1.\bar{k}+=P1.\bar{x}[0]$

(b) Forward section with the derived reverse section in PGAS.

By applying the adjoint mode rule for assignments of Table 3a we end up with the following reverse section in Table 3b.

Due to the incremental assignment in line 3 of the reverse section it does not equate to a Get operation, but has instead become something similar to an Accumulate. As a first guess, we might use an Accumulate on process P2 to add the adjoint $\bar{y}$ via an MPI_SUM operation to the adjoint of process P1. This is not possible, because at runtime, process P2 does not know if and whom to send the adjoints to. Only process P1 has this knowledge based on the forward run. Therefore, the Accumulate has to be on process P1. Unfortunately, MPI only allows an Accumulate where the data is being transferred from the origin to the target, and added to the target's value. What we need, is an Accumulate that gets the value of the target and adds it to the origin's value. This is not supported, hence we need to circumvent this. Note that if we used a Get in the original code, the adjoint operation would have become an incremental put which is a regular

Accumulate combined with an MPI_SUM operation. With Put, the incremental statement is actually an incremental Get which, for now, has to be decomposed into an assignment (Get) followed by a sum. Thus we wrote the adjoint code in Table 4.

Table 4. Reverse section of process P1 and P2 in pseudocode

P1	P2
1 Win_create(NULL,win)	1 Win_create($\bar{y}$,win)
2 Fence	2 $\bar{y}[0]+=\bar{l}$
3 Get(buf[0],P2,0,win)	3 Fence
4 Fence	4 Fence
5 Sync(buf,$\bar{x}$)	5 Win_free(win)
6 $\bar{k}+=\bar{x}[0]$	
7 Win_free(win)	

The increment and the assignment are split up into a Get in line 3 and a synchronization Sync in line 5. The received values of $\bar{y}$ are first buffered in buf. Only after the access epoch has finished, that is after the Fence, the values of buf are added to $\bar{x}$ in a separate synchronization routine Sync. Since we know that each memory location is updated or read only by one RMA operation, we know that we need exactly one increment for each touched adjoint at the end of an access epoch. The same applies to the other two synchronization methods, Unlock and Complete/Wait. This obviously undermines the idea of one-sided communication. If there are several Get's and Put's during an access epoch, the actual synchronization may become a bottleneck as all the increments happen in one single function call of Sync.

Table 5. Adjoint mode rules for one-sided communication involving Put and Get

original	adjoint (now)	adjoint (wished)
Win_create	Win_free	Win_free
Win_free	Win_create	Win_create
Put	Get	Accumulate $\hat{=}$ incremental get
Get	Accumulate	Accumulate
Fence	Fence + Sync	Fence

As a summary, we have developed the rules in Table 5 to adjoin a one-sided MPI code with no overlapping local and RMA's and we added the conversion rules we would like in the future: an incremental get amounting to an Accumulate from target to origin. Allowing overlapping RMA reads only worsens the situation, requiring even more sophisticated synchronization steps and further decreasing the performance.

4   Accumulate

As mentioned before, overlapping local stores and RMA are generally not allowed according to the MPI standard. However, Accumulate is an exception to this rule. Because MPI operations (MPI_SUM,MPI_MAX,MPI_PROD,...) are all commutative, their order of execution has no effect, with the exception of some numerical rounding differences. Hence, in this case, MPI allows more than one Accumulate on one memory location of the target, the sole constraint being that only one type of MPI operation is allowed on that memory location. These operations do not break the determinism of a program. However, there is one exception to this rule. The MPI_REPLACE operation replaces the value at the target with the one from the origin. This renders a given code potentially not deterministic. We will not cover this issue in this paper and stick to the commutative operations. All the adjoints of the commutative MPI operations may be computed efficiently as shown in Table 6. For MPI_SUM and MPI_MAX only the adjoint of the results $\bar{x}_m$ and $\bar{y}$ are needed. Hence, a Get is unavoidable. However, there is one particularity when adjoining the MPI_PROD operation. If we differentiated the product straightforwardly we would end up with $\bar{x}_i += \prod_{j!=i} x_j \cdot \bar{y}$. This however is not efficient, since not all processes do have local access to all x_j's. Therefore, we compute the adjoints with $\bar{x}_i = \frac{y}{x_i} \cdot \bar{y}$. This guarantees that we only need local access to the value of x_i. Yet, as a trade-off, we need access to the global result of y. Hence, we need to save y at the end of all the Accumulate operations and send it back from the target to the origins. This has to take place in the forward section during the computation of the values, since y is a value.

Table 6. Commutative MPI operations and their corresponding adjoint computation

operation	forward section	reverse section
MPI_SUM	$y = \sum_{i=1}^{n} x_i$	$\bar{x}_i += \bar{y}$
MPI_MAX/MPI_MIN	$x_m = \max/\min(x_1, \ldots, x_n)$	$\bar{x}_i += \bar{x}_m$
MPI_PROD	$y = \prod_{i=1}^{n} x_i$	$\bar{x}_i += \prod_{j!=i} x_j \cdot \bar{y} = \frac{y}{x_i} \cdot \bar{y}$

Table 7a is an example code with three processes. Note that it may be extended to an arbitrary number of processes p. Process P1 and P2 send their local contribution x[i] to process P3 where the multiplication will take place. The accumulation amounts to a "*=" operation where the left-hand side resides on a process different than the right-hand side. The adjoint to the "*=" operation has been explained in Table 6. Hence we end up with the PGAS code in Table 7b As mentioned before, we need to somehow transfer the end result of P3.y[0] to the processes P1 and P2 in order to compute P1.$\bar{x}$[0] and P2.$\bar{x}$[0].

We propose to do this in the second Fence operation in the forward section of process P1 and P2. Therefore this time, the forward section of P1 and P2 is structurally different from the original code:

Table 7.

P1	P2	P3
1 Win_create (NULL, win)	Win_create (NULL, win)	Win_create (NULL, win)
2 $x[0]=3$	$x[0]=4$	$y[0]=2$
3 Fence	Fence	Fence
4 Accumulate ($x[0]$, MPI_PROD,	Accumulate ($x[0]$, MPI_PROD,	Fence
5 P3,0, win)	P3,0, win)	$l=x[0]$
6 Fence	Fence	Win_free (win)
7 Win_free (win)	Win_free (win)	

(a) Pseudocode of P1, P2 and P3.

forward section	reverse section
1 $P1.x[0]=3$	1 $P3.\bar{y}[0]+=P3.\bar{l}$
2 $P2.x[0]=4$	2 Fence
3 $P3.y[0]=2$	3 $P2.\bar{x}[0]+=(P3.y[0]/P2.x[0])*P3.\bar{y}[0]$
4 Fence	4 $P1.\bar{x}[0]+=(P3.y[0]/P1.x[0])*P3.\bar{y}[0]$
5 $P3.y[0]*=P1.x[0]$	5 Fence
6 $P3.y[0]*=P2.x[0]$	
7 Fence	
8 $P3.l=P3.y[0]$	

(b) Forward and reverse section in PGAS code

Table 8. Amended forward section of process P1 and P2 in pseudocode

P1	P2
1 Win_create (NULL, win)	1 Win_create (NULL, win)
2 $x[0]=3$	2 $x[0]=4$
3 Fence	3 Fence
4 Accumulate ($x[0]$, MPI_PROD, P3,0, win)	4 Accumulate ($x[0]$, MPI_PROD, P3,0, win)
5 Fence + Get (prod_res, MPI_PROD, P3,0, win)	5 Fence + Get (prod_res, MPI_PROD, P3,0, win)
6 Fence	6
7 Win_free (win)	7 Win_free (win)

The result of the Accumulate and the MPI_PROD operation resides on process P3 in window win at disparity 0. Hence, we can pull this value with a Get on P1 and P2 at line 5. The "+" symbolizes that this Get must happen after the Fence and before the next access epoch begins. As Accumulate is roughly equivalent to a one-sided MPI_Reduce, it becomes clear that what we need here is an equivalent to a one-sided MPI_Allreduce. The final result of the MPI_PROD operation has to be distributed among all the processes. We propose the adjoint code in Table 9.

Table 9. Reverse section of process P1, P2 and P3 in pseudocode

P1	P2	P3
1 Win_create(NULL,win)	Win_create(NULL,win)	Win_create(y,win)
2 Fence	Fence	$\bar{y}[\,i\,]=\bar{l}$
3 Get(buf[0],P3,i,win)	Get(buf[0],P3,i,win)	Fence
4 Fence + Adj_Op($\bar{x}$,buf,prod_res)	Fence + Adj_Op($\bar{x}$,buf,prod_res)	Fence
5 Win_free(win)	Win_free(win)	Win_free(win)

Again there needs to be a separation between the assignment and the increment of $\bar{x}$. This has two reasons. First, as with Put in Sect. 3, there is no way to increment the adjoint from target to origin. Second, we may not do the adjoint operation of MPI_PROD in Table 6 using derived MPI operations, since this is not allowed while using one-sided communication. Therefore, along the same way as before, we introduce an Adj_Op routine which does the incremental adjoint operation. It uses the product result prod_res, the buffer buf where the incoming adjoint P3.$\bar{y}$ is stored and finally the to be incremented adjoints P1.$\bar{x}$ and P2.$\bar{x}$. All in all, we have two requests with regard to the efficient adjoining of Accumulate. We need an equivalent of a one-sided MPI_Allreduce and customizable MPI operations.

5 Summary

This paper examines the structural requirements for adjoining MPI programs using one-sided communication. It concludes that there is a potential performance loss due to the additional synchronization steps when sticking to the current MPI 2.2 interface for the adjoint code. We analyzed in detail the adjoint structure of MPI_Put, MPI_Get and MPI_Accumulate. We drew a wish list of three requests that may potentially provide huge performance gains to the adjoint code of one-sided MPI communication. This is

- an incremental Get essentially amounting to an Accumulate call with the operation MPI_SUM where the data is sent from target to origin and added to the origins value,
- a one-sided equivalent to a MPI_Allreduce,
- and derived MPI operations for one-sided communication.

The current solution, while involving a considerable amount of workarounds, is integrated into the adjoint MPI library (AMPI) at our institute. Although our development is mainly application driven, we realize that applying AD on a one-sided MPI enabled code is still future work. Currently, our in-house AD overloading tool dco together with Adjoint MPI is being integrated into the parallel solver PETSc. A prototype is also in the works via an in-house implemented code for the simulation of a 3D unsteady incompressible flow [6].

References

1. Bendsten, C., Stauning, O.: FADBAD, a Flexible C++ Package for Automatic Differentiation Using the Forward and Backward Methods. Technical report, IMM-REP-1996-17, Department of Mathematical Modelling, Technical University of Denmark, Lyngby, Denmark (1996)
2. Griewank, A., Juedes, D., Utke, J.: Algorithm 755: ADOL-C: A Package for the Automatic Differentiation of Algorithms written in C/C++. ACM Trans. Math. Softw. 22(2), 131–167 (1996)
3. Griewank, A., Walter, A.: Evaluating Derivatives. Principles and Techniques of Algorithmic Differentiation, 2nd edn. SIAM, Philadelphia (2008)
4. Gropp, W., Lusk, E., Thakur, R.: Using MPI-2: Advanced Features of the Message-Passing Interface. MIT Press, Cambridge (1999)
5. Hovland, P., Bischof, C.: Automatic Differentiation for Message-Passing Parallel Programs. In: IPPS 1998: Proceedings of the 12th International Parallel Processing Symposium. IEEE Computer Society, Washington, DC (1998)
6. Lotz, J., Leppkes, K., Naumann, U.: dco/c++ Derivative Code by Overloading in C++. Technical Report AIB-2011-06, RWTH Aachen (May 2012)
7. MPI Forum. MPI: A Message-Passing Interface Standard. Version 2.2 (September 4, 2009), http://www.mpi-forum.org (December 2009)
8. Naumann, U.: The Art of Differentiating Computer Programs. Society for Industrial and Applied Mathematics, Philadephia (2011)
9. Naumann, U., Hascoët, L., Hill, C., Hovland, P., Riehme, J., Utke, J.: A Framework for Proving Correctness of Adjoint Message-Passing Programs. In: Lastovetsky, A., Kechadi, T., Dongarra, J. (eds.) EuroPVM/MPI 2008. LNCS, vol. 5205, pp. 316–321. Springer, Heidelberg (2008)
10. Pascual, V., Hascoët, L.: TAPENADE for C. In: Advances in Automatic Differentiation. Lecture Notes in Computational Science and Engineering, vol. 64, pp. 199–209. Springer, Heidelberg (2008)
11. Schanen, M., Förster, M., Gendler, B., Naumann, U.: Compiler-based Differentiation of Numerical Simulation Codes. In: ICCGI 2011, The Sixth International Multi-Conference on Computing in the Global Information Technology, pp. 105–110. IARIA (2011)
12. Schanen, M., Förster, M., Naumann, U.: Second-Order Algorithmic Differentiation by Source Transformation of MPI Code. In: Keller, R., Gabriel, E., Resch, M., Dongarra, J. (eds.) EuroMPI 2010. LNCS, vol. 6305, pp. 257–264. Springer, Heidelberg (2010)
13. Schanen, M., Naumann, U., Hascoët, L., Utke, J.: Interpretative Adjoints for Numerical Simulation Codes using MPI. Procedia Computer Science 1(1), 1819–1827 (2010); ICCS 2010
14. Utke, J., Hascoët, L., Heimbach, P., Hill, C., Hovland, P., Naumann, U.: Toward Adjoinable MPI. In: Proceedings of the 23rd IEEE International Parallel & Distributed Processing Symposium. IEEE Computer Society, Washington, DC (2009)
15. Utke, J., Naumann, U., Fagan, M., Tallent, N., Strout, M., Heimbach, P., Hill, C., Wunsch, C.: OpenAD/F: A Modular, Open-Source Tool for Automatic Differentiation of Fortran Codes. ACM Transactions on Mathematical Software 34(4), 18:1–18:36 (2008)

On the Usability
of the MPI Shared File Pointer Routines

Mohamad Chaarawi[1], James Dinan[2], and Dries Kimpe[2]

[1] The HDF Group, Champaign, IL 61820, USA
chaarawi@hdfgroup.org
[2] Argonne National Laboratory, Argonne, IL 60439, USA
{dkimpe,dinan}@mcs.anl.gov

Abstract. The MPI-2 standard defines a class of file access routines providing a shared file pointer. All processes using those routines update the same file pointer when accessing the file. Coordination between ranks happens implicitly in the MPI library, relieving the application developer of this responsibility. The shared file pointer routines, however, have found little interest from developers because of several issues ranging from routine usability and portability to performance. We consider the use of these routines in the HDF5 library, a high-level I/O library built on top of MPI, and in Vampir, a performance analysis toolkit. We highlight some of the reasons preventing their adoption and discuss how these routines could be modified to increase their usability. We also propose a novel implementation using the new MPI one-sided routines provided by the upcoming MPI-3.0 standard.

1 Introduction

MPI [11] introduced the notion of parallel I/O in version two of the specification. Although its adoption by end users has been modest, research has shown that, in combination with parallel file systems, MPI I/O can significantly improve the I/O performance compared with other I/O interfaces. Furthermore, higher-level scientific data libraries such as HDF5 [4] and Parallel netCDF (PnetCDF) [10] rely heavily on MPI I/O to provide users with parallel access to the file system.

MPI I/O provides several data access routines that differ in a number of aspects. The first aspect is related to how the offset at which processes access the file is determined: by using individual file pointers or shared file pointers or by explicitly specifying the offset. The second aspect is coordination with independent and collective operations. The third aspect is synchronism with blocking and nonblocking operations. This paper focuses on data access operations that manipulate shared file pointers. We focus on *independent* access with shared file pointers because collective access is something we are trying to avoid in the use cases presented. Furthermore, collective access with shared file pointers can be easily implemented by using a combination of `MPI_Scan` and collective access with explicit offsets. The `MPI_Scan` allows each process to add the amount of data it wishes to read/write to the ones before it (with a lower rank); and, upon

J.L. Träff, S. Benkner, and J. Dongarra (Eds.): EuroMPI 2012, LNCS 7490, pp. 258–267, 2012.

completion, each process knows its subsequent offset for I/O. All processes then call `MPI_File_write_at_all` or `MPI_File_read_at_all` in order to perform the required I/O.

For shared file pointer operations, each rank in the group that opened the file manipulates a single, shared file pointer. Coordinating access to the shared file pointer is handled by the MPI library. Usage scenarios for those operations include generating event logs in parallel applications and organizing individual additions to a file in such as way that subsequent additions do not overwrite older ones (in effect, a distributed form of the POSIX O_APPEND mode). Another scenario could be assigning work to a set of ranks using a common file, where a rank reads in some work to be done from that file and advances the shared file pointer to the next chunk of work. Unfortunately, the actual use of shared file pointer operations by application developers is rare because of issues of portability and performance (discussed in Section 3). Instead, in the case of shared file pointer writes, applications typically resort to writing a unique file per rank, making use of the fact that for a file opened by a single rank, the shared file pointer degrades to an individual file pointer, something that is well supported by all MPI implementations. However, the evolution to increased concurrency in high-performance computing systems is quickly rendering the one-file-per-rank model unsustainable.

The remainder of this paper is organized as follows. Section 2 discusses some of the work done on implementing shared file pointer operations. Section 3 presents two real-life use cases for the shared file pointer routines and analyzes some of the reasons that the routines in their current form cannot be used easily. Section 4 addresses how the shared file pointer routines can be modified to enhance their usability; it presents a novel, library-based implementation of the shared file pointer routines and discusses how the recent MPI 3.0 standard can be utilized for this purpose. Section 5 summarizes the paper and briefly presents plans for future work.

2   Related Work

The most widely used implementation of MPI I/O today is ROMIO [13]. ROMIO is part of the MPICH [3] distribution and is the basis for many I/O libraries used in other public-domain MPI libraries and commercial MPI implementations. To implement shared file pointer functionality, ROMIO stores the value of the shared file pointer in an additional hidden file. It requires this file to be on a file system accessible by all ranks that opened the file. In order to properly serialize access to the shared file pointer (and thus to the hidden file), each access to the shared file pointer by any rank involves locking the hidden file, updating its contents, and unlocking the hidden file. These operations typically have a high cost, severely reducing performance of the shared file pointer routines. Furthermore, not all file systems support distributed file locking; thus, for those file systems, shared file pointer operations will not function correctly.

In order to address those situations, some work has been done to implement shared file pointers without requiring support for file locking. In [9,12], MPI-2 one-sided operations were utilized to atomically update a shared file pointer. Since the MPI-2 one-sided operations do not offer direct support for atomically retrieving and incrementing a value, Latham et al. citeatomics describe how the one-sided operations can be used to build a mutex instead. The mutex is subsequently used to serialize access to the shared file pointer, which is stored at one of the participating ranks.

In [7], three methods are presented for implementing shared file pointer operations without file system support. The first method uses an extra process in order to maintain the status of the shared file pointer; the second uses a separate file per process when writing with shared file pointers; and the third method utilizes also a separate file per process but combines the data of multiple MPI files into a single individual file. Only the first method fully supports implementing the shared file pointer routines as described by the standard. The second and third methods put additional restrictions on the use of the file. Specifically, they require a synchronized clock, and they support only writing with a shared file pointer.

Cope et al. [2], instead of relying on a set-aside process, delegate the management of the shared file pointer to the I/O forwarding layer found in many machines, providing a solution that does not depend on support from the underlying file system or the MPI library. In [8], a similar approach is taken, but in this case the file system itself is augmented with the operations needed to properly implement a shared file pointer.

Despite all the research devoted to implementing shared file pointers, in practice application developers cannot rely on the widespread availability of reasonably performing shared file pointer routines, even though these routines have been part of the MPI standard for over 14 years. Part of the problem is that no single technique will work on all platforms. In addition, the current MPI implementations does not offer the functionality needed to construct a reasonably performing, portable shared file pointer without resorting to a set-aside process or thread, a sacrifice most application developers are not willing to make. As a result, many of the techniques described in this section are simply best-effort solutions.

Chaarawi et al. [1] observe that all known methods for providing shared file pointer support have a narrow usability window, depending on the platform, the underlying file system, the progress model of the MPI library, the set of ranks manipulating the shared file pointer, or any combination of these factors. The researchers describe a framework that, based on the exact circumstances, selects an appropriate technique for providing the shared file pointer routines. Unfortunately, this approach only increases the chances of finding a working shared file pointer technique on a given system. It does not guarantee a suitable method can be found for every supported platform or situation.

3 Motivation

The lack of reliable, well-performing shared file pointer routines has created a situation in which applications avoid using these routines, while MPI implementers don't consider the routines a priority because of the lack of application demand. The rest of this section provides two examples showing that shared file pointer access is an I/O pattern worth supporting.

3.1 Parallel HDF5

Parallel HDF5 [4], a high-level I/O library, is positioned above MPI-I/O in the application's software stack. Instead of treating a file as a simple stream of bytes (the model presented by MPI-I/O), it provides the application with a more structured view of a file. The user organizes a file using different HDF5 objects (groups, datasets, etc.) and dependencies (links) between those objects. The HDF5 library is responsible for maintaining information about the file structure in the form of metadata, which is also stored in the file.

Parallel HDF5 allows all ranks that opened the file to access dataset elements independently or collectively. However, because of synchronization issues, operations that need to modify the structure of the file (i.e., the files metadata) must be collective. Space allocation is an operation requiring careful synchronization between the ranks in order to avoid a situation where multiple ranks attempt to claim the same space simultaneously. When a user creates HDF5 objects, the HDF5 library allocates space to store data values, as well as the necessary additional file metadata. When a user removes HDF5 objects from an HDF5 file, the space associated with those objects becomes free space. The HDF5 library file space management activities encompass both the allocation of space and the management of free space. The HDF5 library implements several file space management strategies; the strategy used for a given HDF5 file is set when the file is created.

Currently, space within the HDF5 file is allocated either from a free list (consisting of previously used and released blocks within the file) or from the end of the files allocated space (EOA). Recycling space within the file is complex as well as unusual in parallel HDF5 applications and therefore typically is disabled for parallel applications. Thus, all space allocation must be performed at the files EOA. In serial HDF5 applications, allocating space at the files EOA is simple. The EOA value begins at offset 0 in the file; and when space is required, the EOA value is incremented by the size of the block requested. In parallel HDF5 applications, however, space allocation using the EOA value can result in a race condition if ranks do not synchronize with each other, causing multiple ranks to believe that they are the sole owner of a range of bytes within the HDF5 file.

Shared file pointer operations have the potential to greatly simplify the space allocation issue in the HDF5 library and to remove the existing collective requirement (an important first step in breaking the collective requirement for all operations that modify metadata); however, such operations have many limitations. In theory, whenever a rank needs to allocate space at the EOA, it would just need to get the current position of the shared file pointer and advance it by the amount of space needed atomically. MPI_File_write_shared can be used to advance the shared file pointer independently of all other ranks (MPI will handle the synchronization issue). However, MPI does not provide any information on where the write actually happened, nor does it indicate the current state of the shared file pointer after the write completes.

While MPI_File_get_position_shared can be used to query the current position of the shared file pointer, this routine does not execute atomically with MPI_File_write_shared. Consider the following example in which two ranks attempt to allocate space, each executing the following sequence of operations:

(1) MPI_File_get_position_shared()
(2) MPI_File_iwrite_shared()

If both ranks retrieve the current position of the shared file pointer at the same time before one of them initiates the write operation, they will both obtain the same value for the position of the shared file pointer. Even though the MPI library will correctly serialize each write operation—resulting in non-overlapping writes—each rank now believes that it owns an allocation starting at the offset returned from MPI_File_get_position_shared, resulting in corruption of the HDF5 file. Any other execution schedule interleaving (1) and (2) likewise results in file corruption. The only valid execution schedules are those where (1) and (2) execute atomically with respect to the other ranks. In order to enforce atomicity, however, extra synchronization (outside of the shared file pointer routines) is required, for example by using a collective operation such as MPI_Barrier. Essentially, then, for the purpose of implementing space allocation, the MPI_File_write_shared is no longer independent, negating its usefulness in trying to break the collective space allocation restriction.

3.2   VampirTrace

Performance analysis is a difficult problem, particularly for parallel software. Many packages aid in this task. One such package is Vampir [6], a sophisticated performance analysis infrastructure for parallel programs. The Vampir toolset relies on event trace recording, which allows detailed analysis of the parallel behavior of target applications. At run time, Vampir's monitoring component collects the events, which include entry/exit events for user code subroutines, message send/receive events, collective communication events, shared-memory synchronization, and I/O events. Event trace data is written to disk at carefully selected times in order to avoid disturbing the behavior of the application being traced. Likewise, to avoid introducing additional synchronization, trace data is typically written by using independent I/O routines. After the application completes, the trace is analyzed. For the rest of this section, we will limit the discussion to the recording of the trace.

At first glance, the I/O pattern of the Vampir tracing toolkit seems to be a perfect match for the shared file pointer functionality: each rank could use the shared file pointer to append a set of events to the trace file. Once again, however, two major issues prevent the use of the shared file pointer routines in their current form. The first problem is that, for an analysis tool, it is vital that the overhead introduced by the tracing layer be kept to a minimum. Unless a relatively efficient shared file pointer implementation can be expected, these routines cannot be used effectively by the tracing toolkit. Unfortunately, on many existing systems the correct behavior of these routines cannot be guaranteed, let alone reasonable performance.

The second problem is more than an implementation quality issue. In order to efficiently analyze the trace file, before the analysis stage begins, an index of the trace file is constructed. In order to do so efficiently, each rank appending events to the trace file needs to know—at the time the data is written—at which offset in the trace log the events were appended. As explained in Section 3.1, the current form of the shared file pointer routines makes it impossible to do so without introducing further synchronization, voiding the independent nature of the routine.

Because of the lack of portable, reasonably performing shared file pointer routines, Vampir resorts to writing a single file per rank. In [5], Ilsche et al. discuss how using one file per rank fails to scale to the current generation of parallel machines. Instead, by employing the technique described in [2], combined with an augmented shared file pointer routine capable of atomically updating and returning its value before the update, they demonstrate the ability to scale Vampir to full system size (over 200,000 MPI ranks) while at the same time improving the performance compared with that of the one-file-per-process model for smaller numbers of processes.

4   Proposed Solution

In this section, a number of improvements to the shared file pointer routines are proposed. We show how these improved routines can be implemented using the recently added MPI-3 one-sided routines.

4.1   Fixing the API

The two use cases detailed in Section 3 required the ability to atomically retrieve and update the shared file pointer. However, the MPI standard only provides a way to either retrieve or update, but not both.

The same problem exists for MPI_File_seek_shared. This routine takes a whence argument and an offset value that indicates by how much the pointer needs to be updated. Using that capability followed by a write operation using explicit offsets (MPI_File_write_at) would appear to provide the atomic operation needed for the use cases; however, the standard states that MPI_File_seek_shared is a collective operation. Furthermore, the routine does not return any information about the current state of the shared file pointer (similar to the access operations). Both restrictions would render this routine useless for our problem.

The easiest and most logical solution is to have the MPI library return the current offset that it is writing to when MPI_File_write_shared is called. The MPI library already needs to have this information, since—to the best of our knowledge—no file systems natively support shared file pointers. No extra work is needed and no performance penalties are incurred if we change the API for shared file pointer operations to return a written-to/read-from offset.

We therefore propose the following new routines, each of which enables retrieving the value of the shared file pointer before the modification:

```
int MPIX_File_write_and_get_shared (MPI_File mpi_fh, void *buf,
  int count, MPI_Datatype datatype, MPI_Offset *position,
  MPI_Status *status);

int MPIX_File_read_and_get_shared (MPI_File mpi_fh, void *buf,
  int count, MPI_Datatype datatype, MPI_Offset *position,
  MPI_Status *status);

int MPIX_File_seek_and_get_shared (MPI_File mpi_fh,
  MPI_Offset offset, int whence, MPI_Offset *position);
```

Except for the extra parameter (position) used to return the position of the shared file pointer before the data was written, these routines are the same as the corresponding MPI routines. MPIX_File_seek_and_get_shared is similar to MPI_File_seek_shared except that it is not collective and that it returns the value of the shared file pointer before the update. This routine enables application developers to claim a region in the shared file without having to read or write the region at the same time or in a single access. Furthermore, this enhanced seek routine can be used in order to easily implement any of the existing shared file pointer routines; and it enables application developers to create their own, specialized shared file pointer routines.

4.2   Scalable and Efficient Shared File Pointers

A closer investigation of the shared file pointer routines reveals that all these functions can be implemented, in effect, by an atomic update of the integer value representing the shared file pointer, followed by the corresponding explicit offset I/O operation. In this section, we investigate how the former can be implemented using one-sided operations, in particular those provided by MPI-3.

In order to support the full range of shared file pointer operations, the shared integer counter representing the current position of the shared file pointer must be able to support asynchronous and atomic *set*, *get*, and *fetch-and-add* operations. Given the need for asynchrony and atomicity, a library-level implementation of shared file pointers using the MPI passive target one-sided communication interface seems natural. Such an implementation was developed for the MPI-2 remote memory access (RMA) interface [9]. However, its space and communication volume grow linearly with the number of processes, and performance was unsatisfactory because the implementation could not leverage fetch-and-add operations, since these were not available in MPI-2. In addition, the algorithm performs poorly when contention is high.

MPI-3 brings several significant enhancements to the one-sided communication interface that enable a library-level shared counter implementation that is more space, time, and communication efficient. In particular, MPI-3 defines several new atomic and accumulate operations, including MPI_Fetch_and_op, which directly provides atomic fetch-and-add through the MPI_SUM operation. The earlier, nonscalable algorithm was constructed specifically to address the lack of atomic fetch-and-add capabilities in MPI-2 RMA. In addition, this operation can provide atomic get and put through the MPI_NO_OP and MPI_REPLACE operations, respectively.

The MPI_Fetch_and_op routine is more restrictive than the new MPI_Get_accumulate function and can be applied only to predefined MPI datatypes (e.g., MPI_LONG). Although it duplicates the functionality of MPI_Get_accumulate, this function was added specifically to enable implementers to take advantage of interconnect-supported atomic operations, which can yield a truly one-sided implementation with low latency and hardware-supported asynchronous progress.

In MPI-2 RMA, multiple concurrent atomic and accumulate operations can target the same location only if the same MPI operation (e.g., MPI_SUM) is used in every concurrent invocation. MPI-3 has relaxed this restriction by allowing all atomic and accumulate operations to target the same location with any operation. Allowing greater concurrency among these operations enables the programmer to relax the synchronization operations used to maintain data integrity and consistency. In the case of a window that holds a single shared-integer location, the programmer can lock the window in MPI_LOCK_SHARED mode and keep the epoch open for the entire life of the shared file pointer. Completion and ordering of individual operations are accomplished with the new MPI_Win_flush operation. Moreover, new request-based, nonblocking RMA operations have been added in MPI-3 that can be used to implement nonblocking shared file pointer updates. The combination of these semantics with new atomic communication functionality enables building an efficient, one-sided shared file pointer that can portably leverage modern interconnect features.

Optimizing for Shared Memory. The MPI-3 standard will also include a portable, interprocess shared-memory interface. This interface extends the RMA interface with a window creation routine that allocates a shared-memory segment and maps it into the address spaces of all processes. Once the shared-memory window has been created, processes can perform "one-sided" load and store instructions to locations in the window. Data consistency and atomic operations are provided by using the existing MPI-3 RMA interface. Given a shared memory window, the MPI implementation can utilize an implementation of the atomic operations that directly performs host CPU atomic operations. In the case of a general RMA window, atomic operations may need to be performed by the network interface, since interconnect-provided atomic operations may not be atomic with respect to the CPU's atomic operations.

The interprocess shared-memory functionality provided by many operating systems requires the use of a special memory allocator. Thus, in order to ensure a portable implementation, the MPI-3 shared-memory window creation routine must also allocate the memory that will be exposed in the window. Traditional window creation, where a user-supplied buffer is utilized as the window buffer, cannot be used to enable optimized host CPU atomic operations. MPI-3 also adds a new window creation routine that allocates and creates the window; however, implementations may not check whether the given window spans only a shared-memory domain because of the overhead of this check.

It is expected that programs utilizing the shared-memory RMA interface will use hierarchical intranode and internode levels of parallelism. When this interface is combined with I/O operations, we anticipate the need for intranode shared file pointers. The new MPI_Comm_split_type routine, combined with the MPI_COMM_TYPE_SHARED argument, can be used to generate a communicator that is able to create a shared-memory window. A shared file pointer implementation can check whether the communicator input to a shared file pointer creation routine is a subset of the shared-memory communicator. If it is, the implementation can create a shared-memory window instead of a traditional window, enabling MPI to use host CPU atomic operations.

5   Conclusion and Future Work

As demonstrated in [5], efficient shared file pointer routines are becoming critical as concurrency in contemporary high-performance computing systems continues to increase. In this paper, we discussed two well-established, real-life candidates for the MPI shared file pointer routines. We have demonstrated why— even when overlooking portability or performance issues0–the inability to manipulate and retrieve the value of the shared file pointer in a race-free manner effectively precludes the use of these routines. We proposed a set of simple extensions improving the usability of the shared file pointer routines. We showed how, for the first time, by building on the new routines provided by MPI-3.0, one can provide a reasonably performing, portable implementation of the shared file pointer routines outside of the MPI library. We outlined the implementation of such a library.

Once implementations of the MPI-3.0 standard become available, we plan to evaluate and release a library implementing the functionality described in this paper, unlocking the improved shared file pointer concept for application developers.

References

1. Chaarawi, M., Gabriel, E., Keller, R., Graham, R.L., Bosilca, G., Dongarra, J.J.: OMPIO: A Modular Software Architecture for MPI I/O. In: Cotronis, Y., Danalis, A., Nikolopoulos, D.S., Dongarra, J. (eds.) EuroMPI 2011. LNCS, vol. 6960, pp. 81–89. Springer, Heidelberg (2011)
2. Cope, J., Iskra, K., Kimpe, D., Ross, R.: Portable and Scalable MPI Shared File Pointers. In: Cotronis, Y., Danalis, A., Nikolopoulos, D.S., Dongarra, J. (eds.) EuroMPI 2011. LNCS, vol. 6960, pp. 312–314. Springer, Heidelberg (2011)
3. Gropp, W., Lusk, E., Doss, N., Skjellum, A.: A high-performance, portable implementation of the MPI message passing interface standard. Parallel Computing 22(6), 789–828 (1996)
4. Hierarchical Data Format Group: HDF5 Reference Manual, release 1.6.3, National Center for Supercomputing Application (NCSA), University of Illinois at Urbana-Champaign (September 2004)
5. Ilsche, T., Schuchart, J., Cope, J., Kimpe, D., Jones, T., Knüpfer, A., Iskra, K., Ross, R., Nagel, E.W., Poole, S.: Enabling event tracing at leadership-class scale through I/O forwarding middleware. In: Proceedings of the 21st International ACM Symposium on High Performance Parallel and Distributed Computing (HPDC 2012) (to appear, 2012)
6. Knüpfer, A., Brunst, H., Doleschal, J., Jurenz, M., Lieber, M., Mickler, H., Müller, M.S., Nagel, W.E.: The Vampir performance analysis toolset. In: Resch, M., Keller, R., Himmler, V., Krammer, B., Schulz, A. (eds.) Tools for High Performance Computing, pp. 139–155. Springer, Heidelberg (2008)
7. Kulkarni, K., Gabriel, E.: Evaluating Algorithms for Shared File Pointer Operations in MPI I/O. In: Allen, G., Nabrzyski, J., Seidel, E., van Albada, G.D., Dongarra, J., Sloot, P.M.A. (eds.) ICCS 2009, Part I. LNCS, vol. 5544, pp. 280–289. Springer, Heidelberg (2009)
8. Lang, S., Latham, R., Ross, R., Kimpe, D.: Interfaces for coordinated access in the file system. In: IEEE International Conference on Cluster Computing and Workshops, CLUSTER 2009, pp. 1–9 (2009)
9. Latham, R., Ross, R., Thakur, R.: Implementing MPI-IO atomic mode and shared file pointers using MPI one-sided communication. Int. J. High Perform. Comput. Appl. 21(2), 132–143 (2007)
10. Li, J., Liao, W.K., Choudhary, A., Ross, R., Thakur, R., Gropp, W., Latham, R., Siegel, A., Gallagher, B., Zingale, M.: Parallel netCDF: A high-performance scientific I/O interface. In: Proceedings of the 2003 ACM/IEEE Conference on Supercomputing, SC 2003, p. 39. ACM, New York (2003), http://doi.acm.org/10.1145/1048935.1050189
11. Message Passing Interface Forum: MPI-2: Extensions to the Message Passing Interface (July 1997), http://www.mpi-forum.org/
12. Ross, R., Latham, R., Gropp, W., Thakur, R., Toonen, B.: Implementing MPI-IO atomic mode without file system support. In: IEEE International Symposium on Cluster Computing and the Grid, CCGrid 2005, vol. 2, pp. 1135–1142 (May 2005)
13. Thakur, R., Gropp, W., Lusk, E.: On implementing MPI-IO portably and with high performance. In: Proceedings of the 6th Workshop on I/O in Parallel and Distributed Systems, pp. 23–32 (1999)

Extending MPI to Better Support Multi-application Interaction

Jay Lofstead[1] and Jai Dayal[2]

[1] Sandia National Laboratories
[2] Georgia Institute of Technology

Abstract. Current scientific workflows consist of generally several components either integrated *in situ* or as completely independent, asynchronous components using centralized storage as an interface. Neither of these approaches are likely to scale well into Exascale. Instead, separate applications and services will be launched using online communication to link these components of the scientific discovery process. Our experiences with coupling multiple, independent MPI applications, each with separate processing phases, exposes limitations preventing use of some of the optimized mechanisms within the MPI standard. In this regard, we have identified two shortcomings with current MPI implementations. First, MPI intercommunicators offer a mechanism to communicate across application boundaries, but do not address the impact this operating mode has on possible programming models for each separate application. Second, MPI_Probe offers a way to interleave both local messaging and remote messages, but has limitations as MPI_Bcast and other collective calls are not supported by MPI_Probe thus limiting use of optimize collective calls in this operating mode.

1 Introduction

The move toward exascale is changing how the scientific computing process works. Currently, one of two approaches is used. Most commonly, separate, independent applications are combined into a single process with scripting or workflow software to ease connecting the output from one component with another as illustrated in Figure 1(a). In a production environment, this is nearly exclusively done using a centralized storage system shared between pairs of connecting components. In general, this is a single storage system. In this approach, each component can scale independently, but is at the mercy of the file system performance for end-to-end scalability. Alternatively, applications can incorporate additional processing pieces, such as analysis or visualization components, in situ as illustrated in Figure 1(b). In this case, these additional processing pieces must scale as easily as the host simulation or scaling the combination will be artificially limited.

The alternative approach to address both of these cases is to use the best of each while avoiding the penalties of both. By using online data processing areas (see Figure 2) to create an online workflow, typically called data staging, hybrid

J.L. Träff, S. Benkner, and J. Dongarra (Eds.): EuroMPI 2012, LNCS 7490, pp. 268–274, 2012.
© Springer-Verlag Berlin Heidelberg 2012

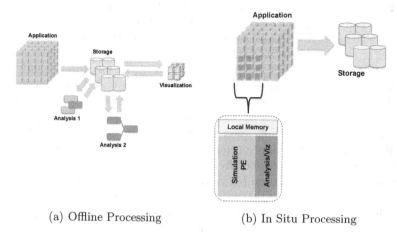

(a) Offline Processing   (b) In Situ Processing

Fig. 1. Traditional Scientific Workflow Architectures

staging, or 'in flight' processing, the speed penalty of a centralized file system is avoided and the scalability limitations of a single, integrated, executable are avoided. This approach, while not without its own challenges, has proven to work well for both tightly coupled and loosely coupled workflows.

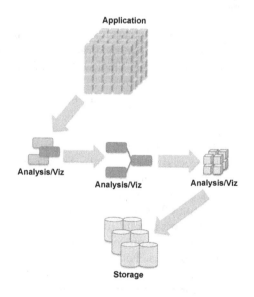

Fig. 2. Online Processing

MPI provides the concept of an *inter-communicator* to connect two applications with MPI messages. This feature works well enough for the inter-application communication, but MPI does not adequately address the potential impact of connecting applications on their operating model. Each application, particularly shared services-style applications, offers a collection of operations to process data. For shared services applications, one or more of these operations may be in process or at least a possible next step at any time. This requires the external interface to seamlessly support any possible message at any time including the corresponding memory use for each of these messages. For all of these cases, if any currently processing task issues a collective call, all processes must participate for the program to continue. The serious implication is that being responsive to messages from the other application requires periodic checks for waiting messages. For a services-style application, this external communication may drive what local processing is performed by different portions of the local application. To optimize the communication between applications, it becomes more efficient to probe for the inter-application messages as well as the local messages on the communicating processes. The lack of complete support of message types in the MPI_Probe call limits the kinds of operations that can be used within these applications.

The rest of the paper is structured as follows. In Section 2 we discuss some of the related work as well as work that motivates the need for these changes. Section 3 discusses the current design and the implications of these decisions for programming of participating application components. The proposed solution is presented next in Section 4. Finally, conclusions are presented in Section 5.

2   Related Work

Separate MPI applications operating as a single workflow using isolated applications to isolate failures has been demonstrated previously. The C-MPI project [11] uses DHTs to connect MPI applications. The LDM [10] offers a similar approach to data staging techniques as demonstrated in the LEAD [2] project. In this case, the various data processing components are linked together to form the processing workflow.

Offline workflows have been built using a variety of tools. For example, Dagman [5], Pegasus [7], and Kepler [4] each provide a way to connect various components in an ordered way to process scientific data. Scientists have also assembled similar systems less formally using scripts. They each work by providing a way to trigger a component at a given time given a set of conditions, such as a prior dependency component has completed processing. In all of these cases, the use of centralized storage as an integration point introduces a performance bottleneck.

The alternative approach of in situ processing, such as is done by ParaView [6] and VisIt [9], has its own problems. For example, the CTH [3] shock physics code in use at Sandia easily can scale to 100,000 cores with an executable size of around 30 MB. When incorporating ParaView for in situ processing and visualization, the executable grows to around 300 MB and has difficulty scaling beyond around 30,000 cores. While ParaView is actively working to correct these scaling limitations, those fixes will not solve the increased memory footprint fully.

PreDatA [12] offers 'in flight' data processing from the simulation to disk by hosting the processing in various locations along the data path. Alternatively,

DataSpaces [1] and the related projects at Rutgers focus on attempting to store data in an online repository for querying by another application. These approaches currently rely on custom connections between components and do not offer the portability offered by MPI intercommunicators. The Network Scalable Services Infrastructure [8] offers an RPC-style interface to efficiently connect between separate applications using native interconnect techniques, but offers no default services.

3   Current Design Attributes

Current applications that wish to participate in an online workflow would incorporate some minor changes. For example, an additional interface that communicates with the related applications is added and then incorporated into the processing loop. This simplifies the application changes by limiting the number of places where code to check for inter-application messaging may occur. This isolates these changes while allowing the application to run as it is originally written. While this is simple in itself, scenarios such as when there is active processing in one or more of the participating applications causes problems. The difficulty with message probing is the lack of support to detect any collective operations. For our motivating example, a mass data transfer from one application to another requires some configuration information to be sent across the inter-application control message interface to indicate the number of variables, their types, extents, and data types. The amount of data in this message is unknown and only slightly bounded. Another message type coming across the same interface will be a variable itself being sent across the application boundary. In this case, the size could be as much as 10% or more of the node's local memory. The kinds of processing that may occur for a variable may require that all pieces of the global variable are processed simultaneously to generate some summary or derived value. Frequently these operations are performed using collective calls as part of a larger processing sequence.

Efficiency strongly suggests that the configuration information is sent across once and distributed out to participating processes locally. This distribution of messages among the processes of one application is generally performed using an MPI_Bcast or similar mechanism to take advantage of the optimizations incorporated into the MPI standard. The difficulty here is two fold. First, the processes operate out of step with each other, so not all subsets of processes will expect the same types of messages. Second, while under the proposed MPI 3.0 standard, it is possible for processes to pre-post for asynchronous collective operations, it is assumed that the processes know what to expect a head of time. In the case of a general processing situation, it is unpredictable what the specifics of the collective call would be rendering this ineffective for this situation. Instead, to implement this functionality, a manual asynchronous broadcast must be implemented. This problem is worse if the processing incorporates other collective operations, such as all-to-all, gather, scatter, or all-reduce operations. None of these pending operations can be detected through the use of an MPI_Probe call.

4   Proposed Extensions

One possible solution to this scenario is relatively straightforward. The current MPI_Probe implementation could be expanded to include all of the collective calls. While this maintains a simpler API, the additional possibilities for types of messages and the change in the behavior that may affect current applications makes this approach less than desirable. Instead, an identical pair of API calls, MPI_Cprobe and MPI_Icprobe that look the same as the MPI_Probe equivalents, would be sufficient. In this case, instead of identifying pending point to point messages, these calls would only detect all of the collective calls that the current probe implementation supports. With this extension, it would be possible to remove re-implentation of collective calls as point-to-point calls and associated operations such as performing the all-reduce operation. Additionally, this would afford potentially leveraging hardware features, such as the collectives network on the BlueGene platform.

The potential performance impact of blocking many or even all processes waiting for a collective call to complete is serious. It is certainly likely that collectives were not included in MPI_Probe for exactly this concern. However, the introduction of asynchronous collective communication largely alleviates this concern. The potential performance penalty of poorly written replacements for the collective calls should outweigh these concerns. Their direct impact of these calls on an MPI application's performance will generally be limited. With sufficient warnings about only using these calls as ways to detect collective calls will cause all processes to stall until the corresponding collective calls are issued.

5   Conclusions

The move to exascale is motivating moving offline workflows online and coupling the various components more tightly while maintaining separate applications to enhance resilience. This communication and processing intensive software architecture requires the ability to both probe for new messages as well as communicate among all of the processes within an application simultaneously. The ability to probe for unexpected messages of all types rather than simply point-to-point messages will enable MPI applications to more easily participate in this software architecture. The inclusion of collective calls such as MPI_Bcast both simplifies the implementation as well as offers the performance advantage of efficient collectives implementations offered by MPI and potentially the ability to leverage hardware features such as dedicated collectives networks.

Acknowledgements. Sandia National Laboratories is a multi-program laboratory managed and operated by Sandia Corporation, a wholly owned subsidiary of Lockheed Martin Corporation, for the U.S. Department of Energy's National Nuclear Security Administration under contract DE-AC04-94AL85000.

References

[1] Docan, C., Parashar, M., Klasky, S.: DataSpaces: An interaction and coordination framework for coupled simulation workflows. In: HPDC 2010: Proceedings of the 18th International Symposium on High Performance Distributed Computing (2010)

[2] Droegemeier, K., Chandrasekar, V., Clark, R., Gannon, D., Graves, S., Joseph, E., Ramamurthy, M., Wilhelmson, R., Brewster, K., Domenico, B., Leyton, T., Morris, V., Murray, D., Plale, B., Ramachandran, R., Reed, D., Rushing, J., Weber, D., Wilson, A., Xue, M., Yalda, S.: Linked environments for atmospheric discovery (lead): A cyberinfrastructure for mesoscale meteorology research and education. In: 20th Conf. on Interactive Information Processing Systems for Meteorology, Oceanography, and Hydrology, Seattle, WA (January 2004),
http://www.cs.indiana.edu/dde/papers/droegemeierIIPS2004.pdf

[3] Hertel Jr., E.S., Bell, R.L., Elrick, M.G., Farnsworth, A.V., Kerley, G.I., McGlaun, J.M., Petney, S.V., Silling, S.A., Taylor, P.A., Yarrington, L.: CTH: A software family for multi-dimensional shock physics analysis. In: Brun, R., Dumitrescu, L.D. (eds.) Proceedings of the 19th International Symposium on Shock Physics, Marseille, France, vol. 1, pp. 377–382 (July 1993),
http://sherpa.sandia.gov/9231home/pdfpapers/issw.pdf

[4] Ludäscher, B., Altintas, I., Berkley, C., Higgins, D., Jaeger, E., Jones, M., Lee, E.A., Tao, J., Zhao, Y.: Scientific workflow management and the kepler system: Research articles. Concurr. Comput.: Pract. Exper. 18(10), 1039–1065 (2006)

[5] Malewicz, G., Foster, I., Rosenberg, A., Wilde, M.: A tool for prioritizing DAGMan jobs and its evaluation. In: 2006 15th IEEE International Symposium on High Performance Distributed Computing, pp. 156–168 (2006)

[6] Moreland, K., Lepage, D., Koller, D., Humphreys, G.: Remote rendering for ultrascale data. Journal of Physics: Conference Series 125(1), 012096 (2008),
http://stacks.iop.org/1742-6596/125/i=1/a=012096

[7] Mullender, S.J., Leslie, I.M., McAuley, D.: Operating-system support for distributed multimedia. In: Proceedings of the 1994 Summer USENIX Technical Conference, pp. 209–219 (1994)

[8] Oldfield, R.A., Widener, P., Maccabe, A.B., Ward, L., Kordenbrock, T.: Efficient data-movement for lightweight I/O. In: Proceedings of the 2006 International Workshop on High Performance I/O Techniques and Deployment of Very Large Scale I/O Systems, Barcelona, Spain (September 2006),
http://doi.ieeecomputersociety.org/10.1109/CLUSTR.2006.311897

[9] Riedel, M., Eickermann, T., Habbinga, S., Frings, W., Gibbon, P., Mallmann, D., Wolf, F., Streit, A., Lippert, T., Schiffmann, W., Ernst, A., Spurzem, R., Nagel, W.: Computational steering and online visualization of scientific applications on large-scale hpc systems within e-science infrastructures. In: IEEE International Conference on e-Science and Grid Computing, pp. 483–490 (December 2007)

[10] UCAR: Local data manager, `http://www.unidata.ucar.edu/software/ldm`

[11] Wozniak, J.M., Latham, R., Lang, S., Son, S.W., Ross, R.: C-mpi: A dht implementation for grid and hpc environments. In: EuroMPI (2009)

[12] Zheng, F., Abbasi, H., Docan, C., Lofstead, J., Klasky, S., Liu, Q., Parashar, M., Podhorszki, N., Schwan, K., Wolf, M.: PreDatA- preparatory data analytics on Peta-Scale machines. In: Proceedings of 24th IEEE International Parallel and Distributed Processing Symposium, Atlanta, Georgia (April 2010)

Versatile Communication Algorithms for Data Analysis

Tom Peterka and Robert Ross

Argonne National Laboratory
tpeterka@mcs.anl.gov

Abstract. Large-scale parallel data analysis, where global information from a variety of problem domains is resolved in a distributed memory space, relies on communication. Three communication algorithms motivated by data analysis workloads—merge based reduction, swap based reduction, and neighborhood exchange—are presented, and their performance is benchmarked. These algorithms communicate custom data types among blocks assigned to processes in flexible ways, and their performance is optimized by tunable parameters. Performance is compared with an MPI implementation and with previous communication algorithms on an IBM Blue Gene/P supercomputer at a variety of message sizes and process counts.

Keywords: communication for large-scale parallel data analysis.

1 Introduction

Large-scale parallel data analysis and visualization often involve intense communication of information in a distributed-memory HPC architecture, for example, when data are analyzed in situ during a computational simulation. Thus, efficient and usable communication algorithms are fundamental to scalable data analysis. While MPI's collectives suffice for some of these tasks, MPI alone does not provide custom domain decompositions, partial reductions, or neighborhood exchanges. Even when a comparable MPI function does exist, configurable algorithms that allow tuning for a target architecture and data movement pattern may outperform MPI implementations for the same task. Our solution is to write such algorithms in a library built on top of MPI.

This paper examines three communication algorithms implemented in such a library. We describe how these algorithms offer capabilities beyond MPI's stock functions. These capabilities include the ability to communicate among blocks instead of processes, so that blocks can be mapped to processes in flexible ways. For example, multiple blocks can be mapped to one MPI process. Reductions are based on configurable radices and rounds and can be either partial or complete depending on these parameters. Neighborhood communication is also included.

Although these communication algorithms have been successfully applied in our prior work to a variety of data analysis tasks, the contribution of this paper is a thorough benchmarking of their performance. We compare with a popular MPI implementation for test configurations where a comparable MPI function can be used. We also compare performance with previous visualization algorithms, in particular, with a highly tuned image compositing algorithm and with our previous implementation of neighborhood exchange in parallel particle tracing.

J.L. Träff, S. Benkner, and J. Dongarra (Eds.): EuroMPI 2012, LNCS 7490, pp. 275–284, 2012.

Table 1. Examples of Communication Patterns in Data Analysis

Analysis Kernel	Communication Pattern
Particle tracing [5]	Neighborhood exchange
Information entropy [6]	Merge based reduction
Morse-Smale complex [7]	Merge based reduction
Computational geometry [8]	Neighborhood exchange
Region growing [9]	Neighborhood exchange
Sort-last rendering [3]	Swap based reduction

2 Background and Related Work

Many algorithms for collectives have been published in the message-passing literature, including [1, 2]. The visualization community has developed similar communication algorithms for image compositing [3].

Parallel scientific data analysis and visualization algorithms share a common set of communication patterns. Table 1 shows a representative sample of data analysis kernels and the communication pattern used in each. Some analyses also generate multiple combinations and iterations of these same core patterns. The right-hand column of the table reveals three common communication kernels: merge based reduction, swap based reduction, and neighborhood exchange. These patterns are described further in Section 3.

Algorithms for these three patterns are implemented in a prototype library called DIY (Do-It-Yourself analysis) [4] that the user calls in conjunction with custom local analysis operations. DIY is lightweight, consisting of approximately 15 K lines of code and 800 KB as a statically linked library. DIY's communication algorithms have hooks for custom reduction operators that act on user-defined data types, as in MPI. Additionally, DIY allows communication among arbitrary subsets of the domain, which are called *blocks*, without the user having to worry about which process actually owns a given block. Blocks are assigned to processes during the initialization of DIY, and a process may own more than one block. In the remainder of this paper, we will follow DIY's terminology and say that blocks communicate with each other rather than processes.

Deciding which communication pattern to select for a particular task depends on several factors. If the operation is not associative and the order of information flow through the domain is data-dependent, then global reduction cannot be used, and neighborhood communication is selected instead. For associative operations, swap based reduction is appropriate when data items are homogeneous, contiguous buffers that can be subdivided, and the user wants a distributed result, as in MPI_Reduce_scatter. When data items are heterogeneous and cannot be scattered, merge based reduction is used, similar to MPI_Reduce.

3 Method

DIY's merge and swap based reductions allow configurable radix messaging. Communication occurs in rounds; and in each round, groups are formed of blocks that communicate with each other. The number of blocks per group in a round is called the *k-value*.

By selecting the number of rounds and the k-value in each round, the user can tailor the communication pattern to the hardware characteristics of the architecture. One also can select a smaller number of rounds than a full reduction would require. Partial reductions are useful for some applications, such as simplification of topological structures [7].

3.1   Merge Based Reduction

The merge based communication pattern is used for associative reduction of heterogeneous data that cannot be readily distributed and instead must be merged in place at a smaller number of blocks during each round. Topological graph structures such as Morse-Smale complexes are reduced this way [7]. Algorithm 1 was first published in 2011 [4]. The inset at the right shows an example of a partial reduction with two rounds of merging using $k = 4$ in the first round and $k = 2$ in the second round.

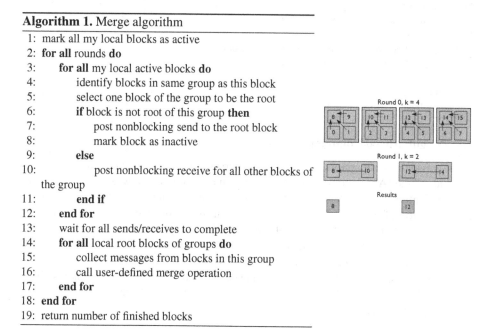

Algorithm 1. Merge algorithm

1: mark all my local blocks as active
2: **for all** rounds **do**
3:      **for all** my local active blocks **do**
4:          identify blocks in same group as this block
5:          select one block of the group to be the root
6:          **if** block is not root of this group **then**
7:              post nonblocking send to the root block
8:              mark block as inactive
9:          **else**
10:             post nonblocking receive for all other blocks of the group
11:         **end if**
12:     **end for**
13:     wait for all sends/receives to complete
14:     **for all** local root blocks of groups **do**
15:         collect messages from blocks in this group
16:         call user-defined merge operation
17:     **end for**
18: **end for**
19: return number of finished blocks

3.2   Swap Based Reduction

The swap based communication pattern is used for associative reduction of homogeneous contiguous data buffers that remain distributed instead of being merged into a smaller number of blocks. This case occurs in sort-last parallel rendering, when multiple image buffers are blended together. In fact, Algorithm 2 is a generalization of the radix-k image compositing algorithm first published in 2009 [10]. The inset at the right shows an example of a partial reduction with two rounds of swapping using $k = 4$ in the first round and $k = 2$ in the second round.

Algorithm 2. Swap algorithm

1: **for all** rounds **do**
2:      **for all** my local blocks **do**
3:          identify other blocks in same group as this block
4:          compute fraction of item to exchange
5:          **for all** member blocks in same group as this block **do**
6:              post asynchronous send of fraction of item
7:          **end for**
8:          **for all** member blocks in same group as this block **do**
9:              post asynchronous receive of fraction of item
10:         **end for**
11:     **end for**
12:     wait for sends/receives to complete
13:     **for all** blocks **do**
14:         collect messages from blocks in this group
15:         call user-defined reduce operation
16:     **end for**
17: **end for**
18: return location of reduced fraction within each block

Round 0, k = 4

Round 1, k = 2

Results

3.3 Neighborhood Communication

For nonassociative operators, information traverses a domain iteratively, one neighborhood at a time. An example is tracing streamlines through a flow dataset, when the communication pattern depends entirely on the input vector field. Algorithm 3 is a generalization of the particle exchange algorithm first published in 2011 [5]. The inset at the right shows an example of two rounds of neighborhood exchange. In the PostMessages procedure, blocks post nonblocking messages to their neighbors, and return to check on the status of received messages in the TestMessages procedure. The number of messages for which to wait during each call to TestMessages is adjustable, and this adjustable level of synchrony is a key reason for the performance improvement of this algorithm over its predecessors.

4 Performance

Our tests were run on *Intrepid*, a 557-teraflop IBM Blue Gene/P supercomputer operated by the Argonne Leadership Computing Facility (ALCF) at Argonne National Laboratory. The test program was compiled with the IBM xlcxx_r compiler using -O3 -qarch=450d -qtune=450 optimizations.

4.1 Reduction

The parameters for our tests were chosen so that our results could be compared against MPI; hence, the merge and swap algorithms performed a full reduction. This means that

---

Algorithm 3. Neighborhood Exchange Algorithm

1: **procedure** PACK MESSAGES
2:     **for all** my local blocks **do**
3:         **for all** all processes in my neighborhood **do**
4:             pack message of block IDs and item counts destined for that process
5:             pack message of item payloads destined for that process
6:         **end for**
7:     **end for**
8: **end procedure**
9: **procedure** POST MESSAGES
10:     **for all** packed ID and count messages **do**
11:         post nonblocking send of counts message
12:         post nonblocking send of payloads message
13:         post nonblocking receive of counts message
14:     **end for**
15: **end procedure**
16: **procedure** TEST MESSAGES
17:     **while** number of arrived messages < desired number of arrivals **do**
18:         wait for some more counts messages to arrive
19:         parse counts message and post blocking send for matching payload message
20:     **end while**
21: **end procedure**

Round 0

Round 1

Results

the number of rounds and k-values per round produced a merged result in a single block, and the swapped result was scattered among all blocks and was equivalent to all blocks communicating with each other. We used one DIY block per MPI process and tested block counts that were powers of two. Tests were run in symmetric multiprocessor mode, one MPI process per node.

Since the swap based reduction is a generalization of the radix-k image compositing algorithm, we also wanted to configure our tests to be able to compare against radix-k. Thus, our reduction operator is the noncommutative *over* operator [11], a linear combination of elements in a floating-point buffer that represents the red, green, blue, and opacity channels of pixels in an image. Our message sizes are based on images of various resolutions at 16 bytes per pixel.

We first disabled the reduction operator and tested only the communication cost. Figure 1 shows this result for merge and swap reduction compared with MPI_Reduce and MPI_Reduce_scatter, respectively. For merging, we found $k = 2$ to perform best; for swapping, $k = 8$ was used. In the merge test, DIY was approximately 10% faster than the BG/P MPI implementation; in the swap test, DIY was up to 60% faster at 1,024 processes.

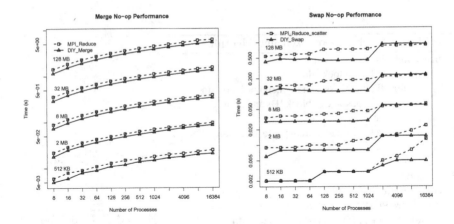

Fig. 1. Communication time only for our merge algorithm compared with MPI's reduction algorithm (left) and our swap algorithm compared with MPI's reduce-scatter algorithm (right)

Next, we enabled the reduction operator, with the results in Figure 2 for $k = 2$ merge reduction and $k = 8$ swap reduction. The difference between MPI and DIY is minimal because the cost of computing the over operator is expensive enough to mask the gains in the communication algorithm. Moreover, when $k = 8$, the computation is performed by looping over the eight blocks that need to be reduced locally, which serializes the computation.

Having eight blocks available for reduction, however, opens new possibilities for thread-level parallelism that did not exist when $k = 2$ or in MPI_Reduce_scatter.

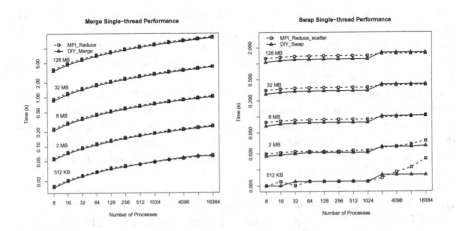

Fig. 2. Communication and single-threaded compositing operator for our merge algorithm compared with MPI's reduction algorithm (left) and our swap algorithm compared with MPI's reduce-scatter algorithm (right)

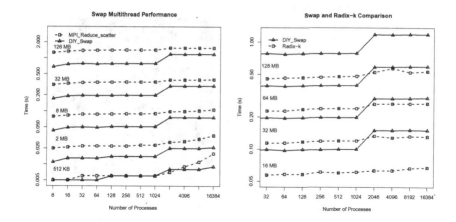

Fig. 3. Communication and multithreaded compositing operator for our swap algorithm compared with MPI's reduce-scatter algorithm (left) and compared with the radix-k algorithm of [10] (right)

When the loop over the eight blocks is multithreaded with openMP in the DIY version, the graph on the left of Figure 3 results. The multithreaded DIY swap algorithm is up to 1.8 times faster than MPI_Reduce_scatter at 1024 processes, and approximately 1.4 times faster than the single-threaded DIY swap in Figure 2.

Within the local *over* operator of the DIY swap version, the outer loop over the blocks that were received was thread-parallelized, and this loop exists only in the DIY version. The inner loop over block elements remained serial in both DIY and MPI. Since the over operator is noncommutative, we wanted to ensure that the same reduction order was maintained in both versions. In our tests, this order is in increasing block global identification number. To maintain this order, we employed a local tree reduction as shown in Figure 4. The idea of reducing local blocks in a tree as opposed to a linear order was introduced by Moreland et al. [12], and we borrowed that idea for our thread ordering.

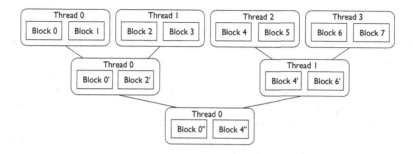

Fig. 4. Local multithreaded tree reduction of eight blocks

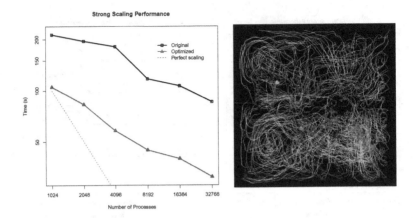

Fig. 5. Strong scaling performance for compute plus communicate time shows three times improvement over previously published results (left) for particles traced in a thermal hydraulics flow field (right)

The right-hand side of Figure 3 compares our multithreaded swap performance with the standalone version of the the radix-k algorithm [10]. It shows that DIY's performance is approximately two times slower than radix-k. Our swap reduction is more general than radix-k because it supports multiple blocks per process and generic data items, and this generality comes with some overhead. We expect that some of this performance gap can be recovered through further optimization of DIY, and some will remain. Motivated by this comparison, we will continue to work to improve performance.

4.2 Neighborhood Exchange

To demonstrate the scalability of the nearest neighbor communication algorithm, and in particular its use of tunable synchronization, we present an example from parallel particle tracing. A common and intuitive way to visualize a static or time-varying flow field is to trace paths that are derived from the trajectory of massless particles injected into the field and advected through it using numerical integration. In a data-parallel distributed-memory environment, the communication pattern that results is a neighborhood exchange. Local computation of integral curves within a block is interleaved with the exchange of particles across block boundaries in an iterative fashion.

The test shown in Figure 5 was run in virtual node mode with one MPI process per core and eight DIY blocks per process. The left side of the figure shows strong scaling of the compute plus communicate time and excludes file I/O. It compares Algorithm 3 with a previous algorithm published in 2011 [5]. The main improvement is due to the adjustable number of arrivals parameter in line 17 of Algorithm 3. This algorithm is approximately three times faster than the original in 2011.

The test dataset comes from a computational fluid dynamics simulation of thermal hydraulics in a nuclear reactor. The problem is large in data size (2048^3 grid points), in the number of particles traced (256 K), and in the computation applied to each particle (1000 integration steps). While 0.25 million particles are too many to visualize, a very dense tracing such as this is necessary for accurate follow-on analysis of the field lines. A much smaller number of particles traced in the same flow field is shown in the right side of Figure 5.

5 Summary

We presented three communication patterns that are common to many data analysis tasks. For global reduction, we designed configurable algorithms for merging and swapping that feature configurable number of rounds and k-value per round. The neighborhood exchange pattern features a configurable degree of synchronization and flexible identification of blocks that constitute a neighborhood. Implemented in a design that communicates user-defined data items among blocks instead of processes, the result is a set of versatile communication algorithms that have proven to be very useful in numerous data analysis applications.

Performance and scalability benchmarks were presented for all three algorithms. We compared the two reductions with MPI. While we designed the experiment to be comparable with MPI's reductions (one block per process and full reduction), it is important to realize that DIY provides richer functionality that in general cannot be expressed by a few MPI calls. Nevertheless, our algorithms were faster than the MPI implementation in almost all the cases tested. The neighborhood exchange was compared with an earlier algorithm, with three times faster performance in a test of parallel particle tracing of a scientific dataset.

DIY's versatility also accounts for lower performance compared with single-purpose algorithms such as radix-k for image compositing. In particular, DIY does not overlap communication and computation deep in the communication loop the way radix-k does, because the reduction operator is in the user's code.

In our ongoing work, we are continuing to look for ways to overlap communication and computation in our general-purpose library, to approach the performance of algorithms like radix-k. We are also continuing to add new features to DIY, including versatile information exchange patterns within a neighborhood. For example, blocks may talk to only a subsets of blocks within a neighborhood, and these subsets can be chosen in various ways. We also continue to build new analysis applications on top of DIY, which in turn drives further innovation in the library.

Acknowledgments. We gratefully acknowledge the use of the resources of the Argonne Leadership Computing Facility at Argonne National Laboratory. This work was supported by the Office of Advanced Scientific Computing Research, Office of Science, U.S. Department of Energy, under Contract DE-AC02-06CH11357. Work is also supported by the DOE Office of Science, Advanced Scientific Computing Research award No. DE-FC02-06ER25777, program manager Lucy Nowell.

References

1. Kumar, S., Dozsa, G., Berg, J., Cernohous, B., Miller, D., Ratterman, J., Smith, B., Heidelberger, P.: Architecture of the Component Collective Messaging Interface. In: Lastovetsky, A., Kechadi, T., Dongarra, J. (eds.) EuroPVM/MPI 2008. LNCS, vol. 5205, pp. 23–32. Springer, Heidelberg (2008)
2. Sack, P., Gropp, W.: Faster Topology-Aware Collective Algorithms through Non-Minimal Communication. In: Proceedings of the 17th ACM SIGPLAN Symposium on Principles and Practice of Parallel Programming, PPoPP 2012, pp. 45–54. ACM, New York (2012)
3. Ma, K.-L., Painter, J.S., Hansen, C.D., Krogh, M.F.: Parallel Volume Rendering Using Binary-Swap Compositing. IEEE Computer Graphics and Applications 14(4), 59–68 (1994)
4. Peterka, T., Ross, R., Kendall, W., Gyulassy, A., Pascucci, V., Shen, H.-W., Lee, T.-Y., Chaudhuri, A.: Scalable Parallel Building Blocks for Custom Data Analysis. In: Proceedings of the 2011 IEEE Large Data Analysis and Visualization Symposium, LDAV 2011, Providence, RI (2011)
5. Peterka, T., Ross, R., Nouanesengsy, B., Lee, T.-Y., Shen, H.-W., Kendall, W., Huang, J.: A Study of Parallel Particle Tracing for Steady-State and Time-Varying Flow Fields. In: Proceedings of IPDPS 2011, Anchorage AK (2011)
6. Xu, L., Lee, T.Y., Shen, H.W.: An Information-Theoretic Framework for Flow Visualization. IEEE Transactions on Visualization and Computer Graphics 16, 1216–1224 (2010)
7. Gyulassy, A., Peterka, T., Pascucci, V., Ross, R.: Characterizing the Parallel Computation of Morse-Smale Complexes. In: Proceedings of IPDPS 2012, Shanghai, China (2012)
8. Schaap, W.E.: DTFE: The Delaunay Tesselation Field Estimator, University of Groningen, The Netherlands, Ph.D. Dissertation (2007)
9. Chen, J., Silver, D., Jiang, L.: The Feature Tree: Visualizing Feature Tracking in Distributed AMR Datasets. In: Proceedings of the 2003 IEEE Symposium on Parallel and Large-Data Visualization and Graphics, PVG 2003. IEEE Computer Society, Washington, DC (2003)
10. Peterka, T., Goodell, D., Ross, R., Shen, H.W., Thakur, R.: A Configurable Algorithm for Parallel Image-Compositing Applications. In: Proceedings of SC 2009, Portland OR (2009)
11. Porter, T., Duff, T.: Compositing Digital Images. In: Proceedings of 11th Annual Conference on Computer Graphics and Interactive Techniques, pp. 253–259 (1984)
12. Moreland, K., Kendall, W., Peterka, T., Huang, J.: An Image Compositing Solution at Scale. In: Proceedings of SC 2011, Seattle, WA (2011)

High Performance Concurrent Multi-Path Communication for MPI

Rashid Hassani, Abbas Malekpour, Amirreza Fazely, and Peter Luksch

Institute of Computer Science,
University of Rostock, Germany
{rashid.hassani,abbas.malekpour,amirreza.fazelyhamedani,
peter.luksch}@uni-rostock.de

MPI is the most generally accepted API in HPC. Today, a typical HPC plat-form provides a hierarchy of parallelism and networks, from OnChip Networks, SMPs, SAN to WAN. The MPI protocol stack has been optimized for shared memory plat-forms, InfiniBand etc. WAN MPI still is an extension of LAN MPI and thus uses TCP. MPI in WANs is important because large cross-site re-source pools often are used in Cloud and Grid Computing. Therefore MPI per-formance/reliability/security in WANs must be addressed, and that's what we do and present here.

Using TCP in WAN environments raises problems: large latencies and the dif-ficulty to utilize the full available bandwidth [1]. Scalability is another significant problem, since a large number of TCP connections have to be established for communication. Therefore, TCP is not well matched of MPI applications in wide area networks. SCTP associations and streams closely match the message order-ing semantics of MPI. For instance, contexts in an MPI program, which identify communicating processes, can be represented as a one-to-many socket in SCTP that establishes associations with that set of processes. Furthermore, mapping associations each with multiple streams to rank of processes within a context in MPI is another significant property of SCTP which directly corresponds with message ordering semantics in MPI. More importantly, the multi-homing feature of SCTP leads to increase the efficient use of all available communication paths and makes it interesting for use in clusters. There is a project which investi-gated the CMT feature of SCTP based middleware in MPICH2 but it is still difficult to schedule messages based on message size in order to minimize latency [2]. The recent innovative concurrent multipath communication method (CMC-SCTP) which is an extension to the SCTP protocol provides an end-to-end fast and efficient use of all available communication paths simultaneously [3]. This method uses the fastest path for exchanging the control and coordination data and provides minimum communication delay but with higher bandwidth up to the summation of all available compute nodes' network injection bandwidth.

The main objective of the proposed project is to improve performance and scalability of communication in wide area network for HPC applications. Due to the striking similarities between SCTP and MPI, we propose to replace TCP by SCTP in the protocol stack of WAN MPI. This is to be achieved by providing a wide area MPI that is based on CMC-SCTP extension protocol. CMC-SCTP will be integrated into the modular structure of Open MPI in order to provide an

J.L. Träff, S. Benkner, and J. Dongarra (Eds.): EuroMPI 2012, LNCS 7490, pp. 285–286, 2012.
© Springer-Verlag Berlin Heidelberg 2012

infrastructure for in-depth evaluation using real-world programs. Open MPI is chosen because it does not impose any restrictions on the communication mechanisms or protocols of the implementation and its modular structure supports easy integration of new modules. We call this project CSM (Concurrent Multipath Communication SCTP for Open MPI). CSM will be a point-to-point concurrent multi-path communication module in Open MPI that supports multi-homing and the ability to stripe and share transferred data across multiple available interfaces. We plan to complement the real-world environment by a simulation-based environment that allows us to evaluate aspects that cannot be addressed appropriately in a real-world. New functions that support re-source management and performance analysis and optimization tools will be provided at little or no extra cost by using monitoring functions of the SCTP protocol. A resource management system allows users to set options for resource allocation that take into account their preferences for a job execution. A performance optimizer might monitor all available resources for communication performance. It may re-allocate resources to the running application if paths with higher bandwidth or lower latency become available. Finally, an application may execute under the control of an automatic performance optimization tool that observes both the application and the available resources and triggers the appropriate actions at run-time. Therefore, an application may be able to reconfigure itself based on performance data.

Since the cost of WAN connections could be an important aspect in a Grid environment, we propose the use of Concurrent Multipath Communication for SCTP as a robust transport protocol extension, which also will provide an automatic performance optimization at runtime that take into account the current load of processors, links and other criteria in order to improve bandwidth, scalability, and especially reducing overall communication delay for MPI in WAN.

Energy costs over the lifetime of an HPC system are in the range of the acquisition costs of the system. Therefore, energy efficiency is an important issue for compute centers and Cloud providers. Our project provides excellent opportunities for the development of a method of applying energy saving techniques in compute centers.Future resource management systems could allow a user to specify minimum energy consumption (and thus minimum cost) under the constraint that the job will be done before a given deadline. They would be able to provide highly dynamic Grid environments with reasonable overhead, reasonable intrusion, and reasonable accuracy for HPC systems.

References

1. Majumder, S., Rixner, S.: Comparing Ethernet and Myrinet for MPI Communication. Los Alamos National Laboratory (2006)
2. Penoff, B., Tsai, M., Iyengar, J., Wagner, A.: Using CMT in SCTP-Based MPI to Exploit Multiple Interfaces in Cluster Nodes. In: Cappello, F., Herault, T., Dongarra, J. (eds.) EuroPVM/MPI 2007. LNCS, vol. 4757, pp. 204–212. Springer, Heidelberg (2007)
3. Malekpour, A., Tavangarian, D.: Concurrent Multipath Communication for SCTP a Novel Method for Data Transmission, I2TS 2010-Rio de Janeiro, Brazil (2010)

Improving Collectives by User Buffer Relocation

Juan Antonio Rico Gallego, Juan Carlos Díaz Martín,
Carolina Gómez-Tostón Gutiérrez, and Álvaro Cortés Fácila

University of Extremadura, Cáceres, Spain
{jarico,juancarl,cgomezt,alvarocf}@unex.es

1 Motivation

According to top 500 list, in November 2010 processors with four or more cores were used in the 92% of the HPC systems, while systems using six or more cores per processor have increased from 19% to 62% until November 2011. In the next years it is expected hundreds of cores per processor competing for memory bandwidth and aggravatting the problem known as *memory wall*, the decrease of memory bandwidth relative to a processor that make applications to reach just a few percent of its peak performance.

Incoming architectures appear to encourage the use of the *Hybrid model*. OpenMP is the representative of the shared memory programming paradigm, avoiding explicit communication. Nevertheless, up to now, the fact is that MPI is still used for building HPC applications and libraries on multicore clusters, due to application portability and performance.

Mainstream MPI implementations such as *MPICH2* and *Open MPI* run each rank as an operating system process. A message between two processes usually goes through a shared memory region mapped by both address spaces, and it therefore needs two copies. This approach can be self-defeating because of cache pollution and memory bandwidth harnessing. This issue gets worse in collective operations whose performance is critical in the global application behavior.

Therefore, mechanisms have been developed for saving copies in the transmission of messages in shared memory, as *SMARTMAP*, based on hardware capabilities, or *KNEM*, based on a operating system module which increases latency because of the cost of system calls, but highly improves bandwidth of medium to large sized messages.

Thread-based MPI implementations propose another model. Implementing an MPI process as a thread fit MPI Standard 1.3 requirements with changes in the code to eliminate static variables and enforcing the use of thread-safe libraries. Benefits coming from one-copy message transfers and in-site reducing operations, besides of improved scalability due to high reduction of memory consumption of the library internals, or better handling of non-contiguous messages.

2 *CAS*: Common Address Space Component

CAS (Common Address Space) is an early implementation of a new Open MPI collective component trying to mimic the performance and algorithms of the

J.L. Träff, S. Benkner, and J. Dongarra (Eds.): EuroMPI 2012, LNCS 7490, pp. 287–288, 2012.

threaded shared memory model. By invoking `MPI_Alloc_mem`, the user allocates the buffer to send in a memory region mapped to all the processes in the communicator. New algorithms avoiding intermediate copies can be devised for improving performance based on this configuration. Up to now, we have implemented broadcast and reduce algorithms. In broadcast, root sends the address of the user buffer to the rest of ranks, while receivers copy data directly from the user buffer in parallel. Message fragmentation is not required. Our Reduce algorithm is similar to current Open MPI SM (*Shared Memory*) component, and it is still to be improved for taking full advantage of the new component facilities. Root process is charged to apply the computation operation on all buffers, but no data movement is needed, because buffers are in common address space. Our position is that allowing all processes collaborate in applying the operation by sharing out buffers, and taking into account the memory placement, performance could be dramatically improved.

First attempts of implementing algorithms in this new component shows an improvement for both operations respect to Open MPI collective SM component, as shown in Fig. 1. Intel IMB benchmark is used on an eight core *Nehalem* machine, without cache effects.

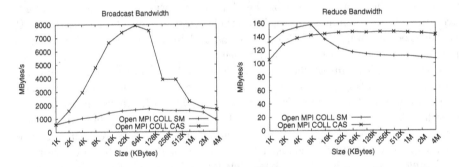

Fig. 1. Broadcast and Reduce bandwidth in a 8-core Nehalem with 8 processes

The most important drawback of the component is the requirement of user involvement in allocating buffers correctly for performance and memory saving. For instance, in `MPI_Bcast` only root needs to allocate the send buffer in shared memory via `MPI_Alloc_mem`. Preprocessing techniques are being faced for assisting on the allocation of buffers and applying different kinds of algorithms based on their arrangement. As these techniques mature, we expect to move them towards mainstream use. In the meanwhile, only buffers with a size greater than a threshold are allocated in shared memory, leaving to double-copy methods the smaller ones. Study of applications and libraries profiles are necessary for clarifying where CAS component can be applied, as well as its overall benefits.

Asynchronous Checkpointing by Dedicated Checkpoint Threads

Faisal Shahzad[1], Markus Wittmann[1], Thomas Zeiser[1], and Gerhard Wellein[2]

[1] Erlangen Regional Computing Center, University of Erlangen-Nuremberg, Germany
[2] Department of Computer Science, University of Erlangen-Nuremberg, Germany
{faisal.shahzad,markus.wittmann,thomas.zeiser,gerhard.wellein}@rrze.fau.de

Abstract. Checkpoint/restart (C/R) is a classical approach to introduce fault tolerance in large HPC applications. Although it is relatively easy as compared to other fault tolerance approaches, its overhead hinders its wide usage. We present an application-level checkpointing technique that significantly reduces the checkpoint overhead. The checkpoint I/O is overlapped with the computation of the application by following a two-stage checkpointing mechanism with dedicated threads for doing I/O.

1 Algorithm and Implementation

With each step closer towards the exascale barrier, the mean time between failure (MTBF) of these futuristic systems reduces. This raises the importance of checkpoint/restart techniques [1]. As IO bandwidths cannot be increased arbitrarily, it is important to investigate approaches which can hide IO time of checkpointing. One of these approaches is to utilize non-blocking asynchronous MPI-IO for creating checkpoints. However, neither asynchronous non-blocking point-to-point communication [2] nor asynchronous non-blocking MPI-IO is supported by most of the MPI implementations. Therefore, we implement asynchronous checkpointing manually by creating a two-stage checkpointing mechanism and a dedicated checkpoint thread (CP-thread) as shown in Fig. 1. Each MPI process is divided into two threads, a worker thread and a CP-thread. The CP-thread of each MPI process is pinned to a simultaneous multi-threaded (SMT) core for the present Intel processor architectures, while the worker threads are pinned to the physical cores. If SMT is not available, physical cores may be oversubscribed. When a checkpoint is triggered, an in-memory checkpoint is made first by the worker thread. The second stage of checkpointing involves the copying of the in-memory checkpoint to the external file system and is carried out by the CP-thread. For benchmarking, we have utilized an MPI application based on a stencil type algorithm with toggle grids. Thus, it is obvious to introduce an additional checkpointing grid (CP-grid) which is responsible for temporarily storing the in-memory checkpoint. By switching the grid pointers, the extra in-memory copy of the CP-grid from the most updated grid is completely avoided.

J.L. Träff, S. Benkner, and J. Dongarra (Eds.): EuroMPI 2012, LNCS 7490, pp. 289–290, 2012.

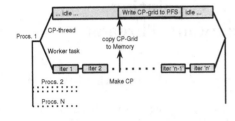 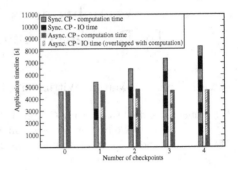

Fig. 1. Diagram of the program flow. Each MPI process is divided into worker and checkpoint threads. At checkpoint iteration, the worker thread signals the checkpoint thread to write the checkpoint.

Fig. 2. Checkpoint overhead for 128 LiMa nodes (1536 MPI-processes, 1 CP-th./SMT-core) with aggregated checkpoint size of 800 GB/checkpoint

2   Results

Benchmarks were performed on an Intel based Infiniband cluster (LiMa)[1], which is connected to a Lustre parallel file system. In a naïve synchronous checkpointing technique, each MPI process interrupts its computation for the duration of writing checkpoints, i.e., the complete IO time is added as overhead to the total runtime. Figure 2 shows the checkpoint overhead comparison between a naïve synchronous checkpointing and our presented asynchronous checkpointing technique for our application on 128 LiMa nodes with an aggregated checkpoint size of 800 GB. Each synchronous checkpoint adds ≈22% overhead to the application, whereas each asynchronous checkpoint costs ≈0.6% overhead, i.e., almost all the IO time is effectively hidden. This significantly reduces the checkpoint overhead. The maximum number of low overhead asynchronous checkpoints can be calculated as: $\dfrac{\text{application runtime without checkpoints}}{\text{IO time for a single checkpoint}}$.

Acknowledgements. This work was supported by BMBF grant No. 01IH11011C (FETOL).

References

1. Hursey, J.: Coordinated Checkpoint/Restart Process Fault Tolerance for MPI Applications on HPC Systems. PhD thesis, Indiana University, Bloomington, IN, USA (July 2010)
2. Hager, G., Schubert, G., Schoenemeyer, T., Wellein, G.: Prospects for Truly Asynchronous Communication with Pure MPI and Hybrid MPI/OpenMP on Current Supercomputing Platforms. In: Cray Users Group Conference 2011, Fairbanks, AK, USA (2011)

---

[1] http://www.hpc.rrze.fau.de/systeme/lima-cluster.shtml

Verification of MPI Programs Using Session Types

Kohei Honda[1], Eduardo R.B. Marques[2], Francisco Martins[2],
Nicholas Ng[3], Vasco T. Vasconcelos[2], and Nobuko Yoshida[3]

[1] Queen Mary & West Field College, University of London, UK
[2] LaSIGE, Faculty of Sciences, University of Lisbon, PT
[3] Imperial College London, UK

Developing safe, concurrent (and parallel) software systems is a hard task in multiple aspects, particularly the sharing of information and the synchronization among multiple participants of the system. In the message passing paradigm, this is achieved by sending and receiving messages among different participants, raising a number of verification problems. For instance, exchanging messages in a wrong order may prevent the system from progressing, causing a deadlock. MPI is the most commonly used protocol for high-performance, message-based parallel programs, and the need for formal verification approaches is well acknowledged by much recent work (e.g., see [1]).

Our proposal for verification of MPI programs is based on session types [3]. The methodology considers the specification of a global interaction protocol among multiple participants, from which we can derive an endpoint protocol for each individual participant, e.g., as in Scribble [2]. A well-formed protocol can be verified in polynomial time and ensures type safety, communication safety, and deadlock freedom [4]. The idea is that we can ensure these properties for an MPI program by verifying conformance of the program against a given session type specification. This contrasts with other state-of-the-art methodologies considered for MPI, like model checking or symbolic execution [6], that require program-level analysis for all properties of interest, and inherently lead to a state-explosion problem as the number of participants grows.

Session type	MPI fragment

```
process r  :
 r in {0, ..., P-1},
 N > 0
= loop {
 float[N] to    (r+1) % P
 float[N] from (P+r-1) % P
 float    allreduce
}
```

```
float err, localErr, sbuf[N], rbuf[N];
int r, P;
MPI_Comm_rank(MPI_COMM_WORLD, &r);
MPI_Comm_size(MPI_COMM_WORLD, &P);
...
for (i=0; i < MAX_ITER && err > MAX_ERROR; i++) {
  MPI_Sendrecv(sbuf, N, MPI_FLOAT, (r+1) % P, 0,
               rbuf, N, MPI_FLOAT, (P+r-1) % P, 0,
               MPI_COMM_WORLD, &status);
  // computation
  ...
  MPI_Allreduce(&localErr, &err, 1, MPI_FLOAT,
                MPI_MAX, MPI_COMM_WORLD);
}
```

To illustrate our proposal we sketch a ring pattern that can be found in many MPI programs, e.g., n-body pipeline computations, shown above. We depict a pseudo-session type specification (left) and a corresponding MPI program fragment (right). The session type specifies that in every turn each participant r should send a float array of size N to its right neighbor and receive another array of the same size from its left neighbor. Then, after some local computation involving the received data, all participants perform a collective reduction (using MPI_Allreduce).

J.L. Träff, S. Benkner, and J. Dongarra (Eds.): EuroMPI 2012, LNCS 7490, pp. 291–293, 2012.

We have identified two key challenges. The first is to refine session type abstractions to capture the general traits of MPI programs, e.g., rank-based communication, collective operations, typical communication patterns (e.g., ring, mesh), and other MPI operations that may correspond to multiple steps in the protocol (like `MPI_Sendrecv` in the example). Other features impose additional complexity, such as nondeterministic operations (e.g., wildcard receives) or the possible choice/coexistence between blocking and nonblocking operations (e.g., an `MPI_Send` operation can be matched by a `MPI_Irecv`/`MPI_Wait` operation pair). Important work such as dependent-types or parameterized multiparty session types [7] can provide insights on these topics.

Session types have already been used to describe and verify parallel programs, e.g., Session C [5]. The proposals so far, however, require that programs are specified using a session type-specific programming abstraction and provide no support for common traits of message-based parallel programs such as collective operations. In contrast, we propose checking the conformance of standard MPI programs against session types. This second challenge is far from trivial. In essence, we need to determine a sound correspondence between a session type specification and the control flow graph of a program *for any* process. The communication flow is dependent on the numerical rank of each process, i.e., for any r in the example the endpoint type must be matched against the concrete control flow of the MPI program when executed for rank r. Moreover, a control flow synchrony needs to be established between processes. In the example we would need to infer that the same number of loop iterations is executed for all ranks, based on the assertion that err and i always have the same value in all processes per each iteration (note that err results from `MPI_Allreduce`). Beyond this simple example, other MPI programs easily make this type of assertions more complex to infer, e.g., manager-worker programs which combine such a parameterization with distinct branches and communication operations for different process groups.

Acknowledgements. This work is partially supported by EPRSC funds EP/G015635/01 and EP/G015481/01, Fundação para a Ciência e Tecnologia funds PTDC/EIA-CCO/122547/2010, and the Ocean Observatories Initiative.

References

1. Gopalakrishnan, G., Kirby, R.M., Siegel, S., Thakur, R., Gropp, W., Lusk, E., De Supinski, B.R., Schulz, M., Bronevetsky, G.: Formal analysis of MPI-based parallel programs. Communications ACM 54(12), 82–91 (2011)
2. Honda, K., Mukhamedov, A., Brown, G., Chen, T.-C., Yoshida, N.: Scribbling Interactions with a Formal Foundation. In: Natarajan, R., Ojo, A. (eds.) ICDCIT 2011. LNCS, vol. 6536, pp. 55–75. Springer, Heidelberg (2011)
3. Honda, K., Vasconcelos, V.T., Kubo, M.: Language Primitives and Type Discipline for Structured Communication-Based Programming. In: Hankin, C. (ed.) ESOP 1998. LNCS, vol. 1381, pp. 122–138. Springer, Heidelberg (1998)
4. Honda, K., Yoshida, N., Carbone, M.: Multiparty asynchronous session types. In: POPL, pp. 273–284. ACM (2008)

5. Ng, N., Yoshida, N., Honda, K.: Multiparty Session C: Safe Parallel Programming with Message Optimisation. In: Furia, C.A., Nanz, S. (eds.) TOOLS 2012. LNCS, vol. 7304, pp. 202–218. Springer, Heidelberg (2012)

6. Siegel, S., Mironova, A., Avrunin, G., Clarke, L.: Combining symbolic execution with model checking to verify parallel numerical programs. ACM TOSEM 17(2), 1–34 (2008)

7. Yoshida, N., Deniélou, P., Bejleri, A., Hu, R.: Parameterised Multiparty Session Types. In: Ong, L. (ed.) FOSSACS 2010. LNCS, vol. 6014, pp. 128–145. Springer, Heidelberg (2010)

Runtime Support for Adaptive Resource Provisioning in MPI Applications

Gonzalo Martín, David E. Singh,
Maria-Cristina Marinescu, and Jesús Carretero

Computer Science Department, Universidad Carlos III de Madrid
{gmcruz,desingh,mcristina,jcarrete}@arcos.inf.uc3m.es

1 Introduction

The work we present in this paper focuses on dynamic provisioning of computational resources depending on the performance requirements of the application and the characteristics of the cluster available for execution. We target applications which exhibit variable performance over time. The idea is to dynamically optimize the cost (total CPU-time) / performance (program execution time) ratio of parallel applications by (1) reducing the number of processors when the computation requirements decrease enough to justify it, and (2) moving computation onto those processors that can compute faster but don't require extensive remapping of the data. This approach adapts well to time-shared platforms in which many applications may need to execute on the same cluster at the same time, and allows users to implement different cost / performance tradeoffs.

The approach we are proposing differs from AMPI [1] in that they exploit process virtualization while we employ non-virtualized MPI processes. It also differs from DynMPI [4], which drops those nodes from computation which most degrade the performance of the application. In contrast, our approach removes processes only when the computation requirements of the application decrease.

2 The Basic Architecture

The main components of our runtime environment are the **decision module**, the **scheduler**, and the **monitoring layer** which tracks the performance of the application and feeds this data to the decision module. The decision module implements heuristics to establish how many resources to assign to the application at different points during its execution. This decision is communicated to the scheduler, which elects the set of processes that will continue executing such that they are located on the compute nodes with fastest execution time and which involve minimum data remapping. For space reasons we skip most details of the runtime environment [2] and focus on the decision module.

We have evaluated our framework for EpiGraph [3], an iterative, distributed simulator for infectious diseases which exhibits a significant variability in the iteration cost during its execution. Our heuristic Throughput-Based algorithm (TB) starts from the assumption that the user provisions a maximum number of

J.L. Träff, S. Benkner, and J. Dongarra (Eds.): EuroMPI 2012, LNCS 7490, pp. 294–295, 2012.

processors (P_{max}) for executing an application. Using this amount of resources, as the iteration time increases the throughput decreases and reaches its minimum value. This is the point where the application reaches maximum speedup, after which this decreases. A low speedup implies using many resources for a low performance improvement. The idea of TB is to reduce the number of processors to meet the cost/performance requirements.

The TB algorithm takes as input from the monitoring layer the current execution time of the program t_s. Based on the previous (t_{s-1}) and current execution times, TB predicts the execution time for the next iteration interval (t_{s+1}). The number of processes that will execute during this interval (P_{s+1}) is computed by the formula $P_{s+1} = P_{max}\frac{t_{s+1}}{\alpha * t_s}$. α controls the program throughput rate such that larger values of α imply fewer processes and, as a result, achieve smaller throughputs. Fig.1(a) shows the aggregated CPU time and the overall program execution time for TB on a cluster of 16 compute nodes. For α=0.2 we reduce the aggregated CPU time by 19% with a degradation in overall execution time of 11% when compared to executing EpiGraph on 16 processes without the support to our runtime environment. For the same setup, Fig.1(b) illustrates the progression of the number of resources used over time and the iteration times.

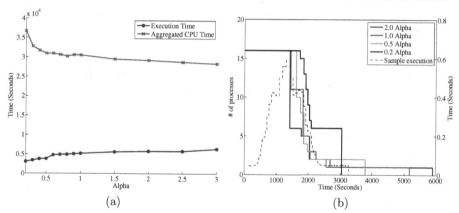

(a)   (b)

Fig. 1. (a) Impact of α on execution time, (b) number of resources for TB

Acknowledgments. This work has been partially funded by the Spanish Ministry of Science and Technology under the grant TIN2010-16497.

References

1. Huang, C., Lawlor, O., Kale, L.: Adaptive MPI. In: Rauchwerger, L. (ed.) LCPC 2003. LNCS, vol. 2958, pp. 306–322. Springer, Heidelberg (2004)
2. Martín, G., et al.: Runtime support for elastic execution of epigraph. Technical report (2012)
3. Martín, G., Marinescu, M., Singh, D., Carretero, J.: Leveraging social networks for understanding the evolution of epidemics. BMC Syst. Biol. 5(3) (2011)
4. Weatherly, D., Lowenthal, D., Nakazawa, M., Lowenthal, F.: Dyn-mpi: Supporting mpi on medium-scale, non-dedicated clusters. JPDC 2006 66(6), 822–838 (2006)

Revisiting Persistent Communication in MPI

Yutaka Ishikawa[1,2,3], Kengo Nakajima[2], and Atsushi Hori[3]

[1] Department of Computer Science, University of Tokyo
[2] Information Technology Center, University of Tokyo
[3] RIKEN Advanced Institute of Computational Science

The implementation of persistent communication provided in MPI is reconsidered to provide low latency and true overlapping communication and computation. In the persistent communication facility, the end-points of both the sender and the receiver are set up by issuing MPI_Send_init and MPI_Send_recv primitives prior to actual communication triggered by the MPI_Start or MPI_Startall primitive. The same communication pattern is reused without reissuing the initialization. Thus, at the start of actual communications in persistent communication, the runtime system already knows all the communication patterns, i.e., peers and message sizes if both sender and receiver have issued persistent communication primitives. Several enhancements utilizing network interfaces can be achieved as follows:

1. RDMA
   If the receiver's buffer address is sent to the sender before the start of the communication, the remote DMA mechanism is utilized.
2. Optimization of synchronization
   If a process does not need to synchronize with other processes upon issuing the MPI_Start or MPI_Startall function, the synchronization at that point can be eliminated. For example, in the case where a reduction function has been issued to check the computational convergence before the start of the persistent communications, it may start without synchronization among peers.
3. Scheduling network interfaces
   Because the runtime system already has known communication patterns, i.e, peers and message sizes, upon starting the communications, it has a chance to utilize network interfaces if each node has more than one network interface, e.g., four DMA engines are equipped in K computer[1]. Moreover, if a low-level network library provides an API for issuing multiple communication operations, low latency communication is carried out.

In order to achieve the first two optimizations, a new communication protocol and an implementation for persistent communication, called PRDMA (Persistent Remote Direct Memory Access), has been deigned and implemented in Fujitsu FX10, a commercialized version of K computer[1].

Information about remote memory address must be obtained prior to issuing a remote DMA primitive. Because the initialization of persistent communication is not a global operation, this information is not always available during the

J.L. Träff, S. Benkner, and J. Dongarra (Eds.): EuroMPI 2012, LNCS 7490, pp. 296–297, 2012.

initialization, but it is informed asynchronously. When this information has not arrived at the first communication, the MPI_Start/MPI_Startall primitives wait for this arrival.

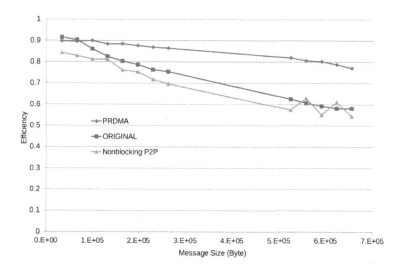

Fig. 1. Efficiency

PRDMA was evaluated using a simple benchmark program, whose communication pattern is parallel two-dimensional stencil computation, i.e., communicating with four neighbors simultaneously during the communication phase, to reveal how the facility carries out overlapping communication and computation. In this benchmark, the persistent communication is initialized by both sender and receiver sides followed by the main computation and communication loop. In the main loop, the start primitive is issued followed by the local computation. After finishing the computation, completion of the communications is waited for.

The results of the benchmark are shown in Fig. 1. These results are derived from executions carried out five times. Efficiency on the y-axis represents how total performance is slowed down if communications are involved during the execution. For example, if the time with communications is 1.25 seconds and the time without communications is 1 second, its efficiency is 0.8 (1 divided by 1.25). The results show that our proposed mechanism, PRDMA, outperforms the original one.

The PRDMA proposed in this paper has a big limitation because it assumes both sender and receiver sides issue persistent communication primitives. The protocol is currently being redesigned to eliminate this limitation.

Reference

1. K Computer, http://www.aics.riken.jp/en/kcomputer/

StarPU-MPI: Task Programming over Clusters of Machines Enhanced with Accelerators

Cédric Augonnet[1], Olivier Aumage[3], Nathalie Furmento[2],
Raymond Namyst[2], and Samuel Thibault[2]

[1] NVIDIA Corporation, Santa Clara, California, USA
[2] LaBRI, CNRS, University of Bordeaux, France
[3] Inria, Bordeaux, France

Abstract. GPUs clusters are becoming widespread HPC platforms. Exploiting them is however challenging, as this requires two separate paradigms (MPI and CUDA or OpenCL) and careful load balancing due to node heterogeneity. Current paradigms usually either limit themselves to offload part of the computation and leave CPUs idle, or require static CPU/GPU work partitioning. We thus have previously proposed StarPU, a runtime system able to dynamically scheduling tasks within a single heterogeneous node. We show how we extended the task paradigm of StarPU with MPI to easily map the task graph on MPI clusters and automatically benefit from optimized execution.

Keywords: Accelerators, GPUs, MPI, Task-based model.

1 Adapting the StarPU Paradigm to Clusters of GPUs

A lot of research has been conducted to allow MPI applications to offload kernels on GPU devices. StarPU [1] is a runtime scheduler for heterogeneous architectures. A StarPU program is written as a graph of tasks, each task working on a set of data. The computation part of the task, the *codelet*, wraps different implementations of the task for each type of device (CPU core, GPU, etc.). StarPU uses a virtual shared memory for automated data transfers between all the heterogeneous processing units to enable scheduling tasks over all these units. By carefully combining StarPU with MPI, we now benefit from both paradigms: scheduling tasks over CPUs and GPUs, and using clusters equipped with GPUs.

The integration of StarPU and MPI uses two strategies, depending on whether we accelerate existing MPI codes, or we add distribution to existing single node applications for exploiting clusters. The first strategy uses a small library we presented in [2], to extend the StarPU's data management layer with MPI-like semantics. The second strategy builds on the task-oriented model of StarPU.

2 Mapping Task Graphs on Clusters

Task graphs are indeed a convenient and portable representation which is not only suited to hybrid accelerator-based machines, but also to clusters of nodes

J.L. Träff, S. Benkner, and J. Dongarra (Eds.): EuroMPI 2012, LNCS 7490, pp. 298–299, 2012.
© Springer-Verlag Berlin Heidelberg 2012

enhanced with accelerators. The first step is to partition the graph into multiple sub-graphs of tasks that will be executed by the different instances of StarPU. Data dependencies that cross the boundary between the nodes are fulfilled by replacing the dependency with a MPI data transfer that is performed by the means of our MPI-like library. In other words, a node that generates a piece of data required by its neighbour(s) makes a *send* call. Similarly, a node that needs a piece of data that was generated on another node makes a *receive* call. Provided an initial partitioning of the DAG, this shows that our task-based paradigm is also suited for clusters of multicore nodes enhanced with accelerators.

The source code below shows the StarPU-MPI version of the Cholesky decomposition. The MAGMA reference linear algebra library is currently being extended to clusters by using this paradigm.

```
1   for(x = 0; x < X; x++) for(y = 0; y < Y; y++)
2       starpu_matrix_data_register(&A[x][y], 0, &A_tile[x][y], ld, tile_s, tile_s);
3       starpu_data_set_rank(A[x][y], (y%Y_BLK)*X_BLK + (x%X_BLK));
4   for (k = 0; k < Nt; k++)
5       starpu_mpi_insert_task(MPI_COMM_WORLD, &potrf, RW, A[k][k], 0);
6       for (m = k+1; m < Nt; m++)
7           starpu_mpi_insert_task(MPI_COMM_WORLD, &trsm, R, A[k][k], RW, A[m][k], 0);
8       for (m = k+1; m < Nt; m++)
9           for (n = k+1; n < m; n++)
10              starpu_mpi_insert_task(MPI_COMM_WORLD, &gemm,
11                                     R, A[m][k], R, A[n][k], RW, A[m][n], 0);
12          starpu_mpi_insert_task(MPI_COMM_WORLD, &syrk, R, A[m][k], RW, A[m][m], 0);
13  starpu_task_wait_for_all();
```

The plot below shows the strong scalability obtained by the Cholesky decomposition on a cluster of machines enhanced with accelerators. Each machine has two Intel Nehalem X5650 sockets with 6 cores each, running at 2.67 GHz, as well as 3 NVIDIA Fermi M2070 GPUs each.

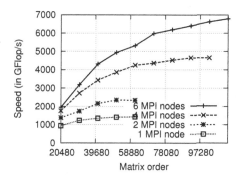

References

1. Augonnet, C., Thibault, S., Namyst, R., Wacrenier, P.A.: StarPU: A Unified Platform for Task Scheduling on Heterogeneous Multicore Architectures. In: Sips, H., Epema, D., Lin, H.-X. (eds.) Euro-Par 2009. LNCS, vol. 5704, pp. 863–874. Springer, Heidelberg (2009)
2. Augonnet, C., Clet-Ortega, J., Thibault, S., Namyst, R.: Data-Aware Task Scheduling on Multi-Accelerator based Platforms. In: The 16th International Conference on Parallel and Distributed Systems, ICPADS (2010)

Author Index